Enterprise Security Risk Management:
Concepts and Applications

Brian J. Allen, Esq.

CISSP, CISM, CPP, CFE

Rachelle Loyear

MBCP, AFBCI, CISM, PMP

Kristen Noakes-Fry, ABCI, Editor

ISBN 9781944480431 PDF

ISBN 9781944480424 EPUB

ISBN 9781944480448 Print

A Division of Rothstein Associates Inc.

203.740.7400

info@rothstein.com

www.rothstein.com

Keep informed about Rothstein Publishing:

 www.facebook.com/RothsteinPublishing

 www.linkedin.com/company/rothsteinpublishing

 www.twitter.com/rothsteinpub

ISBN 9781944480431 PDF

ISBN 9781944480424 EPUB

ISBN 9781944480448 Print

Library of Congress Control Number: 2017953266

A Division of Rothstein Associates Inc.

Brookfield, Connecticut USA

203.740.7400

info@rothstein.com

www.rothstein.com

Dedication

This book is dedicated to all the security practitioners in our industry who relentlessly and professionally practice their craft, at times with sleepless nights, and are so often are not appreciated for the role they play in the environments they work in. Also, to the volunteers who provide their expertise to help guide our profession and clear hurdles for our young professionals. Their unselfish dedication is recognized and appreciated.

Acknowledgments

The authors extend their humble thanks to the individuals and organizations whose support and feedback made this book possible. There are many people in the security industry who deserve praise; in particular, we'd like to acknowledge Ray O'Hara, Jeff Spivey, John Petruzzi, and Professor Martin Gil, each of whom has been a mentor to us both. Most importantly, they have been supportive friends on our journey in creating this book.

We also wish to acknowledge three security industry associations, ASIS, SIA, and ISC2. Each of these societies provided the needed support and avenues to network with peers as we were in the pursuit of the thought leadership needed to compile in this book. They will be the foundational organizations for driving our industry's future from being a trade to being a profession.

This three-year journey also couldn't be accomplished without the efforts of Kristen Noakes-Fry, our editor, and Philip Jan Rothstein, our publisher, who have provided their wisdom and guidance with the patience required to guide us newbies.

Last, we cannot thank Maria Allen and Eric Smith enough for supporting us each through this journey and allowing us to spend so much of our "free time" working on this book rather than spending it with them. We love you both!

Thank you all.

Foreword

Enterprise security risk management (ESRM) has long been in the shadows of the security industry, often mentioned but never documented. With this book, *Enterprise Security Risk Management: Concepts and Applications,* security practitioners will be able to support the growing importance of an evolving global security program for all enterprises around the world. I admire the authors, Rachelle Loyear and Brian Allen, for the work they have put in this book. It's funny how you choose your friends in life, and often they become life-long friends. In our case, we are close friends and business colleagues who all have a desire to share our knowledge with others and to lead our industry. Rachelle and Brian are two professionals with a relentless desire to help others be successful. If I had met them earlier in my career, my life would have been better for it.

Three things stand out for me as the core components of the book: enterprise, security risk, and risk principles. If nothing else, understanding these three concepts and being able to articulate what they mean in a business setting will advance your career and enhance your business acumen. If you are serious about your career and want to lead this industry, this book will help you to do that. We need leaders to take us to the next level – promoting ESRM in your organization and the business community will help to do that. From time to time, all of us have said, "If only I had known this years ago." Through this book, this is your chance to know it now and become that change agent our industry needs!

I am honored to have been selected to write this foreword. Rachelle and Brian would probably say that I mentored them. That may be partially true, but we really mentored each other. Now we are on this journey mentoring others, which is proving to be extremely rewarding as we go along this path. We have formed an alliance called the Global Security Risk Management Alliance (www.gsrma.net/). In GSRMA, our sole purpose is to educate others on the merits of ESRM. Some readers of this foreword may know me, while others might recognize my name, since I am very active in our industry internationally and am a former President of ASIS International. I speak frequently and I am vocal advocate for ESRM in the security industry. I consider this book, the first of its kind in our industry, to be a critical component of our efforts as security professionals to protect our people and assets around the world.

Ray O'Hara, CPP

Executive Vice President at AS Solution
President and Co-founder, Global Security Risk Management Alliance
Past President, ASIS International
Las Vegas, NV
September 2017

Foreword

In their new book, *Enterprise Security Risk Management: Concepts and Applications*, Brian Allen and his coauthor Rachelle Loyear – both seasoned security professionals – present the risk and security community with new opportunities based on an evolving security management framework. Forgetting the "old school" security formulas, the authors describe the global maturation of security risk management models for businesses.

Enterprise security risk management (ESRM) leaves behind the old and limited "guns, guards and gates" constructs of what security has been to explore what security can be as a part of the overall organizational risk management framework.

I urge that all senior management read and discuss Brian and Rachelle's vision of what is possible from an organization supported by the right security risk management program positively impacting the achievement of business goals and therefore elevating shareholder value. Boards of directors, executive management, and business stakeholders will all benefit from exploring ESRM, as described in this book.

The authors describe in detail how ESRM can be applied in many areas of a company that relate to business risk, including business continuity, crisis management, cybercrime, workplace violence, cybersecurity and more. Insights will continue to be gained from the book as readers have new realizations that security risks throughout the organization have a significant positive and negative impact to the achievement of business goals.

Brian and Rachelle have presented a wealth of thought-provoking options for the reader, and I am confident that this book will add bottom line value to the companies which choose to understand and implement ESRM.

Jeff Spivey, CRISC, CPP, PSP

CEO and Founder,
Security Risk Management, Inc.
Board Director, ISACA International
Past President, ASIS International
Charlotte, NC
September 2017

Foreword

Over the years, I have become a big fan of the writings and presentations of Brian Allen and Rachelle Loyear on enterprise security risk management (ESRM). They are outstanding professionals in their field, and the information they have shared is quickly becoming required reading, at least in the circle of security professionals I hang out with. As a board member of ASIS International, I have observed how the organization appears to be using Brian and Rachelle's work to develop material for the global membership to relaunch and refocus their efforts toward ESRM.

Throughout my career, I've tried (sometimes not very successfully) to incorporate many of the principles and practices Rachelle and Brian discuss in this new book, *Enterprise Security Risk Management: Concepts and Applications*. When I met resistance within the organization, I realize now that I was not following the methodology that they describe and illustrate in the following pages. I wish I could have referred to this content about 15 years ago – I could have saved myself a lot of sleepless nights and pointless debates with folks not familiar with security or risk.

This book's understanding of what a successful ESRM program looks like is compelling and represents something we as a profession must strive to achieve. In my opinion, we're past the days when a security professional can develop a security program based on a silo approach to protecting assets. I agree that it's time to replace the views we held in the past with the approach and vision described by Rachelle and Brian. We must change our approach to security and move in the direction of ESRM, or risk becoming insignificant to our organizations in the next 5 to 10 years.

That's a strong warning, but Rachelle and Brian have realized the urgency of the situation, and you can see it in the way their explanation of ESRM unfolds. From exploratory discussions about ESRM program and what it is (and isn't) through to the ongoing maintenance and support of a successful ESRM deployment, the text really develops a methodical approach that a security professional can follow. There's no hype or drama, and their examples bring practical advice we can all use in our journey to ESRM.

If you're a security professional looking toward the future and wondering how we as a profession will succeed – read this book. If you're looking for an opportunity to broaden your understanding of how ESRM truly supports the business – read this book. And if you're looking to create your own path for future success – well, you know my thoughts.

Tim McCreight, MSc CISSP CPP CISA

Director, Strategic Alliances

Hitachi Systems Security

Member, ASIS International Board of Directors

Calgary, Alberta, Canada

September 2017

Table of Contents

Part 1

Why Enterprise Security Risk Management (ESRM)?

In Part 1 of this book, we will discuss enterprise security risk management (ESRM) by exploring the definition of ESRM: what it is, what it is not, and how it differs from the security approaches that many, if not most, enterprises have in place today.

You will find out why ESRM is emerging as the answer to many of the most urgent problems security professionals face today, especially the frustrations they share with the business leaders of those enterprises they are tasked with securing. You will be prompted to think about what the success of your security program could look like when seen through a risk management lens. Finally, as you begin to use ESRM, you will experience personal and professional satisfaction as a security professional and become a recognized and trusted partner in the business-critical effort of protecting the enterprise and all of its assets.

In This Part:
- **What is Enterprise Security Risk Management (ESRM)?**
- **How Can ESRM Help You?**
- **How Can ESRM Help Your Security Program?**

What is Enterprise Security Risk Management?

This book is about an approach to security that is familiar and yet new, philosophical and yet practical: *enterprise security risk management* (ESRM).

How is it familiar? As a security professional, you are probably already practicing some of the components of ESRM. Many of the concepts of ESRM – such as risk identification, risk transfer and acceptance, crisis management, and incident response – will be well-known to you.

How is it new? In our many years of experience in the security industry, we have found few enterprises and few security organizations that apply these familiar principles in the comprehensive, *holistic* way that ESRM represents, much less who communicate them effectively to key decision-makers.

How is it philosophical? ESRM redefines the thinking on role of security in the enterprise, refocusing the security organization's efforts to work in partnership with business leaders and other key stakeholders to identify and mitigate security risks.

How is it practical? ESRM offers a straightforward, realistic, actionable approach to deal effectively with all the distinct types of security risks facing the security practitioner today.

This chapter will help you to:
- Define ESRM.
- Understand why ESRM is important both for your security program and for the entire security profession.
- Explain how ESRM is different from enterprise risk management (ERM) and why your organization needs both.

1.1 ESRM Defined

We will discuss the meaning and implications of ESRM in depth throughout this book, but first a simple, straightforward definition of the term:

> ***Enterprise security risk management*** is the application of fundamental risk principles to manage all security risks – whether related to information, cyber, physical security, asset management, or business continuity – in a comprehensive, holistic, all-encompassing approach.

There are three key factors to that definition: enterprise, security risk, and risk principles.

1.1.1 Enterprise

In this book, we use *enterprise* in the broadest sense of the meaning – a business, organization, or company. That can include:

- Public organizations (municipal, state, and federal).
- Privately held companies.
- Not-for-profit organizations that provide goods, services, or other non-profit activities.
- Stockholder controlled corporations.

When we talk about business, organization, company, or any other similar term in this book, we mean any or all of the enterprises above.

1.1.2 Security Risk

Risk is a very broad term, but ESRM deals specifically with security risk. When we say, "security risk," we mean anything that threatens harm to the enterprise: its mission, its employees, customers, or partners, its operations, its reputation – anything at all. That could be:

- A troubled employee with a gun.
- An approaching hurricane.
- A computer hacker in another country.
- A dissatisfied customer with access to a social media account and a wide audience.

Security risks take many different forms, and new ones are being introduced all the time. Recognizing those risks, making them known to the enterprise, and helping your enterprise business leaders mitigate them is central to the ESRM philosophy.

1.1.3 Risk Principles

The definition of ESRM states that risks are managed through fundamental risk principles. For that, we will reference an existing body of knowledge on how to manage *all* types of risk, and then apply it specifically to the security area.

The International Organization for Standardization, in *ISO Standard 31000:2009 – Risk Management: Principles and Guidelines*, and the American National Standards Institute, in *Principles of Risk Assessment*, both outline similar, highly effective, standards for risk management. A few examples of key principles from the ISO Standard 31000 (2009) are that risk management should:

- Be part of an holistic decision-making process.
- Be transparent and inclusive.
- Be dynamic, iterative, and responsive to change.
- Be capable of continual improvement and enhancement.

These are just a few points from the standard. The entire standard is quite comprehensive and we will describe more from this risk standard and others throughout this book to show you how to apply these fundamental principles of risk management.

On the surface, the definition of ESRM may sound like what you and your security organization are already doing. In fact, we have heard many people say, on first hearing of ESRM, "I already do that." But while you are probably already doing *some* parts of the overall ESRM practice, as you read further you will see how ESRM practiced holistically, according to this definition, is a major departure from traditional, "conventional" security.

Questions for the Security Practitioner
- "What kind of security risks have the potential to cause harm to my enterprise?"
- "Would my manager or the employees who report to me define *managing risks* the same way I do? What about other leaders in my organization?"

1.2 ESRM Overview

We will get into significant detail about all aspects of ESRM in further chapters. But first, we will take a brief look at the mission and goals of an ESRM program, the steps of the ESRM life cycle, and the role of the security practitioner in an ESRM security program.

1.2.1 ESRM Mission and Goals

To truly succeed, every department of an enterprise needs to fully understand why it exists, and what it does or needs to do for the enterprise it operates within. Security is no exception. Sometimes, as security professionals, we forget to think of our department as a *business* function, but it certainly is. ESRM, with its risk-based approach, provides a simple, effective way to frame the business mission and goals of the security organization – for ourselves as security practitioners, for the people in our security organizations working to achieve those goals, and for business leaders.

In 2015, ASIS International's CSO Roundtable group (of which one of us – Brian – was a member at the time) published an early description of ESRM. In their report, the group offered a clear description of the mission and goals of ESRM:
- The **mission** of ESRM is to identify, evaluate and mitigate the impact of security risks to the business, with prioritized protective activities that enable the business to advance its overall mission.
- The **goal** of ESRM is to engage with the business to establish organizational policies, standards, and procedures that identify and manage security risks to the enterprise. (Beheri, A., 2015).

When you embrace the ESRM philosophy, the organization you are tasked with protecting will help you identify what they care about and need protected. Then you will be able to assist them, provide input for them, and enable them to make the right decisions to protect their assets and functions. Ensuring that the organization understands that it is in their best interest to partner with security in identifying and mitigating risks is central to ESRM – and to your success as a security practitioner. The process of building that understanding and partnership is a topic that we will keep returning to throughout this book.

1.2.2 ESRM Life Cycle – A Quick Look

ESRM is a cyclical program. Once begun, the cycle of risk management is ongoing, as seen in Figure 1-1. In Part 2 of the book, you will learn more about each of the steps.

1. **Identify and Prioritize Assets** – Identifying, understanding, and prioritizing the assets of an organization that need protection.
2. **Identify and Prioritize Risks** – Identifying, understanding, and prioritizing the security threats the enterprise and its assets face – both existing and emerging – and, critically, the risks associated with those threats
3. **Mitigate Prioritized Risks** – Taking the necessary, appropriate, and realistic steps to protect against the most serious security threats and risks.
4. **Improve and Advance** – Conducting incident monitoring, incident response, and post-incident review; learning from both successes and failures; and applying the lessons learned to advance the program.

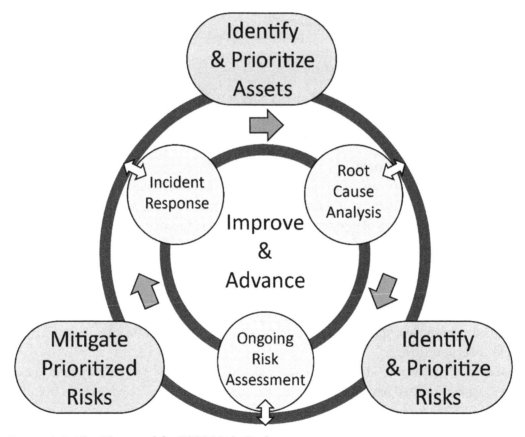

Figure 1-1. The Phases of the ESRM Life Cycle

1.2.3 Your Role in ESRM

Simply put, the role of the security practitioner – your role – in ESRM is to manage security risks. Those three words do encompass some more involved concepts, and that is what you will explore over the course of this book. But, ultimately, everything that the security practitioner, manager, executive, and department does in an ESRM paradigm is done to manage risks to the enterprise, in partnership with department or group leaders who are the stakeholders regarding those risks.

You will notice that we focus strongly on the *role* of the security practitioner as a manager of risk in all our discussions. That is because, so often, security is *not* viewed as an enterprise partner, risk manager, and enabler of business operations, but is, instead, viewed as enforcer, rule-maker, task-doer, and (sadly) at times an obstruction to getting things done. In the next few chapters, we will talk about why that is and how ESRM can help you change that view in your enterprise. For now, the key thing to remember is that the role of security in ESRM is to *manage security risk*.

Questions for the Security Practitioner
- "If I asked my manager or department executive what the role of security is, what answer would I likely receive?"
- "Do I know all of the important assets that need to be protected for my enterprise to accomplish its mission?"
- "Does my security department have a defined mission within my enterprise?"

1.3 Why is ESRM Important?

Unfortunately, in the traditional, non-risk-based security environment in which many of us security professionals work today, businesses often must experience a significant security event and impact *before* they take a close look at their security practice and then decide to give it more support and resources. We hear about this experience repeatedly in conversations with our peers in the security industry. Often, a terrible event must happen first before security implementations are given priority.

However, ESRM, when communicated and practiced consistently, allows your organizational leaders to make more educated security decisions based on identified and assessed risks, rather than letting those same risks go unmitigated until there is negative impact on the enterprise.

Today, we often find that security programs get significant traction and advance through one of four common scenarios:
1. Regulation, such as when a government or a private regulatory body like the Payment Card Industry tells the business it must do something.
2. Liability, such as when the organization is sued because of bad security practices, which leads the business to make changes in security to avoid getting sued again.
3. Major incidents that change the security landscape, such as natural disasters or criminal acts.
4. Executive foresight to avoid the other three.

ESRM avoids use of the "capitalize on tragedy" dynamic by building the enterprise support necessary for better security practices, *before* the significantly impactful event happens that more traditional security programs often find driving their momentum.

Case Study: Could ESRM Have Made a Difference at Chrysler?
In July 2015, *Wired Magazine* published an article about two security researchers, Charlie Miller and Chris Valasek, who hacked into a Jeep Cherokee through its wireless internet-connected entertainment system. Through that attack vector, they could send commands and gain access to more critical parts of the car, including the steering, brakes, and transmission. The controlled experiment, with the *Wired* reporter, Andy Greenberg, voluntarily at the wheel of the car, ended when the hackers remotely killed

the engine and steered the car off the road. It was a shocking article to many who had never considered the vulnerabilities associated with the desired convenience of having their car's entertainment system connected real-time to the internet (Greenberg, 2015). Although this attack was performed for research purposes only, and was, in fact, difficult to accomplish -- *and* there were no reports of accidents related to the exposed vulnerability -- Chrysler certainly had some trouble on its hands.

Quite obviously, this issue became a public relations nightmare for Chrysler as the story was picked up by multiple news agencies and repeated over and over during that news cycle. In addition to the immediate news, Chrysler also faced class-action lawsuits against claims of fraud, negligence, and breach of warranty claims. Adding to the trouble was the need to recall 1.4 million vehicles to receive a software update and close the vulnerability that the researchers used as the attack avenue. The issue even got the attention of Congress, which initiated legislation regulating security controls in vehicles, a subject that will certainly be battled over in the coming years. Clearly, all these things had expensive and disruptive implications for Chrysler's sales and operations.

We do not claim to know what security conversations happened surrounding Chrysler's rollout of the internet-connected entertainment system, and we *certainly* will not claim that practicing ESRM can ensure that *every* vulnerability is identified and mitigated in every project. But we will state confidently that if ESRM is incorporated into the security philosophy and practiced throughout the business, security risks are more likely to be discussed by the right asset owners and stakeholders. Such awareness will enable better security risk decision-making to occur, before the rollout of whatever product or service is under discussion.

Chrysler's internet-connected entertainment system seemed like a great idea for a consumer feature in the vehicle. However, when the project was in the planning stages, the stakeholders in the conversation around security should probably have included:

- Public affairs (public relations nightmare).
- Government affairs (regulatory implications).
- Legal (class-action lawsuits).
- Operations teams and dealer relations (1.4 million recalls).

All the above, at a minimum, should have been engaged in the security-risk decisions during research and development of these vehicle systems. Security subject matter experts could have been engaged right from the beginning of development, looking for security risks proactively and holistically, identifying asset owners and stakeholders who would need to be a part of the conversation.

Would having that foresight allowed Chrysler to avoid these security issues? Maybe or maybe not, but it would have given the business a much better opportunity to identify and engage the right stakeholders in finding risks and vulnerabilities and in making a more educated security-risk decision.

In the incident above, Chrysler clearly faced three of the four scenarios we outlined in the beginning of section 1.3. Would executive attention and support around the role of the security department have helped the company avoid this issue? It is probably not fair to answer that question from our outside perspective, but it is fair to infer that there is opportunity for *many* businesses to be more proactive in defining the role of security within their organization, and use security professionals to avoid a similar situation.

1.3.1 Traditional Corporate Security Scenarios: Something is Missing

Talking to a lot of security managers and practitioners at conferences, meetings, and other industry events, we have learned about a lot of different approaches to security. Discussing both successful and struggling security departments with managers and practitioners, we found:

- Security programs that work successfully in their organizations, even though the program is run largely on instinct or based on the experience of one leader, rather than as a formalized and documented process which could be extended into new areas.
- Security programs that are successfully involved in some areas of the enterprise, but completely blocked from being involved in other areas by business "silos."
- Security practitioners who feel like outsiders in the enterprise because they are called in only when they are "needed" – after something has gone wrong, not before.
- Security managers who are given authority in only one area of security (such as access control), while other aspects of security management (like investigations) are performed by other groups.
- Security managers who spend all their time performing tactical functions -- responding to incidents, implementing password controls, installing and monitoring video or access systems – rather than developing preventative strategies (often referred to as "fighting fires").
- Security programs that fail because they do not have the participation and support they need from the rest of the enterprise.
- Security managers who are "blindsided" by security problems that they were not even aware existed, but are still expected to take the blame for the problems.
- Security managers with organization leaders who admit that they are not sure when to get security involved in their processes, or are not sure of how to ask for help without seeming to have a problem.

While a lot is wrong here, of course, a lot is also right. We will be discussing throughout this book how ESRM can improve all the scenarios above. But for now, we would like to talk about one key component that is *missing* from all these: *consistency.*

Consistency = Trust

Why is consistency in your security function so important? It is because consistency in words and actions are ultimately what builds trust between you and your partners. People do not trust easily when situations are unpredictable. A consistent practice of risk-based security management, working in strong partnership with enterprise business functions, and showing your colleagues that your security group is there to support and assist the organization in fulfilling its mission and purpose will make you and your security department predictably reliable and trustworthy in the eyes of your strategic partners.

1.3.2 ESRM as a Driver for Consistency

In ESRM terms, consistency has two fundamental meanings:

- Consistently applying a security risk management philosophy to every part of the security function and in all security decision-making.
- Consistently communicating and defining security roles and responsibilities to the internal strategic partners who are so critical to the success of your ESRM program.

All the scenarios we listed above could be remedied by first consistently *communicating* to business leaders about the role of the security department (which is, as we have mentioned, to manage all security risks in partnership with the business), and by consistently *practicing* a risk-based program that builds trusted partnerships with those same leaders.

Bringing consistency to your security program is essential to ensuring that all your stakeholders across the enterprise:

- Understand exactly what to expect from you as a security professional and from your security program.
- Recognize and appreciate security's roles in the enterprise and its business value.
- Rely on you and your team to perform your roles as trusted business partners.

Consistency is driven by:

- Following known, documented, well-communicated practices.
- Remembering the proper steps of all security activities and processes.
- Always understanding the true role of the security function as managers of security risk.
- Practicing that understanding as the security leader.

That consistency begins with a structured path to implementing the ESRM program.

Questions for the Security Practitioner
- "Do I practice security in a consistent, transparent, and documented methodology that can be counted on to be the same in almost every interaction?"
- "Do my strategic partners in the enterprise understand my role, what I do, and how I can help them"?"
- "Do I communicate with my strategic partners on a consistent basis about security and the role of security, and not just when an incident of non-compliance occurs?"

Think About It: Where Are You and Your Department Five Years From Now?
It is the interview question everyone who has ever applied for a job hates: "Where do you see yourself five years from now?" It is never easy to answer because it means you must take stock of where you are right now and figure out whether your skills, your responsibilities, and your degree of influence will get you from here and now to where you want to be.

Before adopting the ESRM philosophy as the foundation of our security program, we asked ourselves the same things:

- "In five years from now, do we want to experience the same frustrations in getting things done as we do now?"
- "In five years, do we want the security department to continue to struggle for traction in protecting important enterprise assets?"
- "In five years, do we want our strategic partners within this enterprise to see us as valued contributors to the success of business operations? Or as a cost-center that prevents them from getting things done?"

The answers we gave to those questions led to the development and implementation of a successful risk-based security department in our organization, and, ultimately, to writing this book. Taking stock like this is something we think everyone should do at certain stages of their security careers. Perhaps like us, the answers to these questions may lead you to shift the direction you are going in.

For example, ask yourself how you want to be seen by business partners, senior executives – all the key people who will have influence over the course of your career. Then ask yourself whether you can clearly define your goals for success, and whether you have developed the skills you will need to go to the next level.

1.4 What is ESRM Not?

You have now seen a little about what ESRM is and why it is important to the success of your security practice. The first step on the ESRM journey is explaining the new philosophy to your strategic partners in the enterprise. To do that, you will need to have a firm understanding of the topic. While it might seem counterintuitive, a large part of understanding ESRM is also understanding what ESRM *is not*.

There are two topics that are often confused in discussions of ESRM. The first, which we will discuss below, is ERM – *enterprise risk management* – which is often confused with ESRM due to the similar name. The second is enterprise security convergence, a term you may have heard describing organizational and personnel management model that is not a philosophy of managing security risk. We will discuss convergence in more depth in Chapter 23.

1.4.1 How is ESRM Different from Enterprise Risk Management (ERM)?

ESRM is part of a larger universe of risk. While security risks are, by themselves, significantly important and can have severe impacts on the enterprise, they are not the only types of risk an enterprise can face. When discussing ESRM, we sometimes find that it can be confused with the larger topic of ERM, which includes many types of risk, such as:

- Financial and investment risk.
- Supply chain risk.
- Operational risk.
- Resource risk.

There are a lot of different risk approaches out there; many of them, like ERM, are well-known and widely practiced. When you are working to understand ESRM and communicate its principles to others, it is very important that you *first* understand how and why it is different from those other approaches. ESRM is different from ERM, and it certainly does not attempt to replace it.

The same group of CSOs associated with ASIS International, which we referenced earlier, had the following to say about the difference between ERM and ESRM:

> Enterprise Risk Management (ERM) looks at the universe of risks – financial, strategic, accidental, and so on – that an organization faces. However, ERM does not always fully consider the risks that are traditionally associated with security. Enterprise Security Risk Management (ESRM) is a working philosophy ensuring that these risks are properly considered and treated. (CSO Roundtable, 2010).

ERM is often an established program within the enterprise, sometimes separate, or sometimes part of Internal Audit or Compliance, designed to manage risks for the enterprise. These risks are not, by any means, limited to security risks. They may include virtually any type of risk the enterprise could face – everything from market capitalization problems to the possibility of a hostile takeover.

An ERM program usually has a defined scope, a formal risk assessment process, and often has a dedicated Enterprise Risk Management department as well. ERM also uses risk principles when managing enterprise risks, which include, but are not limited to, security risks. The security organization should always play a role in the ERM program, along with other functions, such as finance, HR, legal, and operations, in order to identify and address the security-related risks that the enterprise may be facing.

By contrast, ESRM uses risk management principles to manage all *security-specific* risks across an enterprise. It does not define an organization, specific job roles, or a required management structure, but simply establishes a management philosophy and process that the security organization can use to guide the enterprise in identifying, managing, and accepting security risks.

To make the differences between ERM and ESRM a little easier to grasp, Table 1-1 shows some of the significant differences between ESRM and ERM for you to be aware of and to communicate to your stakeholders should the question arise of why both are needed.

Table 1-1. What is the Difference Between ESRM and ERM?

Enterprise Risk Management	Enterprise Security Risk Management
It focuses on all aspects of organizational risk – operational, environmental, and especially financial.	It focuses solely on managing *security* risks to organization assets.
It is a defined program with a specific structure, usually a department in and of itself.	It is a working philosophy for managing security risk through traditional risk-management principals, but does not require any specific departmental structure.
ERM programs may or may not include or look at security-related risks as part of the overall risk profile of the organization.	ESRM does not look for risks outside the security realm.
ERM typically must focus on the highest priority risks to the enterprise, leaving focus on less impactful risks out of the risk register.	ESRM assesses and analyzes all security risks, then prioritizes them for mitigation or other responses, allowing for a more granular approach to security risk.

Chapter Review

In Chapter 1, you learned:

- Enterprise security risk management (ESRM) is the application of fundamental risk principles to manage all security risks – whether informational, cyber, physical security, asset management, or business continuity – in a comprehensive, holistic, all-encompassing approach.
- ESRM is performed in a life cycle of risk management that includes:
  - Asset assessment and prioritization.
  - Risk assessment and prioritization.
  - Risk treatment (mitigation).
  - Continuous improvement.
- ESRM helps provide a common operating philosophy that can alleviate frustration when security and business interests are misaligned.
- ESRM is a working philosophy for security practitioners. It is different from traditional enterprise risk management (ERM), which typically focuses on more finance-driven risks and is also different from the more general topic of security convergence.

Looking Forward

In Chapter 2, we will:

- Look at how ESRM can impact security students, professionals, and managers to enable them to be more successful in their careers.
- Discuss how executives who have security practitioners reporting to them can be more effective, by using ESRM to ensure the success of the security department.

Practitioner steps to consider before moving on to Part 1, Chapter 2:

- ✓ Work to understand and define the current security philosophy in your enterprise.
- ✓ Understand the relationship between the existing security department and any enterprise risk management (ERM) program that exists.
- ✓ Begin to look at the structure of the organization with an eye to discovering existing security risks that the organization might be exposed to.

Security Program Self-Assessment

In this self-assessment, you should think about the answer to the questions posed, and then see where your program is on the identified ESRM spectrum.

Question	Y/N	Is This ESRM?
Do you identify assets owned by the enterprise that might be at risk of harm and need protection?	□Yes □No	**NO**: If you have never developed a list of all enterprise assets, this is a preliminary step for an ESRM program. **PARTIAL**: If you are reaching out to internal departments and other groups to get updated asset lists in order to implement camera or access coverage, you are part of the way to an ESRM implementation. **YES**: If you are reaching out to departments and other groups to determine the assets owned by a business function, asking about the impact that losing those assets might have, and then working with the department or group to identify a mitigation plan that the organization wants to implement, you are practicing ESRM.

Questions for Discussion

1. How can the enterprise benefit from including ESRM as a security practice, in addition to using a higher level ERM program?
2. Why is it important to the security program that ESRM is practiced in a cycle that continually feeds back on itself?
3. What do you think the consistent application of ESRM principles could do for your reputation in the enterprise with department leaders and senior executives?

References

Beheri, A. (2015, December). *Enterprise security risk management: A holistic approach to security.* Retrieved from https://www.linkedin.com/pulse/enterprise-security-risk-management-holistic-approach-alaa

CSO Roundtable of ASIS International. (2010, April). *Enterprise security risk management: How great risks lead to great deeds.* Retrieved from https://cso.asisonline.org/esrm/Documents/CSORT_ESRM_whitepaper_%20pt%201.pdf.

Greenberg, A. (2015, July). Hackers remotely kill a jeep on the highway—with me in it. *Wired Magazine.* Retrieved from https://www.wired.com/2015/07/hackers-remotely-kill-jeep-highway/

International Organization for Standardization (ISO). (2009). *ISO/IEC 31000:2009 Risk management – Principles and guidelines.* Geneva, Switzerland: Author.

Learn More About It

For further reading about risk management principles:

Fraser, J. & Simkins, B. (2010). *Enterprise risk management: Today's leading research and best practices for tomorrow's executives.* Hoboken, NJ: J. Wiley & Sons.

Frigo, M. & Anderson, R. (2011). *Embracing enterprise risk management: Practical approaches for getting started.* Available at https://www.coso.org/Documents/Embracing-ERM-Getting-Started.pdf

Lam, J. (2014). *Enterprise risk management: From incentives to controls,* 2nd Edition. Hoboken, NJ: J. Wiley & Sons.

For further reading about enterprise risk management:

Committee of Sponsoring Organizations of the Treadway Commission (COSO). (2004, September). *COSO Enterprise risk management – Integrated framework executive summary.* Available at https://global.theiia.org/standards-guidance/topics/Documents/Executive_Summary.pdf

NC State ERM Initiative. (2017), *Library articles, resources, research.* Article listings available at https://erm.ncsu.edu/library/categories/category/.enterprise–risk–management–erm–basics

2

How Can ESRM Help You?

Now that you have learned about the definition of ESRM and why embracing ESRM is important for security success, in Chapter 2, we want to build on that general definition and delve further into the importance of ESRM. You will see how anyone who is responsible for security can benefit professionally and personally from a clear understanding of ESRM principles, no matter what enterprise, industry, or level, and at any stage of their career.

This chapter will help you to:
- Discover how ESRM can help advance you in the security field, no matter if you are a student, a newcomer, or a professional.
- Identify the challenges at each step of your career development.
- Recognize how all roles and departments in an organization can work together to handle risks using the ESRM model.
- Involve the Board in ESRM and help members see the benefits.

2.1 Security Function Professionals

At this point in your security career, you may be a newcomer, such as a college student looking for your first job or a public sector professional looking to transition to work in private sector security. Or you may already be a security professional, who is:

- An experienced executive leading an entire security program.
- A professional in a single-function security environment.
- A professional in a converged logical and physical security environment.
- An experienced professional seeking the synergies that a converged environment could bring.

No matter what, the ESRM philosophy and practice has a specific benefit to you and your program. We will examine how you can benefit if you are in one of these categories or working with those in one of these categories:

- Security student.
- New security practitioner.
- Security manager.
- Transitioning public sector professional.
- Security practitioner.
- Business function manager.
- Enterprise senior executive.
- Board member.

2.1.1 The Student

As security becomes increasingly professionalized, it is also becoming increasingly attractive as a career choice for a broad range of individuals. With the job market seeing a projected 1.5 million-person shortfall in the cybersecurity workforce by 2019 (Morgan, S., 2015), many people are studying at the undergraduate or postgraduate level to join the security industry in both general security and information security, or in related fields, such as risk management.

As a student in the security field, whether you are interested in pursuing a skillset in cyber/information security, physical security, investigations, threat management, emergency management, or other types of security activities, you will eventually be called upon to discuss the risks associated with the tasks, activities, and processes you are learning to carry out.

2.1.1.1 How Can ESRM Help You?

ESRM can help you add to your current knowledge and skills by defining the key, necessary expertise to become a well-rounded security professional and can help you find the valuable security roles you are looking for.

By applying an ESRM lens to your learning process even *before* you begin working in the security industry, you will benefit from understanding the business-centric and risk-based philosophy of ESRM and how it can be applied once you begin work as a security professional.

2.1.2 The New Security Practitioner

Security practitioners may come into the industry by many paths. Some may specifically go to school to learn security skillsets. Others may find themselves working in security after security responsibilities were given to them as part of a job in human resources, facilities, information technology, or some other enterprise function. These are just two possible paths, but everyone has been "new" to their security role at some point. We believe that understanding ESRM will help you, as a new practitioner, to ultimately have a more successful security career moving forward. It certainly will provide you with a foundation to develop necessary organizational and security management skillsets as you prepare for additional responsibilities and professional growth.

2.1.2.1 How Can ESRM Help You?

ESRM principles can help new security practitioners develop a comprehensive understanding of the value they offer the enterprise and communicate that understanding to their peers and their superiors, both inside and outside the security organization. This will both make you significantly more effective in your security efforts and help you advance in the security organization.

2.1.3 The Security Manager or Executive

As a security practitioner who has the responsibility and professional experience to manage and run a security program, you face the challenge of developing a comprehensive program for identifying real-world risks and protecting the enterprise against them. You may manage a program in a small enterprise where you provide only physical security to a few facilities, or you may manage a wide-ranging program in a large enterprise that covers physical and cyber security, investigations, crisis management, and more. Whatever the scope and size of the program, having a clear understanding of risk-based security will help you and your program support the enterprise more effectively. Having a clear definition of security's role and consistent expectations of the security function allows for a smoother integration of security across the entire organization.

2.1.3.1 How Can ESRM Help You?

ESRM principles offer a strategic framework for developing a security program, communicating its importance to enterprise leaders, and obtaining critical senior-level commitment to security. These are the key aspects of any security program. Risk-management principles will assist you in communicating the value of the security program to your strategic partners in other organizational functions, as well as the executive management of your enterprise.

Questions for the Security Manager
- "Does the management of my organization understand what the security department does?"
- "Does the management of my organization support the security mission and see my department as a valuable contributor to business success?"

Think About It: The "Seat at the Table"

A statement we hear often in the security profession is about the need to get "a seat at the table," to have your ideas heard and taken seriously on how to best protect the enterprise you have been tasked with securing. ESRM is a program and path that can lead to the security leader having that all important access to the CEO or executive level. How?

1. ESRM clearly defines the role of the security department in managing security risks to enterprise assets, does not simply perform daily tasks to "make things safe."
2. ESRM brings the security leader into the discussion of furthering and supporting the mission and goals of the enterprise.
3. ESRM allows both business and security leaders to discuss, in business terms, the costs and benefits and various security risk responses and to align those responses with business-defined tolerance levels for risk.

Those three points will allow you to clearly and confidently explain your role in the enterprise and your business value to business leaders. The "seat at the table" is reserved for discussions of enterprise strategy, direction, and goals. An ESRM security program elevates the security discussion from the day-to-day tasks performed to a strategic discussion of aligning security-mitigation planning to overall risk tolerances – making security leadership part of the business discussion and fully a part of enterprise leadership.

2.1.4 The Transitioning Public Sector Professional

Many security practitioners come to the private security profession from previous careers in public sector positions such as the military, law enforcement, or public emergency management. These public roles provide a significant amount of experience for the transitioning professional in many aspects of security management. However, the world of private sector security is a very different environment than the public realm and ESRM can truly help the former public professional to adapt to the realities of a corporate environment. Public sector professionals often function in a world of command and control, where strict chains of command are in place and the decisions made at the top are carried out without question by those below them. Additionally, former law enforcement professionals usually operate in an enforcement mode, where they have a clear mandate to catch wrong-doers and ensure they are punished for transgressions. As you are seeking to transition, you may speak with colleagues who have already transitioned and heard their experiences in how private sector is "different." ESRM can help you with that.

2.1.4.1 How Can ESRM Help You?

If you are a transitioning public sector professional and are more used to working in the environment we described above, you will find that understanding ESRM will be an invaluable help in navigating the different ways of doing things in a private sector organization. Often you will find that your recommendations as a subject matter expert might be negated by a budget decision, or a functional leader might refuse to let you investigate an incident in their area because they do not want to have their business interrupted. The risk management approach of the ESRM philosophy will enable you to navigate the bureaucratic obstacles that can cause so much frustration for transitioning public sector security practitioners.

Questions for the Security Practitioner
- "What are my expectations of how my security decisions will be received and implemented in the private sector?"
- "Have I discussed how the management in the enterprise understands of the role of security?"
- "What issues have I heard from other transitioning public sector colleagues as they have moved into the private sector?"

2.2 Business Functional Professionals

Every enterprise must eventually face that it will encounter risks of harm to enterprise assets, personnel, and operations. The impact from these security risks may be minor, such as a vandalized broken window in a retail center. Or the risks may be major, such as a significant cyber-intrusion to the network, which brings down operations on an entire computerized manufacturing line for a week. Neither of these possible scenarios can be solely the responsibility of the security team. As business function leaders, you must be aware of the security risks your area of responsibility faces to make sure that the impacts from potential risks are mitigated according to your business tolerances. Ultimately, in the risk-based philosophy of ESRM, it *must be* a business decision to identify what security risks are acceptable and what impact must be avoided. The ESRM-based security function will assist in that and help you build a true strategic partnership with your security team to protect the enterprise.

2.2.1 The Business Function Manager

Business function managers, whatever their area or level of responsibility, will eventually need to interact with the security function. All areas of the enterprise have some exposure to risk of harm. Some functions will have an acceptable level, while others may require actions to mitigate the impact of those security risks. Whatever the case, business function managers who do not understand the risk-management role of the security department too often look upon the security department as simply an enforcement mechanism or as the group solely responsible for protecting the company's assets. Neither view is strictly correct, and both can lead to an unhealthy and unproductive partnership. ESRM principles can help managers collaborate effectively with security professionals in managing security risks that threaten their assets and their business goals.

2.2.1.1 How Can ESRM Help You?

If you are a business function leader who interacts with the security organization in any way, or perhaps has oversight of the security function under your area of leadership, learning about ESRM and the risk-based philosophy of security will build an understanding of what you should expect from a security practitioner and organization. In addition to understanding what to expect from the security professionals in your enterprise, understanding ESRM will enable you to recognize and appreciate your own role in managing the security risks your function is exposed to. You will gain a clearer picture of what it means to be an asset owner and risk stakeholder in an ESRM program and what input and activities will be expected from you in managing security risk.

2.2.2 The Senior Executive

Senior executives in the enterprise have ultimate responsibility for all business functions and for enterprise success overall. The company senior executives must manage all enterprise risk – security risks as well as other types. However, many senior executives come up through the company through an operational or financial path, and as such may not have the in depth understanding of the security function needed to properly deal with enterprise *security* risk. Senior executive support for the security organization is critical to ensure a successful security function and to prevent harm to enterprise assets. ESRM will help with this.

2.2.2.1 How Can ESRM Help Your Organization?

As a senior executive, by understanding ESRM, you will gain a clear and actionable overview of security's role in the enterprise, what to expect from a successful security program and a baseline to define success, how to position the security leader and department to be successful, and what are the core competencies needed in a security manager and a security organization. ESRM will help you learn what your responsibility is in guiding the security organization in managing threats to the company's assets. It will enable you to know what to look for, what questions to ask, and what kinds of metrics and reports you should expect to measure the impact of the security group in your organization.

2.2.3 The Company Board of Directors

The Board of Directors is the guiding body of the enterprise. In the security realm, it is the responsibility of board members to understand and ensure all types of risk are managed in line with enterprise risk tolerance levels. As with the senior executives, many board members have less exposure to security topics than other risk areas. An understanding of ESRM will assist in managing these less familiar types of risk. The Board plays a significant role in ensuring that throughout the business, security risks can be communicated and escalated with proper transparency. They also play a role in ensuring that the security department and the security leader have independent reporting lines, which allow for proper security risk management and independence in executing those functions.

2.2.3.1 How Can ESRM Help Your Organization?

By understanding ESRM, members of boards of directors of companies will gain a greater appreciation of security's role in the business, and especially how a security organization can limit shareholder liability. They will learn the importance of a security governance model that delivers transparency and accountability, how to incorporate security risks into a practice that is based on risk principles, and how to identify obstacles to security risk issues that are being identified, accepted, and mitigated. Reporting security risks and metrics to the Board under an ESRM practice will help identify and communicate if risk tolerance levels are changing or being impacted and allow Board members to make more educated decisions on security risks.

Questions for the Board Member
- "Does the board have a focus on security topics as part of the regular agenda?"
- "Do I understand how my role as a board member impacts security risks of the organization?"
- "Does the board focus on security risks to the enterprise holistically? Are we focused on one or two narrow topics like data breaches?"

Chapter Review

In Chapter 2, you learned:

- How ESRM can help security practitioners at every stage of their career to be more successful in managing security risks to their enterprise.
- How business function and enterprise leaders can enhance their understanding of security risk and how it impacts the enterprise by working with their security department in an ESRM model.
- How both security and other business functional professionals can benefit from learning more about ESRM.

Looking Forward

In Chapter 3, you will:

- Contrast the traditional view of the security function in business organizations with the ESRM view of security.
- Explore common security frustrations and how embracing an ESRM philosophy can help alleviate them.
- Define what constitutes success in the security area.

Practitioner steps to consider before moving on to Part 1, Chapter 3:
- ✓ Analyze where you are in your career and consider how the benefits of ESRM might assist with your career development.
- ✓ Evaluate how your relationships in the enterprise might be improved by applying an ESRM philosophy.

Security Program Self-Assessment

In this self-assessment, you should think about the answer to the questions posed, and then see where your program is on the identified ESRM spectrum.

Question	Y/N	Is This ESRM?
Does the Board of Directors, or the executive management, of your organization have a regular report on security activities?	□Yes □No	**NO**: If the Board of Directors has no security topics on the agenda and leaves the security topic to company management, this is an excellent place to target for an eventual ESRM implementation. **PARTIAL**: If the Board of Directors requests ad-hoc updates on the overall enterprise state of security, or regular updates on one narrow aspect of security, like cyber security, your enterprise is part of the way towards practicing ESRM. **YES**: 1) If the security function presents to the Board of Directors on at least an annual basis on the state of overall security risk for the enterprise, 2) If the Board has a clear understanding of the security department's role as managers of security risk, not just the tasks it is assigned, 3) If the Board and/or executives have played a direct role in aligning the security department within the organization to risks that can be communicated through a transparent process, then you are practicing ESRM.

Questions for Discussion

1. In what ways can the security practice be different in public and private sector security?
2. How can the security practitioner use this book to assist strategic business partners in the enterprise to better understand the security role and responsibilities to the organization?
3. How can executives with security responsibilities better understand the security practitioners in their organization?
4. How does an understanding of ESRM benefit both the security and business function professional?

References

Morgan, S. (2015, July). Cybersecurity job market to suffer severe workforce shortage. *Cybersecurity Business Report.* Retrieved from http://www.csoonline.com/article/2953258/it-careers/cybersecurity-job-market-figures-2015-to-2019-indicate-severe-workforce-shortag

3

How Can ESRM Help Your Security Program?

So far, you have seen a little bit about the basics of ESRM: What it is, what it is not, who can benefit from it, and how. Now, before we start getting into the deeper fundamentals of the practice, we want to cover some of the benefits of ESRM.

In Chapter 3, we will discuss some of the frustrations we hear from security professionals and their strategic partners across the globe, some of which you may find familiar. We will also talk about how ESRM can help alleviate many of those frustrations and at the same time, improve the overall success of your security program.

This chapter will help you to:

- Explore how security has traditionally been viewed both inside and outside of the security profession.
- Understand how ESRM can change the perception of security in your enterprise to help you better communicate the value of security risk management.
- See how ESRM is the best methodology to meet the changing global security risk climate.

3.1 The Traditional View of Security and Why the Industry Must Change

When we first began discussing and exploring the concepts and ideas that eventually led to the development of ESRM security management principles, we talked to a lot of security professionals about their programs. We discussed things like:

- What they did.
- How they did it.
- When they felt like they were being successful.
- Whether they felt supported.
- When they felt like they were not getting the job done in the way they wanted to get it done.
- If they felt valued in their companies.
- What obstacles they faced.
- What helped them to get things done.

During these discussions, we heard a lot of security professionals repeatedly express frustration with some of the same topics, even though they managed very successful programs:

- Security budgets being cut without reason.
- Projects not prioritizing security until the last minute, if at all.
- Department leaders refusing to allow security investigations in their areas.
- Clear cases of wrongdoing not dealt with appropriately.

These same themes were mentioned repeatedly by our peers in the security industry. We came to realize that much of what we considered to be wrong in our own security program, as well as what they said was wrong in theirs, had to do with the *perceptions* of security by organizational leadership – and within the security group. We began to think of that perception as the "traditional" view of security. The concepts of ESRM evolved to respond to that perception and the need to change it. ESRM is a way to help both security practitioners and business leadership understand the true role of security in an enterprise. All this builds the trust needed to truly make security an integral part of an enterprise and help the organization carry out its mission of managing security risk.

3.1.1 The Traditional View of Security

Here is an exercise that we did repeatedly. Try it. We think you will be surprised at the results. The next time you are in a room full of security professionals, ask this deceptively simple question:

"What does security do?"

3.1.1.1 What Does Security Do? – The Answer from the Security Practitioner

Chances are, you will get as many different responses as there are people in the room. Here are just a few of the kinds of comments we heard, and similar to what you are likely to hear during the discussion:

- "Security's job is to protect the company's business assets."
- "Information security – making sure sensitive personal information, like credit card data, is protected."
- "We're focused on physical security."
- "Investigating breaches of company security policy."

These responses are not wrong, exactly. In fact, with the traditional way of approaching security, they are all correct – specifically to the person talking – and that is the heart of the problem. The answers are all very different, and they are all *incomplete* as a definition of the security *profession*. That is because they are all describing security *jobs.*

The other problem with these types of common answers is that they do not touch on what the role of security is – only what the answerer *sees* security do. The definitions feel like they are incomplete because they do not start with and consistently define the role of security – they just talk about tasks.

Questions for the Security Practitioner
- "Have I ever asked stakeholders in my organization an open-ended question like, 'What is security's role here?'"
- What would the answers be like if I did? Would they vary, by department or title?
- "What benefit might I get, both from asking the question and from the answers?"
- "How would I answer if someone asked me the same question? Would my answer change, depending on the circumstances (for example, who was asking the question)? Would I just be listing the tasks that my security program performs? Or would I have a broader answer describing my role in the company?"

3.1.1.2 What Does Security Do? – The Answer from the Board of Directors and Senior Executives

Now imagine you left that room full of security professionals and walked next door to ask the same question of a group of board members, line-of-business owners, or senior executives. You would almost certainly get an equally wide-ranging, equally "correct" – and equally incomplete – set of answers, perhaps like:

- "Security manages the physical security on our property, like the guards and gates."
- "Security protects our data, through things like password management and network monitoring."
- "It is all about protecting our people on campus, and making sure our systems and data are safe."
- "They help keep us up and running if something goes really wrong, like a natural disaster."

Again, these answers, in and of themselves, are not wrong. They are based on these key decision-makers' perceptions, their mindset, their experiences, and what they observe security doing every day. But, just like the security practitioners' responses, these are not adequate to define what security is. The ESRM definition of security and our role goes beyond what we see in both sets of answers above, not simply describing the tasks we are responsible for, but clarifying security's role in the enterprise overall.

3.1.2 Why the Security Industry Needs to Define "Security"

Reactions like the ones we have listed above clearly do not reflect a comprehensive, accurate view of the important work you do – and we imagine they do not reflect the way you want yourself and your role as a security professional to be perceived. But they are all too common, and they are damaging to your effectiveness, and your success, as a security professional.

That is why defining security – its role, its objectives, and the most appropriate ways of measuring success – is so important. If we in the security profession cannot define what we do, how we do it, and why we do it, we:

1. Cannot possibly be sure we are successful.
2. Cannot ensure that security is recognized seriously as a serious professional business discipline.
3. Will be leaving it to others to define security through their perceptions and experiences (and define it in ways that we are not likely to agree with).

Significant issues can come from letting people outside the security organization define security:
1. It often results in the security practice within an enterprise being broken up, or "siloed," so physical and investigative security responsibilities are handled separately from information/cybersecurity responsibilities (although when you are using ESRM as your security philosophy, the process of protecting assets, whether they are physical or logical, is precisely the same).
2. It can lead to some clear security responsibilities being handled by groups entirely outside of security (for example, HR performing investigations or facilities handling guard services).
3. It can lead to security functions being cut from areas where it is assigned as a responsibility but is not central to the core department mission, and then the enterprise misses key aspects of a comprehensive security program entirely.

Why, then, do security practitioners, business executives, operational managers, and ordinary employees still have so many different answers to the question of what security is, and such different expectations of what the security department should be doing? To us, the answer lies in several problems we have discussed already in Part 1 of this book and will continue to focus on going forward. They are:
- The absence of a consistent "philosophy" of security management.
- A focus on tactical functions – daily operational tasks – rather than strategic, risk-focused, decision-making that leads to our programs being defined by those functions and assigned tasks.
- A view of the security practitioner's role that centers on enforcement of rules, rather than on management of risks.

These problems can lead to weakened security that can compromise the enterprise and lead to frustration for both security practitioners and their strategic partners in the organization. They can all be addressed mostly effectively by the application of ESRM principles.

3.1.3 The ESRM View of Security – A Profession, not a Trade

In this book, we will be taking a close look at that deceptively simple question, "What does security do?" The varying responses and reactions we saw when security practitioners and enterprise leaders were asked to define security suggests that it is a difficult question, but it really is not. At least, not when ESRM principles are applied. ESRM offers a very simple, highly definitive, and extremely useful answer:

"Security manages the enterprise's security risks – all of them – using basic risk principles."

Looking back at the earlier exercise of asking, "What does security do?" to a roomful of security professionals, we can see that – whether they recognize it or not – their responses to the question can be distilled down to, "Manages security risks."

Table 3-1 shows what their statements mean when they are looked at through the lens of ESRM. The bottom line always comes back to a risk that needs to be managed through sound risk management principles.

Table 3-1. Traditional Views of Security Reconsidered Through ESRM

Traditional View	ESRM View
"Security's job is to protect the company's business assets."	To be precise, security means protecting the company's assets – all of them, physical, logical, and human – against the many risks presented by a fast-changing and increasingly dangerous world. All the security measures we take are aimed at managing and mitigating known and emerging risks.
"Information security makes sure that sensitive personal information, like credit card numbers, is protected."	A seemingly endless series of high-profile data security breaches shows the risks of inadequate information security – risks that can literally be fatal for a enterprise. ESRM principles recognize the entire range of security risks, and help security professionals and their strategic partners in the enterprise address them appropriately while understanding each other's roles in the management process.
"We're focused on physical security."	Physical security is the practice of protecting the company's physical property from a variety of security risks, ranging from theft to damage to misuse. The ESRM approach, however, views this as an aspect of risk. Those physical security activities being done are there to *mitigate a risk or multiple risks*, not just done for the sake of doing them.
"Investigating breaches of company security policy."	When security policies are not followed, whether intentionally or unintentionally, the company is exposed to an enormous range of risks, ranging from legal liability to fines for regulatory noncompliance to reputational and brand damage. Investigation is the first, necessary response to an indication of a breach of policy. It is also the first step in understanding root causes and mitigating the risk(s) involved.

3.1.3.1. Managing Security Risks

Managing security risks enterprise-wide is your role and your responsibility as a security professional. ESRM, because it is comprehensive, holistic, and all-encompassing, is what makes that possible. Because no matter what type of security risk is being discussed, the practice of managing those security risks is essentially the same. Treating all security risks in the same manner will mean your program is completely consistent in its approach to, execution of, and messaging about all parts of the security program. Describing what you do to manage security risks will close gaps in awareness of how you are perceived by your peers inside the organization. This consistency makes it easier for others both to understand what you do and to be more willing to partner with you in protecting the enterprise.

3.1.4 ESRM-Based Security – Moving from Task Management to Risk Management

At the heart of ESRM is the recognition that security is an *overarching strategic concern*, not a set of tactical, operational tasks to be performed.

3.1.4.1 Security Task Management

In today's security world, every practitioner is busy. There are threats to monitor, video cameras to repair, investigations starting up, gates to guard, executives to protect, data to encrypt, metrics to analyze and report on, and employees to manage. So, it is not surprising, as we saw earlier in our "questions" exercise, that the tasks we perform every day are used to define our discipline. These are the first things that come to mind when we are asked to explain what we do for the organization. It is not surprising, but it is a mistake. It is a mistake that damages our effectiveness and credibility as security professionals and, even more importantly, compromises the security of the people and assets we are tasked with protecting.

Why? Because when you define your role as doing things – completing tasks – then it is easy for people to view that task as unimportant, or not their problem, or not something that should come out of their budget. It is just one task or item, after all. But ESRM can change that definition by ensuring that your role is clearly defined as managing security risks. Describing your role as managing risks means that those risks must at least be *considered* when security decisions are made, or else the decision makers are not performing due diligence to protect their operations, or even more simply, are not making educated security decisions about their assets.

3.1.4.2 Security Risk Management

Risk management is the identification, assessment, treatment, and monitoring of security risks to the organization. It is fundamentally different from task management because it means looking at ways to protect the company at a strategic level, as well as at a tactical level. It is deeply concerned with allowing the enterprise to complete its mission with minimal interruption from security-related incidents. Of course, risk management can still involve tasks, but these are tasks with a higher purpose. These are tasks that are given to personnel with tactical security expertise so that they can mitigate an identified risk. In this way, the role of the security group is to carry out a program that helps the enterprise to protect itself, not merely to be a gate or a guard or an access control method. This may seem like playing with words, but truly this small difference in approach can lead to a very big change in the way you, and your security team are perceived.

3.1.4.3 The ESRM Solution: A New Philosophy

Implementing ESRM brings with it a holistic view of securing the enterprise through a consistent philosophy and management methodology. This view extends far beyond the day-to-day operational tasks that are assigned to the security organization.

It seems obvious, and yet many security professionals routinely do these tasks – assess risks and implement risk mitigation plans, perform root cause analysis, make proactive recommendations – without considering that they are, in fact, aspects of overall, enterprise-wide security risk management. That lack of consideration about how the tasks impact overall risk means that moving from a task-oriented, performance-based security program to a comprehensive, holistic ESRM program requires a *fundamental* shift in how many security professionals think about both security and risk. It also requires a shift in how they think about how their current responsibilities fit with the overarching role that security plays in the enterprise. When we, as security professionals, change the way we think, we change the way we present ourselves, and it follows that we also change how others see us – from task-doers to risk managers.

3.1.5 Why Is the Traditional Approach to Security So Frustrating for So Many People?

One of the most critical issues we have found in our discussions with our peers in the security profession and with their strategic partners inside their organizations is that almost everyone involved with security (whether the practitioner or the impacted stakeholder) often feels frustration at the process and the experience. This frustration can manifest in many ways. For example, an internal business partner has overturned or dismissed a security proposal, the security requirements have been dictated to the security practitioner against their recommendation, or a business leader has decided that security requirements are onerous and interfering with getting their work done.

When we looked at all the various frustrations, however, we found that they are often the result of one of two things:

1. The security practitioner is not fully aware of what their role is.
2. The strategic partner is not fully aware of what security's role is.

Both situations are avoidable and are the responsibility of the security practitioner to correct. First, by understanding that the role of security in the enterprise is to be mangers of security risk. Second, by communicating a comprehensive understanding of that role and appropriately setting the expectations of what security and the business leaders should be doing in the security risk management process.

3.1.5.1 The Missing Network Switch: A Story of Security Frustration

Let us look at a fictional story to examine this all-too-familiar problem from the perspective of both the security practitioner and a business function leader. Although this is fictional, it is something that happens in real life all too often. In the next two sections, we will examine a security risk and incident as played out in the "traditional" security environment.

3.1.5.1.1 The Traditional Security Environment

The Security Practitioner

Rick M., is a security manager for Aspect Insurance, a multibillion-dollar health insurance provider. Rick has been assigned the task of protecting one of his company's data centers, which is undergoing a major upgrade involving an independent contractor. Data security is a critical concern for the company because its operations are subject to rigorous regulatory compliance requirements. The data center handles massive amounts of personally identifiable information, and a security breach would be a disaster, exposing the company to regulatory scrutiny, legal liability, and serious reputational damage to its brand.

Rick knows all this, and he is deeply concerned about the security risks inherent in having outside contractors onsite in such a sensitive location. In keeping with established industry best practices, he recommends that the company conduct background checks for all the contractor's employees involved in the project.

When the data center's facility and finance managers see the plan and the associated costs, they are not convinced that it is necessary or worth the cost, since the cost is not covered in the project budget and would require that they find new funding. They also do not see the issue as "their problem." To them, personnel security is somebody else's concern. The company has technical solutions for Information Security with intrusion detection and prevention technologies, all managed by IT. The facility and finance managers point to that and to the physical security measures that are already in place – guards and gates, video cameras and card readers – so they do not see the need for more. They reject Rick's recommendations.

Rick comes away from his presentation feeling that his expertise is not being valued and that he is not being allowed to do what he was hired to do: protect the company. More significantly, he comes away still concerned about the security of the data center – and it does not take long for his fears to be realized.

Three months after his presentation, a network switch is stolen from a server rack in the data center by a contracted employee (whom they later learn has burglary convictions on his record). The switch is valued at only a few thousand dollars, but during the theft, several active servers are badly damaged, and months of critical data has been compromised. The data is possibly destroyed. Also, it could have been possibly copied, stolen, and then corrupted to hide the data theft – for which the stolen network switch could even have been a cover! All the elaborate cybersecurity measures the company had put into place were meaningless because someone simply walked into the data center with a malicious intent.

When he learns of the incident, Rick has an "I told you so" moment. (Of course, as a professional, he keeps it to himself.) But his sense of satisfaction does not last long, since, as the security manager, he is the one held responsible for letting the intrusion happen. He begins an investigation and quickly identifies an employee of the independent contractor who was onsite at the same time as the theft. But by then, the employee is no longer working for the contractor, who claims to have no knowledge of his whereabouts.

The Business Function Leader

Paul K. is the network and systems vice president responsible for the systems that were damaged in the theft of the network switch. His team is under intense pressure to repair the damage, get the servers back up and running, and determine whether the data was destroyed (which would be a bad outcome) or stolen (which would be even worse). He must also determine whether any of the compromised data was covered by mandatory reporting regulations. If he cannot definitively establish that the data was not stolen, he must begin the reporting process for a potential violation. Additionally, while this is going on he must restore regular business operations and must recover the lost data, some of which was not backed up real-time and will have to be re-created from scratch. Angry at what he sees as a clear security failure, Paul calls Rick in and demands to know what went wrong and why.

Rick explains that the theft could have been prevented if the background checks he recommended had been in place – checks that the facility and finance manager at the data center rejected because they were too expensive. Instead of being appeased by this, Paul is now angrier than ever. He accuses Rick of not fighting hard enough for the security controls he believed were necessary – and that, by not fighting harder for those controls, he has not done his job. Rick was tasked with protecting the data center, and, from Paul's perspective, he obviously failed to do that.

At the end of this story, both Rick and Paul are unhappy and frustrated at the security organization's seeming inability to "get things done." And the main reason for their frustration, and for the security failure that brought it to a head, is a fundamental, and very common, situation: A security professional was given the responsibility to undertake an assignment but not the means to carry it out.

These problems – both the security failure and the frustration and "blame game" that go along with them – could have been prevented by the application of ESRM principles. In the next section, we will look at how this situation might have played out in a company, and a security organization that based its decision on the ESRM philosophy.

3.1.5.1.2 The ESRM Security Environment

The Security Practitioner

When Rick is tasked with "protecting" the data center, he views the assignment not simply as a security problem to be solved, but as a security risk issue to be managed. He begins by identifying the serious risks – regulatory, legal, and reputational – that the company would face in the event of a security failure during the data center upgrade. Then he identifies the key stakeholders who would be impacted by a security failure and realizes that they include an extraordinarily broad range of roles and organizations within the company. (One of the most important is the risk of regulatory violations if the data has been stolen.) For that reason, instead of presenting his recommendations for background checks on all the independent contractor's employees, Rick goes to where he believes the risk *lives*: first to Paul, the network and systems vice president and then to the General Counsel, who would own the regulatory risk.

The Business Function Leader

At first, Paul does not understand why Rick has come to him about background checks, since the facility and finance managers have already said they believe Rick's recommendations will be too expensive. But when Rick lays out in detail the possible consequences of a security failure, Paul sees that the risks would, in fact, impact him directly, far more than either facilities or finance. He decides that the risks are unacceptable to his network and data security, and that the costs of background checks are small compared to his data security risks. He brings in the human resources (HR) and legal departments, and asks Rick to collaborate with them in designing and conducting background checks on all the independent contractor's employees assigned to the project. Rick and Paul are both satisfied: Paul is because his risk is mitigated, and Rick is because the correct risk owner made the risk mitigation decisions.

3.1.5.1.3 The ESRM Difference

Our scenario, as we left it above, could have two different endings:

1. The background checks could reveal that several of the employees who the contractor was planning to have onsite in the data center had misrepresented their employment histories, some had exaggerated their technical qualifications – and one had an extensive criminal record. The contractor would immediately remove those employees from the project, and the network switch would never be stolen, or the data compromised, because the thief was never allowed into the data center.

2. Events could have played out differently. Paul might have listened, understood the risk, and still chosen not to accept the additional project costs of background checks, and the theft and damage might still have occurred.

Crucially though, with ESRM principles in place:

- The responsibility for the security risk would have resided in the appropriate place – with the owner of the business assets at risk.

- Paul, as an executive, would have been on record as accepting the security risk.

- It would have been difficult, if not impossible, for anyone to lay the blame on Rick or the security organization, because it was clear that it was Paul who owned the risk and made an educated risk decision.

This fundamental concept – the acceptance of risk by its true owner – is an essential component of ESRM. As security professionals, we know that security incidents are always going to happen.

Information assets will be lost, physical assets will be stolen or damaged, and business processes will be interrupted. There is no such thing as perfect security, and there never will be. However, we believe that when security professionals are not practicing ESRM as the basis of their security program, the wrong people can often be making security and risk decisions, whether based on right information and criteria or not.

Most often we see that they are the wrong decision-makers, not because they should have no say in the decision, but because they are not the *sole* asset owner or stakeholder, and they should not have the *only* say. Sometimes, as we saw in the example above of a function or department making a security decision based solely on financial details, the decision maker is not a true stakeholder in the *risk* at all.

Unfortunately, when things go wrong, as they inevitably will, it is the security professional who often takes the blame. This blame was mostly because there was no clearly defined understanding of what the security practitioner's role was in the first place. ESRM principles, however, can significantly reduce the number of stories like Rick's and Paul's by shifting the security practitioner's defined role from task management to risk management.

Questions for the Security Practitioner
- "What is the source of frustration in my role as a security practitioner?"
- "Are my recommendations being accepted and implemented? If not, why not?"
- "Can I be more involved in the security decision process?"

3.2 The Evolving Global Risk Environment is Driving Industry to Risk Management Postures

As members of the security profession, we driven to focus on risk management rather than simple security tasks by the rapidly changing security risk situation across the globe. Technology, globalization, social media, rapid change, and faster travel make us all much closer together than we used to be, and these changes increase the potential for business disruption. ESRM incorporates a flexible response to this changing environment because continually assessing and managing risk puts you in a better position to respond quickly to security incidents, whether anticipated or unforeseen.

3.2.1 Security and Risk Threats are Real

The security and risk issues that will be discussed in this book – the issues that ESRM addresses – can threaten an enterprise's competitiveness, its profitability, and even its very survival. In the year 2014, data breaches like the ones at Target, JPMorgan Chase, and eBay compromised the sensitive personal data of millions of people, exposing them to the possibility of identity theft and other kinds of fraud (Roman, 2014). These security breaches cost those enterprises millions of dollars, as well as damage to reputation and brand that, while difficult to calculate precisely in dollar terms, was probably even worse. Board members and senior executives can face lawsuits, regulatory liability, even criminal charges if they fail to protect the interests of shareholders, customers, and employees. Damage to physical infrastructure (factories, roads, bridges), like the catastrophic destruction caused by the earthquake and tsunami that struck Japan in 2011, can disrupt supply chains, forcing factories and stores thousands of miles away to close. The workplace violence that is now all too common threatens not only employees' lives, but also their morale and their productivity. Even small-scale problems, like employee theft, can seriously impact an enterprise's bottom line.

In Table 3-2 below, we show just a few examples from the 2016 annual global risk report from the World Economic Forum. Many of today's critical risks include terrorism, random acts of violence, fraud, natural disasters, and – especially prevalent in the evolving security environment – cyber-attacks and other kinds of information security risks. We have included the risks from this report that we consider especially applicable to security professionals, but we encourage you to visit the WEF site for risk trend awareness.

Table 3-2. Global Risks by Category

Category	Risk
Economic	• Failure/shortfall of critical infrastructure. • Illicit trade (e.g. illicit financial flow, tax evasion, human trafficking, organized crime, etc.).
Environmental	• Extreme weather events (e.g. floods, storms, etc.). • Major natural catastrophes (e.g. earthquake, tsunami, volcanic eruption, geomagnetic storms). • Man-made environmental catastrophes (e.g. oil spill, radioactive contamination, etc.).
Geopolitical	• Failure of national governance (e.g. failure of rule of law, corruption, political deadlock, etc.). • Large-scale terrorist attacks. • State collapse or crisis (e.g. civil conflict, military coup, failed states, etc.).
Societal	• Large-scale involuntary migration. • Profound social instability.
Technological	• Adverse consequences of technological advances. • Breakdown of critical information infrastructure and networks. • Large-scale cyberattacks. • Massive incidents of data fraud/theft.

Source: World Economic Forum (2016), *Global Risks Report,* pp. 85-86.

The reality is, the security and risk issues we will be talking about throughout this book are virtually life-or-death questions – for people and for enterprises.

3.2.2 The Risk Conversation is Changing Rapidly

The world is a rapidly changing place, and the pace of change is getting faster each year. Risk items that have the utmost importance and impact in one year are supplanted the next year by new and different threats. We cannot tell exactly what the future of security will hold, but we can predict with a measure of certainty that it will be different from what we know now, and likely will different from anything we can imagine today. That shifting ground is what makes the conversation about risk and risk management so important in today's security realm. Tasks, technologies, standards, practices, and skills can become obsolete, but risk is a constant threat. Being able to understand risk, examine environments, and discover how they are vulnerable to harm, are skills that will never be obsolete, even in a rapidly changing world.

While the future of security is unknowable, we certainly can say that as a security professional, embracing an ESRM philosophy will make you and your security program:

• More nimble.

• Quicker to become aware of new threats and risks.

• More able to respond to changing environments.

• Better positioned to assist the enterprise in responding to threats of harm to the business.

3.3 What Does "Security Success" Look Like?

Here, we will take a moment to discuss what security success means in the context of this book. We all want our security efforts to be successful, and of course we all want successful security careers. But security success is not necessarily easy to define, or even to recognize. That is a genuine problem, because if we do not know what success looks like, we can never be sure we have achieved it.

To explore this, try a simple thought experiment:

> You have been put in charge of setting up a brand-new security program for your entire company. When you are six months in, the senior executives who gave you that responsibility want to know whether the program is a success. How will you determine how successful the program has been so far, and how will you communicate your conclusions to those high-level decision-makers?

3.3.1 Success is Not Just Measured by Numbers

Maybe you will look for key performance metrics. Those metrics could measure anything from the number of investigations your organization has conducted, to the dollar value of the reduction in losses from fraud. They could represent the number of intrusion attempts that you have intercepted. Or maybe they would show a reduction – or at least rationalization – of your security budget because the right people with the right skillsets were assigned to the right tasks, and some previously manual tasks were automated. Those are all great data points, and they are all useful, even necessary. But do any of those numbers, individually or in the aggregate, really define "success?" We do not think so.

They are necessary because they define scope, scale, efficiency, and effectiveness, all of which are important. However, they do not communicate whether a risk tolerance threshold has been clearly established by the appropriate stakeholders. Nor do those numbers measure and communicate a changed threat level that exceeds the set tolerance in a way which would require the business to adapt the mitigation approach for any specific risk. That is why, in this book, we will present a novel approach to defining the success of your security program.

3.3.2 In Security Success, Intangibles are Important

ESRM success – not just security success – is measured at least as much by intangibles as by those metrics above. To figure out what those intangibles are, it is imperative to assess your current processes and your overall approach to how you practice your security responsibilities and finally to determine how that practice is perceived in your environment.

Here are a few questions to consider when making that assessment:
- "Do my counterparts in the business see me as a true partner?"
- "Is leadership including me at the beginning of new projects, to help identify risks and develop mitigation plans from the outset?"
- "When changes in business processes and business models are being considered, am I involved?"
- "Do the metrics and reports that I send out truly align with security risks and my strategic partners' concerns?"

Success is not just a question of how well your organization is performing (which is, of course, important). It is also about how much personal and professional satisfaction you are taking in your role as a security practitioner.

You should also be asking yourself some fundamental questions about how you feel about your job:

- "Do I truly feel valued by my superiors, my security colleagues, and my peers in the enterprise?"
- "Does the company offer me the career path I desire? Am I doing everything I can to advance along that path?"
- "Am I communicating the importance of what I do?"

3.3.3 Your Answers Create Your Definition of "Success"

There is an important reason we have based our definition of success on questions – and your individual answers to those questions. As much as you might like a straightforward way of defining your goals and determining whether you have achieved them, it is not that simple. It is a little like a child asking a parent, "When will I be a grownup?" It is easy to reply, "When you are eighteen years old," or "When you are at least five feet eleven inches tall." But, as is so often the case, the easy answer is not necessarily the right one. As we all know, lots of grownups are not five feet eleven, and lots of people over eighteen (or thirty, or even fifty) are not really grownups.

Questions for the Security Practitioner
- "What does success really mean to me? Is it in the form of a promotion, a higher salary, a bigger budget, more responsibility – or is it simply that my work is more satisfying?"
- "Do my colleagues in the security organization, my manager, and my business partners see security success the same way I do? If not, what can I do to make our perceptions align better?"
- "Are we on a path to properly recognize security's role in the organization, and gaining the necessary partnerships and respect to be successful?"

Your ESRM program will not be perfect from day one. (In fact, it will never be perfect, and recognizing that fact is a key component of being able to define success realistically.) Furthermore, it will not be measured by security or risk metrics, at least not in the meaningful way that ESRM requires. How will you know when you are successful? In some ways, it is like trying to define how mature you are. How mature is your organization? How mature are you at your security craft? How mature do you need to be or want to be, so that you can accomplish your personal and professional goals? Of course, even when you feel like you have matured – either you individually, or your entire program – it always feels like there is room for improvement.

ESRM is, in fact, a process of continuous improvement. As your security program becomes more successful, your strategic partners will rely on you more, and you will know you are doing what needs to be done. That is part of what success looks like – always recognizing that there is more to be done.

A good benchmark question for a security professional would be:

"Is our security program or my individual practice more mature today than it was yesterday?"

The answer will not be based on how many viruses you have blocked or how many dollars you have saved with your guard contract. It will be far more meaningful than that.

3.3.4 The Security Professional and the Business Leader: Using ESRM to Move Beyond Frustration to Success

As previously discussed, it can be frustrating when the business does not accept our decisions, our recommendations, or the plans we are trying to implement. And security can be every bit as frustrating for business leaders, who often see it as an obstacle to getting things done. Part of the problem, of course, is that business leaders do not necessarily recognize the importance of what we do and what we are trying to do. To put the problem in its simplest terms, they do not recognize our role in the enterprise.

ESRM will help us gain recognition because we, as the security professionals, also have a responsibility to recognize what our role is, and what it is not. In ESRM, at its most basic, we learn that our role is simply to manage security risk. That means guiding the business through the risk decision-making process, not making the decisions ourselves.

It is vital that we, as security practitioners, recognize that this is not avoiding responsibility or shifting blame. In an ESRM environment, our value as security practitioners comes from guiding our strategic partners in the organization through a proper decision-making process about the security risks to their business assets. That aspect of ESRM allows us to build the true partnerships, enabling us to succeed in the mission of protecting those assets the business deems important to protect.

There are two sides to this process:
1. Helping the business understand security.
2. Helping security understand the business.

The place to start with both sides of the process is understanding what your enterprise internal partners want and need from you. You can best do that by the simplest means possible: asking them. We will talk in Chapter 4 about how to do just that.

The payoff for the security practitioners comes when the business recognizes the true value of security and embraces it as something that adds real-world business value. This recognition reduces that frustration we have all experienced and makes the overall security program more successful.

Questions for the Security Practitioner
- "Do my colleagues in the security organization view their role the same way I do mine?"
- "Do we base our view on the business priorities of the enterprise? If not, why not?"
- "Is security updated regularly to address changing business needs?"
- "How often does the whole enterprise review its business priorities, and how often (if at all) are those priorities communicated to the security organization?"
- "Are you and the rest of the security organization properly aligned with the business? If not, why not?"

3.3.5 The ESRM Philosophy of Security Success

In 2010, ASIS International's CSO Roundtable conducted a benchmarking study of security professionals to determine the extent to which ESRM concepts were being accepted in the security and business communities. Comments by professionals participating in the study show that ESRM principles are very much top-of-mind for both security and business executives.
- According to Timothy Williams, Director of Global Security, Caterpillar, "With ESRM's holistic approach to security came the understanding that a whole host of business issues that were not

traditionally associated with "security" – think, for example, of Sarbanes-Oxley or HIPAA – were now firmly part of security's bailiwick, underscoring again how important it is for security professionals to be business professionals first" (CSO Round Table, 2010, p. 3).

- Dr. Erwann O. Michel-Kerjan, Managing Director, Risk Management and Decision Processes Center, The Wharton School of the University of Pennsylvania, explains, "The growing recognition of Enterprise Security Risk Management (ESRM) as a holistic view of risk – all risks – throughout an organization is important; this holistic view helps ensure that the threats that might typically not be recognized in an enterprise risk management program focusing primarily on financial risks (such overlooked risks, for example, might include: risks to brand and reputation; physical supply-chain risks; or loss of consumer confidence if your data is stolen or networks attacked) are now more and more fully identified, prioritized, and mitigated" (CSO Round Table, 2010, p. 5).

These comments, and many others from security and business thought-leaders, show an emerging consensus that ESRM is necessary for security success – now and in an increasingly complex and dangerous future. Central to ESRM is the recognition that security success is simply, business success.

As a security professional, you are operating in an environment driven, for the most part, by profit and value. This is not the whole story, of course. For example, there are government and nonprofit organizations that are not profit-making entities, and even many private-sector businesses that have goals other than profit (such as, contributing to the wellbeing of their employees or their communities). But most enterprises, certainly, are interested in protecting and increasing the value they deliver to their owners, their shareholders, their customers, and others. Every enterprise, whatever its mission, has a critical interest in protecting the assets it views as important. These two points come together in the ESRM philosophy, and understanding them and applying them is crucial to your success as a security professional.

Questions for the Security Practitioner
- "Looking five years into the future, what role do I see ESRM playing in my success as a security professional?"
- "How can ESRM help me identify the strategic partners who will be critical to my success? How can I communicate and collaborate more effectively with them?"

3.3.5.1 Security Becomes Strategic

The ESRM philosophy can be considered fully in place when basic risk management principles are accepted throughout the entire security program and when those principles mesh consistently and comprehensively into the daily thought processes of all the security practitioners in the department. Over time, this change will mature how the security organization functions and will turn security managers into security and risk professionals. Just as importantly, it will change the perceptions of other stakeholders across the enterprise – including internal business partners, senior executives and board members. That means the difference between being defined as a tactical, operational problem-solver, to being regarded, eventually, as a strategic partner.

3.3.5.2 Security Becomes a Business Function

We are focused on risk management as a philosophy, but we are not suggesting that security management doesn't also involve managing operational tasks or implementing security processes and systems. It always has, and it always will. Nevertheless, security task management becomes ESRM when those security processes and systems are put in place, enterprise-wide, according to a strategic framework of risk mitigation and response, developed with input from business function leaders. Those leaders are the people with the most at stake in protecting those assets; they are ones who must take responsibility for them; and they are the ones who must decide on the return on investment (ROI) of any risk mitigation plan. The risk treatment plan that is chosen may be – almost certainly will be – assigned to the security organization to implement and manage. But the plan itself will be the result of a carefully considered business decision. Embracing ESRM means ensuring that security is a *business function*, based on a clear-eyed understanding of business risk. When we see security as a business function like any other – one that delivers real-world business benefits – our strategic partners will see it the same way.

Questions for the Security Practitioner

- "When a task is assigned to me, or when I assign a task to someone else, does everyone involved clearly understand why the task is important, what asset is being protected, how that asset impacts the business, who and what will be impacted by it, and what standard of performance is expected?"
- "Is our understanding of an assigned task based on a common, consistent philosophy that is clearly understood by both the security organization and our business partners?"

Chapter Review

In Chapter 3, you learned:

- Security professionals and other business professionals do not always agree on what "security" is or understand the role of the security professional in the larger organization.
- ESRM is a path to managing security risk in an ever-changing global risk environment.
- Measuring the success of a security program is complex and will mean different things to different people and organizations. The ESRM philosophy can help the security practitioner understand their own program's best measure of success and meet it.

Looking Forward

In Part 2 of this book, we will:

- Begin an in-depth discussion of all the steps of the ESRM life cycle and look at the best practices surrounding an ESRM implementation.

Practitioner steps before moving on to Part 2:

✓ In your own words, answer the question, "What does security do?"
✓ Ask some of your business partners and executives the question, "What does security do?" What answers did you get?
✓ Think about some of the new risks your organization will face in the changing security environment.

Security Program Self-Assessment

In this self-assessment, you should think about the answer to the questions posed, and then see where your program is on the identified ESRM spectrum.

Question	Y/N	Is This ESRM?
Do you understand what your enterprise requires to consider your security program a success?	☐Yes ☐No	**NO**: If you have never explored the benchmarks of success for your program, this is a preliminary step for an ESRM program. **PARTIAL**: If you have some metrics identified to define success, but they involve documenting tasks and metrics based on efficiency, you are part of the way to an ESRM implementation. **YES**: If you have specific understandings with your strategic partners regarding the risks you manage and your role, as well as methods to measure adherence to the risk tolerance, you are practicing ESRM.

Questions for Discussion

1. What security issues can you think of that might be caused by operating security in corporate "silos?" Are there benefits to silos that could outweigh these issues? What do you think?
2. Can you identify three security tasks that could be operationalized to free up time and resources to address strategic risk issues? How might this impact the business?
3. How could you communicate ESRM principles and their importance to your peers, both inside and outside the security organization?

References

CSO Roundtable of ASIS International. (2010, April). *Enterprise security risk management: How great risks lead to great deeds.* Retrieved from https://cso.asisonline.org/esrm/Documents/CSORT_ESRM_whitepaper_%20pt%201.pdf

Roman, J. (2014, December 30). Top data breaches of 2014, infographic: Lessons learned from year's top incidents, *Bank Info Security.* Retrieved from http://www.bankinfosecurity.com/top-data-breaches-2014-a-7736

World Economic Forum. (2016). *The global risks report 2016.* Retrieved from http://www3.weforum.org/docs/GRR/WEF_GRR16.pdf

Learn More About It

For further reading about security management:

Walters, D., Fischer, R. J., & Halibozek, E. P. (2013). *Introduction to security.* Burlington, MA: Butterworth-Heinemann.

Fay, J. (2011). *Contemporary security management.* Burlington, MA: Butterworth-Heinemann.

Part 2

The Fundamentals of ESRM

In Part 1, you gained an overall view of what ESRM is and how it can benefit your security program. Specifically, you saw how it can benefit in your ongoing security career. Now we will delve into how to begin your ESRM journey. In Part 2 of this book, you will learn about activities to get you, your department, and your enterprise ready to follow an ESRM program. You will also explore further details about the ESRM cycle that was introduced in Part 1.

In This Part:
- **Before You Begin**
- **The ESRM Cycle – An Overview**
- **The ESRM Cycle – Step 1 – Identify and Prioritize Assets**
- **The ESRM Cycle – Step 2 – Identify and Prioritize Security Risks**
- **The ESRM Cycle – Step 3 – Mitigate Prioritized Risks**
- **The ESRM Cycle – Step 4 – Improve and Advance**

4

Preparing for an ESRM Program

Now that you have a start on understanding ESRM and how it differs from traditional security management methods, you are ready to move into the implementation process. In this chapter, we will help you begin your ESRM journey by covering the preparation steps to follow as you introduce ERSM into your security organization. We will also discuss the people across the rest of your enterprise whom you will need to involve in ESRM and how you can get their cooperation for your program.

This chapter will help you to:

- Do the up-front research to embark on an ESRM program.
- See how to relate your security program to your business environment.
- Identify the stakeholders in your security program, and understand their needs.
- Understand the difference between an asset owner and a risk stakeholder, and determine how to best work with each.
- Understand corporate culture, which will be the foundation for a risk-based security program.

4.1 Understand the Business and its Mission

The first activity in an ESRM implementation process, before even entering the steps of the cycle itself, is to spend time investigating your enterprise and truly *understanding* it. It is impossible to know the measures you will need to take to evaluate, mitigate, and protect against enterprise risks unless you know what those risks are. You cannot understand those risks unless you understand the business, what it does, and why it does it.

An analysis by the leading consulting firm PricewaterhouseCoopers explains in detail why risk management activities (like ESRM) need to consider the overall business context:

"It is important to begin by understanding the relevant business objectives in scope for the risk assessment. These will provide a basis for subsequently identifying potential risks that could affect the achievement of objectives, and ensure the resulting risk assessment and management plan is relevant to the critical objectives of the organization....The focus on business objectives helps ensure relevance and facilitates the integration of risk assessments across the organization." (PwC, 2008, p.21-22).

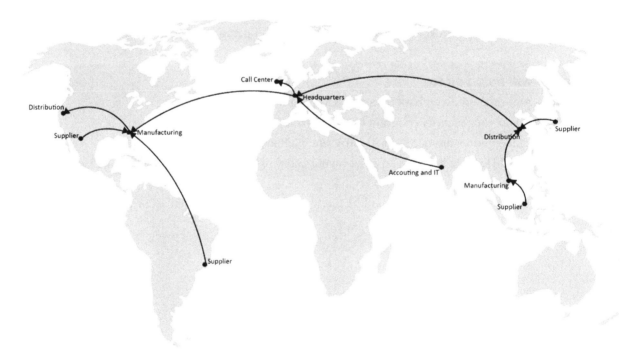

Figure 4-1. Businesses in the global economy are complex and highly interconnected and require an understanding of many "moving parts."

4.1.1 Holistic Understanding of Risk

Figure 4-1 shows why understanding your business is going to be a complicated undertaking that involves many complex and interconnected parts. But that understanding is necessary for implementing a successful security program.

For example, to protect the supply chain that begins with parts in Asia and ends with a finished product on the shelf in Canada, it is imperative that you know:

- The path that the parts take.
- The environments they are moving through.
- Which parts are time sensitive and critical, and which have schedule flexibility.
- Who in the business is dependent or interdependent on the parts.
- What the finished product is and does.
- How consumers use the product.
- Whether the product is an essential good or a luxury item, and how the customers view it.
- How disruptive it would be if the supply chain were interrupted.

Those are just *a few* of the things you need to understand about *one* type of business. A financial firm or a bank has aspects to understand that are different from a chain of convenience stores, and understanding an entertainment company is far different from the discovering the details of a medical facility.

The common link that they all have is:
- A product or service that they provide (or other reasons for conducting operations).
- Employees (or volunteers) doing tasks that contribute to the enterprise objective.
- Consumers or recipients of the end-product or service.
- An environment they operate in.
- People who are authorized to make decisions on behalf of the organization.
- Risks.

Finding the specifics of your organization is the starting point of implementing an effective, risk-based security program.

Even if you have been working at a company for a very long time – perhaps especially if you have been working there for a very long time – it is imperative to take a good look at how the business is functioning *now*. Enterprises' missions change constantly. Some of the ways in which your organization might have changed since the last time you assessed it might be:
- Older products and services become less valuable, and so less critical in the business risk profile.
- New products and services are brought to market.
- Industry drivers such as supply-and-demand change constantly.
- Competitive threats and opportunities change along with these other changes.

You should think about all these factors during any business assessment; your understanding of the business needs to be continuously updated, revised, and refined to ensure that the program can align with business changes up front, rather than as an afterthought.

4.1.2 The Needs of Your Business

Through years of managing security organizations and speaking with countless security practitioners, an important lesson we have learned is:

> **If your security program is not clearly and realistically aligned with the needs of the business, it will be considered out of touch at best, and a liability at worst.**

If you cannot show that you fully grasp the needs of your potential strategic partners in protecting the enterprise, they will have no real reason to trust or rely on you to help them continue those operations.

Case Study: Understanding the Unfamiliar

Carol D., a very experienced IT security manager, spent years working for a company in the midwestern US that specialized in cloud-based hosted network services. She was responsible for securing the internal network and data center, the hosted data and applications, as well as disaster recovery. Her success got her noticed, and a headhunter approached her about a very different job: director of security for SecStat, a company helping small-to-midsized businesses (SMBs) to deploy and integrate physical security systems on their premises.

Overnight, Carol went from protecting mostly intangible virtual assets, using electronic means like encryption and intrusion detection systems, to being responsible for securing SecStat's offices, making sure the company's employees were safe, running background checks on installation personnel, and many more of the usual "traditional" security practices. While Carol did have a solid background in overall security management and was familiar with many of the more physical-based security disciplines from her years in the industry, her knowledge was not at the level her new position required. "The first time I talked with one of the senior business leaders," she remembers, "I felt like Alice stepping through the looking glass. He was talking about camera apertures and lumens of lighting and security bollards – stuff I didn't know about in any kind of detail, but that they knew intimately because it is the product and service they sold."

Carol knew she needed a "crash course" in what her new company did and how it did it. To her credit, she wasn't afraid to go to her new colleagues and managers and ask questions – even questions that were so simple, so basic, that they embarrassed her. ("A little honest ignorance will take you a long way," she says now.) And, somewhat to her surprise, she found that people – from design engineers, to product marketing managers, to senior executives – were more than happy to talk about what they did, why it mattered, and what was most important to them.

The result was that she developed strong working relationships with her new business partners, understood and prioritized their needs, and developed effective risk mitigation methods to recommend to them. She even found that a lot of her "virtual" security expertise could be leveraged to protect physical business assets.

4.1.3 Sources of Information

There are many ways to approach understanding an enterprise and its mission, but through years of working in our own business environment and talking with other security professionals, we can distill the process to three basic ways of understanding the enterprise and the associated risk environment:

1. Listen to insiders.
2. Examine the enterprise's internal and external messaging.
3. Listen to outsiders.

4.1.3.1 Company Insiders

The simplest, most straightforward way to understand what is critical to the business is to engage with the people who are running it day-to-day. They know how the business works; they know what is important; they know what assets represent the greatest business risks and business opportunities. Hearing what key executives and managers say about the business's mission and objectives is essential. It will help you understand other strategic partners' priorities, and understand how their concerns and priorities fit in the overall work of the enterprise.

It is not always easy to communicate with people in other parts of the enterprise who have vastly different responsibilities. To make it easier to start the conversation, below are a few examples of key stakeholders, and some questions you could use, or adapt, to open a meaningful dialogue.

The Chief Risk Officer (CRO):
- "What are the risks you are most worried about right now, and what is just at the edge of your radar screen?"
- "What risks are you possibly spending extra time and effort on that may not be so important as to justify that extra time and effort?"

The Chief Compliance Officer (CCO):
- "What regulatory and other compliance bodies and frameworks do you have to report to and interact with?"
- "How are those relationships working? Are some especially difficult or sensitive?"
- "What are the consequences of failing to meet certain regulatory requirements?"

The Chief Operating Officer (COO):
- "How does security impact the overall efficiency of the business?"
- "Is security helping, or hindering, or some of both?"
- "How do you think security is perceived by line-of-business managers and other operational heads?"

The Corporate Legal Counsel:
- "What are your biggest concerns related to security and risk?"
- "What legal liability could our security measures potentially be exposing the company to?"
- "Should we involve the legal department each time we suspect criminal activity? If not, how serious should the alleged infraction be before we contact you?"

- "How can we assist with the legal mission, and how can we support or assist with litigation and liability reduction efforts?"

One simple, powerful question – which has certainly helped us repeatedly in our security careers -- that you can use when speaking with any stakeholder at any level is:

"How can I help you to be successful?"

Once you have heard what the executives have to say, talk to the people who run the enterprise's various lines of business. Here are a few sample questions you can ask them:
- "What product or service does your organization deliver, and what role does that play in the business's overall mission and goals?"
- "What is your organization's most important contribution to the business?"
- "How does your product or service work, and what resources – for example, skills, physical assets, or intellectual property – does your organization need to make it work?"
- "What are your organization's most urgent priorities, and what environmental factors do you see potentially changing those priorities?"
- "What security risks are you most concerned about right now?"

In many cases, your internal strategic partners are already aware of many of the risks they face, and can lay them out for you very clearly. In others, your discussions will be a starting point to educate you about the business, and to educate your partners about risks and about your role in security risk management.

This process of getting to know your internal business partners and what they need is a critical building block of the relationships – the *strategic partnerships* – that ESRM both creates and depends on to drive success in the security program.

Questions for the Security Practitioner
- "Who are the critical internal partners I should speak with to learn more about the enterprise I work for, the business it is in, and the environment it operates in?"
- "Would the security organization benefit from an inventory of information sources which everyone in security could consult, from experienced practitioners to new hires?"
- "What topics do I already know I should talk to company subject matter experts about to learn more? What topics do I think my strategic partners might benefit from hearing more about from me?"

4.1.3.2 Company Published Communications
Enterprises today spend an enormous amount of time, effort, and money communicating with the outside world. They communicate with their:
- Customers.
- Clients.
- Partners.
- Vendors.
- Regulatory agencies.

- Government bodies.
- Shareholders if they are publicly traded.
- Industry analysts.

All the information your corporate communications and public relations teams produces is important to the business. These can include press releases, annual reports, marketing collateral, and regulatory filings. These documents, though intended for others, can also be valuable to you as a security practitioner to help you understand the business environment.

Many enterprises also have internal communications organizations that work to provide information to employees about distinct aspects of the company. The information they produce – on intranet sites, in training materials, and in policy manuals – can be an invaluable resource for the security practitioner.

Some examples are:
- Vision, mission, and business goals.
- Values (often expressed in a mission statement).
- Organizational structure.
- Business plans and budget projections.
- Policies and procedures.

4.1.3.3 Outsiders and The Media

A third way to understand the enterprise business organization is to see what other people – customers and clients, industry analysts, or the public – are saying about it. An online search will reveal many different perspectives on the enterprise and help identify some of the less easy-to-find reputational or industry-specific risks that exist.

Here are just a few of the places you can begin looking:
- Mainstream news sources, like newspapers and online news sites.
- Specialized industry publications focusing on your enterprise's target markets (or adjacent markets).
- The financial media.
- Consumer and lifestyle publications and websites that feature both professional and nonprofessional product and service reviews.
- Competitors' advertising, especially if it offers different product or service comparisons
- Online user communities.
- Social networks, like Facebook and Twitter.

Of course, the relevant sources of information, and the types of information available will vary depending on the enterprise and the industry. But one thing that will not vary is your need to seek out external points of view, which can broaden and deepen your understanding of the business you are in, and how it is being perceived in the real world.

4.1.3.4 Observing Non-Verbal Communication – The Underlying Culture

We mentioned three sources of information that you can seek out and gather input from, but there is also one last, non-verbal, usually undocumented source that you should pay attention to. Every enterprise, every organization, has its own very specific culture, and the rules of that culture are not always, if ever, written down anywhere. There tends to be an assumption that "everybody knows" how things work, and for that reason, there is usually no formal documentation of the enterprise culture.

Here are a few questions you could ask yourself while you are observing everyday interactions in the business:

- "Is this a suit-and-tie enterprise, or more of a jeans and tee-shirts outfit?"
  - Dress codes can offer a clue to corporate culture. Be aware that a highly regimented, disciplined enterprise like a financial institution will likely be more receptive to a rigorous set of policies and procedures to mitigate security risk. A more casual, freeform environment – possibly like a technology startup – may take more persuasion when it comes to accepting security edicts.
- "Is the enterprise historically resistant to change, or does it willingly embrace innovative ideas and ways of thinking?"
  - Because security changes are like any other type of change – new, uncomfortable, and sometimes threatening – you need to understand how open to change your strategic partners really are. You may observe that they are more open to new ideas in their own technology than they are with new policies and procedures handed down from above.
- "How much risk is the company willing to take regarding certain vulnerabilities?"
  - Understanding how risk-averse or risk-tolerant the enterprise and its decision-makers are will be central to the effective application of ESRM principles.
- "Will some business units and other internal organizations be more responsive to the idea of working with the security organization than others? If so, why?"
  - This is an especially vital concern, because you need a clear-eyed view of where you can begin your ESRM efforts and where you can assist the business by most effectively prioritizing security investments.

Corporate culture is not necessarily uniform or consistent. The unspoken, undocumented attributes that we are talking about can vary widely across the enterprise and even within internal organizations. The larger and more complex the enterprise is, the more likely this is to be the case. Part of your role as a security practitioner will be recognizing – and accommodating – the differences in these cultural environments.

Corporate culture matters because you cannot expect to force a security culture onto the business. A security organization operating on ESRM principles needs the skills to adapt the security culture to the business culture. Cultural understanding is essential to reaching that point.

Case Study: Adapting to the Culture
Since around the year 2000, for a retail outlet to operate without an online presence has become an unworkable business model. Mac B. was an accomplished security professional who spent years in the retail industry running a world-class loss prevention program for a significant department store chain in Canada. During the initial migration from brick-and-mortar storefronts to maintaining that critical web presence, he found himself in a completely new security environment. He was hired to implement a security program at SymDev, a new and fast-growing startup company that was moving into the market of selling vitamins and supplements online. The corporate culture came as a real

shock to him. He was used to making rules and having people obey them without question in his old environment, but that wasn't the way things worked at SymDev.

Mac started out doing things the way he always had: making sure doors were locked, that access was restricted, and that employees were where they were supposed to be and nowhere else. He ensured that the warehouse was secure and that products were tracked meticulously. But SymDev's employees – most of whom were decades younger than Mac – simply were not cooperating. They were hired to work in an environment based on collaboration, openness, sharing, and teamwork, and they did not want to change. In fact, the founder of the company even encouraged employees to take samples of the product from the warehouse to share with friends. Mac very quickly realized that he was the one who had to change and adapt.

How did he do that? By trying to understand what was going on around him. Now clearly, some of the behaviors he observed in SymDev's culture presented serious security risks. The company knew that – and the leadership especially knew they had both physical and intellectual property that had to be protected if the company were to stay ahead of its competitors. After all, that was why they hired a security professional. But before Mac could work to secure the company's critical business assets, he had to understand what they were and how they were created. The "looseness" that was so alien to him was essential to the company's creative processes. As he gained that understanding, Mac came to realize that some doors – literally and metaphorically – simply had to be left open. But he was also able to show SymDev's business leaders that some security risks were unacceptable – that some doors had to be closed, for example, to prevent access by outsiders. And even though employees were encouraged to give out product samples, those needed to be tracked properly to prevent other types of loss. He showed that the security measures he was recommending were both appropriate and acceptable.

4.2 Understand the Business Environment

When we discuss the environment that you need to understand, it encompasses a number of significant factors, which can include:

- The building or buildings that the business operates in.
- The physical environment (urban/rural, foreign/domestic, subtropical/arctic, etc.).
- The geographic environment (city/state/country).
- The accessibility needs of employees, customers, and others.

Enterprise environments vary widely, and as a result, their required levels of security vary widely. For example, compare the security environment on a university campus with that of a defense contractor's manufacturing plant. A university is explicitly intended to be open, to encourage social interaction and the free exchange of ideas and has the dual responsibility of ensuring the safety of both students and visitors, while protecting information assets. On the other hand, a defense plant is almost exactly the opposite: a closed environment where workers, materials, and intellectual property are closely monitored to protect against espionage (including industrial espionage), sabotage, industrial accidents, and other disruptions. Security professionals designing policies and practices for such widely varying environments cannot do that effectively unless they understand those environments.

4.2.1 Examining the Environment the Business Operates In

As with the questions to ask about the business organization and mission, you will need to ask key questions about the environment in which the enterprise operates. Here are just a few basic questions you could ask about the environmental aspects of the enterprise to understand more about how to protect it from harm:

- "What kind of area is the building or campus located in?"
  - o Many universities – however open and welcoming they may try to be – are in areas with high crime rates that need to be considered.
- "Is there a significant amount of traffic – on foot or in vehicles – in and out of the environment?"
  - o In some environments, people will be permitted to move freely on and offsite, while in others, IDs will have to be checked and possibly bags searched.
- "How many authorized people need to be on the site each day?"
  - o Some enterprise environments, like shopping malls and government offices, are de facto public spaces, and will be visited by thousands of people every day – people who do not need explicit authorization to be there. Security measures for these environments, though obviously still very important, will necessarily be much more relaxed than in truly private environments.
- "How much public access is required for the business to operate?"
  - o A defense plant can afford to keep visitors waiting while their identities are checked and to escort visitors while onsite, but a retail store cannot.
- "How sensitive and critical are the business processes and assets that are onsite?"
  - o The more sensitive the operation, the more likely it is that risks will need to be mitigated rather than accepted.
- "What are the expectations of the employees and management?"
  - o Many employers go to great lengths to accommodate the lifestyle choices of their employees, as a way of recruiting and retaining the best and the brightest. (This is especially true of high-tech firms and their young knowledge workers, who can often pick-and-choose in a highly competitive market for talent.) That means it is essential to use non-intrusive security measures.
- "Will there be significant numbers of special needs persons coming in and out?"
  - o Accessibility sometimes requires special entrances and special accommodations, such as checkpoints with ramps and wide enough openings to accommodate wheelchairs, or personnel available to guide people with visual or auditory impairments.

This environmental understanding will be constantly evolving, because environmental aspects and needs can change very significantly, especially after a dramatic event. For example, Virginia Polytechnic Institute and State University (Virginia Tech), like most universities, had an open environment. Following the mass shooting on April 16, 2007, that cost 32 people their lives, the administration and the campus security team certainly reassessed their environment and approach to security. Elementary schools now routinely issue panic buttons to teachers and practice lockdown drills with students, especially following the murders of 26 students, teachers, and administrators at Sandy Hook Elementary School in Newtown, CT, on December 14, 2012. As you can see from these examples, even places like schools, which have historically been dedicated to openness and freedom of expression, must now balance those values against the need to protect the environment, the people, and assets within.

Decisions balancing openness, access, and security aren't always easy, and neither is understanding the environment in which they will be made. Here's an example of two environments with very similar demographics – both completely centered around children – but with almost diametrically opposed security and risk requirements.

Case Study: Environmental Differences Drive Security Concerns

Here are two environments with some striking similarities: They are both designed to accommodate children and their parents, they are both high-volume, high-traffic, and high-density. They both have a profound interest – professional, operational, and ethical – in protecting children. Yet it is almost impossible to imagine two more diverse environments from a security and risk perspective.

Figure 4-2. An amusement park is an open environment that must protect patrons while still ensuring a free flow of traffic.

The amusement park (see Figure 4-2.) is a vast, sprawling space that can function only with high, mostly unrestricted traffic flow through open spaces. Its visitors do not want to feel that they are constantly watched or followed, nor to have their access in any way restricted. That is not the experience people are looking for when they take their families to such a park, and a restricted experience would not be good for an amusement park's business.

A children's hospital, by contrast, is a far less open space, with far more barriers to entry, both external and internal (see Figure 4-3). Many of the areas in the hospital will be restricted to cardholders or other authorized personnel, and many will be openly monitored by uniformed security personnel and video cameras. Most visitors will not be bothered in

Figure 4-3. A children's hospital must allow access, but at the same time restrict traffic to sensitive areas of the facility and provide enhanced levels of security for patients.

the least by these security measures. In fact, they will likely expect to show ID before being allowed to visit a child's room, and they may well feel comforted by the presence of visible signs that their children are being protected.

These approaches to security and risk management couldn't be more different, but neither is right or wrong. They are simply different – and the difference is based entirely on an informed understanding of the differences in the two environments.

4.3 Understand Your Stakeholders

Once you have developed an understanding about the "what" of the business – the mission, processes, goals, and environment – it is time to work on the "who" of the business. That means asking questions like:

"Who *owns* the business, or a specific segment of it?"

"Who *runs* the business and which parts?"

"Who controls the assets that need to be protected?"

"Who makes the final decisions about those assets?"

These are critical questions because they will help you identify the people who are the key stakeholders in the process of protecting the business.

4.3.1 What is a Stakeholder?

Stakeholder is a word we will use throughout this book. It is a central ESRM concept. It can mean different things in different environments, but here is one excellent business-oriented definition:

> Stakeholders are individuals or groups who have an interest or some aspect of rights or ownership in the project, can contribute in the form of knowledge or support, or can impact or be impacted by, the project (Bourne, 2005).

A stakeholder is also a person who ultimately has a primary responsibility for an asset involved in a project or business. That asset can be almost anything: money, data, brand reputation, or even a relationship (for example, with a regulatory agency) which could be damaged if it is not managed appropriately. Because many individuals and roles can have that "concern or interest" noted in the definition above, a single asset can have many stakeholders.

Whoever owns a business asset will ultimately be a risk decision-maker, either individually or together with others, sometimes many others. It is imperative to identify these people because ESRM is built on the concept of placing security and risk decision-making in the hands of people who are responsible for those assets. You cannot do that if you do not know who they are.

4.3.1.1 Finding Your Stakeholders: A Closer Look

Learning about and understanding the enterprise will give you a very good start on identifying your key ESRM stakeholders, but it is only a start. Think of all the people or groups who will be impacted by the security program or any specific project: Who will have influence over the completion of your projects? Who will have an interest in the success or failure of the program? These stakeholders may have a range of roles, including senior executives, individuals within the project, within client organizations, or system developers.

Consider who is impacted by the enterprise security program or specific project, and ask yourself:

"Who stands to gain from this project, and who might be worried about losing?"

"Who controls the necessary resources, and who has the ultimate authority for the risk decision? Are they different people or roles?"

"Who has influence – as opposed to authority?"

"What is my relationship with the stakeholder? Am I able to influence this person? Is it a reporting relationship?"

"How much will I need to rely on influence – as opposed to direct authority – in working with the stakeholder?"

It is important to identify stakeholders who have a vested interested in the success of your program. But it is every bit as important to identity any who may see security practices, specifically your recommendations, as an impediment to the success of their goals.

Stakeholders are, as defined above, the people who have primary responsibility for various business assets, or are the additional risk decision-makers associated with those assets. There may – in fact, there probably will – be times when you find that an asset does not have a clear owner. In the ESRM process, it is *essential* to identify an asset owner who is also a risk stakeholder, to have an appropriate person to make decisions about risk tolerance, acceptance, or mitigation options. If an asset has no identified stakeholders, you must search for the right person. At times, this may mean you must go up the organization's hierarchy to identify the asset owner or stakeholder, or to have the ultimate business function leader designate one. It is not your role as a security practitioner to decide who is an asset owner; that decision must come from the enterprise. As with most of ESRM, your role is to work through the process to ensure that each asset that needs protection has an asset owner identified, and that your discovery process for stakeholder identification is thorough.

Think About It: Customer Personal Data – Whose Asset is It?

Customer data is a critical asset for almost every business organization in existence, but here we will be more specific, considering an account-based service: your local phone company. It stores and manages – and must protect – an enormous amount of sensitive personal data about its customers, including names, addresses, calling records, metadata, billing information, credit information, and stored payment methods.

Clearly, all this customer data is a critical business asset; so it is crucial to find the appropriate stakeholder or stakeholders to make the risk decisions associated with it. But who is that?

    Is it the CIO, because the data resides on the IT organization's servers?

    Is it the Customer Care department because it owns the customer relationship?

    Is it sales, because sales mostly gathered the information in the first place?

    Is it the Chief Privacy Officer, because that role is to ensure that the company is protected from privacy liability issues?

What is the answer? All the above (and probably quite a few more).

If there were a data breach, for example, all those people and organizations would be engaged because they would all have a role to play in the response, control, and aftermath of the event. If they have a role to play in a breach response, then they clearly should also have a role in the decisions about how to protect, mitigate, and/or accept the risks associated with the data asset.

4.3.2 Why Stakeholders Matter

As we have discussed, stakeholders are essential decision-makers. Knowing their level of risk acceptance is crucial to your ESRM program because ESRM is both art and science. It requires you to balance an extraordinary range of security and risk priorities – to protect the enterprise against threats while still allowing it to function. To take an extreme example, the simplest way to protect a building is to not allow anyone into it, or near it. But, of course, that is almost always out of the question, because it would completely choke off the business's ability to operate and meet its objectives.

In ESRM, your role is to listen to your risk stakeholders, then design and implement security measures that they believe address their risks without impinging too far on their business mission. You must balance the need for acceptable security risk protections against the needs of the business and the people who make it work. That balance – and recognizing that the tipping point is stakeholder risk acceptance – is a major part of the art and science of ESRM practice.

Think About It: Stakeholders and Decision-Making

One problem that many food service companies face these days, from the nationwide franchise operations to neighborhood mom-and-pop places, is that in which locations do you offer delivery services? It is an especially tricky question to answer in transitional neighborhoods, with wealthy and safe enclaves right next door to high-crime areas. If your nationally known pizza company has an outlet in an area like this, and some of your delivery people have been robbed or even assaulted, can you, as a security practitioner, decide to deliver to some addresses in the area but not others?

It seems like a simple enough decision – especially if you have had problems at some of those addresses – but it really is not simple. For one thing, refusing to offer business services to certain addresses could be defined as race-based "redlining," which is explicitly prohibited by US federal and state law and covered under the EU right against indirect discrimination. And yet, you still have a responsibility to protect your employees' safety to the best of your ability.

Balancing those concerns while avoiding the brand damage that could come from your company being perceived as accepting racial profiling will be a complex process involving stakeholders across many parts of the company, including the legal, compliance, safety, HR, corporate communications, and public relations organizations.

4.3.2.1 Risk Stakeholder Conflict

The role of the stakeholder in ESRM is vital – making the crucial decisions on questions of risk treatment, risk appetite, and risk acceptance. But as a security practitioner, what do you do when the stakeholders cannot all agree on the appropriate treatment of risks?

For example, consider a customer data scenario in an online stock trading service. In a service-based model like online trading, where the customer data is a key asset of the firm, the company's chief privacy officer will specifically want to ensure that customer data is securely protected and accessed appropriately, by the right people, at the right time, for the right reasons. He or she may request an extensive login or validation process with several steps (possibly involving two-factor authentication). But the customer service department has a different key focus; they have a critical interest in ensuring that the customer has a pleasant user experience which is informative, timely, satisfying, and hassle-free. This means easier access to personal information. They may request a streamlined online experience. Clearly, these two stakeholders have very different, possibly even opposing, interests.

What is your role as a security practitioner in this scenario?

It is hard not to take sides with one stakeholder or another, but it is vital that you take into account the objectives of the business as a whole. If your advice is objective, given in the context of a risk based conversation, and you identify the potential costs and impacts for both parties, then you are also free – and expected – to give your professional security opinion on the best mitigation. However, the ultimate decision must come from the stakeholders. To keep consistent with ESRM practice, you must manage the security risk process using risk principles:

1. You have identified the asset at risk – the customer data.
2. You have looked at the risks to that data.
3. You have properly identified the risk owners: the chief privacy officer and the leader of the customer service department (and probably others, as well).
4. You have identified their business needs and concerns about the asset in question.

Now, finally, you can help those stakeholders find the best, most balanced, most workable solution to all their issues.

Helping stakeholders find the balance among their differing needs is the essence of ESRM. For example, as the security professional in this scenario, you might suggest enforcing a password strength-level that would satisfy the chief privacy officer while permitting the customer to use only a single authentication step. Whatever the final decision, the best way to reach the goal is by facilitating a conversation and reaching agreement. If no agreement is reached, you may need to escalate the decision to the appropriate management level for a final decision. More senior management will have a broader view of the business with a wider focus, thus avoiding a decision determined by the more personal goals of the disagreeing stakeholders.

Key Thought: Risks That Cannot Be Accepted

We have talked a lot about risk acceptance in this chapter and in earlier ones, but there is one thing that about which we must be absolutely clear.

Some risks should NEVER be accepted by *any* risk owners.

We like to call these "orange jumpsuit risks" because they have legal or regulatory implications that could result in someone going to jail. One of the most important and necessary parts of your role as a security professional is to be aware of the kinds of activities that are 100% illegal and to prevent your strategic partners from conducting them, or attempting to conduct them. If you are ever unsure, or if it is not clear whether an activity has serious legal implications, it is important to appropriately escalate to a knowledgeable stakeholder.

Sometimes, your role in ESRM compels you to step in and prevent something from happening. For example:

You work for a financial institution, and someone reports to you that funds from new investors are being used to pay off earlier investors and make their returns appear better than they really are. If someone – anyone, right up to the CEO – tells you that this is okay and that you shouldn't investigate further, you simply cannot accept that answer. What is going on is known as a "Ponzi scheme," and it is completely illegal. If people are signing off on false statements, even if they are completely unaware that the statements are false, they could go to jail.

In the course of handling a routine technical support issue, an IT department found child pornography on a company-owned computer used by an employee. Following established procedure, they have reported this to human resources (HR). An HR manager calls you, understandably disturbed, and tells you that she wants to send the files to the police immediately. This sounds like the right thing to do, right? Except that – because of the content – transmitting those files electronically, no matter what the reason, would be a very serious criminal offense in almost any jurisdiction. You cannot allow HR to do that.

You might want to ask yourself whether orange is a good color for you. Picture this: If you know that illegal activity is going on and do nothing about it – or do the wrong thing, as in the case of the employee with child pornography on his computer – you could be wearing a jumpsuit yourself.

Chapter Review

In Chapter 4 you learned:

- To successfully manage security risks, it is important for you to understand the business: who owns the assets, who the security risk stakeholders are, and what the stakeholder role is.
- As successful security practitioner in an ESRM environment, you need to understand the environment, the business mission, and who the strategic partners and enterprise decision-makers are.
- As a security practitioner, to be considered a strategic partner, you must communicate your role in the business environment. Your partners must understand what the security department's role is.

Looking Forward

In Chapter 5, we will:

- Explore the ESRM life cycle and introduce what each segment of the cycle entails. Further chapters will explore details of the steps individually.

Practitioner steps to consider before moving on to Chapter 5:

- ✓ Reach out to operational groups and ask if they have job shadowing programs, which would allow you to experience their operations for a day. This is especially useful to learn about business processes that you are less familiar with.
- ✓ If you do not already have a background in business finance, take an online course on the subject to gain understanding.
- ✓ Review risk and the aspects of the *risk triangle*, if you do not already know them.

Security Program Self-Assessment

In this self-assessment, think about the answer to the questions posed to see where your program is on the identified ESRM spectrum.

Question	Y/N	Is This ESRM?
Does your security program regularly reach out to business functions to understand their security needs?	□Yes □No	**NO**: If you have never reached out to an internal department to inquire how security can help them, this is a great place to start your ESRM program. **PARTIAL**: If you are reaching out to internal business units to get updated asset lists for protection, personnel access needs, or updated floor layouts for video coverage, you are part of the way to an ESRM implementation. **YES**: If you are reaching out to determine the goals of their business operation, the environment they operate in, and what they consider are the priorities for protection, you are practicing ESRM.

Questions for Discussion

1. Under what circumstances should stakeholders be ignored in favor of your security expertise? What are the ramifications of that? How might it damage the relationship between stakeholders and your security program if you attempt to override their decisions?
2. If a stakeholder opts out of the risk management process, how can this harm your program and the enterprise by leaving them out?
3. Can you think of examples where an organization would have security needs in one location that are different in another location? How might this cause conflict in setting security risk priorities?
4. What are some effective ways to manage the conflict between a stakeholder's risk tolerance and their needs? How do you ensure that all stakeholders understand the ultimate outcome of any security decision?

References

Bourne, L. (2005). *Project relationship management and the stakeholder circle* (Doctoral dissertation). Retrieved from http://www.stakeholder-management.com/Papers/P021_L_Bourne_Thesis.pdf

PricewaterhouseCoopers (2008). *A practical guide to risk assessment: How principles-based risk assessment enables organizations to take the right risks.* Retrieved from https://web.actuaries.ie/sites/default/files/erm-resources/A%20practical%20guide%20to%20risk%20assessment.pdf

Learn More About It

For further reading about risk assessment, see:

American National Standards Institute (ANSI)/ASIS International /The Risk Management Society (RIMS). (2015, August). *Risk assessment.* Alexandria, VA: ASIS International.

Committee of Sponsoring Organizations of the Treadway Commission (COSO). (September 2004). *COSO enterprise risk management – Integrated framework (2004).* Durham, NC: American Institute of Certified Public Accountants [AICPA].

ISO/IEC, (2009). *ISO/IEC 31000:2009 Risk management – Principles and guidelines.* Geneva, Switzerland: ISO/IEC.

National Institute of Standards and Technology (NIST). (2012). *Guide for conducting risk assessments (NIST Special Publication 800-30).* Gaithersburg, MD: Author.

For further reading about stakeholders, see:

Bourne, L. (2008, May). *SRMM: The five stages of stakeholder relationship management maturity.* Available at http://www.stakeholdermapping.com/index.php/download_file/view/30/92/

Kenny, G. (2014, March). Five Questions to Identify Key Stakeholders. *Harvard Business Review.* Available at https://hbr.org/2014/03/five-questions-to-identify-key-stakeholders/

5

The ESRM Cycle – An Overview

In Chapter 4, you explored the things that you need to do to prepare yourself and your security program to implement a risk-based management model. Now that the preliminary steps are taken care of, you are ready to move into the ESRM cycle itself. In the next four chapters, you will get a detailed look at what is involved at each step of the process. However, before that, we will introduce you to the cycle at the holistic level, and walk through an example of how the ESRM life cycle differs from the more traditional approach.

This chapter will help you to:
- Understand the overall ESRM life cycle.
- Compare the ESRM life cycle to other industry life cycles and models.
- Get a view of the ESRM cycle in action.

5.1 What is ESRM? – A Closer Look

In the last chapter, we covered the steps of how to prepare for an ESRM implementation. Now we will take a closer look at exactly what ESRM is, how it impacts your job as a security practitioner, and how it will protect your enterprise. ESRM represents a fundamental change in the way many enterprises – and organizations and individuals within those enterprises – conduct security operations. The implementation of an ESRM program takes time and commitment; above all, it is a process – an ongoing life cycle, as shown in Figure 5-1.

Figure 5-1. The ESRM Life Cycle

This is a life cycle, not a linear, one-time process. These steps are all critical to protecting the enterprise. They are conducted on an ongoing basis, sometimes in line, sometimes simultaneously, always continuously. (That's why they are shown as a circle in Figure 5-1.)

The steps in the ESRM life cycle will look familiar to you as an experienced security practitioner, and those shown in the diagram may appear to be fundamentally basic. For example, if you manage network security and you are configuring firewalls, you are *already* implementing a mitigation plan. The same is true if you manage an enterprise continuity program and have plans in place to respond to certain identified risks. But this is crucial to holistic ESRM practice: doing any of these steps individually without continuing with the others – without taking into account the *entire* life cycle – is merely managing or performing a security task. However, simply performing tasks is not practicing security in a risk-based management paradigm. When you implement the complete, holistic program life cycle, you realize the full benefits of ESRM, and move from task-based security to risk-based management.

5.1.1 Similarities to Industry Life Cycles

The ESRM life cycle is like other risk management cycles with which you may already be familiar. In Table 5-1, we present a few similarities between the ESRM life cycle and other life cycle models.

Table 5-1. Risk Standards with Life Cycle Models Like ESRM

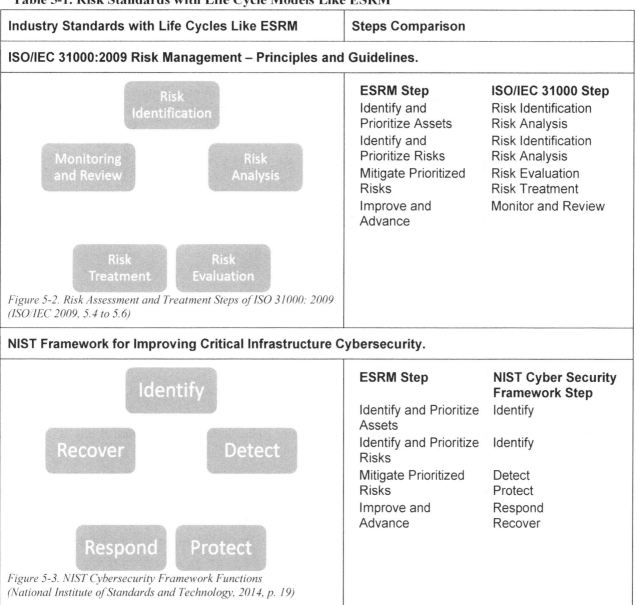

Industry Standards with Life Cycles Like ESRM	Steps Comparison
ISO/IEC 31000:2009 Risk Management – Principles and Guidelines.	

Figure 5-2. Risk Assessment and Treatment Steps of ISO 31000: 2009 (ISO/IEC 2009, 5.4 to 5.6)

ESRM Step	ISO/IEC 31000 Step
Identify and Prioritize Assets	Risk Identification / Risk Analysis
Identify and Prioritize Risks	Risk Identification / Risk Analysis
Mitigate Prioritized Risks	Risk Evaluation / Risk Treatment
Improve and Advance	Monitor and Review

NIST Framework for Improving Critical Infrastructure Cybersecurity.

Figure 5-3. NIST Cybersecurity Framework Functions (National Institute of Standards and Technology, 2014, p. 19)

ESRM Step	NIST Cyber Security Framework Step
Identify and Prioritize Assets	Identify
Identify and Prioritize Risks	Identify
Mitigate Prioritized Risks	Detect / Protect
Improve and Advance	Respond / Recover

NIST Guide for Conducting Risk Assessments

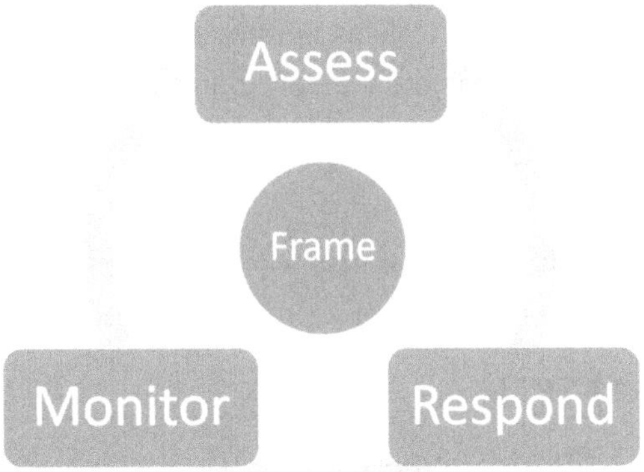

ESRM Step	NIST Risk Management Step
Identify and Prioritize Assets	Frame Assess
Identify and Prioritize Risks	Assess
Mitigate Prioritized Risks	Respond
Improve and Advance	Monitor

Figure 5-4. NIST Risk Management Process
(National Institute of Standards and Technology, 2012, p. 4)

COBIT 5: A Business Framework for the Governance and Management of Enterprise IT.

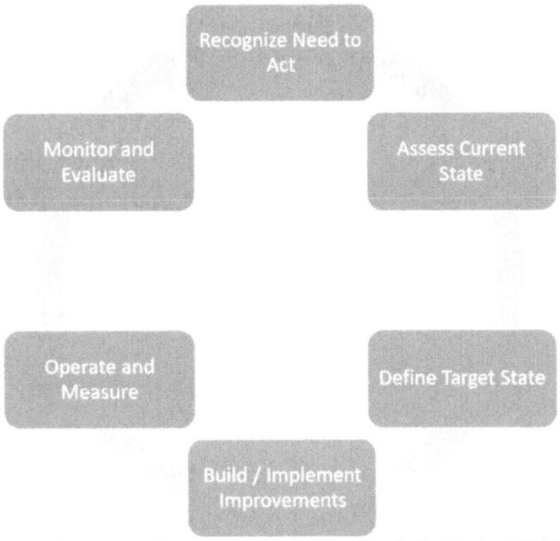

ESRM Step	COBIT 5 Step
Identify and Prioritize Assets	Assess Current State Define Target State
Identify and Prioritize Risks	Assess Current State Define Target State
Mitigate Prioritized Risks	Build / Implement Improvements
Improve and Advance	Operate and Measure Monitor and Evaluate

Figure 5-5. COBIT 5 Continual Improvement Life Cycle (ISACA, p. 37)

Table 5-1 shows that the underlying concepts of ESRM and other standards are not particularly different – these other models have distinct similarities to ESRM. However, the ESRM model is a distillation of what we and other industry experts have been working with over many years in the security industry, and it is *uniquely suited* to the overarching management of enterprise *security* risk.

In Table 5-2, we list a few more widely used security models. You will see similarities between all these models in the ways they identify assets and risks, set priorities, create and implement mitigation plans, and respond to security incidents.

These other models are all very useful, and offer the security practitioner great insight. (We hope you will refer to them as you enhance and refine your understanding of security and risk principles.) But the ESRM model has different priorities, different applications, and different goals from these other models. ESRM represents a comprehensive method of engaging asset owners and other stakeholders in the process of making security risk decisions. It also facilitates partnering with other business function leaders to make security work an integral component of the enterprise.

Table 5-2. Other Widely Used Risk Models

Model	Web Site
European Union Agency for Network and Information Security (ENISA) Risk Management/Risk Assessment (RM/RA) Framework	https://www.enisa.europa.eu/topics/threat-risk-management/risk-management/current-risk/enterprise-process-integration/the-enisa-rm-ra-framework
Carnegie Mellon Operationally Critical Threat, Asset, and Vulnerability Evaluation (OCTAVE) Framework	http://www.cert.org/resilience/products-services/octave/
Federation of European Risk Management Associations (FERMA) A Risk Management Standard	http://www.ferma.eu/app/uploads/2011/11/a-risk-management-standard-english-version.pdf
EU Solvency II Directive (2009/138/EC)	http://eur-lex.europa.eu/legal-content/EN/TXT/HTML/?uri=CELEX:32009L0138&from=en
OCEG GRC Capability Model 3.0 (Red Book)	http://www.oceg.org/resources/red-book-3/

5.1.2 Application of the ESRM Model

Part of applying the ESRM model – and one of the ways it differs from other models – is that the cycle requires a security practitioner to manage security risks both proactively and reactively. ASIS International's CSO Roundtable Group published some of the earliest papers on the topic of ESRM, stressing this same idea, that ESRM is:

- Proactive in that it continuously assesses the full scope of security-related risks to protected assets.
- Reactive in how it responds to security incidents. It mitigates the impact, and then assesses residual risk to minimize exposure to recurrence, while learning how a risk may have changed, and how it could affect the risk assessment progress and thinking, all over again. (CSO Roundtable, 2015)

This double approach enables you and partners within your organization to work together to develop security strategies and address unacceptable risks, accept minimal risks to the enterprise, and continually monitor both for any changes. ESRM principles help the enterprise to take advantage of risks, and add real value to the business by doing so.

Questions for the Security Practitioner
- "Where could the ESRM process begin in my working environment?"
- "Which parts of my existing security program align with the steps of the ESRM life cycle?"
- "How can I communicate the tasks that I perform in my security role through the lens of the ESRM model?"

5.2 The ESRM Life Cycle Model in Action

To see how the ESRM model functions in a working environment, we will look at two examples of using the life cycle approach vs. not using the cycle, in two different disciplines:

1. Physical security with the task of assigning a security guard to a new facility.
2. Cyber security with the task of securing information in a point of sale system.

5.2.1 A Task Management Approach

In a task management approach, the security department may be told of a new retail facility that is coming online that requires security services.

Physical Security Responds
The facility is a high value retail location and has requested security guards to protect the facility. An assessment is done to determine hours of operation, needed coverage, level of officer skill needed, and more. The guards are assigned and begin covering the location when it opens, according to the post orders given to them.
Cyber Security Responds
The facility will process sales on site, as well as allow customers to come in to make payments or inquiries on billing accounts. The IT team assesses the requirements, then designs and installs an encrypted network and role-based access system, which meets the stringent requirements of the payment card industry and the internal company requirements for protecting customer personal information.

In the task-managed approach to security, these are both fine outcomes. Protections have been put in place and the facility's project manager is happy to check off the project task of security implementation.

5.2.2 An ESRM Approach

In the ESRM life cycle, it is imperative to think of implementing a risk mitigation such as assigning a guard to a facility or implementing strong customer information protections as a series of steps, which will ensure the tasks performed by the security team are always optimal and necessary. While the application and assessment of facts will change, and the mitigation actions for the risks will be different, the thought process and steps will always remain the same.

In the ESRM life cycle model, you would:

- **STEP 1: Identify and Prioritize Assets.**
  - Determine what the asset priority is by asking questions, such as:
    - What functions are in the facility?
    - What is stored there?
    - What is sold there?
    - What information is processed there?
    - What data is stored there?
    - Who are the stakeholders?
    - Who has a stake in making sure it is secure?
    - What's the importance of this asset?

- **STEP 2: Identify and Prioritize Security Risks.**
  - After determining the stakeholders and the impact of the asset to business operations, an assessment of the risks is next, with questions like:
    - What could cause harm to this facility?
    - Is it a target for certain types of crime?
    - Is it in a location with physical risks?
    - Are there regulatory requirements that must be met?
    - How would a data theft or breach impact the enterprise?
- **STEP 3: Mitigate Prioritized Risks.**
  - Working with the stakeholders previously identified in Step 1, determine the stakeholder's tolerance for risk.
    - Determine if that tolerance justifies less physical security.
    - Tailor the levels of security guard activity and assign the number of guards needed to mitigate any of the risks identified in Step 2.
  - The Payment Card Industry rules require certain technology mitigations, so:
    - Determine the requirements to protection of the network and data processing.
    - Propose a cyber security implementation, which meets the required levels of
    - protection as defined by the enterprise stakeholders.

It is likely that as an experienced security practitioner – even in a task-managed security environment – you have done something like the three steps above, whether thinking of it as risk management or not. Security assessments are generally performed to determine security needs. Security is applied according to the assessment results. So far, in ESRM, we are merely *formalizing these steps* that you are probably already doing, and ensuring that they happen in every security endeavor. We are also ensuring that they are done in partnership with functional leaders as mitigations to risks that fall outside their acceptable tolerance. (Although, you will notice that the security risks were all discussed together, not in a siloed, separate approach that sometimes comes in the more traditional model.

The next step in the life cycle, is where ESRM *truly* comes into play as a risk-management model. Without Step 4, you would not really be managing the risks, merely putting in needed protections and moving on to the next task on the list. If you never revisit the risk that caused you to make the initial decision, then eventually your mitigation plan may no longer be appropriate for the risk. Thus, ESRM includes the "Improve and Advance" phase.

- **STEP 4: Improve and Advance.**
- **Incident Response.**
  - If an incident occurs, in addition to responding immediately to the incident, you also investigate to define the underlying root cause that allowed the incident to happen.
- **Root Cause Analysis and Assessment.**
  - As part of the overall improvement process, analyze each root cause to determine if it has changed the security equation. This enables you to find new risks, or to see that perhaps some previously acceptable risks are now falling outside of tolerance.
- **Ongoing security risk assessment.**

- Is the location is no longer important enough, or sensitivity enough, to justify the cost of a guard?
- Has the location become more sensitive, meaning that the guards in place do not have the skills, training, or experience appropriate to the new risk profile?
- Has the company determined that billing or payment activities will no longer happen at the location?
- Have regulations become more stringent about protecting information?
- Is there emerging technology, which makes it easier to break into networks that previously met the original design parameters, but have not been upgraded?
- Has the company profile changed in some that increases or lessens it as a target to bad actors?

Every enterprise is different, with different security and risk requirements, and that means there will always be variations in the design and implementation of the ESRM life cycle, and especially in the level of detail involved. But there are some things that every application of the ESRM life cycle will have in common, and one of the most important is that it will be a step-by-step process, with every step having an influence on all the steps that follow. If you keep this basic principle in mind – if you always think in terms of moving through the steps of the life cycle in order – it will become an ingrained habit that you can apply to every security and risk issue you deal with, however large or small.

The example above is just a high-level walk-through of the cycle. In the following chapters, we will dive more deeply into all the steps.

5.3 ESRM is Cyclical, But Not Always Sequential

Throughout this book, we will refer to the beginning and end of the ESRM life cycle, but it is important to understand that you will not always begin with Step 1. (As you can see in Figure 5-6, your organization may already have completed Step 1 [Identifying and Prioritizing Assets], possibly without even thinking about it in those terms.) In addition, you may find that after you have completed Step 2 [Identifying and Prioritizing Risk], a new risk will materialize or be identified, perhaps because of an unforeseen event, or because someone read something concerning in the news. Or crucially, a new risk may be identified simply because of the ongoing activities in the ESRM program – for example, as the unexpected result of an investigation into an unrelated event.

Figure 5-6. The Life Cycle Doesn't Always Start at Step 1.

The ESRM cycle can also be engaged when there is a change in management mindset, whether the change is driven by a security practitioner, a business leader in the enterprise, external pressure from customers, clients, or the community, or even government or regulatory pressures.

Think About It: Changing Risks, Changing Minds

As an example of how a change in mindset can cause a re-engagement of the ESRM cycle, consider how differently security threats were treated and tolerance levels were established in the United States on September 10, 2001, compared and contrasted to September 12, 2001.

Parts of one very significant external action, the attacks on the World Trade Centers in New York City and on the Pentagon in Washington DC caused risk tolerance levels to shift dramatically among multiple groups overnight. Enterprise managers, shareholders, boards of directors, customers, clients, and government officials suddenly placed an enormous focus on physical security and organizational continuity. Laws were passed, policies changed, and responsibilities were increased. That kind of systemic change has an immediate impact on security risk decisions. While a task-based security program might respond to a significant event with recommendations about budget, personnel, and equipment, the ESRM model would instead call for a re-examination of assets, risk, tolerance levels, and priorities. This would lead to recommendations for risk owners to make decisions, and become educated about a changed state of security risk.

While 9/11 is a significant example of this level of immediate and high impact mindset change in relatively recent history, there are other examples of events that have had significant impacts on organizational risk tolerance and required a new risk examination in line with the steps of the ESRM model. In 2013, Edward Snowden's revelations about the NSA certainly had a global societal impact on the conversation around privacy and government access to personal data. The concepts of privacy and information security were redefined in 2013 with the Snowden release. Companies around the world had to reassess how they secured and potentially shared (or would share in the future) any personal information with their governments.

Chapter Review

In Chapter 5 you learned:

- The ESRM life cycle is always ongoing.
- ESRM is a working philosophy to manage and respond to security risks, and it will guide the practitioners through every aspect of their daily functions.
- ESRM helps the security practitioner remain closely tied to the enterprise and consistently focused on the most relevant roles and responsibilities.
- The ESRM life cycle can start and end at any point. The process is flexible, should always be adaptable, and it should never come to an end.

Looking Forward

- In Chapters 6 through 9, we will delve more deeply into the steps of the ESRM cycle and look at some of the techniques and standards that apply to fully implementing the ESRM cycle.

Practitioner steps to consider before moving on to Chapter 6:

✓ Ensure a clear understanding of why managing risk, in partnership with enterprise stakeholders, is so important to overall organizational success and begin to communicate that to your stakeholders.

Security Program Self-Assessment

In this self-assessment, you should think about the answer to the questions posed; and then see where your program is on the identified ESRM spectrum.

Question	Y/N	Is This ESRM?
Do you review security programs that are in place and then adjust them to meet changed needs?	☐Yes ☐No	**NO**: If you do not have a regular annual review or any process in place to adjust security implementations in response to enterprise needs, or if changes only occur when budget changes dictate them, this is a suitable place to start your ESRM program. **PARTIAL**: If you have regularly scheduled risk reviews or adjust programs when the enterprise makes requests, you are part of the way to an ESRM implementation. **YES**: If you have regularly scheduled risk reassessments, you proactively reach out to your enterprise partners to ensure your program is meeting organizational needs, and you are regularly adjusting your security program based on risks identified or changes in asset priority as part of security incident reviews, you are practicing ESRM.

Questions for Discussion

1. In the ESRM life cycle, in which areas can you identify potential starting points, other than the initial identification of assets?
2. What documented standards do you currently use in your enterprise or security environment? Can you relate the ESRM life cycle to any or all of them?
3. How is continual improvement the key to risk-based security management?
4. Does the ESRM life cycle always work in a linear fashion? Why or why not?

References

CSO Roundtable of ASIS International. (2015*). Enterprise security risk management: A holistic approach to security*. Retrieved from https://cso.asisonline.org/esrm/Documents/Enterprise%20Security%20Risk%20Management--Overview%20and%20Case%20Studies%20pt%202.pdf

ISACA. (2012). *COBIT 5: A business framework for the governance and management of enterprise IT*. Rolling Meadows, IL: Author.

ISO/IEC. (2009). *ISO 31000:2009, Risk management – Principles and guidelines*. Geneva, Switzerland: Author.

National Institute of Standards and Technology (NIST). (2014). *Framework for improving critical infrastructure cybersecurity*. Gaithersburg, MD: Author.

National Institute of Standards and Technology (NIST). (2012). *Guide for conducting risk assessments. NIST Special Publication 800-30, Version 1*. Gaithersburg, MD: Author.

6

The ESRM Cycle – Step 1: Identify and Prioritize Assets

In the last chapter, you saw how the steps of the life cycle work together as a whole, and that each step of the cycle has its own set of considerations to look at. In this chapter, you will begin to work through the life cycle at Step 1 to identify and prioritize all the assets in your enterprise that eventually will need to be protected through the rest of the ESRM risk assessment and management process.

This chapter will help you to:

- Explore and identify what is an asset for risk management purposes.
- Find all the stakeholders associated with any specific asset.
- Assign business value to assets, in partnership with the asset owners.
- Recognize the role of security, and the role of the asset owner in determining asset priorities.

6.1 Step 1 – Identify and Prioritize Assets

The first step in the ESRM cycle is to identify the enterprise assets that will need to be protected by your security program, and understand why they are important to your strategic partners for meeting their business goals and objectives (see Figure 6-1.)

Figure 6-1. The first step *of the ESRM Life Cycle is to identify and prioritize assets.*

In Chapter 4, we discussed the difference between the primary asset owner and the other risk stakeholders who might have some interest or interaction with the assets. We also discussed who might also need to be involved in the risk process. Excellent books, such as *The Manager's Guide to Risk Assessment: Getting it Right* by Douglas Henderson (Rothstein Publishing, 2017) take you through risk assessment processes in detail. Step 1 of the ESRM cycle deals with both asset owners and other stakeholders. In this step, you:

1. Find all the assets.
2. Identify the primary asset owner.
3. Find all the stakeholders who should be involved in risk decisions for those assets.
4. Finally, work with all of them to understand the actual business impact, and importance of each asset.

Most enterprises want to protect the most critical assets before those with less impact on the enterprise. Prioritizing enterprise assets, in partnership with the asset owners and stakeholders, is the beginning of that decision-making process.

6.2 What is an Asset?

When looking for assets, some will be unmistakably clear and easy to find and understand. These could be things like computer hardware, retail inventory, manufacturing facilities: these are called *tangible* assets. Unfortunately, other assets might be tougher to define as assets. These are *intangible* assets – for example, the way a company carries out business processes, critical data, the good reputation of the firm, or proprietary training materials. These are also assets that need to be protected, even if they do not take up physical space. A thorough exploration of all assets will provide you with new perspectives on the enterprise, mission, and resources needed to do business.

6.2.1 How Do You Identify Business Assets?

Critical to the ESRM process is a systematic effort to discover all the assets, and a continual review of the assets within the context of how the business uses them. The enterprise's business assets will change over time, and this asset discovery will be an ongoing process. This is where the relationships you have built inside your company can help. Your strategic partners can help you find the less obvious assets, but you will need to be diligent in your asset investigation.

> ### *Case Study: Counting All the Assets*
> George P. has just been hired as the director of the new security organization at Vancouver Pool Supply, a Canadian manufacturer of pumps, hydratic systems, and other technologies used in swimming pools, saunas, and fitness facilities. He has worked to identify the enterprise assets – spread across the company's corporate headquarters in Vancouver, three warehouses across Canada, seven sales offices in Canada and the US, and a manufacturing plant in China.
>
> He believes it is a comprehensive list. When he takes it to his boss, Leslie U., the company's general counsel, she points out that the list does not include one critical technology asset that she is aware of – a significant amount of customer data in a data warehouse/sales platform, which not only stores critical information but has an online ordering component as well. All that data is valuable in terms of marketing and customer care and even in terms of regulatory compliance. Leslie wanted to know why George had not listed that IT system and the included data as an asset to be protected.
>
> George went back to investigate further and eventually came up with an answer. When doing the asset identification process, George had spoken to both marketing and customer care, and neither organization had identified the ordering system as an asset. In his discussions with IT, they had identified company computers, servers, local network hardware in facility data rooms, as well as the applications that all that hardware ran, including the internal billing system. So why had no one mentioned this business-critical system?
>
> It turns out that the data warehouse and online order platform are part of a third-party software-as-a-service (SaaS) model, accessed via the web and hosted by the SaaS provider – a vendor. Nobody at Vancouver Pools considered themselves the *owners* of the systems; so, when asked about *their* assets, nobody ever mentioned it. But clearly, this asset was real and needed to be considered and assessed for risk.

You cannot have a comprehensive understanding of the risks you will need to address until you have the same complete understanding of the assets you need to protect. This understanding does not come without digging past the more obvious assets and truly understanding all the parts and pieces of the enterprise.

6.2.1.1 Finding Tangible Assets

When you are examining your enterprise to find all the tangible assets, you can look for and ask your strategic partners about these categories:

- Accounts receivable.
- Buildings and facilities.
- Cash and cash equivalents.
- Computer equipment.
- Equipment.
- Fixtures.
- Furniture
- Inventory.
- Investments.
- Land.
- Machines.
- Manufacturing materials.
- Plant.
- Stored resources.
- Vehicles.

6.2.1.2 Finding Intangible Assets

Finding intangible assets is harder, but when you are looking for intangible assets, your investigation can include these types:

- Brand related:
  - Brand reputation.
  - Internet domain names.
  - Logos.
  - Mastheads.
  - Name recognition.
  - Trademarks.
- Contract related:
  - Licensing agreements.
  - Service contracts.
  - Leases.
  - Franchise agreements.
  - Use rights.
- Customer related:
  - Customer lists.
  - Goodwill.
  - Relationships.
  - Customer reputation
- Intellectual-property related:
  - Trade secrets
    (such as secret formulas and recipes).
  - Processes and procedures.
  - Institutional knowledge.

- Technology related:
  - Patents on technology.
  - Computer software/code.
  - Data.
  - Critical access credentials.

6.2.2 Who Really "Owns" an Asset?

Once you have identified stakeholders and assets, you can begin to determine who the *owner* of any given asset really is. Figuring out who that person is isn't always easy. Many assets will have a primary asset owner (often the person with budgetary control over the assets), but these assets may also have many stakeholders who could be impacted by any incident or action involving that asset, and they all need to be consulted on questions of security risk. We will often refer to the impacted decision-makers interchangeably, using the terms "stakeholders" or "owners."

In the following sections are a couple of seemingly simple examples that show how complicated it can be to identify an asset owner and stakeholder.

6.2.2.1 A Building

This might at first seem like an easy answer. It is a physical asset, and the facilities organization mostly takes care of maintenance, upkeep, that sort of thing, so facilities should be the asset owner, right?

But what if the building is leased? Is the landlord the asset owner? Or is it the department that holds the contract with the landlord?

Now, think about what goes on in the building: the people, processes, and business functions that are housed there. If it is a manufacturing plant or a warehouse, then procurement management may be the primary owner of the asset, because of the building's place in the company's supply chain. But if it is a call center, the customer service organization may have the biggest stake. If the building houses a data center, then IT and information security must be considered as potential asset owners. If the building contains multiple internal organizations (as shown in Figure 6-3) there are certain to be multiple assets owners and stakeholders. Of course, Human Resources would be stakeholders in any building that houses employees, and ultimately (mostly as an escalation point in any risk decision conflict), senior executives would be the final layer of responsibility for the entire company. The question can be quite complex of who owns a facility as the most responsible stakeholder. and what other stakeholder might also need to have input on any security risk discussions.

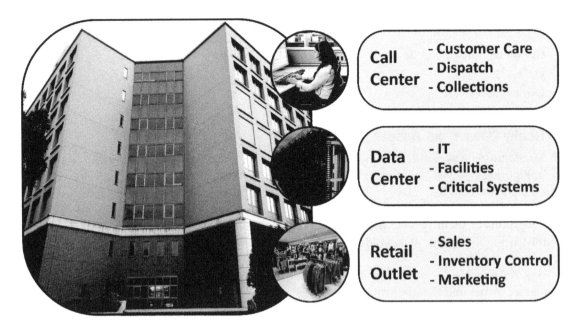

Figure 6-3. A facility can have multiple asset owners, depending on what functions are housed in it. Retrieved from https://commons.wikimedia.org/wiki/File%3AGeneral_Research_Building%2CKyutech.JPG

Figure 6-4. A server or other data center device will have multiple asset owners, depending on the function of the device and the data housed on it. By Michael Jastremski. Retrieved from https://commons.wikimedia.org/wiki/File%3AServer_Linux.jpg

6.2.2.2 A Server

This server example, at first glance, seems even simpler. As you can see in Figure 6-4, a server is simply a computing device; so, the assumption is often that its owner should be someone in the IT organization that is responsible for keeping it up and running.

But all that changes when you start to think about the applications that may be running on the server, the processes that depend on it, and crucially, the information that passes through it.

Does the server hold payroll software? Then the accounting department obviously has a stake, and so does HR. Is it running computer-aided design (CAD) software? Then the design, engineering, and manufacturing organizations may all be owners or stakeholders. And if the server stores sensitive personal data, it is almost certain that the regulatory compliance organization is one of the stakeholders, along with the legal organization, and possibly the government relations organization.

6.2.2.3 The Web of Assets and Asset Owners/Stakeholders

Sometimes the *obvious* asset owner and the risk stakeholder are the same person or the same organization. But that is not always the case. Enterprises are complicated webs of interdependencies on many levels. Oftentimes, assets provide benefits to multiple processes, workflows, and organizations. Assets typically work together in a system where, if one asset is compromised, the impact can cascade through multiple areas waiting on upstream and downstream inputs and outflows. Figure 6-5 is a simple diagram of interactions between a few departments and activities, showing that flow.

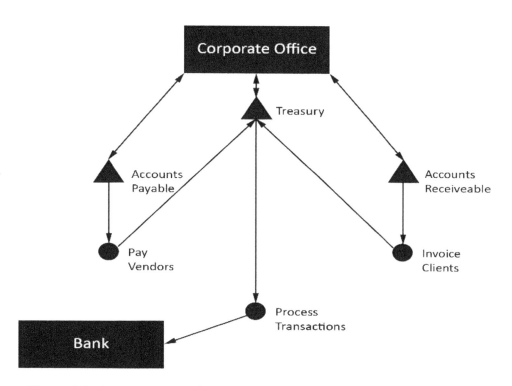

Figure 6-5. Assets, teams, and processes work together in a web of inflows and outflows.

When you are determining who needs to have input about any one asset to the enterprise, you will need to consider many pieces. Otherwise, an asset that seems unimportant to one person in the web (and therefore able to handle more exposure to risk) might actually be important in another context and be impacted by an unmitigated security risk. In such a situation, during the time needed for the impact to the asset (which was deemed not critical by *one person* in the chain) to be corrected, every other process it affects in the web will come to a halt.

Questions for the Security Practitioner
- "What are some examples of assets in my organization whose owners might be different what is initially apparent?"
- "Do I have a method for determining who in my organization is *most responsible* for assets/facilities/processes?"

6.3 How Do You Assign Value to Assets?

Your enterprise cannot determine its tolerance for risk to assets that they do not know the value of. The value of some assets – especially tangible ones – is easier to determine than others, using common quantitative methods. We will not go into detail about this process here – partly because these methods are discussed in any basic accounting book, and partly because this is a process that must be worked out with the business asset/risk owners, and probably with the finance organization as well. The following is an overview of some widely used valuation methods that your business probably uses.

6.3.1 Simple Tangible Asset Valuation (Two Methods)

- **The Cost Method.** This method – probably the easiest to use – values an asset based on its purchase price. It is most useful when applied to stand-alone assets that have no complex dependencies on other assets (for example, in a supply chain).
  Example: This shipping container full of manufactured plastic widgets cost the company $3 million. Therefore, because of the cost, the asset is valued at $3 million.
- **The Market Value Method.** This approach values an asset based on its current market price, determined by one of two standards:
  1. **Replacement Value** – how much it would cost to replace the asset.
     Example: This software cost us $400,000. But the company went out of business; so, if this program needs to be replaced, we will need to pay a new company $650,000. Therefore, the asset is valued at $650,000.
  2. **Net Realizable Value** – how much the asset could be sold for.
     Example: This painting on the wall in the office cost us $500. But the artist became very popular and then died. We could now sell the painting for $375,500. Therefore, the asset is valued at $375,500.

6.3.2 Complex Tangible Asset Valuation

Sometimes assets carry special dependencies – circumstances that make valuing them more complicated and more difficult. Look at Figure 6-6, as an example. A gear in a machine used on a manufacturing assembly line may have cost just $300 when purchased from a custom manufacturer. But if it fails, or is damaged from some risk impact, ordering a new one could take days, weeks, or even months, resulting in significant downtime and disruption, not to mention the work involved in replacing it and any other parts that might need to be replaced. And the manufacturer's customers may have service-level agreements (SLAs) written into their contracts that set financial penalties for failure to deliver products on time. Any one of these factors would make the gear's business value far higher than the $300 replacement cost. That is why you need to take all associated costs and expenses into account. And getting that right depends heavily, if not entirely, on input from the business owner.

Figure 6-6. The value of a seemingly simple piece of hardware can escalate, depending on the impact of the item on the systems around it.

6.3.3 Intangible Asset Valuation (Three Methods)

As discussed above, valuing tangible assets can be a complex process. However, valuation of intangibles is far more difficult.

While tangible asset methods of valuation all rely in some way on the principle of economic substitution (the ability to swap another asset in the place of the one you are valuing at some price point or cost), that is not possible with many intangible assets. In fact, the process is nearly impossible with intangible assets, such as goodwill or reputation, and is still difficult with others, like the value of an existing customer base.

To ensure the proper valuation of intangible assets – information, brand reputation, regulatory compliance, and other types – you will need to involve a broad range of stakeholders, including (but not be limited to):

- Business leaders.
- The legal organization.
- The customer service organization.
- The corporate communications, public relations, and public affairs organizations.
- The corporate compliance organization.

Once these people are engaged in the conversation around valuing the intangible assets, questions that should be answered include:

- What is the life of this asset? (Is it to the end of a contract, or to the perceived horizon that a specific reputation status will remain?)
- What portion of your business mission or function is enabled directly or indirectly by this asset? (Can a monetary value be put on it?)
- Is this asset listed anywhere with a value on the company financial reports?
- In the case of intangible assets like goodwill or reputation, how much would you pay if this item were something you could specifically purchase for the firm?

Intangible assets might be more difficult to value, but there are some generally accepted practices that can help, even here.

1. **The Market method**. This valuation method involves doing some research and attempting to find transactions in the market where a similar asset was involved in a transaction. A similar value can be assigned to the asset.
   Example: The company name is registered as a domain name. A recent sale of a registered URL that is a common misspelling of a competitor's name was completed for $235,000. Therefore, the asset can be roughly valued at $235,000 to $250,000.

2. **The Income method**. If the intangible asset generates income or significantly contributes to activities that generate income, then the estimated future income generated can be used as the value.
   Example: By owning the licensing rights to a song, the royalty payments from its use are expected to be $25,000 over the next 5 years. Therefore, the asset can be roughly valued at $25,000.

3. **The Cost method**. For assets such as intellectual property created by the firm, the cost method allows you to compile the associated costs such as development man hours, research costs, etc.
   Example: This internally developed engineering design required 560 man-hours to develop at a cost of $240 per hour. Therefore, the asset can be roughly valued at $135,000.

Just as in the methods we described for tangible asset valuation, these methods are common accounting practices that your organization's accounting group ought to be able to assist with.

> **Think About It: Valuing Data in the Real World**
> Here is a real-world example of assigning value to intangible assets. The retail chain Target suffered a massive, highly publicized data breach during 2013 holiday season, with the credit and debit cards of more than 40 million customers exposed to potential fraud. Target's CEO eventually valued the cost of the data breach at $148 million (Prince, 2015). It is extremely difficult to say how he arrived at that figure. Did it reflect just the value of the information that was compromised, at the time it was compromised? Did it factor in the presumed impact of the breach on Target's revenue? The fines the company would be exposed to? The cost of legal actions? The loss of customer confidence? It is impossible for us, as outsiders, to answer those questions with any certainty. But we as security professionals can still learn from Target's experience by understanding that even things that are hard to place a value on will certainly reflect a value if they are harmed as part of some security risk impact.

6.3.4 Business Impact Analysis (BIA)

Another methodology for determining the value of assets – one that is used in many different risk-related programs – is the *business impact analysis* (BIA). In an ESRM program, a BIA focuses mainly on assets, to determine how critical it is to protect an asset, based on the impact that the loss or compromise of that asset would have on the business's identified requirements, objectives, and needs. Like the other asset valuation methods that we discussed, BIA is the subject of entire books and websites. You may have teams in your company, or even already reporting to you in the security group, who perform disaster recovery, business continuity, financial, or other types of risk management, and who can help you with the BIA process. The International Organization for Standardization (ISO) has a standard, ISO 22301, that goes into the BIA process in depth. Also, books such as *Business Continuity Management: Global Best Practices*, 4th edition, by Andrew Hiles (Rothstein Publishing, 2014) can provide valuable insight. In addition, we list other resources in the Learn More About It section at the end of this chapter.

> ### Think About It: What Is "It" Really Worth?
> Did you know that in October 2014, a lost Apple iPhone prototype sold online for $84,000? (Walker, 2014) Seems like a lot for a smartphone that, when completed and released, would retail for $500 or so. But somebody obviously thought it was worth a lot more. Why might that have been? Was the buyer just a collector with more money than sense? Or was it another smartphone manufacturer that wanted an advance look at where the market was headed, and maybe even the opportunity to reverse-engineer some of the technology in the prototype? We do not know the answer to those questions, but here's one thing we do know: Someone thought that iPhone was worth more than $500. A lot more.
>
> Additionally, many industry observers felt that Apple completely overreacted to the loss (which it considered a theft of valuable intellectual property), obtaining a search warrant for the home of at least one person suspected of being responsible. The public and media backlash to their reaction was harsh and immediate – and Apple's director of security resigned in the face of intense criticism of the company's perceived overreaching. When you consider the damage to Apple's corporate reputation and brand image, clearly there were more assets involved in this incident than an iPhone prototype; and they were more valuable than Apple's security organization and stakeholders recognized.

6.4 How Do You Prioritize Assets for Protection?

The outcome of the asset valuation process is a figure, which can be used to determine the priority or level of protection needed for each asset. It seems obvious that assets with little or no real-world impact on the business should have less rigorous protections than high-impact assets. Although it might be tempting to simply list all the assets in ascending value order, and then protect them accordingly, the priority of assets is, of course, ultimately up to the business owners. That is one of the most fundamental principles of ESRM, and one we cannot lose sight of. However, the list of assets and associated values is a key piece of information that you, as a security practitioner, can share with your strategic partners to help them make the right decisions in the risk mitigation process.

Your role is to help the asset owner understand the information you present, and its implications. That means making sure the business units:

- Are aware of the impact of a possible security failure.
- Are aware of all the different opinions on the impact.
- Are aware of your professional security-based opinion about what protecting that asset might include.
- Consider any future impact of the asset.

6.5 How Do You Deal with Conflicts in Asset Valuation and Prioritization?

As we have seen, a specific enterprise asset can have multiple owners and stakeholders. Unfortunately, owners sometimes disagree on the value of the asset. As a security practitioner, your role in the valuation process is to guide the business and stakeholders through a conversation that is informed by your analysis of asset value and associated risk. Then you must help them find agreement on the appropriate level of risk the business is prepared to accept, and the appropriate protections to put in place to address that level of risk.

> ### Case Study: Asset Valuation Conflicts at Waters & Frank Sporting Goods
> Matt M. is a security manager with a small sporting goods company, Waters & Frank (W&F), which does some of its sales online. The online sales manager, Karen P., considers W&F's public-facing website her top asset. Her annual sales performance bonus is 75% of her total compensation, and it is based almost entirely on website traffic and sales. This is obviously what makes the website absolutely her top priority. She urgently wants the asset to be protected with significant data security and business continuity controls, including fully redundant servers and continuous backup of databases. But Fred C., the IT director, thinks the existing failover backup solution is adequate and does not want to incur the significant costs of the additional protections.
>
> Matt knows these assets need to be valued in real-world business terms. So, he consults senior business leaders, and he discovers that the website accounts for less than 10% of the company's total sales. The online sales that are so important to Karen simply aren't a core part of the company's current strategy – at least for now. Therefore, Matt is faced with the challenge of helping the business balance the costs of protections against the potential risk impacts.
>
> Matt sets up a meeting with Fred, Karen, and other relevant stakeholders to allow them to discuss what the protections she wants would cost vs. the amount of revenue that online sales brings in. Karen agrees to a suggestion that Fred makes to leave the protections in place that he thinks are adequate for now and to revisit revenues on a quarterly basis to determine the cost/benefit ratio of increasing security on Karen's asset.

As shown in the example above, it is important to prioritize resources in line with the overall business mission and with goals that have already been thoroughly investigated and are clearly understood by the asset owners and all other stakeholders.

Chapter Review

In Chapter 6, you learned:

- Asset valuation and prioritization is the first step of the ESRM life cycle.
- Many common accounting and risk assessment methodologies can be employed when valuing your enterprise assets.
- The security practitioner plays a vital role in collecting asset value information, ensuring all stakeholders are engaged in the valuation and prioritization process, and mediating conflicts in asset prioritization.

Looking Forward

In Chapter 7, you will:

- Explore Step 2 of the ESRM process – Risk identification and Prioritization.

Practitioner steps to consider before moving on to Chapter 7:

✓ Reach out to your strategic partners in finance or risk, to determine whether some or all assets are covered in an existing asset registry for the company.

✓ Research common finance/accounting methods, to become familiar with terms you'll need to discuss with your strategic partners in the finance world.

Security Program Self-Assessment

In this self-assessment, you should think about the answer to the questions posed, and then see where your program is on the identified ESRM spectrum.

Question	Y/N	Is This ESRM?
Do you have a list of assets and the associated impacts, values, and priorities for your enterprise?	☐Yes ☐No	**NO**: If you have never compiled a comprehensive asset valuation list, this is a suitable place to start your ESRM program. **PARTIAL**: If you have a general understanding of the company priorities on protecting assets, and understand who the most impacted groups are for each asset, you are part of the way to an ESRM implementation. **YES**: If you have a formal process for compiling and regularly re-assessing a list of the value of company assets, in partnership with the key asset stakeholders, you are practicing ESRM.

Questions for Discussion

1. In a business environment, what factors might get in the way of gaining a true understanding of all the enterprise assets?
2. Why might an asset have more than one asset owner? Can you think of more examples of this?
3. How might corporate "politics" interfere with the security practitioner's ability to understand all enterprise assets? Can you think of any ways to work through these issues?
4. In your opinion, what is the best place to start when developing asset valuations: Begin with the simplest ones, or with the ones that you intuitively think are the most important?
5. What is the role of the security practitioner in determining asset prioritization? What is the role of the security practitioner in mediating conflicts in asset prioritization? How do these roles work to help the asset owners in their areas of business?

References

Prince, B. (2015, February 26). Target data breach tally hits $162 million in net costs. *Security Week.* Retrieved from http://www.securityweek.com/target-data-breach-tally-hits-162-million-net-costs

Learn More About It

For further reading about asset valuation and other accounting methods see:

Bragg, S. (2013, October 24). *Fair value accounting.* Available at http://www.accountingtools.com/questions-and-answers/fair-value-accounting.html

CGMA. (2012). *Three approaches to valuing intangible assets.* Available at http://www.cgma.org/Resources/Tools/DownloadableDocuments/valuing-intangible-assets.pdf

Maher, M., Stickney, C. P., & Weil, R. L. (2012). *Managerial accounting: An introduction to concepts, methods and uses.* Mason, OH: South-Western Cengage Learning.

For further reading about business impact analysis see:

ISO/IEC. (2012). *ISO/IEC 22301:2012 Societal security – Business continuity management systems.* Geneva, Switzerland: Author.

ISO/IEC. (2009). *ISO/IEC 31000:2009 Risk management – Principles and guidelines.* Geneva, Switzerland: Author.

Hiles, A. (2014). *Business continuity management: Global best practices* (4th ed.). Brookfield, CT: Rothstein Publishing.

7

The ESRM Cycle – Step 2: Identify and Prioritize Security Risks

Now that you have asset identification and prioritization taken care of, it is time to determine the risks that the prioritized assets are exposed to. Then, also, to determine the priority that those risks have in the overall risk picture for your enterprise. The combination of Steps 1 and 2 will leave you with a comprehensive view of the assets that are most important to your enterprise strategic partners and the most critical risks that those assets are exposed to. This will prepare you for the next step of planning how to treat and mitigate the risks.

This chapter will help you to:

- Clearly communicate the difference between a threat and a risk to your stakeholders.
- Follow a clearly defined risk assessment process based on an industry standard.
- Prioritize risks in partnership with the business leaders of your organization to protect your enterprise in line with set tolerances.

7.1 Identify and Prioritize Security Risks

Once you have the prioritized list of assets, you can use it to determine which of the assets are important enough and have sufficient impact on the enterprise to move into Step 2 – assessing the risks to each asset (see Figure 7-1).

The ESRM risk assessment approach recognizes that not all enterprise assets are equal. The time and resources needed to do a risk assessment are not trivial; spending them assessing risk on assets that the business has already determined are less important is not the best use of limited bandwidth. Assessing risks on enterprise assets in the order of identified priority is one way that ESRM makes the security organization more efficient and responsive to the overall needs of the business.

Figure 7-1. ESRM Life Cycle Step 2 is Identifying and Prioritizing Risks.

7.2 What is Risk?

At first, this question might seem entirely self-evident. However, we want to quickly revisit the topic of what exactly constitutes a true risk to an asset. Some risks might have a significant impact, but may be very unlikely to occur, while others might have a small impact, but occur all the time. Your strategic partners will need your help in understanding just exactly what kinds of risk their assets face.

One way to make sure that your audience understands the risk messages you are conveying is by using the concept of the risk triangle.

7.2.1 The Risk Triangle

To understand the risk to their assets, your internal strategic partners need to understand the components that make up the risk triangle – seen below in figure 7-2.

- **Threat.**
  - Something that could potentially cause harm to the asset.
  - Examples: theft, cyber-attack, fraud, fire, flood, vandalism, data breach, etc.
- **Exposure.**
  - The level to which any specific threat might actually happen to the asset in question.
  - Example: a technology asset not connected to any network has lower exposure to hacking.
- **Impact.**
  - A consequence of the threat happening.
  - Example: financial or operational, or even an intangible impact such as reputational damage.

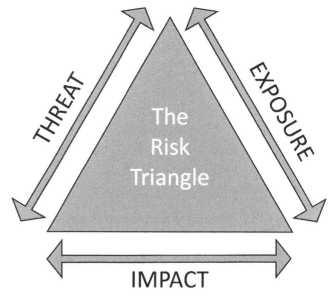

Figure 7-2. The Risk Triangle

For a perceived or thought-of risk to be a *true* risk to the business, it must have all three sides of the triangle to stand on. The threat of flood, for example, does not impact an asset that is far from any flood zone. This is because there is no second part of the triangle – Exposure. But exposure is also not enough. An asset may be near a river, and therefore exposed to the threat of flood, but if it is submersible, or housed in a watertight unit, there is no impact to it and thus still no risk. Only when the three aspects come together does the risk materialize as an item to be considered in the assessment process.

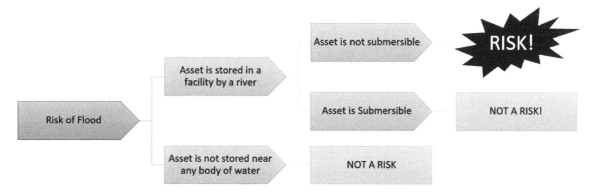

Figure 7-3. All three sides of the risk triangle must exist to be considered "a risk."

In Figure 7-3, we show a decision tree that walks through how to determine whether something is a risk that must be mitigated. Visual decision trees like this one can help you to communicate these risk concepts to any of your partners who may not be familiar with risk assessment.

7.3 The Risk Assessment Process

The process of identifying, associating, and prioritizing risk – most commonly known as *risk assessment* – is a common topic in many disciplines, not just ESRM. For example, the International Organization for Standardization (ISO) Risk Standard 31000 is applicable to many disciplines (ISO/IEC, 2009):

- Financial risk.
- Operational risk.
- Project risk.
- Resource risk.

Risk assessment and management are not limited to the security function, and as security risk managers, we can learn valuable lessons from other risk management disciplines and standards, and apply them to security risks as well. The ISO 31000 is the most comprehensive standard, with the widest application across industries and the globe, but we have listed several web sites at the end of this chapter with additional standards.

7.3.1 ISO Standard and Good Practices

The ISO Risk Standard (ISO/IEC, 2009) defines a risk assessment as, "the overall process of risk identification, risk analysis, and risk evaluation."

- *Risk identification* is finding, recognizing, and detailing the risks that could impact the asset under consideration, or the objectives that it is used to reach.
- *Risk analysis* is understanding the nature, causes, and origination points of the identified risks, and estimating the level of risk. Analysis also includes determining the potential impact of the risk to the business, whether financially, or through operational impacts, or even intangible impacts, such as reputational effect. Finally, it includes identifying any existing controls that the business might already have in place for the risk.
- *Risk evaluation* compares the results of the analysis with the overall defined company risk tolerance level and management acceptance criteria, then determines if a risk is tolerable or must have mitigation steps identified.

In the next few sections, we will break down how you perform these steps to devise a plan that will allow business owners to understand the risks, and either accept or mitigate the discovered security risks.

7.3.1.1 The ESRM Difference

Although the ISO standard provides good guidance and best practices in risk management principles, we show in Table 7-1 that it is not precisely the same as the ESRM process.

Table 7-1. ISO 31000 Risk Assessment Steps vs. ESRM

International Standards Organization Risk Assessment	ESRM Risk Assessment
1. Risk Identification 2. Risk Analysis	1. Risk Identification
3. Risk Evaluation	2. Risk Prioritization

In the ESRM life cycle, we *first* look at risk identification, which is a simpler and somewhat more accelerated process than the ISO way of breaking things up. ESRM combines the first two ISO concepts of identifying and analyzing risk into the single step of Risk Identification – those two ISO recommended steps are easily combined when you consider all risk from the outset using the risk triangle model. ISO's concept of risk identification is truly more like listing potential threats, while the analysis part determines whether the threat has exposure, and impact, and is truly a risk. ESRM simply combined this.

Once the risks are identified, ESRM then looks at risk prioritization. This is called risk evaluation by the ISO standard, but is essentially the same process of determining the level of risk vs. the enterprise tolerance for risk, and then prioritizing treatment based on the gaps between the two.

Questions for the Security Practitioner
- "What might be the best published standard to apply to my enterprise?"
- "Could I leverage the work of other people in my enterprise who manage other types of risk to begin my security risk assessment?"

7.4 Risk Identification – Finding all the Risks

Just as you saw when identifying the assets owned by your enterprise, the process of identifying all the potential risks to those assets is an investigative one that involves, among other things:

- Research into historic security incidents to determine existing risks.
- Discussions with asset owners to identify their risk concerns.
- Identifying risks from existing risk registers – local threat data from government agencies, or insurance companies.

Some risk assessments are simple and straightforward. Tangible assets, like buildings, are exposed to a readily identifiable set of environmental risks, based on their location. Some risks are obvious, simply because of the nature of the enterprise's business. A defense contractor that handles classified government data must be deeply concerned with information security, while a gold or diamond mine is likely far more concerned with the risk of physical theft.

Not all risks are as obvious as these, however. An effective way to find the less obvious risks is to approach risk assessment from the point of view of some other key stakeholders. Looking at your organization from other's points of view allows you to see what their priorities are, and to focus on threats that could potentially harm their ability to meet those priorities.
- Think like a CEO.
  - The CEO's "big picture" point of view will center around security risks that could impact the company's ability to carry out its mission, cause it to lose customers or market share, and keep it from being profitable.
- Think like a shareholder.
  - Of course, the first concern of most shareholders is the profitability and sustainability of the company they've invested in. But another thing to consider is that many investors today are "activist" investors. Is your firm one that fits a profile, such as being "green," which could be an exposure to consider?
- Think like a customer.
  - Put yourself in the place of your organization's customers, and imagine what their major concerns might be. Is it their personal safety when they are on your premises? Is it keeping their personal information out of the hands of thieves?

These are all numerous ways of looking at assets that might be at risk, and of seeing what the impact might be if exposure to a threat caused an occurrence of that threat – a security incident. These do not necessarily contradict one another. The CEO, the shareholder, and the customer – and many other stakeholders – all have their own "right" ways of looking at a risk to an asset. From an ESRM perspective, what matters is considering all their viewpoints so that, as a security practitioner, you can conduct a thorough and meaningful risk assessment.

Questions for the Security Practitioner
- "Do I have any direct contact with my enterprise's customers or clients, so that I can fully understand their view of my organization?"
- "How can I leverage my information gathered prior to beginning the ESRM program, so that it will assist me in identifying all the risks?

7.5 Prioritizing Risks for Mitigation

So far in the ESRM process, you have:
- Developed a comprehensive understanding of your enterprise.
- Identified your strategic partners and stakeholders.
- Identified and placed a business value on enterprise assets, in partnership with your stakeholders.
- Examined and identified risks to those assets.

That all feeds the next activity – placing priorities on the risks to plan for appropriate mitigation. It's time to ask:
- Which risks are the most impactful to critical assets?
- Which risks most urgently require mitigation plans?
- Which risks might be less impactful than thought at the beginning of the risk identification?
- Which risks might be within risk tolerance and acceptable to the business?

You have gathered the information about corporate culture, acceptable levels of risk, what is most important to the stakeholders, what exposures each asset has, and what impact the loss of the asset might be on the business. That all comes together now to inform you in planning a security strategy to protect your enterprise, to make recommendations about the importance of any risk, and to prioritize the order in which it should be considered.

Of course, your strategic partners in the business – business function leaders and other stakeholders – must be fully engaged in discussions at this point, to determine how the business sees the risk, and whether they are willing to accept the risk or they wish to find a method for dealing with it.

7.5.1 Presenting a Risk Matrix

It can be very helpful to build a risk matrix or a threat "heat map" to present to your strategic partners to inform their decisions while determining the need for security risk mitigation strategies. These documents simplify what can often be a complex message. The simpler you make your security risk message, the easier it will be for your non-security colleagues to understand. In turn, this will make it easier for you to explain your recommendations, and enable the risk owners to be *truly* educated on the risk topics prior to making your decision.

7.5.1.1 Education vs. Fear

In ESRM, 100% of the goal is to ensure that your risk owners are fully educated, and that they truly understand the risks that could affect their business objectives. In the past, we have unfortunately met occasional security practitioners who use security jargon, confusing terminology, inflated numbers, and hyperbole to convince the enterprise to implement their security recommendations. This is a common tactic used in sales called, "The FUD Factor." It stands for:

- Fear.
- Uncertainty.
- Doubt.

FUD is a disinformation strategy that is designed to manipulate the human fear of the unknown, rather than letting the person reach a factual and educated decision. Using this technique is a real danger to your credibility as a security professional, since you are making a case for a security strategy based on fear, rather than on concrete assessments of potential impacts. Using FUD communicates a lack of business modeling and acumen, and it is difficult to defend when questions come up about hard facts.

Additionally, there is plenty of ammunition for security mitigation planning using real-life risk information, with no need to play on any fears or use confusing tactics. Of course, people do *like* to hear stories of why they should consider things, and executives are no different. There is a time and place to use anecdotes, to point out incidents in other companies, and imagine risks that might apply to your own enterprise. As we will discuss in Chapter 9, this is part of ongoing risk awareness. But relying too much on "The FUD Factor" is never a winning approach.

Questions for the Security Practitioner
- "Have I ever used scare tactic to describe a potential impact from a threat, because I thought the facts of the risk were not sufficient to have my plan implemented?"
- "How do I communicate the existence of security risks to my stakeholder audience currently?"

7.5.1.2 Building a Matrix

In Figure 7-4, we show a simple, factual, risk matrix that you can use to educate your strategic partners about:

- Risks that could impact their critical assets and business goals.
- The identified potential exposure to and impact of the risk.
- Potential mitigation options for each risk, and the associated costs and effects. (This is also related to Step 3 in the ESRM cycle – Mitigating the prioritized risks.)

Critical Asset Risk Matrix

Asset: _____   Risk Stakeholders: _____

_____

_____

_____

Completed By: _____   Date Completed: _____

Ref #	Risk Description	Impact Rating	Exposure Rating	Notes on Impact/Exposure Ratings	Mitigation Options	Post Mitigation Impact Level	Post Mitigation Exposure Level	Notes

Figure 7-4. Risk Matrix.

This type of matrix is the starting point of discussions with your strategic partners. It can be quite simple, or you can add additional information as needed for your enterprise environment. The choices you make must be based on your organizational culture. For example, the impact and exposure ratings we recommend are:

- High.
- Medium.
- Low.

These make sense to most people and the meaning is easily communicated. However, some organizations might want impact measured on a scale of 1 to 10, or in financial terms such as:

- <$50,000.
- $50,000–$100,000.
- $100,000–$500,000.
- > $500,000.

The message you present must be the one best heard by your audience. The business leaders in your organization should be the main drivers in defining any risk measurement thresholds and terminology – this is a natural extension of their role in the process as the ultimate decision makers on all security risks.

7.5.1.3 Building a Heat Map

While a risk matrix can be a very simple way to educate your strategic partners on the risks that could impact their assets, an even simpler and predominantly visual way to show them the risks they face is a heat map.

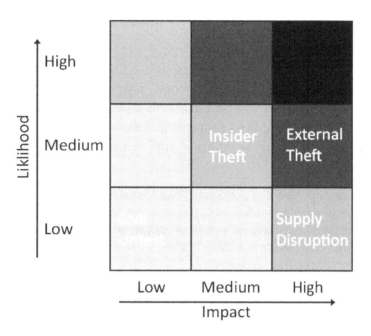

Figure 7-5. Risk Heat Map

A heat map is typically a grid with colors ranging from green in the bottom left to red in the upper right, along axes of impact and likelihood. In Figure 7-5, you can see a typical heat map with some example security risks that would be common to a shipping and receiving warehouse for a pharmaceutical company. In this image, we depict the colors in shades of grey, but we would recommend using colors to call attention to the most serious threats in red.

7.5.1.4 Security Risk Decision-Making

Once you have presented your strategic partner with a picture of the risks that their assets are exposed to, and depending on the level of formality within your organization, you may need to move forward with a decision paper on each mitigation plan. This is a formal written yes/no statement from the business owner regarding the mitigation plan. Alternatively, you may be able to simply have a verbal "go ahead" from the risk owner to move forward with the plan. Whatever the case, the key in ESRM is that you have the risk conversation. The owners of those risks are the ones who make the final decision on whether to implement a mitigation plan, and how to go about it. As long as you provide them with correct, clear, factual information, in the ESRM paradigm, you have done your job, no matter what their final decision may be.

7.5.2 Conflicts in Risk Prioritization

Of course, the world of decision making is not always so black and white. Just as we saw in asset prioritization, you may run into any number of issues when you have these risk prioritization conversations with your colleagues. You might see any or all of the following:

- Different risk owners finding different levels of risk tolerable.
- Partial or non-risk owners attempting to use finance/budgets to control risk priority decisions.
- Different risk owners wanting specific risks considered over others.
- Personnel without the authority to state risk tolerance attempting to accept risks as tolerable.

As you implement and work through the ESRM process, we can practically guarantee that you will see all these conflicts, and probably others. However, as the security practitioner, the ESRM philosophy gives you the authority to work with all those involved, and reach a solution which will meet all the needs of the enterprise. In fact, in ESRM it is your main requirement as the security practitioner, to manage the risk process in partnership with the enterprise. Managing risk includes resolving conflicts that are based on differing viewpoints.

Think About It: Varying Views of the Same Risk Picture

Different assets will have different risks, but there can be different risks, even for the same asset, based on the stakeholder's point of view when looking at the risk and the surrounding circumstances. Here is a thought exercise that shows how different the risk priorities can be and how they can change.

Let's say you are working for a major lending institution. A mortgage broker is suspected of setting up fraudulent accounts, collecting sales commissions on the mortgages associated with those accounts, then letting them go into default for nonpayment.

An investigation establishes that the broker did, in fact, commit the fraud, and he is immediately fired.

Now, from your security perspective, does that mean there is no longer any risk, or is it still a priority?

You, the brokers in that department, their managers, the sales executives, company executives, and your security investigators all see this from their own unique, and very different, perspectives.

The Sales Team

The salespeople, brokers, and sales managers probably just want to get back to work; so they're likely to see that all was needed was the firing of that one employee, and that action would mitigate the risk that the fraud presented. They might see the risk as a low priority. But is that their decision to make? Or, to put the question in ESRM terms, do they own the risk?

The Senior Executives

What if further investigation showed that more than just that one employee was using the same fraudulent process? What if the fraud represented something close to 5% of company sales? Would that make the risk a higher priority and warrant escalation of the issue to senior executives? What if the fraud was on such a large scale that it might force the company to restate its quarterly earnings? This would clearly not be the low priority that the sales team might consider it.

The US SEC and DOJ

And it could grow beyond that scope. What if the investigation showed that certain managers on the sales team had known about the fraud and covered it up so that the company wouldn't have to restate its earnings? Wouldn't everyone's perspective change at that point? Remember that senior corporate officers in the US sign off on Sarbanes-Oxley forms, saying that those earnings reports are accurate. If they are not, the managers and the company both face liability for very serious civil and even criminal penalties from the SEC and DOJ.

These are a lot of "What if?" questions and speculation. But asking "What if?" is what risk identification and prioritization is all about. As the security practitioner, you must ensure that the "what if" does not wander into "FUD Factor" territory but that it still explores the realistic and possible risks that the enterprise faces every day.

Wells Fargo – Fraud Scandal

The example we described here was echoed in real life events in 2016, when the CEO of Wells Fargo was called to testify in front of the US Congress regarding a decade's worth of fraudulent account activity related to sales processes in the firm. The Wells Fargo fraud scandal led to the CEO stepping down and the company paying roughly $185 million in fines and restitution, in addition to enormous stock value losses. Each step along the way, the sales personnel, managers, and executives all had their own perspective on the practices being performed. But ultimately, the impact was larger than likely any of them anticipated it would be.

As you can see, there are a lot of moving pieces in the risk prioritization discussion. There are a few things to keep in mind, though.

- The enterprise can tolerate and accept risk, and can consider it to not be a priority at all, if the person with *authority* to do it chooses to.
- Conflicts *will* eventually occur with personnel who all have a legitimate stake in the risk priority decision.

Questions for the Security Practitioner
- "Is there disagreement in my enterprise over prioritizing one risk over another when leadership is planning budgets, and so on, around security?"
- "If I needed to at this time, would I be able to impartially mediate a disagreement between two equally authorized stakeholders on a risk priority? What if I agreed more with one, but both had the same authority?"

7.5.2.1 The Role of Security

We discussed some of the concepts in handling stakeholder conflict in chapter 6 when exploring conflicts in asset valuation, but the risk discussion is slightly different, more complicated, and the stakes of putting the right security measures in place to mitigate risk can be much higher than a conflict in how much an asset is worth to the organization. Your role is to help the business come to an agreed upon decision accepted by the people with authority to do so. All final risk priority decisions, while heavily influenced by the expertise of the security leader, must be made by the business function leaders whose assets and objectives are impacted by the risks.

The various risk decision roles are outlined below in Table 7-2.

Table 7-2. The Role of the Security Practitioner in Risk Decision Conflicts

	Your Role as a Security Risk Manager		Not Your Role and a Security Risk Manager
Yes	Provide clear, factual risk descriptions, and outline possible mitigation options.	No	Make unilateral risk priority decisions without stakeholder involvement and agreement.
Yes	Ensure that all stakeholders who are exposed to the risk are part of the risk priority decision.		
Yes	Ensure that stakeholders have the appropriate role and authority to make any risk decisions.		
Yes	Coordinate meetings between stakeholders who have conflicting opinions on risk prioritization, and mediate the conversation to allow them to come to agreement.	No	Make final risk priority decisions in situations where stakeholders disagree.
Yes	Escalate to higher management when risk priority conflicts cannot be resolved.		
Yes	Escalate to higher management when persons without true authority to make a risk tolerance decision attempt to accept a risk outside of their role.		

In some cases, the roles as outlined above can be tricky to perform. Conflict can inherently get into the murky waters of organization politics, and competing stakeholder interests can certainly make for contentious discussions sometimes.

The work you have done of building a professional reputation and solid relationships with all the stakeholders will facilitate your role of providing the best information, and any mediation needed. This will ultimately ensure that the enterprise is protected appropriately, according to the tolerance for risk and the need for critical asset protection.

Case Study: Risk Tolerance – When Priorities Collide

Shawn R. has recently been promoted to the position of chief security officer (CSO) with Draper Logistics, a London-based firm that specializes in assisting small and midsize businesses with logistics, transportation, and resource issues. He has been with Draper for three years in a series of increasingly responsible security positions, and in that time, he has consistently communicated his view that security risk belongs to everyone in the company and that his colleagues must be the key drivers in protecting the company assets from harm. When he began his tenure as CSO, it was with a clear understanding from the company's CEO, Phil C., that his mission was to implement and sustain a risk management-based security culture.

Shawn's first step in this direction is to revisit the company's business impact analysis, which was completed right before he joined Draper. His team works with functional leaders across the company to identify the assets they are responsible for, and to determine how critical each one is to the business. The result is a report sent out to the managers of those assets, letting them know how heavily the company relies on the assets. To Shawn's surprise, that turns out to be his first big challenge in his new role.

Draper's chief technology officer (CTO), Tony K., disagrees with the criticality ratings that the report assigns to several of the IT systems he is responsible for. The report says that those systems require higher availability, with stronger backup and recovery capacity, than they currently have. Tony simply changes the ratings and sends the report back to Shawn.

Shawn immediately meets with Tony, explaining that the risks outlined in the report were gathered directly from business leaders, and that the ratings can't simply be changed without further discussion and input. Tony's reply is a stark contrast to Shawn's collaborative approach. He says he has been in IT for decades, that he knows what is important and what is not, and that the IT systems belong to him.

Shawn makes it clear that this is unacceptable, He says he will point out to the CEO that Tony has changed the report over his objections, that Tony has disregarded the input of the impacted business leaders and is exposing the company to risks that aren't his risks to accept. The discussion becomes quite heated, with Tony repeatedly saying that the business leaders just don't "get" IT. This eventually emerges as Tony's overriding concern, that other department heads have no idea how much it costs to maintain their systems in the highest classification tier.

Finally, Shawn offers to arrange meetings between Tony and the individual business leaders, whose classifications he does not agree with. That way, the business leaders can explain why they consider the applications to be critical, and Tony can discuss the costs associated with that tier. In the course of these meetings, one business leader does acknowledge that the cost of criticality on her application is not worth the return. Two others show Tony that their applications support critical business, and he was unaware of the value of those applications. He also learns that a failure of those applications would cost Draper millions. With Tony's initially reluctant approval, those leaders and Tony go to Phil and find the necessary budget to apply additional risk mitigations to the systems.

It is an awkward situation and an uncomfortable one for Shawn. After all, he is still very new to his job. But the outcome is the right one: All the impacted stakeholders have come to an agreement about risk acceptance. And although he was prepared to, Shawn didn't need to take the uncomfortable step of escalating the issue to the CEO.

The role of the security practitioner in ESRM can sometimes be complicated. But ultimately, the bedrock foundation of the ESRM philosophy is knowing that you have provided the best information you can to the decisions makers and that you have helped them come to the final decision of how to handle a risk.

7.5.2.2 The Role of the Asset Owner

In making a risk decision in the ESRM model, the role of the risk owner/stakeholder can be easily described, but it still a significant responsibility in protecting the enterprise from the harm that might come from security risks.

Quite simply, the role of the risk owner is to make educated decisions. That simple statement involves the roles as outlined below in Table 7-3.

Table 7-3. The Role of the Risk Owner in Risk Priority Conflicts

	Role of the Risk Owner/Stakeholder		Not the Role of the Risk Owner/Stakeholder
Yes	Fully understand the risk to the enterprise as presented to them by the security leader.	No	Make unilateral security risk priority decisions, without all stakeholders' involvement and agreement.
Yes	Escalate the decision, or accept the escalation of the security manager, when the level of risk decision-making exceeds their authority.	No	Exceed their authority in risk tolerance decision-making.
Yes	Come to agreement with other risk stakeholders on all security risk priority decisions.	No	Make security risk decisions, without involving security or other stakeholders.

According to ESRM, risk owners and stakeholders must understand both their roles, and the role of the security practitioner in security risk management. This is the reason it is critical that you communicate the role of security consistently and clearly, and also the roles of your strategic partners on a regular basis.

Chapter Review

In Chapter 7, you learned:

- The risk triangle requires a threat, exposure, and impact for a threat to be considered a real risk.
- The ESRM cycle calls for identifying all possible risks, and then working with business stakeholders to prioritize the risks.
- Conflicts can occur when prioritizing risk, and the role of the security professional is to help the business leaders and stakeholders come to agreement on a priority.

Looking Forward

In Chapter 8, we will move on to the next step in the ESRM cycle – choosing and implementing the appropriate response to the identified and prioritized risks.

Practitioner steps to consider before moving on to Chapter 8:

✓ Consider looking at language used to communicate risk in other risk or financial documents in your organization to best describe, identify, and prioritize risks.

✓ Consider asking other departments that deal with risk in your enterprise whether risks are typically accepted, transferred, or mitigated to get a better understanding of typical decisions.

Security Program Self-Assessment

In this self-assessment, you should think about the answer to the questions posed, and then see where your program is on the identified ESRM spectrum.

Question	Y/N	Is This ESRM?
Do you ask department leaders in your organization to provide support at the executive level during annual budgeting processes?	☐Yes ☐No	NO: If you have never engaged internal departments to support you in implementing a new program, or in supporting the budget of an existing program, this is a suitable place to start your ESRM program. PARTIAL: If you ask for input from impacted departments when implementing a program, but do not engage ongoing support from strategic partners when budgeting for security, you are part of the way to an ESRM implementation. YES: If you present your strategic partners with risk matrices and maps to educate them on their risks, and also have a formal process for internal departments "sponsoring" each policy, standard, or program in your department, and you can call on strategic partners to defend the programs to senior management if needed, you are practicing ESRM.

Questions for Discussion

1. How can the reputation of the security practitioner impact perceptions of the risk information that is presented to the asset owners and risk stakeholders?
2. Why are conflict-resolution skills important in the risk prioritization process?
3. How can the security practitioner best ensure that the asset owners and stakeholders truly understand the security risks that the enterprise faces?

References

ISO/IEC. (2009). *ISO/IEC 31000:2009 Risk management – Principles and guidelines*. Geneva, Switzerland: Author.

Learn More About It

For further reading about performing risk assessments see:

Tucker, E. & Broder, J. (2012). *Risk analysis and the security survey* (4th ed.). Waltham, MA: Butterworth-Heinemann.

Vellani, K. (2007). *Strategic security management: A risk assessment guide for decision makers*. Waltham, MA: Butterworth-Heinemann.

For further reading about risk standards see these web sites:

- Carnegie Mellon Operationally Critical Threat, Asset, and Vulnerability Evaluation (OCTAVE).
  - http://www.cert.org/resilience/products-services/octave/
- European Union Agency for Network and Information Security (ENISA) Risk Management/Risk Assessment (RM/RA) Framework.
  - https://www.enisa.europa.eu/topics/threat-risk-management/risk-management/current-risk/business-process-integration/the-enisa-rm-ra-framework
- National Institute of Standards and Technology (NIST) Cybersecurity Framework.
  - https://www.nist.gov/cyberframework
- ISACA Control Objectives for Information and Related Technology (COBIT 5) Framework.
  - https://www.isaca.org/cobit/pages/cobit-5-framework-product-page.aspx
- ASIS/RIMS ANSI Risk Assessment Standard.
- https://www.asisonline.org/Standards-Guidelines/Standards/published/Pages/Risk-Assessment.aspx (available for purchase).

8

The ESRM Cycle – Step 3: Mitigate Prioritized Risks

In Step 3 of the ESRM cycle, the identification and prioritization of assets and risks comes together, and allows security professionals to take action to deal with the identified risks. This is called risk *treatment* in many risk management standards. We refer to this step as risk *mitigation* because this step will *primarily* involve putting in place mitigating plans and actions, which will lower the exposure and impact of identified threats. However, your strategic business partners might sometimes choose another treatment option. We will review those options in this chapter as well, to ensure that you are familiar with the other available choices.

In this step of the ESRM cycle, you can really communicate the difference between ESRM and traditional security to your partners. Risk mitigation activities, such as physical security, investigations, access management, etc., are often the processes used to define the security department and its role. In this step, you can discuss these mitigation processes as part of the ESRM model and risk paradigm – focusing on aspects of overall security risk management, rather than on the tasks that define the security function.

This chapter will help you to:
- Clarify the definition of risk mitigation within the larger context of risk treatment.
- Explore the ESRM approach to presenting mitigation activities as risk response.
- Explain to your strategic partners the roles of security and of the business stakeholders in making risk mitigation decisions.

8.1 Mitigate Prioritized Risks

Step 3 of the ESRM cycle, as shown in Figure 8-1, is to mitigate the prioritized risks. It means working with your strategic partners to choose and implement the preferred business response to the risks that you have identified and prioritized with them.

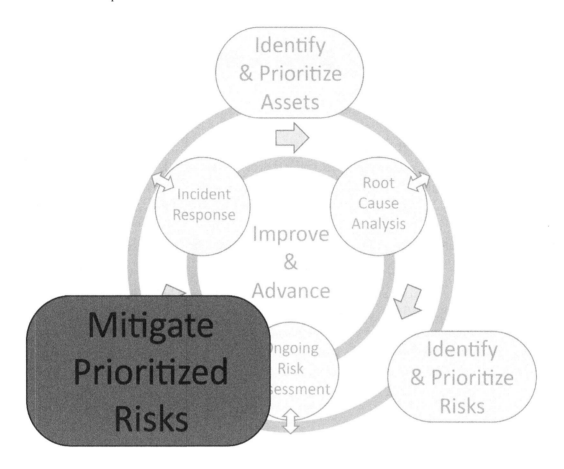

Figure 8-1. Step 3 of the ESRM Life Cycle is to mitigate the prioritized risks

Some examples of risk mitigation plans and activities are:
- Maintain access control.
- Use locks and keys.
- Install network firewalls.
- Post guards.
- Use and manage passwords.
- Plan for crisis management and response.
- Conduct investigations.
- Monitor facilities with closed circuit video.

These are tasks that you and your security team are likely already doing. This part of the ESRM cycle allows you to reframe the tasks through the risk mitigation lens, and it helps you to validate with the stakeholders that the correct activities are being done to meet risk tolerance. We cannot to tell you exactly what the mitigation response should be used for your enterprise security risks. At this step in the cycle, you and your stakeholders will come together to determine those choices.

8.2 Risk Management and Mitigation Responses in Existing Industry Standards

Risk mitigation planning is not only a critical component in security, but in many business functions. Many published standards deal with risk mitigation, and many industries and professions that deal with risk regularly have their own specific standards and practices. In Table 8-1, we outline a few profession- and industry-specific risk management standards. Use these for additional ideas on handling risk and understanding how your strategic partners in other functions within your organization look at risk.

Table 8-1. Professional Standards for Risk Mitigation

Profession	Organization and Standard	Excerpt on Risk Management
Project Management	**Project Management Institute (PMI)** www.pmi.org *A Guide to the Project Management Body of Knowledge, 5th edition,* 2013, pp. 310-311.	**11. Project Risk Management** Project risk management includes the processes of conducting risk management planning, identification, analysis, response planning, and controlling risk on a project. The objectives of project risk management are to increase the likelihood and impact of positive events, and decrease the likelihood and impact of negative events in the project…. To be successful, an organization should be committed to address risk management proactively and consistently throughout the project. A conscious choice should be made at all levels of the organization to actively identify and pursue effective risk management during the life of the project.
Internal Audit	**The Institute of Internal Auditors (IIA)** www.theiia.org *International Standards for the Professional Practice of Internal Auditing Standards,* 2012, p. 13.	**2120 – Risk Management** The internal audit activity must evaluate the effectiveness and contribute to the improvement of risk management processes. *Interpretation:* Determining whether risk management processes are effective is a judgment, resulting from the internal auditor's assessment that: • Organizational objectives support and align with the organization's mission. • Significant risks are identified and assessed. • Appropriate risk responses are selected that align risks with the organization's risk appetite. • Relevant risk information is captured and communicated in a timely manner across the organization, enabling staff, management, and the board to carry out their responsibilities.
Fraud/Accounting	**Chartered Institute of Management Accountants** (CIMA)	**Analyzing Fraud Risks** Fraud risk is one component of operational risk. Operational risk focuses on the risks associated with

	www.cimaglobal.com *Fraud risk management: A guide to good practice*, 2009, p. 21.	errors or events in transaction processing or other business operations. A fraud risk review considers whether these errors or events could be the result of a deliberate act designed to benefit the perpetrator. As a result, fraud risk reviews should be detailed exercises conducted by teams combining in-depth knowledge of the business and market with detailed knowledge and experience of fraud. Risks such as false accounting or the theft of cash or assets need to be considered for each part of the organization's business. Frequently, businesses focus on a limited number of risks, most commonly on third-party thefts. To avoid this, the risks should be classified by reference to the possible type of offence and the potential perpetrator(s). Fraud risks need to be assessed for each area and process of the business, for example, cash payments, cash receipts, sales, purchasing, expenses, inventory, payroll, fixed assets, and loans.
Human Resources	Society for Human Resource Management (SHRM) www.shrm.org *The SHRM Body of Competency and Knowledge 2016*, p. 54.	**Functional Area #13: Risk Management** HR develops and implements strategies to prevent and reduce the occurrence of risks and adverse events, and to minimize associated harm to the organization and its employees. Key Concepts: • Approaches to qualitative and quantitative risk assessment (e.g., single loss expectancy, annualized loss expectancy). • Business recovery and continuity-of-operations planning. • Emergency and disaster (e.g., communicable disease, natural disaster, severe weather, terrorism) preparation and response planning. • Enterprise risk management processes and best practices (e.g., understand context, identify risks, analyze risks, prioritize risks) and risk treatments (e.g., avoidance, reduction, sharing, retention). • Legal and regulatory compliance auditing and investigation techniques. • Quality assurance techniques and methods. • Risk sources (e.g., project failures) and types (e.g., hazard, financial, operational, strategic). • Security concerns (e.g., workplace violence, theft, fraud, corporate espionage, sabotage, kidnapping and ransom) and prevention. (SHRM, 2017. P54)

All these standards provide helpful information to the security professional as background research. However, the ESRM philosophy does not require any one specific standard or practice when mitigating the risks faced by your enterprise. ESRM is a flexible philosophy, and can easily leverage any specific risk mitigation standard that you choose as applicable to your organization. For example, the health-care field has vastly different security risks from the financial field. If your business is in manufacturing, it will have a different outlook on risk than a business in the services or retail industry. The requirement from the ESRM standpoint is that some kind of response to risk must be undertaken. The one thing we cannot do as security professionals is ignore the risk – that is never an appropriate option.

Questions for the Security Practitioner
- "What industry or professional standard might be the most appropriate to consider for my enterprise?"
- "Are there specific laws in my country or specific regulations in my industry regarding risk that I must consider at this point in the ESRM cycle?"

8.2.1 The ISO Risk Management Standard

It is important to understand that ESRM is agnostic in how it chooses a standard to follow in your enterprise risk model. With that in mind, we will once again discuss the ISO Risk Management Standard 31000:2009 as the closest thing to a universally applicable standard.

The ISO considers *mitigation* as part of a larger topic of "risk treatment." The standard tells us that risk treatment is a "process to modify risk." It goes on to modify that broad definition with a few clarifying notes.

Note 1: Risk treatment can involve:
- Avoiding the risk by deciding not to start or continue with the activity that gives rise to the risk.
- Taking or increasing risk to pursue an opportunity.
- Removing the risk source (2.16).
- Changing the likelihood of risk (2.19).
- Changing the consequences of risk (2.18).
- Sharing the risk with another party or parties (including contracts and risk financing).
- Retaining the risk by informed decision.

Note 2: Risk treatments that deal with negative consequences are sometimes referred to as:
- Risk mitigation.
- Risk elimination.
- Risk prevention.
- And risk reduction.

Note 3: Risk treatment can create new risks or modify existing risks (ISO, 2009).

8.2.2 The ESRM Difference

Slightly different from the ISO standard, the ESRM life cycle model refers to "mitigation" rather than "treatment," because mitigation is the most typical response to security risk when using the steps of the ESRM cycle. Why? Because the ESRM process of identifying asset and risk priorities *before* the mitigation step means that items which make it to the priority list will typically fall outside of the tolerance of any option other than a mitigation action. However, since it is still possible that your strategic partners might choose not to mitigate the risks, we will briefly explore the other options outlined in much of the existing risk management literature.

119

8.3 Risk Treatment Options

The final decision on how to treat a security risk is up to the asset owner and the risk stakeholders of that risk. Still, it is important that you are able to provide options to assist the business owner in making that decision.

Typically, you have four options for dealing with any security risk.

1. **Accept the risk.**

   The business owners have ultimate responsibility for their own areas, and the risks associated with them. They may choose to accept a given risk, if they think it is appropriate, and if they have the proper authority to accept the risk

2. **Stop the activity that causes the security risk.**

   This is always an option that may be considered by the enterprise when faced with a risk – security or otherwise. Is the activity that the business is engaged in worth the risk inherent in doing that activity? For example, is it worth the risk to operate a retail store in a high crime area when the business handles cash and other valuables? Perhaps the answer is yes. The outlet may be highly profitable, or there may be legal or regulatory obstacles to refusing to operate in an under-served area. For many reasons, the business might decide to operate that outlet, despite the risks. But if the impacts from risk outweigh the gains, the risk owner could also decide that some risk is unacceptable, and mitigate it by simply ceasing operations.

3. **Transfer the risk to another party.**

   Simply put, this is typically a matter of purchasing insurance to share the monetary impact of a risk with a third party. Alternately, a partnering company could indemnify your enterprise against a risk. The impact might still occur, but if the asset in question is easily replaced and not time-critical, transferring the risk might be a good option.

4. **Mitigate the exposure to or impact of the security risk**.

   Mitigation is the area where your skills and knowledge as a security practitioner will likely prove to be most valuable, and it is the option that will be taken most of the time in the ESRM cycle. You can identify the threat, and then you can determine what security measures could lessen the enterprise's exposure to the threat. This will reduce the likelihood that it will occur, and will lessen the impact if it does happen. This requires developing business-case-based mitigation recommendations for the risk owners to consider.

8.4 Risk Mitigation Decisions

As a security practitioner, your role is to manage the process of dealing with risk, so that the risk owner can make the final decision on the appropriate risk mitigation plan. However, that means that you are the *subject matter expert* in security plans, and the one who implements the security tactics, programs, and tasks that are chosen by the business to be put in place. Because of the trusting relationships you will have with your colleagues as part of the ESRM program, they ought to understand that your recommendations and solutions are key to the process.

You have the expertise to show your stakeholders what options will provide protection to the business. Sometimes, small steps might provide enough protective benefit. Your risk owners might feel it is enough and will not implement a larger project. If it is truly their risk to decide about, and if they truly understand what they are accepting, then implementing their chosen option is the correct path.

In Table 8-2 and Table 8-3, we outline the roles of the security risk manager, the asset owners, and risk stakeholders in the risk mitigation process.

Table 8-2. The Role of the Security Practitioner in Risk Mitigation Decisions

	Your Role as a Security Risk Manager		Not Your Role and a Security Risk Manager
Yes	Provide clear, factual risk descriptions, and recommend mitigation options.	No	Make unilateral risk mitigation decisions without stakeholder involvement and agreement.
Yes	Provide subject matter expertise and experienced advice in all security mitigation planning decisions.		
Yes	Ensure that all stakeholders exposed to the risk are part of the risk mitigation planning.		
Yes	Ensure that stakeholders have the appropriate role, and authority to make any risk mitigation decisions.		
Yes	Coordinate meetings between stakeholders who have conflicting opinions on appropriate risk treatment plans, and mediate the conversation to allow them to come to agreement.	No	Make final risk mitigation decisions in situations where stakeholders disagree.
Yes	Escalate to higher management when risk decision conflicts cannot be resolved.		
Yes	Escalate to higher management when persons without authority to make a risk mitigation decision attempt to do so outside of their role.		

Table 8-3. The Role of the Asset Owner in Risk Mitigation Decisions

	The Role of the Asset Owner/Stakeholder		Not the Role of the Asset Owner/Stakeholder
Yes	Understand fully the risk to the enterprise, and the mitigation options as presented to them by the security leader.	No	Make unilateral security risk decisions without all stakeholder involvement and agreement.
Yes	Decide on mitigating the risk that best protects the enterprise assets within the risk tolerance level of the organization.	No	Exceed their authority in risk tolerance decision making.
Yes	Escalate the decision, or accept the escalation of the security manager, when the level of risk decision making exceeds their authority.	No	Make security risk mitigation decisions without involving security or other stakeholders.
Yes	Come to agreement with other risk stakeholders on all security risk mitigation decisions.		

8.4.1 Conflicts in Risk Mitigation Decisions

In Chapters 6 and 7, we discussed the types of conflicts you might run into Steps 1 and 2 of ESRM life cycle. Step 3 of the cycle is no less prone to creating conflict. Some of the conflicts you might run into when choosing mitigation tactics are listed here:

- Finance or budget owners who attempt to cut security implementations, even though they are not the only impacted stakeholders.
- Stakeholders having different opinions on the best mitigation tactics.
- Risk stakeholders who might not truly understand the risk, or see no need to mitigate it.

- Risk stakeholders without the authority to make mitigation decisions, but who think it is their decision to make.
- Potential mitigation activities that might slow other projects, causing risk stakeholders to object.

Unfortunately, managing security risk involves many moving parts – different assets, stakeholder interests, people, personalities, and budget limits – making running into conflicts an inevitable part of the decision-making process. This is to be expected, but the ESRM practice and philosophy makes dealing with conflict less contentious. That is because your role in managing the risk process is to ensure that the correct people come to the table, are properly educated on the risks, and that they make the decision that best serves their business interests. As the security professional, you will be able to provide expertise and a mediation role when faced with conflicting opinions about the right thing to do. We discussed tactics for dealing with such conflicts in the last two chapters. These tactics work just as well with mediating conflict over mitigation as they do with other risk stakeholder conflicts you might run into.

Remember that in Chapter 3, we talked about Rick M and the missing network card in the data center. His mitigation recommendations were denied. Then when the risk he was trying to mitigate occurred, he had the feeling of "I told you so." ESRM frees the security practitioner from that feeling, because security risk mitigation decisions are always made by the person who is most responsible for it, with the proper processes followed, and known tolerances kept in mind. The asset owner knows the stakes, so the security expert can rest assured, knowing that no matter whether any recommendation is followed or not, the ultimate decision will agree the way the organization wishes to manage their risk.

Questions for the Security Practitioner
- "Do I feel like I am able to escalate security risk mitigation conflicts to the appropriate level in the organization if necessary?"
- "Do I have a clear understanding of the risk tolerance of my enterprise, and do I know what level of the organization is proper for risk decision making when it exceeds stated tolerance?"

Chapter Review
In Chapter 8, you learned:
- Step 3 of the ESRM cycle is to choose and implement the appropriate response for dealing with the risks as prioritized by the business.
- Options for treating risk include accepting the risk, stopping the risky activity, transferring the risk, or mitigating the risk.
- In risk mitigation, the security practitioner's role is to work with the business to find the most appropriate risk solution for the enterprise.

Looking Forward

In Chapter 9, we will move on to the last piece of the ESRM cycle – Improve and Advance. This step is the ongoing activity that will enable your program to continually improve, identify, and mitigate new risk, and protect your enterprise on an ongoing basis.

Practitioner steps to consider before moving on to Chapter 9:

   ✓ Think about the culture of your organization, and imagine how needed escalated risk decisions might play out in different parts of your enterprise.

   ✓ Consider the security programs you already have in place. How are those already mitigating risks to critical assets of the enterprise?

Security Program Self-Assessment

In this self-assessment, you should think about the answer to the questions posed, then see where your program is on the identified ESRM spectrum.

Question	Y/N	Is This ESRM?
Do you have a process for documenting risk management decisions in your organization?	☐Yes ☐No	**NO:** If your department has no formal risk management process or documented steps for risk decision making, then this is a suitable place to start your ESRM program. **PARTIAL:** If your department sometimes requires written documentation of a risk decision (normally when you disagree with the decision), then you are part of the way to an ESRM implementation. **YES:** If you have a formal documented process where all risk response decisions and activities are documented with the response and approval, and if the activities and tasks are perceived as mitigation steps in managing security risks, and if the organization doesn't define the security organization solely based on those tasks, then you are practicing ESRM.

Questions for Discussion

1. In the security area, why is the most common response to risk to mitigate the risk? Are there places where other options might be acceptable if explored? How might risk acceptance with monitoring sometimes be a better option?
2. As a security practitioner, how does having a trusted relationship with your strategic partners benefit the business when conflicts arise between stakeholders?
3. If you are dealing with a risk stakeholder who is attempting to accept a risk that exceeds their authority, what are some ways you can think of to escalate the risk decision to the appropriate level, without damaging the relationship with the stakeholder?
4. If a risk owner refuses all your security risk mitigation recommendations, and they have the appropriate authority to do so, then in the ESRM philosophy, you have successfully completed your role. How does that differ with the traditional security role?

Learn More About It

For further reading about standards for risk mitigation, see:

ISO/IEC. (2009). *ISO/IEC 31000:2009 Risk management – Principles and guidelines.* Geneva, Switzerland: Author.

Lees, G. (2012, January). *Fraud risk management: A guide to good practice.* London, UK: Chartered Institute of Management Accountants.

Project Management Institute. (2013). *A guide to the project management body of knowledge.* Newtown Square, PA: Author.

Society for Human Resource Management (SHRM). (2017). *The SHRM body of competency and knowledge 2017.* Available at https://www.shrm.org/certification/Documents/SHRM-BoCK-FINAL.pdf

The Institute of Internal Auditors. (2012, October). *International standards for the professional practice of internal auditing (standards).* Available at https://na.theiia.org/standards-guidance/Public%20Documents/IPPF%202013%20English.pdf

For further reading about conflict resolution, see:

Moore, C. (2014). *The mediation process: Practical strategies for resolving conflict* (4th ed). San Francisco, CA: Jossey Bass.

Patterson, K., Grenny, J., McMillan, R., & Switzler, A. (2011). *Crucial conversations: Tools for talking when stakes are high.* New York, NY: McGraw Hill Education.

Stone, D., Patton, B. & Heen, S. (2010). *Difficult conversations: How to discuss what matters most.* New York, NY: Penguin Books.

9

The ESRM Cycle – Step 4: Improve and Advance

Now that you have worked through the beginning steps of your ESRM cycle, it's time to move into the ongoing operational phase of ESRM. Step 4, Improve and Advance, is the ongoing, day-to-day activity that will enable your ESRM program to be nimble, responsive, and above all, to continually improve to meet the needs of your enterprise strategic partners.

That we are moving on does not mean you will never revisit Steps 1 to 3. If you need to reassess the entire enterprise, if you have an identified enterprise change, or when you receive a request from a business leader to add security coverage to a new segment of the business, these steps will need to be taken at regular intervals.

This chapter will help you to:
- Understand how the ESRM cycle continues to identify and mitigate new risk.
- Discover how root cause analysis as the primary driver of investigations helps protect the enterprise from residual risk.
- Identify ways of detecting new risks in the enterprise environment.

9.1 Improve and Advance

Unfortunately, risk mitigation is not the end of the risk process. Risk to the organization and business processes can never be eliminated, and however sound your security and risk process and practices are, bad things will, inevitably, happen. That is simply the nature of the security business.

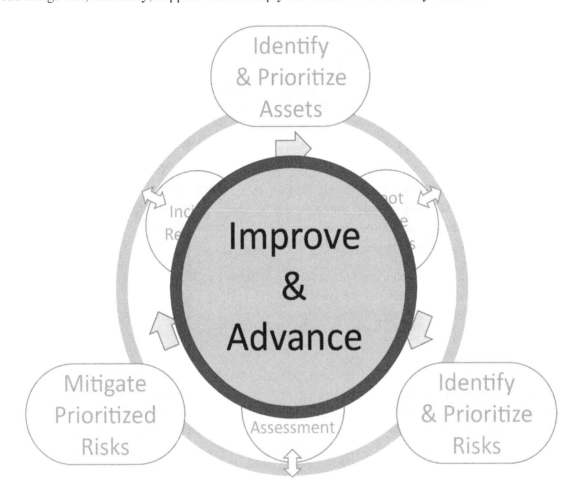

Figure 9-1. ESRM Life Cycle Step 4 is to Improve and Advance the program.

The last step in the ESRM cycle is the core of your program. It is a cycle-within-a-cycle of improving and advancing your program in the face of what will be a continually shifting security risk landscape. As shown in Figure 9-1, improving your ESRM program is a continuous, ongoing process, involving:

1. Incident Response.
2. Root Cause Analysis and Improvement.
3. Ongoing Security Risk Assessment.

9.2 Incident Response

Continually improving and advancing your ESRM program requires that you and your strategic partners in the organization recognize the inevitability of security incidents occurring, and have plans to respond to them when they do.

128

Incident response can mean one of two things:
1. A **reactive response** is reacting to an incident of harm coming to the enterprise.
2. A **proactive response** is reacting to the identification of *potential* harm that could occur, due to some activity that is actively occurring, and then mitigating it.

In the first type, an "event" will occur and need to be dealt with in some way. This could be anything. It could be an angry customer in a retail environment who needs to be escorted off premises. It might be responding to a bank robbery (if your security team is trained and tasked with such things). It could even be responding to a DDOS attack, or a data breach. All these kinds of events must be addressed *in the moment.*

The second type of incident response is where information is brought to the security department about behavior or activity that is not *actively* causing harm (that is known of), but has the *potential* to do so if it is not dealt with. Examples that fall into this category are reports of concerning behavior in the "red flags" zone on the workplace violence spectrum, or perhaps it is a report of network activity that looks suspicious, but may or may not be an actual cyber-attack.

Both types of incidents are things that the security team will react to and provide protective action for the enterprise. We call it an incident response because the activity is brought to the attention of the security team and a response is made.

Questions for the Security Practitioner
- "Are all security or security-related incidents being reported to my security department for response? If not, what types of incidents are directed to other groups, such as HR or Audit?"
- "What methods of reporting exist within my enterprise to ensure that employees can escalate potential incidents and concerning behavior to the security team?"

Incident response is one way to create and maintain awareness of impacts to the enterprise from previously unknown or residual risk.
- **Previously unknown risk** is something that you will inevitably run across in your security program, unfortunately. This is simply a security impact that went undiscovered in the asset identification phase, or it is a risk from a threat that was completely unforeseen. Your security incident response program should always be ready to handle these unexpected impacts.
- **Residual risk** is an impact from a risk that was considered, and it was either accepted as within tolerance, or it was partially mitigated. Just because a mitigation plan is in place or a risk is acceptable does not mean that the impact associated with that risk will never occur. There is no "perfect" mitigation, and accepting a risk means just that – accepting that the impact might occur. In either case, your security incident response team will typically be the first line of defense or of recovery.

When an incident has occurred, after the *immediate* response of life safety and damage control, and once the active impact is stopped, the next step in the continual improvement process is to perform an investigation to discover the root cause of the incident.

9.3 ESRM Investigations and Root Cause Analysis

Investigations are a core part of all security programs, not only ESRM. They can drive overall improvement of the security environment in any organization. However, in the ESRM model, the goal is slightly different. Although investigations to determine the perpetrator of an incident are part of the security incident response, the main goal of all ESRM investigations is to discover the underlying root cause of the incident – to understand the risk that was behind it, to determine whether residual risk still exists, and if it does, to work through a re-assessment process by following the risk cycle again.

Just as we discussed two types of incident response, we need to consider two types of investigations:

- A **reactive investigation** is performed to analyze either a reactive or proactive incident response. These investigate the facts surrounding an incident impact, such as determining who perpetrated a theft, what circumstances may have contributed to an incident occurring, an investigation into reported suspicions based on a tip about possible sales fraud, or time-card issues based on questionable management of forms.

- A **proactive investigation** is the process of scanning the environment for threats from inside or outside. These could involve gathering intelligence on internal personnel who may be exploiting vulnerabilities of the business, looking at the changing demographics of an area that may lead to new risk, monitoring virus registries to understand emerging cyber threats, or learning about the latest social engineering hacks.

In the ESRM paradigm, the goal of both types of investigation are driven by the need to determine the security risk at the foundation of the incident or potential incident. According to Fred Forck's *Cause analysis manual: Incident investigation method & techniques*, a *root cause analysis* (sometimes called a "postmortem report" or "incident investigation") is a "structured search for the underlying fixable reasons explaining the…factors that resulted in an adverse condition or critical incident" in the interests of preventing such conditions recurring in the future (Forck, 2017, p. 296). Thus, such an analysis is vital to continually improve your enterprise security program by identifying and mitigating residual risks.

> ### Think About It: Why Do We Dig Deeper?
> As security professionals, we already understand that bad actors will never stop finding new and imaginative ways to do bad things; so, a crucial part of preventing bad actors from exploiting that specific situation again is to dig into each incident, and then determine exactly what circumstances allowed it to happen.
>
> As an example:
>
> A software engineer inserted some malicious code (malware) into a mobile app she developed – a backdoor that would allow criminals to access or even take control of a user's phone or tablet. Then, when her employer's quality control processes caught the bad code, an investigation identified the guilty party. She was quickly fired, and the malware removed.
>
> That is a good outcome, but it is also an incomplete one.
>
> Rather than stopping at the point of identifying and firing the guilty party, a root cause investigation (also called a postmortem analysis) could identify residual risks that did not disappear once the rogue employee was walked out the door.

A look at the company's hiring practices, for example, might show that a background check was never conducted on her. The postmortem might show that she had a criminal record that no one was aware of.

The *residual* risk in this instance – which is the goal of the postmortem – was not that one "bad actor" was hired, but that the employee who was caught may not be the only criminal who is writing apps for the company, because a risk mitigation process of checking backgrounds was not in place.

A root cause analysis of process-based risk might find that the company's coding and QA processes themselves were at fault and should have caught the malware before it could go live. That leaves open the possibility – the residual risk – that more undetected bad code could be hidden in the app.

Neither of these findings is designed to blame or point fingers, but it is merely to assist the enterprise in closing potential gaps in the security posture.

9.3.1 Performing a Root Cause Analysis

A root cause analysis includes asking follow-up questions, and delving into the answers to determine root cause, uncovering residual risk left from that cause, and actions that might prevent the incident from reoccurring. The follow-up questions may include:

- What happened?
- What were the time lines of the event?
- How did it happen?
- Could this happen again?
- What was the threat?
- Has the threat changed?
- What was the exposure?
- Has the value of the asset changed?
- What was the attack path or vector?
- Were there any controls in place?
- If so, what controls were circumvented or failed?
- Do the same vulnerabilities still exist?
- Could the same vulnerabilities be exploited again?
- Do changes need to be made to mitigate the probability and potential impact?
- Is accepting the same risk acceptable again?

Once the root cause analysis is complete, you will provide a report to the impacted business units, and other asset and risk stakeholders, as part of your ongoing strategic partnership to continue the cycle of improvement to enterprise security. The report will make your partners aware of any previously unknown or residual risks that were discovered in the investigation. It will also allow them to assess and potentially treat those risks (either to mitigate or accept them), just as they had that opportunity in the first pass through the ESRM cycle. This is how the enterprise remains vigilant for new risks, and can protect operations from new or previously unknown threats.

Think About It – A Legal Responsibility to Find the Root Cause
Root cause analysis not only protects the enterprise from residual risk, but it is essentially a legal requirement for proper business practice due to two legal concepts.

Foreseeability
- This concept means that a reasonable person or entity ought to understand the likely consequences of an action (or lack of action). Root cause analysis will allow you to understand the root action that led to the consequence under investigation.

In the legal system, this concept is tied to:

Heightened Liability
- Liability means that a person or organization is responsible for harm caused to another. In the case of heightened liability, it refers to something that has already happened once. Thus, by the definition of foreseeability, if it happens again, it makes the responsible party "more" responsible, since the responsible party ought to have been able to understand the consequences and should have done something to avoid the cause or action.

9.4 Ongoing Security Risk Assessment
Incident responses, investigations, and a root cause analysis all feed directly into the last piece of continual improvement, which is constantly assessing and updating the company's picture of risk.

Ongoing risk assessments involve the same parts of the original assessment process that we discussed in Chapter 7. A reassessment identifies the assets, threats, and impacts, and then drives out what is truly a risk, prioritizes the risks, and presents them back to the risk stakeholders for their decision on how to deal with them. Ongoing risk reassessments are also good for the program overall, because if ESRM is a continual process, each iteration involves less time and effort than a full assessment "from scratch" would require.

When doing a reassessment, some of the questions to ask are:
- What's new in the environment?
  - What assets have been purchased?
  - Has the business mission changed?
  - Has the business reorganized into different business units?
  - Has the business launched any new products?
  - What new projects are in the beginning phases that the security group could provide input on from the start?
  - Have new regulations from external agencies been released?
- Are there any new risks?
  - Have previously identified risks become more significant?
  - Are there new mitigation tools that would be more effective and efficient to minimize risk?
  - Have previously implemented mitigation plans and/or tools become outdated and no longer effective against an existing risk?
  - Are there any emerging risks that should be anticipated?
- What's been depreciated or retired since the last assessment?
  - Have any products been pulled from the market?

- o Are some services no longer being offered?
- o Have any systems been replaced or retired completely?
- o Have policies or procedures been retired or changed?
- Have postmortem recommendations been followed or completed?
  - o Has the mitigation process been completed for risks found through the last assessment?
  - o If not, why are open issues still open?

The answers to these questions will lead you to new stakeholders to talk to, or perhaps will help you identify stakeholders who can be removed from the list. They will help you narrow down where to look for new assets, or will allow you to remove some assets from the assessment list. You can use these questions to drive discussions with business units to see if their goals and objectives have remained the same, and if their appetite for risk has been impacted by any of the changes.

Questions for the Security Practitioner
- "Do I have a defined reassessment program for assets in the enterprise that have been through an initial assessment?"
- "Once a security program is implemented, have I gone back on a regular basis and reviewed the metric of efficiency or effectiveness of that program?"

9.4.1 Sources of Risk Awareness

Investigations and reassessing internal processes are one way to find new risk, but there are many external sources of risk awareness that you can use daily to determine what might be a potential impact to your enterprise. Some examples are:

- Media
  - o Daily TV and radio news shows, newspapers, and websites are excellent sources of identifying new risk. In the security business, we must unfortunately recognize the fact that risk is often discovered through impact. News stories will help you learn about risks that have impacted other enterprises, and think about whether those same threats might impact your own, and to what extent.
  - o Popular culture can also impact your organization's tolerance of risk. Movies and TV shows can make what might have seemed a small risk loom much larger in the minds of executives. Keeping an eye on what is in the media can help you prepare for questions about risks shown in fictional works as well.
- Legal Opinions/Regulatory Trends
  - o If a new law or regulation is released or passed, it is important to be aware of the ramifications for the enterprise.
- Government Sources
  - o Many government entities provide feeds of new and emerging security situations. Law enforcement agencies and other defense groups in many countries are excellent sources of awareness.
- Security Industry Associations

- o Security industry organizations often provide valuable information and analysis of emerging security risks to their members, as a benefit of membership. There are organizations for many different disciplines.
- Industry Publications
  - o Most industries have specific publications, journals, magazines, and web sites that provide news, and updates specific to that industry. We encourage you to pay close attention to the ones that are aligned with your enterprise to ensure an overall awareness of industry trends.
- Subscription Awareness Tools
  - o There are many firms that provide security incident awareness emails or real-time feeds of information from around the globe. While we do not endorse any specific tool, we would recommend considering the available options.

9.4.2 Reporting and Employee Vigilance

One of the most effective ways of ensuring that you receive early warnings on new internal risks is through a mandatory reporting program and a security awareness campaign. If employees understand that they are also responsible for ensuring the security of the enterprise by following good security practices and reporting violations, then they will be valuable allies to you in the job of protecting your enterprise from harm.

One note to remember about encouraging reporting. With awareness efforts, you will often find that reporting increases, and so do your false alarms. However, in risk management, it is better to investigate 10 false reports to find and mitigate a true risk, than it is to have no awareness of the potential threat at all.

Chapter Review

In Chapter 9, you learned:

- Responding to and investigating incidents that harm the enterprise is the beginning of discovering new risks or residual risk, leading to further improvement of the risk management program.
- Root cause analysis is the key goal of ESRM investigations, driving further risk decision-making by your strategic partners.
- Continually scanning the internal and external environment to discover new potential threats to your enterprise is an ongoing activity in the ESRM paradigm.

Looking Forward

In Part 3 of the book, we will look at designing and building an ESRM program that specifically fits your organization's culture, mission, and needs. In Chapter 10, we will look at a concept called *design thinking*. We will examine how businesses use it for process development and see how design thinking can help you to roll out an ESRM program that your strategic partners will accept and embrace.

Practitioner steps to consider before moving on Chapter 10:
- ✓ Consider joining relevant industry associations.
- ✓ Update information feeds and subscriptions to include new risk information.
- ✓ Find out if your enterprise has a stated non-retaliation policy for incident reporting. If not, consider implementing one.

Security Program Self-Assessment

In this self-assessment, you should think about the answer to the question posed, and then see where your program is on the identified ESRM spectrum.

Question	Y/N	Is This ESRM?
Do all events that your security group responds to go through a formal root cause analysis?	□Yes □No	**NO:** If your department has no formal process for analyzing root causes to flush out residual risk, this is a suitable place to start your ESRM program. **PARTIAL:** If your department sometimes does a root cause analysis, depending on the event and severity of impact, or for "political" reasons, you are part of the way to an ESRM implementation. **YES:** If you have a formal documented process where all events undergo a root cause analysis and a report is made to impacted stakeholders, you are practicing ESRM.

Questions for Discussion

1. Why is root cause analysis so critical to security program improvement? Do you think it's possible to improve and advance without this aspect?
2. Why is it important to the ongoing improvement of the security program that all security practitioners continually scan the internal and external environment for new risks?
3. What are some ideas for encouraging all enterprise personnel to take an active role in securing the environment and to report any incidents or potential security issues they are aware of?
4. What is your best source of information on internal threats and potential risks? How do you make sure you are hearing the information?

References

Forck, F. (2017). *Cause analysis manual: Incident investigation method & techniques.*
   Brookfield, CT: Rothstein Publishing.

Learn More About It

For further reading about Security Incident Response and Management, see:

Fay, J. (2011). *Contemporary security management* (3rd ed.). Burlington, MA: Butterworth-Heinemann.

Kral, P. (2012). *The incident handlers handbook.* The SANS Institute. Available at
   https://www.sans.org/reading-room/whitepapers/incident/incident-handlers-handbook-33901

Roberts, S. J., Maxwell, K. R., & Brown, R. (2017). *Intelligence-driven incident response: Outwitting the
   adversary.* Sebastopol, CA: O'Reilly Media.

For further reading about Investigations see:

American National Standards Institute (ANSI) & ASIS International. (2015, August). *ANSI/ASIS
   investigations standard, ANSI/ASIS INV.1-2015.* Available for purchase at
   http://webstore.ansi.org/RecordDetail.aspx?sku=ANSI%2FASIS+INV.1-2015

Association of Certified Fraud Examiners (AFCE). (2017). 2017 *Fraud examiners manual, U.S. edition.*
   Austin, TX: Author.

Ferraro, E. F. (2012). *Investigations in the workplace* (2nd ed.). Boca Raton, FL: CRC Press.

For further reading about Root Cause Analysis, see:

ABS Consulting. (2008*). Root cause analysis handbook: A guide to efficient and effective incident
   investigation* (3rd ed.). Brookfield, CT: Rothstein Publishing.

Part 3

Designing a Program That Works for Your Enterprise

Now that you have the fundamentals of the enterprise security risk management (ESRM) cycle down, it's time to get specific. ESRM is not a one-size-fits-all standard. Your knowledge of your own enterprise and the partnerships inside your organization will allow you to tailor the ERSM philosophy to fit the needs of your business. In this part of the book, we will explore some theories for designing security business processes that fit your enterprise.

In Chapters 10 and 11, we are going to take a closer look at a different aspect of ESRM implementation: We will explore designing, developing, and rolling out an ESRM program that your strategic partners will embrace, and one that will also enhance the standing of the security program within the enterprise.

In This Part:
- **Designing Your ESRM Program**
- **Rolling Out Your ESRM Program**

10

Designing an ESRM Program to Fit Your Enterprise

A key driver for putting your enterprise security risk management (ESRM) program into practice enterprise-wide will be learning to think and communicate more like your partners on the "business" side of things.

In this chapter, you will learn about a widely-used business concept called "design thinking," which product and process developers across many different industries and organizations use to roll out products, services, and internal programs. You can take this theory of process development and tailor the concepts into a phased, iterative rollout plan for your ESRM program.

This thought and program design process will make developing and releasing your ESRM program much easier, while you learn to interact more effectively with your strategic partners in developing security programs that meet their needs as well as yours.

This chapter will help you to:
- Think about business process development in a new way.
- Understand the business concept of *design thinking* and how to use it.
- Start developing a security program that your strategic partners in the business will embrace.

10.1 Design Thinking – A Conceptual Model for Your ESRM Program

Business process development can be approached in many ways. One way that we have found very useful is what business organizations refer to as *design thinking*. Design thinking is used widely by development teams as a way of helping decision-makers to identify problems and issues, and to develop and implement creative, yet focused, solutions to them.

One reason that design thinking has become so popular among business leaders is the constantly increasing complexity of business operations and risks. Business assets have multiple owners, often with competing agendas and varying views of risk. Many of the current risks were unimaginable until very recently, and new risks are constantly emerging. These complex business environments call for a creative approach to ensure that processes align with the environment. Design thinking – while it is not the only method, by any means – is something we have found most useful in our security careers.

The History of Design Thinking

Design thinking has its roots in architecture and the visual arts, and it first became widely used in business as a product design methodology. But it can be used to define a business process or program – including a security program – just as easily as it can be used to design a new car or mobile phone. Many businesses are adopting this thinking style to build processes and procedures in a collaborative format in which all impacted parties will have a voice in the eventual model.

Design thinking, as it is thought of today, was developed in 1991 by David M. Kelley, a design specialist and professor at Stanford University for 25 years. It is based on a set of basic principles, including empathy with other people (those critical relationships we have talked about), the creation of "road maps," the use of prototyping (also known as trial and error), and a willingness to make mistakes and learn from them.

In their article, "Reclaim your Creative Confidence," David and Tom Kelley wrote about the importance of creativity and design thinking for many of the most successful businesses around today:

> …we know that creativity is essential to success in any discipline or industry. According to a recent IBM survey of chief executives around the world, it is the most sought-after trait in leaders today. No one can deny that creative thinking has enabled the rise and continued success of countless companies, from start-ups like Facebook and Google to stalwarts like Procter & Gamble and General Electric (Kelley & Kelley, December 2012).

This creativity and method of thinking will serve you well as you begin putting your ESRM program in place. In Figure 5-1, we offer a visual model of the cycle of design thinking. As you can see from the diagram, design thinking represents an iterative model, one that allows programs and processes to develop, mature, evolve, and change as conditions change.

We wish to acknowledge the work of David M. Kelley at Stanford University in developing the "design thinking" methodology we are using. We are also grateful that Kelley has made it available freely, via Creative Commons, for the use of scholars and business professionals

(For more information about design thinking, see the "Learn More About It" section at the end of this chapter.)

In security and any other discipline, design thinking begins with an attempt to understand the needs and desires of the people and organizations involved in the process or program to be developed. We already touched on this concept of involving your strategic partners in the business in earlier chapters, when we discussed relationships with asset and risk owners, and with stakeholders. But design thinking takes this a giant step further, by *obliging* us to work hard to understand what those people – individually and in groups – want and need from us. In design thinking, this is referred to as *empathy*.

10.2 The Phases of Design Thinking

Figure 10-1. The design thinking process begins with, and returns to, empathy. (Hasso Plattner, 2013).

10.2.1 Empathize Phase

At its core, empathy is the ability to understand and share the feelings of another person. It is very important to every human being. We all need to be listened to and understood, in business and our personal lives, whether we are the consumer of a product or service, or the provider. Empathy allows us to get along better with our fellow human beings, because we can put ourselves in their shoes and see things through their eyes. In earlier chapters of this book, we talked about how it feels when other people in the enterprise do not understand and appreciate the value of what we do as security professionals. In part, that is a result of a lack of empathy. It is important for security professionals to ensure that this is not what other people feel when dealing with us.

Tasks of the Empathize Phase

1. Fully understand which process or aspect of the program you are designing.
2. Talk to people in your organization about how they feel about the current process.
3. Ask key questions:
    o What can be improved?
    o What do they like about the current process?
    o How will changing the process or implementing a new process impact them?
4. *Listen* to your partners.
5. Understand their point of view.

In design thinking terms, empathy means first recognizing the people who will be most impacted by whatever you are trying to accomplish. These can be the stakeholders whom you have already identified, other impacted groups like the general employee population, or the supervisors who will have to enforce a new policy. Then make a serious, honest attempt to understand what each group needs and wants from you and your program. not just as strategic partners, but as human beings. Above all, it means *listening* (Hasso Plattner, 2013).

In ESRM-specific terms, empathy is essential to your program because human beings are essential to your program. We cannot stress too strongly that this is not just some vague, nice-to-have concept. In Chapter 11, we will share our real-world experience in rolling out an ESRM program, and you will see that empathy was critical to its success.

Questions for the Security Practitioner
1. "Are there instances in my life and work when I was talking to a person and thought that they had no idea how I felt or what I was thinking? Did that make me want to interact with them more, or less?"
2. "Can I think of any current processes that I ask personnel to do which even I find troublesome? How do employees who do not understand the risk being mitigated feel about those processes?"
3. "How does it make me feel when others ask for my feedback on their ideas? Am I more likely or less likely to embrace the final decision?"

10.2.2 Define Phase

In design thinking, definition means taking what you have learned from the empathy phase and concretely defining in your own mind the problem that needs to be solved based on what you learned from the stakeholders. (Hasso Plattner, 2013). Once you have done that, you can craft (define) an actionable statement that can be communicated effectively back to your stakeholders.

Tasks of the Define Phase

1. Review the results of your conversations in the *empathy* phase.
2. Review and redefine your own understanding of the issue at stake.
3. Clearly define the problem that needs to be solved in language that everyone can understand.

10.2.3 Ideate Phase

Ideation is the brainstorming process of moving beyond identifying a problem to begin working with your partners and defining potential solutions (Hasso Plattner, 2013). This is a phase in which it is essential not to limit your thinking or that of anyone else. Be as creative as possible, and encourage as much creativity as possible. so that you can generate a broad range of ideas, no matter how unrealistic.

Of course, this is the real world and the final process will certainly need to be based on a realistic proposal. When designing security-related processes, you will inevitably run up against several legal, regulatory, ethical, and logistical requirements, which will need to be considered for the final process or procedure. However, during this brainstorming phase, the notion of "throwing out there" every single idea that you and your partners can think of to solve the problem may lead to some solution that has never been tried as a response to a security risk. In fact, this unique approach may be a perfect solution for your enterprise environment, even though it is not taught in any traditional security models.

Tasks of the Ideate Phase

1. Set up brainstorming meetings with security personnel and stakeholders.
2. Clearly communicate the problem defined in the last step and look for solutions.
3. Record all ideas without judgement to get beyond the obvious solutions.
4. Narrow the ideas down until you arrive at what seems like the best, most workable solution for everyone.

10.2.4 Prototype Phase

The Prototype phase is where you begin to build, whether in real life or virtually.

The prototype (sometimes called a pilot project) does not need be polished or even complete. It could be as simple as a storyboard or outline presentation that people can look at, or "walk through," and provide feedback about how it meets the needs they have identified up to that point. (Hasso Plattner, 2013).

Once the prototype has gone beyond being a design on paper, and you decide to do a pilot, start small, involving stakeholders who have been part of the project all the way through. This way, the original stakeholders are invested in making sure the process is workable for everyone.

Tasks of the Prototype Phase

1. Build the model or template of the final process.
2. Present the model as a walk through to your stakeholder, or run a limited pilot trial of the process.
3. Make sure your stakeholders have many opportunities for feedback.

Questions for the Security Practitioner
1. "In the past, when starting a new project, have I formally defined the goals of the project and the problem to solve? How was that different from projects where I did not do that?"
2. "When I roll out new processes or procedures, do I look for feedback after they have been in place for a while? Am I willing to change them based on that feedback?"

10.2.5 Test Phase

Testing in the design thinking model means actively soliciting feedback about your prototype, actively listening to that feedback, and then recognizing where it does and does not meet the needs that you and the other stakeholders have identified. (Hasso Plattner, 2013).

Tasks of the Test Phase

1. Allow the prototype to run for a set period.
2. Gather feedback from all stakeholders at the beginning, at set points along the way, and at the end of the test.
3. Modify the process or procedure, based on the feedback from all parties.

And when these phases are complete? *The entire process begins again.* You circle directly back to the beginning of the process, using *empathy* to understand how the people involved in the testing process feel about the prototype, *definition* to confirm that your identification of the problem is correct, *ideation* to identify potential changes that will solve the problem, and finally re-*prototyping* and *retesting*. It is an ongoing cycle that will continue until you and the test stakeholders have reached agreement about the solution to the original security risk or problem.

10.3 ESRM Program Rollout in a Formal Design Thinking Model

Design thinking is a general theory and model. Now we will talk about how to tailor that model to a security focused and ESRM-specific program rollout. This is a much larger topic than a single process or procedure. Designing an entire security program is a significant undertaking. We recommend an iterative rollout, rather than attempting to do the whole program all at once.

When you are rolling out an ESRM program, it is critical to make the process as simple as possible. Security is a complex discipline, with many moving parts; you cannot simply scrap your existing practices and start from nothing, since there is far too much risk exposure involved. While the transition is taking place, the enterprise must continue operating in a secure manner. Access will still need to be controlled, investigations will still need to be conducted, surveillance will still need to take place. The security organization will need to continue functioning effectively while you transition from security task management to security risk management.

It is a clearly defined path that allows you to start with the core concepts and implement them. Then, once those are in place, you will expand the program to the next phase, taking incremental steps to success, until the entire program is moved into the ESRM way of managing security.

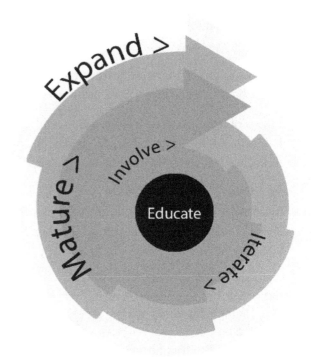

Figure 10-2. An Iterative Design Thinking Model for ESRM

Figure 10-2 shows a model of how you can use design thinking concepts to implement your ESRM program in a phased approach.

10.3.1 Educate and Involve the Stakeholders (Empathy)

The first element of design thinking is empathy. In rolling out your ESRM program, beginning with empathy means taking some very concrete steps. First, you need to educate yourself and your security team, and then involve your stakeholders and educate them as well.

The step of educating yourself, which comes at the very beginning of the iterative process, is the most complex, but it is essential to your ESRM success. To do this, you must:

- *Completely* challenge your current security management program and your current security practices. That means taking a step back and determining what is truly security risk management practice and what is not - as defined by the ESRM paradigm. To do this, you must look at every security role, position, policy, practice, and thought process to determine its fit in the overall security model.
- Understand the "why" of all the things your program is doing – what needs are you trying to meet?
- Conduct a gap analysis for every process that you perform, and find the difference between what it does and what it should be doing to meet your strategic partners' needs.
- Understand all the moving parts of your program. Then add an understanding of what each part does for your stakeholders, and how they mesh with what your partners truly need and want from you.

To get that final piece of understanding about what your strategic partners need and want, you will need to work to educate them as well. You will want to:

- Explain to them the concept of ESRM, and educate them on the roles of the security group and of the asset owner in managing enterprise security risk together.
- Educate them on how security can help them to ensure their ongoing business mission by protecting their assets from harm.
- Show them the need for some security programs, while also making clear that risk decisions are up to them in the business.
- Reach an agreement about roles and responsibilities regarding protecting their assets.

Why are these points critical to the first step of rolling out an ESRM program in your enterprise?

1. Your partners are not going to understand the value of your program unless they understand and agree with the role of security in the company. It is that base understanding of the ESRM philosophy about who "owns" security risk (them) vs. the role of security in identifying and helping them understand that risk.
2. You cannot be successful in your security management if you and your stakeholders do not first come to an agreement about the definition of "success." We are not suggesting this will happen overnight, but the focus of your program must be consistent and comprehensive in order to build partnerships and understanding.

Case Study: When Success Is Not Successful

How do you agree on the definition of "success?" Here is an example from Jack G., a security professional we know. He was given the responsibility of implementing a business continuity management (BCM) program for a warehouse/distribution company in New Jersey. (We will call it Northeastern Logistics.) This was in the post-9/11 years, when many companies realized that BCM was an important thing. The company decided to assign the task of writing a plan to a security manager, assuming that it was an easily accomplished one-person job. Jack rolled out a "typical" BCM program. He deployed planning software and held some training sessions. And then he waited for departments in the company to complete their business impact analyses, risk assessments, and plans. This would then enable him to assure the executives who had given him the assignment that the company was ready for a business disruption.

He had a long wait. The rest of the business saw BCM as his (or security's) responsibility. He had rolled out his program and given people in each group information about how to use it to supply him with the documents he needed. But those people had other work to do, and inevitably, that work came first. When they got their regular work done, maybe then they could get those plans written up.

Jack followed up, pestered, gave deadlines, extended deadlines, begged, and sometimes even wrote the plans himself (if/when he could get the subject-matter experts to at least tell him what he needed to know). He did his best, and eventually there was at least some information from each internal group entered in the BCM plan book. As the other enterprise groups saw it, they had jumped through the hoops that security had put in their way. Now they could stop hearing about this BCM thing that security was bothering them about.

And that was all just fine – sort of – until a devastating hurricane called Sandy struck. Northeastern Logistics got hit very hard. Fuel shortages kept its trucks from making a lot of deliveries, and the company lost important contracts. It also lost a lot of inventory and other business assets to floodwaters in their warehouses that were built within 500-year flood zones (and it certainly had not been 500 years since the last flood).

Once the storm was over, the floodwaters had receded, and a lot of ad hoc fixes were in place, the Northeastern Logistics' senior executives went to the impacted groups and asked them, "Why weren't you ready for this?" Everybody's answer was, of course, some variant on "That was security's job." Jack responded by showing the executives documentation of all his BCM efforts. He pointed out that not one department had asked for the BCM plan as part of the recovery process.

It is not a very happy story, but it does have a happier ending for both Jack and his strategic partners. Before Sandy, they had defined business continuity "success" as "having plans in the system." Security assumed those plans would be used, while the business departments "checked the box," moved on, and then forgot that the plans even existed. They certainly did not remember them at the time of crisis. The hurricane changed all that. Department leaders recognized there were very real risks to their business assets, and they saw the benefits of participating in the BCM program. They asked for help in making sure their plans were both workable and up-to-date. They went to Northeastern Logistics' executives and asked that resources be given to the security organization to assist the business with BCM planning. Both sides now saw that the success of the program would require plans that were maintained and tested on a regular basis.

The case study above provided a valuable lesson for all involved, but it was a difficult and very expensive one. Perhaps if Jack had known about ESRM principles before a once-in-a-generation hurricane struck, the up-front discussions about asset risks and risk ownership would have led to the success criteria being defined as more than just completing the plans on paper. Instead, success would have been defined as ensuring that all risks were met and mitigated to the tolerance satisfaction of the risk owners, and this success criteria would have been met before the crisis, not after.

To help your strategic partners grasp the value of your program, it is essential to use second step in iterative design thinking when rolling out your ESRM program. This step gets everyone who is touched by the program or may be part of it in the future involved and identifies those who need to be added into the conversation. Iterative design thinking helps to communicate with all stakeholders, clearly and effectively, throughout the process.

10.3.2 Iterate the Process (Your Definition and Prototypes)

When you begin the process of iteration, you combine the definition and prototype phases of design thinking into a step that will happen several times over. This is where you apply what you have learned from all those stakeholder conversations about their wants and needs, and put into place ways of meeting the needs and solving the problems. Using design thinking, a product designer working on a new mobile phone might start with a mockup or a working model that shows the direction the project is going in. This is prototyping, and it can be applied just as easily and effectively to an ESRM program as to a product.

As we discussed above, the rollout of the ESRM program should be done one process at a time, where any aspect of your existing program transitions from simply being a task that your group does, to an accepted and business-driven mitigation of a security risk. It would involve the appropriate asset owner in determining the correct risk response. Each piece can be taken and reworked into a prototype process or policy, which your stakeholders can step through and provide feedback on.

Prototyping an Access Control Process
Let's imagine you have been tasked with securing a facility. In response to what you see as the risk of intrusion into the critical data center, you are considering installing biometrics authentication – fingerprint readers – for all employees. But while you initially

explored this and talked with various stakeholders, you heard concerns expressed about this approach being intrusive and possibly violating employees' privacy.

How can prototyping this solution help your program rollout?

One simple way could be to set up a pilot project in just one area with the identified risk. You may choose to make it an opt-in project in which only employees who are comfortable with the program are involved, and then you can see what kind of adoption you will get.

The result: You can find out whether it will face significant resistance from the people involved and what their privacy concerns may be. An added benefit is that you can do all this without the cost of implementing a full-scale program that you might end up canceling.

Once you have the small-scale prototype up and running, the feedback from your stakeholders and end-users will allow you to continue to refine the process until it is something that is acceptable and able to be fully rolled out (or perhaps unacceptable and not implemented, depending on the final decision of the asset/risk owner). The important thing is to start small, get feedback, make adjustments, and iterate – and keep iterating until you have it right.

10.3.3 Mature the Process (Testing and Feedback)

Maturing your prototype and program is the next step in the ever-expanding circle you saw in Figure 10-2. The human element (empathy/involvement) does not go away once the prototype is agreed upon and your project is under way, and you cannot stop listening to the people impacted just because your prototype seems to be a success. Testing and feedback is an integral part of design thinking. The feedback you get at the beginning of an implementation may change more than once as it goes on.

Because the security program, processes, and procedures all primarily impact stakeholders and personnel outside of the security department, it is not possible for you alone to judge whether your process is a success. That feedback must come from the impacted people in the enterprise. As people interact with the process, they will begin to see different better ways that things could work, and you can learn from their changing perceptions as your program builds.

If we return to the case on the biometric authentication project, imagine how this might go. The process is working, you haven't seen any problems with the technology, and you haven't heard any complaints from participants about their privacy, or about the time it takes to use the system. But still, you should proactively reach out to everyone involved, and find out what they really think about having their fingerprints read to get to their workstations. They may not be complaining to you. They may not be complaining to their managers (many people are understandably reluctant to do that). But that does not necessarily mean that they are comfortable with what you have asked them to do. And the only way to know for sure is to engage with them, in a way that lets them know you are serious about their views, anonymously if necessary.

10.3.4 Expand the Process (Begin Again with a Larger Scope)

As you follow the iterative process, each project you do will eventually mature and run smoothly. At that point, it is time to expand your scope into another area – to bring another process into the ESRM model. Bringing in a new process expands your whole ESRM program, which can mean:

- Expanding to other locations.
- Addressing a new type of risk.
- Working with an entirely new set of stakeholders.
- Converting another task your program performs to a risk-based approach.
- Assessing other security policies and practices.
- Re-evaluating set risk tolerances.

Each expansive round is made up of the same exact steps. You start back with education and involvement, ensuring that you use empathy to understand the people involved, then iterate your designs and prototypes, and finally mature the new aspect of the program through feedback. This process is why the diagram in Figure 10-2 is an ever-expanding spiral of the same steps. It keeps going, getting larger and larger as you engage more stakeholders, bring in more processes, identify more risks to mitigate, and build more and better partnerships.

Where does the design thinking cycle end? That's a trick question. In fact, it does not. Not ever. It is a continuous, ongoing cycle of listening, learning, trying new things – sometimes successful, sometimes failures, sometimes a mix of the two – and then using what you learn to mature and expand. And it never stops.

Chapter Review

In Chapter 10, you learned:

- Design thinking represents an iterative model, one that allows programs and processes to develop, mature, evolve, and change as conditions change. The steps of design thinking are: *empathize*, *define*, *ideate*, *prototype*, and *test*.
- Rolling an ESRM program out will work best if you follow an iterative process, including:
  - Educating yourself and others.
  - Involving others in your design process.
  - Iterating and maturing the process rather than attempting to roll everything out at once in final form.
  - Once maturity is reached in one area, expanding the rollout to a new area until eventually your whole program operates in an ESRM model.

Looking Forward

In Chapter 11, we will look at a real-life example of rolling out an ESRM program following the concepts discussed in Chapter 10.

Practitioner steps to consider before moving on to Chapter 11:
- ✓ Consider having a small design thinking session with your security team and begin to show them how it can help improve your program.
- ✓ If your enterprise has design teams, go to them, and discuss the design thinking theory to see how it applies in product design.

Security Program Self-Assessment

In this self-assessment, you should think about the answer to the questions posed, and then see where your program is on the identified ESRM spectrum.

Question	Y/N	Is This ESRM?
Do you ask for feedback from personnel who interact with security processes about how the process is working?	☐Yes ☐No	**NO**: If you never get feedback from persons impacted by your security implementations, this is a suitable place to start your ESRM program. **PARTIAL**: If you are willing to listen whenever someone approaches you proactively with feedback on your security program, you are part of the way to an ESRM implementation. **YES**: If you actively reach out to impacted parties and solicit feedback on your program in a non-punitive listening environment, and you consistently review your existing program, policies, and processes to ensure alignment with the ESRM philosophy, you are practicing ESRM (or at least, design thinking).

Questions for Discussion

1. Where could you potentially involve design thinking in your everyday life? Are there aspects of the process, like empathy, testing, and feedback, that could provide benefits outside of the business organization?
2. Identify and discuss areas of business that you think could benefit from the design thinking process. Are there areas that might not benefit from a formal, iterative design process? Why or why not?
3. When is the ideal time to start involving your stakeholders in the process of designing your ESRM program? When should you reach out to them and begin to talk about the topic?

References

Hasso Plattner Institute of Design at Stanford University. (2013). *Bootcamp bootleg.* Retrieved from
https://static1.squarespace.com/static/57c6b79629687fde090a0fdd/t/58890239db29d6cc6c3338f7/1485374014340/METHODCARDS-v3-slim.pdf

Kelley, D. & Kelley, T. (2012, December). Reclaim your creative confidence. *Harvard Business Review.*
Retrieved from https://hbr.org/2012/12/reclaim-your-creative-confidence

Learn More About It

For further reading about design thinking:

Brown, T. (2009). *Change by design: How design thinking transforms organizations and inspires innovation.* New York, NY: HarperCollins.

Brown, T. (2008, June). Design thinking. *Harvard Business Review.* Available at
https://www.ideo.com/images/uploads/thoughts/IDEO_HBR_Design_Thinking.pdf

Brown, T. (2009, July). *Designers – Think big!* [Video File]. Available at
https://www.ted.com/talks/tim_brown_urges_designers_to_think_big

Kelley, T. & Kelley, D. (2013). *Creative confidence: Unleashing the creative potential within us all.* New York, NY: Crown Business.

Martin, R. (2009). *The design of business: Why design thinking is the next competitive advantage.* Boston, MA: Harvard Business School Publishing.

11

Rolling Out Your ESRM Program

In the last chapter, you learned about *design thinking*, a theory of program and process development. Now we want to move beyond the theory to give you some real-world stories and practical examples of rolling out an enterprise security risk management (ESRM) program across an enterprise.

This chapter will help you to:

- Develop an ESRM implementation plan tailored to your enterprise, which provides clear value for your strategic partners.
- Convince key enterprise decision-makers that ESRM offers them real-world benefits.
- Build a base for lasting success, and for continuing evolution and maturity for your ESRM program.

11.1 Rolling out ESRM in the Real World – A Story

The ESRM method is more than merely a philosophy to us. We have lived it, operate in it, and have rolled programs from the traditional model over into an ESRM paradigm. We did this often through trial and error, making mistakes and correcting them along the way. With some of those mistakes, we veered off course and slipped back into old, comfortable – traditional – ways of thinking. In some, we forgot to incorporate our design thinking lessons of empathy, understanding, and feedback. Although we managed through this process ourselves, we want to help you to avoid those same mistakes. That is why we think our real-world experience is so important. It is why we are willing to share it in this book, and talk openly about our own lessons learned.

11.1.1 Step 1: Understanding the Current Environment and the Current Challenges (Empathy with Our Security Team)

At the beginning of that first ESRM journey, we recognized that we had a couple of problems in the daily management of our program. Unfortunately, we had not yet discovered how to fix them. Some of the issues we experienced might sound familiar to you in your security role.

- **Issue 1:** We knew that the security practitioners in our enterprise felt frustrated by the way business leaders responded to their efforts to provide security, and how those leaders perceived our role in the business (often complaining about security processes interfering with business operations).
- **Issue 2:** Leaders of other departments did not seem to understand why we had many of the security processes we used. Even when we were investigating an incident (which would benefit the business), we were thought to be sticking our noses where we did not belong, rather than seen as problem-solvers trying to identify risk issues.

But why did those other groups and leaders view us that way? After some self-reflection, we saw that we did not have actual, meaningful relationships with these other departments. Instead, we were largely limited to interactions based on the security tasks we were performing – badging, security guards, continuity planning. We did not perform the role of risk identification and management that we *needed* to play. We had not defined our role properly. The disconnect was either in the way we explained it, or in how our actions colored the perception. Either way, it was our fault, and our responsibility to correct the perception.

> **Case Study: Issues in How Functional Leaders View Security**
> This example of some of the same kinds of issues we experienced was told to us by a security leader, Don C. He worked for a major retail chain – Big Box Furniture – that offered its customers long-term financing on all purchases. Most of Big Box's sales were financed this way, and its salespeople received commissions whether the customer paid or not. This business practice gave sales personnel no incentive to be extra thorough in the credit check process, and it led to a considerable amount of outright fraud. On occasion, a salesperson would accept a fake name, address, or social security number from a customer just to make the sale.
>
> Don's team was brought in to investigate fraudulent accounts on multiple occasions and quickly identified the problem. There was a lack of financial control at Big Box in the sales process, with no separation of duties between the sales and the financial decision to extend credit.
>
> Don's investigators recommended that to end the fraud, Big Box needed to stop having salespeople handle customers' credit applications. Furthermore, the company should check sales records to identify salespeople with unacceptably high rates of customer

default. Unfortunately, sales management didn't want to implement a new policy or to fire sales people who were "making numbers;" so the sales process stayed the same.

Don heard the investigators say that they had discovered the problem, but they had not been listened to when they recommended a solution. In his effort to stop the fraud, he went over the sales managers' heads and had process changes put in place.

And what happened? Well, there *were* fewer fraudulent purchases – and fewer *legitimate* ones, too. The credit process became much more time-consuming – having to bring in finance – and qualified customers were walking away from purchases. Big Box, and its salespeople, were losing sales. Sales managers complained that security was making it impossible to do business, and eventually all the changes were rolled back completely.

So, by the end of this entire story:
- The sales team members were frustrated, and they communicated their frustration to senior management.
- The security team members were frustrated because they were not listened to.
- The customers were lost.
- The "solution" that was implemented was removed anyway.

Why? Because one of the critical design thinking steps was missing: empathy.

Rather than learning why the initial recommendation was not taken or finding a solution that everyone involved could agree on, Don bypassed the sales organization, not considering the views of his strategic partners. Don just went ahead and made the decision that he thought needed to be made. The effect was disastrous, not only for the business, but for the security organization's credibility as well.

In the beginning, we had our roles and our tasks just like Don at Big Box Furniture. We had our ideas of what security should be doing. We had processes and policies in place, but we had put them in place because "we were protecting the company." We created policies in response to something that *we* saw as a security risk to an asset. What we lacked was the support of our internal strategic partners, the very people whose interests we were trying to protect – lacked an understanding of why this was the case.

The solution to this issue seems perfectly obvious now, because we work using an ESRM model that makes it possible to correct this gap in understanding. But at the time we first tried to address the problem, all we knew was that there *was* a problem. Then, we started exploring workable solutions, by reaching out to other security professionals, consulting with industry experts and other outsiders to brainstorm, reading articles on security programs, and meeting with our peers. That led to many conversations where we asked: What do we do? Why do we do it? How do we fix this? All that background did not bring us any closer to effectively communicating with our colleagues in the enterprise about our reasons for doing what we were doing.

Questions for the Security Practitioner
- "If asked, could I outline everything my security group is responsible for? Do I know all the processes that we are performing?"
- "Do I hear complaints about security processes being intrusive or troublesome?"

11.1.1.1 A Deeper Dive (Even More Empathy)

Once we looked for the reasons behind our issues, we knew that we needed to do a deep analysis of our program. We stopped trying to just "get things done" and reassessed everything: policies, processes, metrics, reporting, education, training, job descriptions, expectations, and everything else we did. We asked ourselves *why* we were doing what we were doing, examined the reasoning behind it, and then determined whether it was *really* providing any value to anyone.

Case Study: Understanding the "Why"

Another example of a security task that was undertaken without involving stakeholders was one we heard from an IT professional. We met George Z. at a conference, where he told us that his management had instructed him to run regular vulnerability scans on all the company's systems. He did that and then sent the resulting reports to the system administrators, with instructions to "fix the problem." The system administrators, who were as busy as everybody else in the company, put the reports in their "to do" folder. Maybe an identified vulnerability got fixed in a timely manner, and maybe it did not.

This process did not involve the strategic partners, whose systems were running on these machines. No one was identifying the risk impact to assets, and no one was following up on the results. This was, quite simply, a task being done for the sake of "checking the box" on vulnerability reports.

And whose name was next to the box that was checked? That's right: George's. Eventually, when a vulnerability that was not fixed led to a serious impact on the company's point-of-sale (POS) systems, he was the one who took the blame. This made him frustrated, and it frustrated the impacted stakeholder who had never been made aware that there was a problem.

The common theme we have heard when talking to many security practitioners is that they are performing tasks, but only because the task:

- Has been done for years.
- Has been called a "best practice" by a think tank.
- Is something that someone used to do at their old company.
- Is something their boss told them to do, with no reasoning provided.

On their own, none of these are good reasons for doing these tasks and more importantly, none of them are built on a strategically thought out and consistent philosophy.

How could design thinking have helped? Well, suppose George had asked:

- Why are we doing this?
- Who is impacted by it?
- How important is it to them?
- Who should be involved in the decisions regarding this task?

Had that happened, the result would likely have been very different. The business owners of the system would have probably wanted a concrete method of ensuring vulnerability remediation on their platform, and they could have helped the IT group prioritize the security task on that critical system. This is another case where taking a moment to stop simply doing a task, and taking the time to truly understand who and what is involved would have made an enormous difference.

11.1.2 Step 2: Communicating with the Business and Other Stakeholders (Empathy with Our Strategic Partners)

In Step 1 of our process, we practiced some internal empathy, when we:

- Stopped and took a long look at what we were doing as a security organization and why.
- Understood the issues as we saw them, from inside our organization.
- Discussed the issue we were having with experts and industry peers.
- Came to the idea of risk-management-based security as our solution.

Once we defined the problem as we understood it, and matured our idea of ESRM as a solution, we began "socializing" the business leaders with the ESRM philosophy. In meetings with everyone – from the Chief Executive Officer (CEO) to department executives, from human resources (HR) to engineering – we discussed ESRM, what it meant to us, and what it would mean to them.

> ### Case Study: Educating the Organization on ESRM
> When we knew that we needed to get the ESRM message out, we started with the executives – specifically, the CEO and the general counsel, since both were jobs that require an understanding of risk.
>
> First, we explained how we understood the security role, in ESRM terms, and asked them whether they agreed with our view. Of course, agreement did not come overnight. These were tough-minded people who were perfectly comfortable saying no if they thought that was the right answer. They asked us hard questions about ESRM, about what managing security risk meant and about how the process worked. They finally came to agree with our ESRM-based definition of security's role.
>
> Still, we did not stop there. In particular, we kept reminding the CEO at the beginning of every meeting, "This is how we see our role. Do you still agree?" (It eventually became a running joke, because the CEO always knew how the meeting was going to start.) We did this to make sure that there was a *clear and accepted understanding* of our role before we discussed other security business. This was because those further discussions had to be based on the buy-in of our strategic partners.
>
> By getting executive buy-in, we firmly established the much-needed scope of responsibility and authority of the program. It also established how we would be going about our business. Scope and authority are two key factors in security program success, and we will discuss them further in the next chapter. Once we had agreement at the highest levels in the company, we could go to other leaders and partners in the enterprise and explain to them what ESRM was, what it meant for us, and how it could help them.

Having these discussions with our partners meant taking a deeper dive into some of their specific trouble spots, and *especially* working more closely with people and groups who we were having real problems with. We looked for ways to use ESRM to solve those specific problems. Once again using empathy and listening, we got input from our stakeholders on how to tailor our program to better meet their needs.

11.1.3 Step 3: Creating a Roadmap for the Program Rollout (Ideation and Brainstorming)

One thing our discussions made clear, both internally to the security organization and externally with our strategic partners, was that we needed an entirely new strategy for security – one based on partnerships and risk management, rather than task management. You might recognize that this was a huge task; so we had to:

- Stop what we were doing.
- Take concrete steps to understand who we would need a buy-in from.
- Decide where we would start, and where we would be most effective.
- See who would manage the individual elements of the program.
- Understand whether our employees had the skillsets and the risk management mindset they needed.
- Explore what training would be required to get employees up to speed, if they were not.
- Determine how we would implement each task – and on what timeframe.
- Redefine how to recognize and measure success or failure, and ensure that we did not fall back into old habits and old mistakes.
- Rethink how we would measure and report on the security program.

That is a lot (and it is all covered in the rest of this book).

We approached this part of the process as if we were creating an entirely new system – because we were. But we knew that it had to be a gradual process, and that it could not be an overnight transformation. By this time, we also knew we had to have real acceptance from all our strategic partners. We met several times with our internal personnel and with our partners outside the security department. By the end of this stage – which was really the brainstorming/ideation step of design thinking – we had a broad consensus and commitment on the way to move forward. In addition, we had built a lot of trust, both inside and outside the security organization.

> ### *Case Study: Partnering with the Business to Find Solutions*
> We told one of our security industry peers, Kate M., about the ESRM program we were rolling out, and she decided to apply it to a problem she was having.
>
> Kate worked as a security manager for a company called Kitchens Direct. They do direct sales in customers' homes. The company recognizes the significant legal and publication relations (PR) risks involved in possibly having someone with a criminal record in a customer's home; so the security policy required a rigorous, no-exceptions set of background checks, which took about seven business days to complete.
>
> Kate learned that the sales organization was beginning a very large year-long special project, and the sales managers wanted to bring new people into the training program quickly. For the sake of expedience, they were bypassing the background check process, and there were personnel working in the field without credentials. (In ESRM terms, this means that the sales managers were accepting the associated risk, whether or not this was within their authority in the enterprise.) After our conversation about ESRM, Kate decided to sit down with the leaders of the sales organization to explore the issue.
>
> She explained that if they did not want background checks, they would have to involve the legal and PR organizations in that decision. Those groups were the stakeholders in the risks – such as possible criminal charges, lawsuits, and reputational damage – that came from using in-home salespeople who were not cleared.

She also asked them *why* they felt that they couldn't wait seven days to get new people onboarded. She learned that they were seriously understaffed, and as a result, they were having a tough time meeting their sales targets. Instead of going through the entire security process, they were bringing new hires onto the business premises using someone else's badge, and then training them, which included visiting customers' homes.

Kate and the sales leaders had this discussion using design thinking – listening, empathizing, and working together to brainstorm – and they found a solution.

After some inevitable back-and-forth (design thinking's ideation), they developed a fast-track process that security, sales, legal, and HR could all accept.
1. Security would conduct a basic background check that took about three days and then would issue a probationary clearance so that the new employee could begin training.
2. Sales agreed that if problems were discovered in the deeper check, which took the full seven days, the probationary employee would be dismissed.

The sales leaders were willing to accept the three-day delay, and the security team and the other stakeholders were willing to accept the limited risk of a partially completed background check.

Questions for the Security Practitioner
- "Will all of the personnel in my security department be able to perform their functions in an ESRM environment?"
- "Are the appropriate skill sets in place?"
- "Will I need to help some of the department employees with training on unfamiliar concepts, like the risk assessment and the risk management process?"
- "Could I use design thinking methods inside the security department to design new job descriptions and requirements with the existing employee base?"

11.1.4 Step 4: Piloting the Program (Prototyping and Feedback)

Once we had a detailed roadmap for the program, and the buy-in that we needed from partners and executives, we began introducing pilot projects in selected areas (the iterative rollout, as we discussed in the last chapter). With our strategic partners and security personnel, we identified the most urgent needs, and began by piloting an investigation postmortem program. We chose that one because it dealt with incidents impacting our partners in the business directly. This increased their investment in the new program.

We also chose to start there because the incident postmortem process had historically been quite contentious. Before the ESRM program was put in place, business units would call on security to investigate a problem. Then they would essentially fire whoever was responsible. That made sense from their point of view, and they were happy to let it end there. But it did not make sense from our perspective. We wanted to dig further to see how the person responsible had done whatever it was he or she had done, and why. This would enable us to find ways to keep it from happening again. This required a postmortem analysis of the incident, to determine the root causes and to fix them. Unfortunately, before we applied ESRM principles, identifying a problem and fixing it meant the security organization was telling the business to change processes or to close gaps which made their work go faster. The perception was that we were delaying them from their work. We were not seen as educating our partners about the risks they owned; they saw us as telling them they were doing things wrong. It should be no surprise that they did not like that, and they characterized us as a barrier to getting things done and an impediment to be avoided if possible. This was our issue, and it was what we needed to overcome when we implemented the new postmortem reporting process as a pilot with some of our most skeptical partners.

Case Study: Using ESRM to Change Minds

When we began piloting a new process that would provide root cause analysis on incident investigations, we knew that we needed to change the old incident postmortem process to work in the new model. We designed a prototype process, based on our understanding, and we rolled it out. But our strategic partners still didn't like it! Oops, we had forgotten to re-engage at the beginning with empathy and to truly understand the business needs.

When we looked for feedback and tried to understand our partner's point of view, we asked them what their issues were with our investigations and recommendations. They told us that we did not understand the business, that they either did not understand or did not agree with the root causes that we pointed out, and that our recommendations were not feasible.

At that point, we took the feedback and went back to refine our process, based on that feedback. After a lot of back-and-forth, we ended up with a post-incident report that our strategic partners were happy to receive because it allowed them to make changes chosen by them, *not us*, which would mitigate risks in their processes without breaking them or wouldn't cause too much business interruption during the change. This let them show their leaders, executives, risk management departments, and internal auditors that they were proactively fixing security risk issues. We were finally perceived as problem-solvers by our partners, who had previously told us that we had no clue how their business worked. It made a notable difference in how they worked with us compared to when we were perceived merely as "rule enforcers."

What is the best part of this pilot program and its eventual full rollout? We ended up with several strategic partners who ran their *own* analytics reports on a regular basis, and they sent them to our investigators to review. This way, they were able to expose and mitigate risk even before there was an incident to investigate. They trusted us to know our roleand to let them handle theirs. Now *that* is our definition of "successful" ESRM.

As shown in the case study above, with careful thought, education, and persistence, it is possible to develop and roll out a program that will change the minds of those who might not have the most accurate view of what security does. We did it, and if you follow this design thinking model when rolling out your ESRM program, we think you can do the same.

Questions for the Security Practitioner
- "When I imagine the future of my security program, two to three years from now, what will that look like?"
- "If I asked my strategic partners how they would like to interact with my future security department, how might they respond?"

It took almost two years, from beginning to end, to turn those pilot projects (or "prototypes") into a strategic ESRM practice. We learned a lot of valuable lessons along the way. We kept identifying concerns, and fine-tuning our processes and practices. We figured out how to communicate with, and educate, everyone involved. There was a lot of trial and error – "testing," in design thinking terms – and a lot of back-and-forth with the security organization and the stakeholders.

After we had a few successful pilot projects under our belts, we started mapping out how it could be applied with complete consistency across the security organization, and the across the entire enterprise. We needed to figure out who in security would have what responsibilities, who had the necessary skill sets, and who currently had the necessary understanding to grasp what we were trying to accomplish.

11.1.5 Step 5: Implementation and Evolution Across the Enterprise

With several pilot projects tested, we prepared to roll the program out across the enterprise. We had enough information and feedback to know that we had a good, workable model that fit our strategic partners' needs. If senior executives and other key decision-makers supported it, ESRM would fit into any area or any kind of security risk within the enterprise. Through our experience, we understood that ESRM applied to all security risk, cyber security, physical security, crisis response, fraud management, and so on.

None of this was simple. We had to ask ourselves these questions:
- What do we want to accomplish?
- Is it feasible?
- How will we know if we achieve it, and when?
- What obstacles will we face?
- How will ESRM principles help?

By that point, we had learned a lot about having these conversations, internally and externally (through testing and feedback), and we were getting better at anticipating and addressing stakeholders' concerns.

Eventually, we were operating fully in an ESRM model. We trained our security personnel in the ESRM philosophy. We made it a vital component of their roles, their training, and their day-to-day tasks. We wrote new job descriptions for them that clearly identified ESRM principles, and defined associated skillsets for them as a measure of their success. Everyone on the team was expected to accept the philosophy, and were responsible for practicing it.

Crucially, this staff training and development was an ongoing process. We conducted annual ESRM training. We constantly reaffirmed with executives and strategic partners what our role was, and what our value was. We regularly and consistently reassessed our roles and our practices. We always looked for ways to measure our success – both quantitative and qualitative – and to communicate those successes to all our stakeholders.

Questions for the Security Practitioner
- "What sort of access do I have at the executive level to begin a discussion of risk-based security management?"
- "Am I comfortable initiating these discussions, or would I prefer to start by finding a leader in my chain of command to champion the topic at higher levels?"

11.2 ESRM Program Rollout Checklist

In the last two chapters, we provided a lot of information about models and examples. We walked you through diagrams and cycles, and we discussed an ESRM rollout using real-world terms and examples.

By this point, we hope that you have a clear idea of ways you might approach rolling out a risk-based security management program in your own environment.

Theory and practice are two different things, however. To make the potential rollout of an ESRM program in your organization a little easier to plan and manage, we are including a checklist of steps in Table 11-1 that you can use to design and document an ESRM project plan.

The principles of this approach are clear and consistent. Success will be driven by a multistep approach, consisting of many small steps over an extended period, rather than a few big steps all at once. An excellent way to ensure that nothing gets missed is to create a plan to follow as your team moves from one phase to the next. Of course, if part of the checklist does not fit your enterprise culture, stakeholders, and needs, you should tailor the checklist to fit your situation.

Table 11-1. ESRM Rollout Checklist

Phase	Action/Step
Empathy • **Educate** yourself. • **Understand** your existing program. • **Challenge** current notions of security.	**STOP** 1. Take a step back, and examine your program and what you are doing. 2. Challenge your current notions of what security is, and why you are doing what you are doing. **Understand the Existing Situation** 1. Assess each aspect of your program against the ESRM paradigm of risk-based security decision-making. Determine whether it is operating under a risk management model, according to the principles outlined in this book. 2. List all the security tasks that you manage. 3. Know where each aspect of the program and each process fits into the ESRM cycle. Is it part of assessing? Of mitigating risk? Of ongoing awareness? 4. Tie the existing functions of your program to defined business assets that are being protected. 5. Identify the security risks that the tasks you perform are mitigating. Identify all the owners and stakeholders of those risks. **Set the Stage** 1. Envision what your security program would look like if you applied ESRM principles to all your processes. 2. Consider what steps you would take to execute ESRM throughout the program. 3. Identify who you would need to engage, and how they might respond to the idea of ESRM. 4. Strategize around hurdles that you may face, and make a plan to take them on. 5. Be ready with responses to anticipated challenges about the ESRM philosophy.
Define • **Assess** what the enterprise needs from security in agreement with your partners. • **Educate** your partners.	**Discuss** 1. Explore the idea of ESRM with your close co-workers outside of security, get comfortable with the terminology, listen to their counterpoints, and understand what they may or may not agree with. 2. Identify key line-of-business executives who are critical for success. Explore the ESRM practice with them, and how it would benefit their goals. Start with trusted strategic partners. Start simple and get everybody on the same page.

• **Involve** business executives.	3. Define your success criteria.
	Present
	Meet with the highest level of executive that you can reach. The CEO is the best place to start, of course. If that is not possible, start as high as you can get in your organizational structure, and make that person aware of the need to take this discussion as high as it can go.
	  1. Explain the philosophy of ESRM (see Chapter 20 for an executive-friendly format for doing this).
	  2. Explain the role of security in managing – not owning – security risk.
	  3. Reach agreement with the executive that the role of security in the organization is to identify risks to business assets, and to work with the asset owners to respond to those risks, either through a mitigation program, or by acceptance from the person with the necessary authority.
	    NOTE: If you cannot get this philosophical agreement, the ESRM program is not going to get very far. It is a relatively "easy sell," if you point out the business risks and the ESRM methodologies we lay out in this book (especially in Chapter 20). But if you do not get the agreement you need, keep trying with that same person, in another round with more backup information, or with a different person of influence who might be able to advance the ESRM cause.
	  4. Once you have agreement, continually stress in every interaction with the executive that your role is to point out and manage security risk in partnership with the business asset and risk owners, until his or her perception of you and your organization is ingrained.
	Document
	1. Develop a written ESRM-based security policy that outlines the agreed upon role of security, and ensure that it is endorsed by the executives in charge.
	2. Charter a security council (more on that in Chapter 13) to govern the ESRM program and help drive adoption.
	Do Not Forget the Details
	1. Start with the mission and goals. Break down the goals for processes by incorporating the ESRM principles.
	2. Incorporate the practice into roles and responsibilities.
	3. Assess current skillsets and job descriptions to see if they fit the program, and ensure that personnel have the skills to be successful.

Brainstorm • **Prototype** and develop an outline of the essentials of a program. • **Test** and engage stakeholders. • Incorporate **feedback** and **iterate** with changes.	**Take It One Step at a Time** Start with a program or part of an existing program, and develop a strategy on how to implement the ESRM practice. Invite stakeholders into those strategy sessions. **NOTE:** For each aspect of your program, pick a process or standard that can be converted to an ESRM model. In Chapters 8 to 12, we will go into details on ESRM fits with specific aspects of your security program. But here are the basic steps to bring any individual process or procedure into the ESRM model. **Prototype a Pilot Process** 1. Involve the strategic partners who are the most impacted by the specific risk mitigation process you are piloting, and brainstorm with them on where to start to create a program that would be satisfactory to all stakeholders.

	2. Work from scratch through a prototype of one existing function or task in your overall program. Some of your current tasks may fit right into ESRM, but it is important to identify why they fit, what they are mitigating, and who is responsible for deciding on the risk response. 3. Identify what processes and steps would be different in the new ESRM model, and what the program would look like moving forward. If there are no changes, identify that as well. 4. Educate the security team and asset/risk stakeholders on the prototype, and on the anticipate challenges. Focus on the long-term benefits, beyond individual programs or projects. Take and incorporate feedback as necessary. 5. Develop ongoing reporting and metrics for the process. 6. Ensure that the model is repeatable and adaptable.
Iterate • **Expand.** • **Develop** Goals. • **Integrate** into roles and responsibilities. • **Reinforce.**	**Listen and Respond** Incorporate a feedback process, sticking to the agreed upon ESRM philosophy. The business and security processes will fit into the ESRM practice if applied appropriately. **Implement the Process** 1. Pick a date to start using the new process in daily work. 2. Announce the change, and ensure that all strategic partners know it is beginning. 3. Seek feedback from executives, impacted business units, and security practitioners outside your organization. Continue to iterate the methodology, and practice as needed. **Keep Going!** 1. Consistently reinforce the ESRM principles through education, conversation, and program maturity. 2. Expand the practice into strategy, and more areas of program development. 3. Pick a new process, procedure, or aspect of your program and begin another round of ESRM implementation.

Chapter Review

In Chapter 11, you learned:

- An ESRM program can be complicated to roll out, but using a design thinking methodology to organize your project will make it easier.
- A clear checklist can assist in organizing the project rollout.

Looking Forward

In Part 4 of the book, we will discuss the critical factors you will need to ensure that you can run a successful ESRM program in your enterprise.

Practitioner steps to consider before moving on to Chapter 12:
   ✓ Put together a plan for implementing an ESRM rollout.
   ✓ Consider which processes in your program could be pilot projects for conversion.
   ✓ Create a list of the best strategic partners to work with when beginning your ESRM implementation.

Security Program Self-Assessment

In this self-assessment, you should think about the answer to the question posed, and then see where your program is on the identified ESRM spectrum.

Question	Y/N	Is This ESRM?
Have you ever stopped and truly examined all the processes, policies, procedures, and functions that your security department does, and asked yourself why it is doing them?	□Yes □No	**NO:** If you have never done a functional review, then this is a suitable place to start your ESRM program. **PARTIAL:** If you have reviewed and revamped parts of your overall security program to better align them with business needs and risk management, then you are part of the way to an ESRM implementation. **YES:** If you have already reviewed your entire program and aligned it with the security risk management needs and tolerances of your business, then you are practicing ESRM.

Questions for Discussion

1. What are some strategies you can use to engage executives and other strategic partners in learning about ESRM?
2. How does working with functional leaders who have the most complaints and issues with a process benefit the enterprise? Can you think of concrete benefits from engaging your most difficult partners first, before even beginning a program rollout?

Learn More About It

For further reading about design thinking:

Brown, T. (2008, June). Design thinking. *Harvard Business Review*. Available at
https://www.ideo.com/images/uploads/thoughts/IDEO_HBR_Design_Thinking.pdf

Brown, T. (2009). *Change by design: How design thinking transforms organizations and inspires innovation*. New York, NY: HarperCollins.

Brown, T. (2009, July). *Designers – think big!* [Video podcast]. Available at
https://www.ted.com/talks/tim_brown_urges_designers_to_think_big

Kelley, T., & Kelley, D. (2013). *Creative confidence: Unleashing the creative potential within us all*. New York, NY: Crown Business.

Martin, R. L. (2009). *The design of business: Why design thinking is the next competitive advantage*. Boston, MA: Harvard Business Press.

Part 4

Making ESRM Work for Your Organization

So far in this book you have seen how ESRM can help make any security program more successful and learned how to put an ESRM program into place. In this part, you will explore how to make your ESRM program a success, and look at some of the issues you will need to consider once your ESRM program is in place to make sure it performs the way you intend it to. In Chapters 12, 13, and 14, we will cover topics to make sure your ESRM implementation is a success, and to ensure that it's recognized by your executives and leadership as a success.

In This Part:
- **ESRM Essentials for Success**
- **Concepts of Security Governance**
- **Optimizing the Security Organization**

12

ESRM Essentials for Success

So far in the previous chapters, you have learned how to implement an ESRM program. But implementation is only the beginning. Many factors go into the ongoing success of a risk-based security program. A few factors that will be critical to your ongoing program are:

- Transparency.
- Independence.
- Authority.
- Scope.

When representing your security program in the enterprise, you will need to completely understand the role that each of these foundational elements plays in security success. Then you must be able to explain their importance to others, in business terms rather than technical or security terms. This chapter will enable you to do that.

This chapter will help you to:

- Identify the key attributes of a successful ESRM program.
- See how transparency of risk and process enables you to better engage with your strategic partners in the enterprise.
- Explain why independence is critical to risk management.
- Understand the appropriate level of authority that the security organization requires to be effective.
- Define the appropriate scope for your ESRM program.
- Understand the parallels between the security program and other risk-based programs that exist in many enterprises.

12.1 Transparency

Few concepts are as central to ESRM success as transparency is. The ESRM philosophy is fundamentally based on collaboration and cooperation with security risk stakeholders. Their responsibilities for security risk have significant potential consequences for their areas of business and for the entire enterprise. You cannot expect your strategic partners in the enterprise to make a serious commitment to long-term working relationships with security, or to accept their role in the ESRM paradigm, if the security team is not open, honest, and clear with them about:

- What security is doing.
- Why security-related tasks are being performed.
- What risks those tasks are mitigating.
- Who (which risk stakeholder) made the decisions to perform the security tasks.
- What we need from them to ensure the ongoing protection of enterprise assets.

Transparency takes many forms, but in ESRM terms, it has two key dimensions:
1. Risk transparency.
2. Process transparency.

12.1.1 Risk Transparency

The first critical dimension of transparency in ESRM is *risk transparency*. That is simply the idea that security risks cannot be hidden or ignored for any reason.

We have met some practitioners who are afraid of the repercussions of having risks exposed because pointing out a risk may somehow make it "their fault." Some feel that exposing security risk could bring repercussions from business owners who want to keep those risks hidden. Whatever the reasons, the lack of transparency about legitimate security risks to the enterprise represents a serious threat to the maturity and success of any security program. As a security professional conducting an ESRM program, you are responsible for transparently reporting all security risks to impacted company assets. This means that if you do not report to an asset owner or any other stakeholders that a real security risk exists to a given asset, you are depriving stakeholders of the opportunity to make a business decision about that risk.

The resistance to risk transparency is a common problem. Sometimes, you will run into business leaders who do not want to involve others in "their" risk assessment and treatment decisions. Again, there can be many reasons for business functional leaders who want to be exempted from the security processes. Sometimes the business needs things done in a hurry, and the leaders think stopping to assess risk will slow them down. Some leaders who are not fully educated on risks may think a specific risk is "just not that big a deal." Some may believe that finding risks creates work for personnel who already have plenty to do. However, these attitudes clearly limit the enterprise's ability to make sound risk decisions, and expose the enterprise to even more unknown risks.

Neither the security team nor the business can use these types of excuses in an ESRM environment. It is critical to stick to ESRM principles, maintaining transparency as part of the security role under ESRM, and to educate others on security risk. Of course, arguing with a stubborn business stakeholder is difficult and unpleasant. You will need to pick your battles and understand from the beginning that you will not always win. A risk may not always be mitigated. But if you apply ESRM principles of risk transparency, at least you will have evidence that you have carried out your responsibilities and that the enterprise is aware of risks and is facing them.

12.1.2 Process Transparency

When managing the security risk identification-prioritization-mitigation process, the second aspect of transparency – and a critical part of the security practitioner's role – is being transparent about the entire security decision-making process.

In ESRM terms, this *process* transparency means:
- Being open and honest about real security risks, neither exaggerating them to get a project approved, nor minimizing them for "political" reasons.
- Ensuring that all asset and risk stakeholders are aware of a given security risk and can participate in discussions about accepting or mitigating risk.
- Exploring all the elements of a risk, not simply the obvious aspects.
- Offering risk treatment options commensurate with the level of risk.
- Receiving, and documenting in writing, the risk owner's final decision on the mitigation or acceptance of the risk.

These straightforward principles offer real value to everyone involved in security risk decisions. They will protect you and everyone else, inside and outside the security organization, against finger-pointing and blame-shifting, by ensuring that risk and risk ownership are clearly defined, that the person making the decision is the right one, and that the decision-maker is fully accountable for the outcome.

If the security risk management process does not have transparency, both the security manager and the security organization may be accused of not managing the risk process appropriately. Others in the enterprise will not understand how or why decisions are being made. And there is another problem: A lack of process transparency may alienate key stakeholders, those whose cooperation and collaboration you may need in the future.

Below we see an example of repercussions from a lack of process transparency at an online service firm: Gwendolen's Online Gifts

> ### Case Study: The Problem of a Stakeholder Who Was Excluded
> Gwendolen's Online Gifts (GOC) is a fast-growing online retailer that creates and ships customized gift baskets. The company has two security managers, each with a separate, clearly defined set of responsibilities. Jessica H., the information security manager, is charged with risks related to the company's digital systems, which are obviously mission-critical. Cynthia W. is the corporate security manager, tasked with operational and physical security risks.
>
> The company's rapid growth is placing serious strains on GOC's order processing and fulfillment capacity. One day over lunch, John C., the director in charge of the customer care organization, tells Jessica in passing about a plan to increase order-handling capacity cost-effectively by outsourcing to a third-party call-center in Ireland.
>
> Jessica immediately recognizes that exposing customer information to a third party represents a security risk and tells John she will need to conduct a security assessment before any contract is signed. Her team looks at the outsourcer's information security policies and procedures, checks its technical standards, and even had the company agree to penetration testing of its network. When the outsourcing project is announced to

the entire leadership group, Jessica reports to the VP of operations that the call-center can be trusted to handle GOC's customer data. It seems like all is well.

But in terms of interpersonal concerns, all is not well. After the meeting, Cynthia takes Jessica aside and asks why she was not included in the assessment.

Jessica replies that since Cynthia manages onsite physical and operational security, and the outsourced call-center is not part of that, she did not think it was necessary to bring her in.

But Cynthia disagrees, saying she has some concerns about the project – and she is clearly not happy.

At first, Jessica feels bewildered by Cynthia's reaction. After all, she took a close look at the potential risks to the company's customer data, and found that all the technical protections more than adequate. But as she gave it more thought, she realized that she did not think much about the actual physical protections around the data center, the background checks of personnel, or even the physical access control. Once she understood why Cynthia was upset, she assured her that the next time an assessment was done, she would bring Cynthia in as a partner in the risk process.

In the case study above, we saw Jessica complete a security assessment, but really, she assessed only the security risks associated with the tasks she managed in her department's area of expertise – the risks for which she was responsible for the mitigation. This means that although she told the business function leaders that a full security risk assessment had been done and passed, she in fact did not *fully* explore the risks associated with the outsourcing project. She did not make sure that all the appropriate stakeholders were informed, aware, and involved. She was not transparent about the process. In effect, the result was that she accepted a risk that was not hers to accept.

Of course, it is entirely possible that outsourcing the call-center *could* work out just fine, without involving Cynthia from a physical security perspective in the assessment. But what if did not? If you recall from Chapter 3, we discussed the story of Rick M., a security manager responsible for a data center in which a network switch was stolen, due in part to lax background checking of personnel. What if that same scenario happened at GOC? Suppose that, instead of hacking his way in through the logical controls that Jessica's security review considered adequate, a thief simply walked into the outsourcer's call-center and stole a massive amount of customer data due to inadequate physical protections. Suppose this thief physically accessed a computer terminal and copied the contents to a thumb drive. If that happened, who do you think would be blamed for the data breach? Would it be:

- Jessica, who signed off on the outsourcing project without taking physical security into account?
- Cynthia, who never even had the chance to comment on the risks she might have seen?
- John, who set up the contract with the outsourcer?

In truth, it could be any or all of them depending on the organization. That ambiguity and lack of accountability is due to there being no process transparency in the decision-making process.

One additional note about both process and risk transparency. Sometimes you will encounter a business leader who will want to perform an investigation themselves when faced with a security event or incident in their area, when it exposes a risk and requires investigation. This is usually not an attempt to hide the risk. More likely it is due to a desire to ensure a thorough treatment of the issue. Unfortunately, it still results in a lack of transparency around both the risk and the process, because these leaders often do not have the skillset or experience needed to fully investigate a security breach or issue. They are well-meaning, but they are circumventing transparency, none the less. You have the same duty to educate these leaders about the challenges of them attempting to manage their own risks, as if they were creating a lack of transparency for some unethical reason.

One of the most important and effective ways of ensuring transparency is by having an explicit, formal security policy that is clearly understood by all stakeholders. This policy can literally be as simple and as basic as a statement that anyone who sees a security issue is required to report it to the security organization. What matters is that there is no confusion on anyone's part about what is expected and required.

Transparency – around both process and risk – is required to perform proper security in an ESRM model. The greater the transparency across both process and risk from you and your security department, and from your strategic partners, the more successful your program will be in identifying and mitigating security risk for the enterprise. Without transparency, risks are hidden, unconsidered, unknown, and unmitigated. Ultimately, your security program will fail to protect the enterprise, because you will not have a good understanding of what you are trying to protect.

12.2 Independence

The second critical component of ESRM success is the independence of your security practice. This means you have the capacity and ability to perform your security risk management without interference from outside influences.

Your ESRM program will have many different stakeholders involved in security risk decisions, and those stakeholders can often have competing, even contradictory, agendas and interests. This can translate into pressure to change the assessments and recommendations that you make concerning security risks. The potential for that kind of pressure makes independence for the security organization essential for security success. You must be able to:

- Consider security vulnerabilities wherever they exist.
- Identify risks and maintain risk transparency.
- Understand all business operations and the business' assets.
- Respond to an incident, investigate, and clearly identify its root causes in any area of the enterprise. This independence is the same principle that does not allow an internal audit team to report to an organization that it is auditing.

There are many reasons why a business leader might resist efforts to identify and expose security vulnerabilities and security risks. They may think a security threat will be interpreted as a weakness in their management, or in their processes. In a worse scenario, they may be deliberately doing something that is against the enterprise's interests. In cases like these, the business manager may pressure you not to expose the risk or its root cause, possibly threatening you or your future career prospects, either directly or indirectly. It is a bad scenario when a leader outside of your management structure attempts to pressure you. It is even worse if the individual in question is in the chain of command of the security organization.

Imagine attempting to expose an operational risk when the security function reports up through operations, or a financial fraud risk if the security function reports up to finance. What could happen to either your risk assessment, or even your job, if a person covering up a risk truly wanted to keep it hidden? In a truly independent reporting structure, there is much less chance that this kind of pushback will have an adverse impact on you and your career.

Following are two examples of why independence is essential for your success in ESRM.

Case Study: The Costs of a Lack of Independence

Geri H. works as a security manager in the western region of a financial services company called Stalbridge. The company is highly competitive, and its salespeople, their managers, and all the company's executives are compensated primarily based on the closing sales of various financial instruments. Geri reports to the regional services group, which ultimately reports up through the finance organization to the company's senior vice president of the western region. Recently, Geri's counterpart in the southern region called to make her aware that some salespeople there were taking advantage of a loophole in the change order process. This allowed them to fraudulently inflate their sales numbers and earn higher commissions. Geri began an investigation and found compelling evidence that several salespeople in her region were doing the same on a significant level.

Geri brought the results of her investigation to the sales manager who was responsible for those employees. She expected to be commended for this and to see those employees fired immediately. Instead, she received a call the next day from the VP of Finance, Kevin T. He told her to stop the investigation because exposing it would mean restating the results for the quarter, and he needed to have those numbers up to remain as the number one region in the company. He made it clear that the president of the region would not like to lose that place and that it would be a serious, even career-ending, mistake for Geri to make him unhappy.

Eventually, Geri decided that her ethics were more important than one job, and she escalated the issue to Stalbridge's general counsel, Stanley M. The general counsel immediately grasped the seriousness of the issue, and he ensured that the investigation went forward. However, now she would be investigating not only those employees who had been inflating their numbers but also investigating what levels of management might have been complicit. Escalating the issue outside of her reporting structure to Stanley was a gamble on Geri's part. She did not know whether the reaction would be to commend her or fire her. After this incident, Stanley decided that he would bring the investigations function into his compliance group to prevent a situation like that ever happening again.

A situation like the one at Stalbridge places the security practitioner in an extremely difficult position. Geri had been given a direct order, from someone in her own reporting structure who had a strong personal, professional – and yes, financial – interest in the security issue.

Geri knew that the right thing to do, the thing called for by company policy, was to conduct a more thorough investigation. If she failed to do that, she could be accused of sweeping a serious problem under the rug. But by continuing, she could be threatening her own career. She was caught in an untenable position. But with a clear independent reporting structure, she would not have been. Stan saw that and fixed the problem, granting Geri the independent reporting structure her job required. Had he not, you can imagine the environment that Geri would have had to continue working in, with an executive leader whom she had challenged so openly.

The second example comes from the IT world.

Case Study: The Costs of a Lack of Independence

Sean L. is the information security manager for VitaCorp, a small chain of pharmacies. He reports to the IT organization. The CIO, Simon F., wants to implement a new software application that is expected to save the retail ordering group several million dollars over the next seven years. Time is of the essence because Simon has promised sales, finance, and operating executives that the application will be up and running in just two months. When Sean reviews the project, he identifies several security vulnerabilities that could expose customer data. Those vulnerabilities need to be studied and possibly mitigated, and he tells Simon that. Simon responds that the vulnerabilities are unlikely to impact the project, and there is no time for further study. The project will move forward without further discussion (and without proper risk acceptance).

An organizational structure like the one at VitaCorp, with IT security reporting inside IT, represents an inherent conflict of interest, one that threatens the security professional's needed independence.

Most IT projects have tight budgets and timelines, and those demands are often driven by executives – powerful ones – outside the IT organization. In this example, Simon's financial incentives were likely based on his performance in executing against budget, and in implementing the project commitments that had been made. Simon's insistence on pushing the project through was understandable, as was Sean's reluctance to see it happen. But an information security manager has very little independence in this scenario. If you, as an IT security professional, have identified a security vulnerability that would significantly slow up a major project and potentially impact the CIO's appearance of success, would you feel comfortable escalating that risk outside of your chain of command? Many people – including Sean – would not. That is not to say that even with an independent reporting structure, the project timelines would not have trumped the security risk. However, in the ESRM model, those risks would have been escalated and properly accepted as part of a transparent risk management process.

12.3 Authority

Authority, in the ESRM paradigm, is not about telling people what to do, nor about "enforcing" the will and ideas of the security leader. It refers to the ability of the security manager to:

- Access the appropriate level of business leader to discuss security risk issues.
- Escalate security risk decisions to higher levels of leadership, if necessary.
- Discuss security risks with complete transparency at all levels of the organization.
- Investigate security incidents in any area of the enterprise, as needed.

Having the appropriate authority for the security function is important, and is beneficial to all involved, but it can sometimes feel threatening to people and organizations that may not be used to this type of working relationship. Simply having the kind of access necessary to identifying security risks, expose those security risks, and help manage the mitigation planning process means you have reach into another organization, and that can feel like a threat to some business leaders.

However, if used properly and with discretion, the authority held by the security organization can help foster the kinds of close relationships needed with your strategic partners. Using the authority of the security role to fairly and consistently apply the ESRM model in all areas of the enterprise, with all business partners will show your strategic partners that your organization is:

- Trustworthy.
- Professional.
- Fair.
- Equitable.
- Dedicated.
- Responsible.
- Consistent.

Showing your strategic partners that they can count on you to respect both their role and yours in the security risk management process strengthens both sides of the relationship.

Case Study: Why Authority Matters

Diana P. works as a security manager at Finehart Home Theater, an installer of top-of-the-line custom home electronics systems. Her security function reports to the facilities group. Recently, Diana had been following a high-profile local news story. It was a sexual assault case involving another local retailer, Appliance Galaxy. An Appliance Galaxy employee had been accused of attacking a customer in her home while making a delivery. The police investigation revealed that the employee had a criminal record for a similar offense. The result was an avalanche of bad publicity, with threats of lawsuits for Appliance Galaxy.

Diana realized that Finehart could easily find itself in the same situation; so she approached the installations manager, Susan G., to discuss the possibility of doing background checks on installers. Susan told her that none of her installers would ever be a problem because she hired them all personally and knew how to read people. And besides, finding skilled technicians was hard enough already. Why would she want to add an extra layer of difficulty to the process? She made it clear that she had no intention of making any changes.

Diana described the conversation to her boss, Harold B., who reminded her that nothing like the Appliance Galaxy incident had ever happened at Finehart, meaning that Susan "must be doing something right." And he added, "We are facilities; what are we supposed to do? Just drop it." Diana was frustrated, and she was still very concerned, but there was no one left in the company for her to turn to, at least not without risking her job. So, she moved on to her next project and hoped for the best.

In the Finehart case, Diana clearly does not have the authority to escalate inappropriate risk acceptance in the organization. Rather than take the risk of going outside her chain of command, Diana dropped the issue. It is obvious that "hoping for the best" is never the most effective risk mitigation strategy. An ESRM risk-based approach would have given Diana the ability to continue to pursue the background check issue with the appropriate and true argument that she was fulfilling security's role of exploring all the security risks for the company.

Questions for the Security Practitioner
- "Have I ever seen a security practitioner abuse their position of authority and overstep their bounds? What form did that take?"
- "Have I ever seen a security practitioner in a position of not being able to discuss a risk because they did not have enough authority to point it out to a higher level than their reporting structure?"

12.4 Scope

The final aspect of ESRM success to discuss is scope. In ESRM, scope is the extent, and the limits, of the department's work in managing security risks.

A vital question to consider in the setup of your program, and a necessary one to get approved by your executive structure, is what the defined scope of the security program is. The answer can vary somewhat, depending on the department, the individual, and what the business feels is important. Your role, however, remains fundamentally the same: To manage security risks of all types across the enterprise, using risk principles. Scope is the direction given to your department by the business about which risks fall into the realm of "security risk" and which do not.

How can the definition of security risk and scope vary based on the enterprise? In Chapter 1, we discussed the definition of security risk: Anything that *threatens harm* to the enterprise, its mission, its employees, customers, or partners, its operations, its reputation. That is a broad definition and all the possible threats to the enterprise should at least be *considered* by your overarching security program.

However, in certain industries or businesses, there are functions that, due to regulations or organizational structure, might fall into another area. Some examples where this might happen are:

- Financial fraud in a bank or financial enterprise might belong to a specialized fraud group.
- Policy violation investigations in some organizational structures might belong to the legal compliance group.
- Sexual harassment investigations often specifically belong to HR or employee relations rather than security.
- Unionized environments sometimes have special considerations for any incidents involving union employees.
- Enterprises that deal with materials requiring government clearances might need special handling of some cases outside of the security group.

All the above certainly fall into the category of security risks. And in many smaller, non-specialized, or less-regulated environments, they would be included in the scope of the ESRM program. However, your organization might have legitimate reasons to exclude certain types of risks or certain areas of the organization from the general security risk management scope of activities. As we have shown already, if authorized by the proper level of authority in the organization, these decisions are perfectly acceptable in ESRM.

Nevertheless, what is not acceptable in an ESRM program is defining the security team's scope as performing one or two types of task, which aligns with old perceptions of the role of security. An example would be limiting the scope of the security risks that are managed by the program to only risks that could impact the tangible assets of buildings, because the most visible tasks performed by the personnel in the current security group are camera management and identification badges. Scope simply cannot be predefined as "what the security group is already doing" when implementing your overarching ESRM program.

This does not imply that the tasks performed by security personnel are not influenced by program scope or that they do not have a place in ESRM. But in ESRM, the reason for performing day-to-day security tasks is to service risk management and mitigation; it's not just a job description. All security tasks are taken on *in response to the prioritized risks to organization assets*, and are then assigned to the subject-matter experts in security to carry out. It is a subtle difference, but an important one, because the mitigation activities might *also* be assigned to the business group or owner, as a process change or some other plan.

As we mentioned above, we cannot define those limits or boundaries of scope for you. You will have to do that yourself, in partnership your organization's leadership. Unfortunately, your program may not always have the scope that is necessary and appropriate for you to effectively carry out your program, at least not at the outset. There will always be issues, such as inappropriate job titles and descriptions, enterprise politics, or "siloed" (isolated) organizational structures, which could make the process of defining and establishing scope more difficult. Practicing ESRM does not mean you will get, or should push for an increased scope of responsibilities. But using ESRM principles also doesn't mean there must be any *inherent* limits on program scope. The more effectively you apply ESRM principles, the more likely it will be that you are assigned the scope you need in the context of your organization.

One advantage of using ESRM principles, even if some mitigation plans or risks are outside of the defined scope of your program, is that you can still interact with the other groups who have ownership of certain risks to ensure all risks are covered, and know that your discussions will be centered only on the management of those risks. These conversations are appropriate and necessary discussions about mitigations for identified security risks. No matter what the defined scope of your security program, the critical ESRM principles of security risk management still apply to the entire enterprise.

Questions for the Security Practitioner
- "What concrete steps could I take to understand the scope of my security program, and what should the scope of my ESRM program be?"
- "Can I identify certain tasks that I am performing now that are not appropriate for me and my organization, tasks that could be performed better by someone else within the enterprise?"

12.5 Parallels with Other Risk-Based Functions

We have outlined the four necessary elements required to have a successful ESRM program:

- Transparency.
- Independence.
- Authority.
- Scope.

Now we will discuss how best to communicate the need for these elements across the enterprise. Change can be difficult, and communicating the need for change must be clear and factual. Oftentimes, even perfectly reasonable requests for transparency, authority, or scope can be perceived from the outside as "kingdom-building" or a "land grab." But an ESRM program is only interested in protecting the business in the way that the business organization deems appropriate. Therefore, drawing parallels with other areas as you explain the need for these four elements is appropriate and an effective communication tool.

Security, practiced following ESRM principles, shares many traits with legal, audit, compliance, and other risk management functions. In fact, because security's responsibilities sometimes overlap with these functions, it is important that security professionals understand these other functions. After all, nobody would expect an auditing team to do an effective job if the organization being audited were not open and honest, and were in a position of authority over the audit team. The reverse is also true, the auditors must be equally open and honest about what they are doing and have the authority and scope to do it.

You will benefit greatly if you are able to articulate what audit, legal, and compliance teams do, why and how they do it, and what *their* success factors are. From them, you can learn how to promote transparency, independence, authority, and scope in your ESRM program.

Questions for the Security Practitioner
- "Do I have strategic partners in internal audit or the compliance office, whom I could speak to on the topics of transparency, independence, authority, and scope?"

12.5.1 What Are Audit, Legal, and Compliance?

To start, consider the definitions that some audit and compliance organizations use to describe themselves:

Audit

From the Institute of Internal Auditors (IIA):

> Internal auditing is an independent, objective assurance and consulting activity designed to add value and improve an organization's operations. It helps an organization accomplish its objectives by bringing a systematic, disciplined approach to evaluate and improve the effectiveness of risk management, control, and governance processes (The Institute of Internal Auditors, 2015).

From the Association of Certified Fraud Examiners website:

> Internal auditors verify internal controls are in place and functioning properly to deter fraud. Internal auditors conduct compliance and operational audits, offering solutions for weaknesses in internal controls and verifying that all laws and regulations are upheld (The Association of Certified Fraud Examiners, 2017).

Legal

From the Association of Corporate Counsel (ACC) website:

> In-house counsel in the United States are responsible for a wide range of legal and business duties.…It often requires familiarity with a variety of areas of the law, including contracts, intellectual property, labor/employment, litigation, tax, antitrust, ERISA, corporate/securities and privacy matters, among others…They proactively assess and manage risks and deal with the routine legal matters a corporation confronts (ACC Legal Staff, 2010).

Compliance

From the United States Sentencing Commission, 2012 Federal Sentencing Guidelines Manual:

> [A] compliance and ethics program shall be reasonably designed, implemented, and enforced so that the program is generally effective in preventing and detecting criminal conduct.…An organization's Program should include monitoring and auditing systems that are designed to detect criminal and other improper conduct (US Sentencing Commission, 2012).

The compliance officers and auditors in organizations are charged by law with implementing and carrying out these programs.

12.5.2 What do Legal, Audit and Compliance Functions Need for Success?

The foundational requirements for success in audit, legal, and compliance are remarkably like the ESRM success factors we discussed above. Even if they do not use the same words, you will see independence, transparency, authority, and scope are constant themes in the legal, compliance and audit professions.

Donna Boehme, with the industry group Compliance Strategists, wrote in *Compliance Today* (2012) about essential features of the chief ethics and compliance officer (CECO) position, singling out some qualities that mirror our discussion here.

> Line of sight – The Chief Ethics and Compliance Officer (CECO) must have unfettered access to relevant information to be able to form independent opinions and manage the program effectively. Where important areas of risk … are "carved out" from the CECO's line of sight, the CECO will be unable to perform adequate oversight of the program for that risk.… (Boehme, 2012, p. 24).

This idea parallels what we have been calling *risk transparency*: It is the ability to see and have access to what you need.

Empowerment – The CECO must have the appropriate unambiguous mandate, delegation of authority, senior-level positioning, and empowerment to carry out his/her duties (Boehme, 2012, p. 23).

The word that Boehme used is *empowerment*, but it is essentially what we discussed above, about needing the authority to carry out your defined role.

Independence – The CECO must have sufficient authority and independence to oversee the integrity of the compliance program (Boehme, 2012, p. 23).

Here we even see the same terminology used. This is to be expected, since ESRM is not alone in espousing the idea that a risk-based function needs these essential foundations. In our model, we simply expand the sphere of risk-based functions to include security.

The IIA mentions several similar points on its webpage detailing the *Core Principles for the Professional Practice of Internal Auditing*, stating that "…for an internal audit function to be considered effective, all Principles should be present and operating effectively." In the IIA's list of core principles, we also find parallels with independence, scope, and authority:

- Is objective and free from undue influence (independent).
- Aligns with the strategies, objectives, and risks of the organization.
- Is appropriately positioned and adequately resourced (The Institute of Internal Auditors, 2017).

In the legal department and in-house and general counsel, we continue to see similar themes. From an article reprinted on the Ethic-Intelligence website by Daniel Lucien Bühr and Herbert Wohlmann:

The General Counsel has a dual role: She/he is a business partner who assists management in achieving the operational goals of the company. At the same time, the General Counsel is a guardian to the company. If a conflict between both roles arises, the interests of the company must prevail. The guardian role of the General Counsel is an important element of the checks and balances of a company. The General Counsel can only be a guardian to the company, if she/he is independent. The key elements of organizational independence of the General Counsel are a direct (solid) reporting line to the CEO and a (dotted) strategic reporting line to the board (Bühr & Wohlmann, 2013).

These are just a few examples of risk-based enterprise functions that have foundational concepts and principles in common with ESRM. They are all functions that address business-critical issues of risk, and they all need the same kinds of enterprise commitment and support – that is, the support of executives committing to independence, transparency, authority, and scope.

Chapter Review

In Chapter 12, you learned:

- The four essential elements for a successful ESRM are:
  - Transparency
  - Independence
  - Authority
  - Scope
- Audit, legal, compliance, and other risk-based programs required similar elements to function properly, and these functions can provide parallels for your executive audience to understand why security needs them, too.

Looking Forward

In Chapter 13, we will continue to define what needs to be in place to ensure success for your ESRM implementation and examine the principles of ESRM governance.

Practitioner steps to consider before moving on to Chapter 13:
- ✓ Examine your role in your organization. Does it have the appropriate independence and authority? Identify ways in which the impartiality of ESRM could increase independence and authority.
- ✓ Look at the current scope of the tasks performed by your organization. Does it align with what the ESRM-based scope will be once rolled out?

Security Program Self-Assessment

In this self-assessment, you should think about the answer to the questions posed, and then see where your program is on the identified ESRM spectrum.

Question	Y/N	Is This ESRM?
Does your security program have the necessary independence and authority to avoid repercussions and conflicts of interest in doing your work?	☐Yes ☐No	**NO**: If you feel that there are limits on the security function that occur, due to inappropriate authority and independence, then correcting this is a suitable place to start your ESRM program. **PARTIAL**: If you have an informal recourse method in your chain of command or in contacts outside your chain of command, who can assist in escalating security problems with business leaders in the organization, then you are part of the way to an ESRM implementation. **YES**: If you have a formal policy, approved by the executives, documenting the independent role, authority, and scope of the security program in maintaining risk transparency and have an independent reporting line of organization, then you are practicing ESRM.

Questions for Discussion

1. What are some reasons a business leader might not want a security risk identified? How can you work around some of these issues?

2. Why is it important to have examples of what other risk-based organizations need to properly perform their duties, when explaining ESRM to executives or other business function leaders? Are the examples different, depending on whether the security function reports to operations, HR, risk management, or IT?

3. How does security benefit from transparency? Can you think of any instances in an ESRM program where transparency of risk and process (not investigations or private details) would not be a benefit? Are there arguments against it?

4. How would you define authority and scope within your department's area of responsibilities? What would you do if other groups were attempting to limit your scope in areas they think they should control?

References

ACC Legal Staff. (2010, September). The role of in-house counsel: Global distinctions. *Legal Resources.* Retrieved from http://www.acc.com/legalresources/quickcounsel/troicgd.cfm

The Association of Certified Fraud Examiners (ACFE). (2016). *Internal auditor.* Retrieved from http://www.acfe.com/internal-auditor.aspx

Boehme, D. C. (2012, December). Five essential features of the chief ethics and compliance officer position. *Compliance Today.* Retrieved from http://compliancestrategists.com/csblog/wp-content/uploads/2013/12/Compliance-Today-December-2012.pdf

Bühr, D. L. & Wohlmann, H. (2013, July). Top five governance principles for the corporate legal function. *Ethic-Intelligence.* Retrieved from http://www.ethic-intelligence.com/experts/318-is-there-a-need-for-good-governance-in-the-corporate-legal-function/

US Sentencing Commission. (2012). *2012 Federal sentencing guidelines manual.* (§ 8B2.1(b)(1)). (2012). Retrieved from http://www.ussc.gov/guidelines-manual/2012/2012-8b21

The Institute of Internal Auditors (IIA). (2016). *Core principles for the professional practice of internal auditing.* Retrieved from https://na.theiia.org/standards-guidance/mandatory-guidance/Pages/Core-Principles-for-the-Professional-Practice-of-Internal-Auditing.aspx

The Institute of Internal Auditors (IIA). (2015). *The framework for internal audit effectiveness: The new IPPF.* Retrieved from https://na.theiia.org/standards-guidance/Public%20Documents/The-Framework-for-Internal-Audit-Effectiveness-The-New-IPPF-Brochure.pdf

Learn More About It

For further reading about audit functions, see:

Chambers, R. F. (2014). *Lessons learned on the audit trail.* Altamonte Springs, FL: The IIA Research Foundation.

The Institute of Internal Auditors (IIA) website. Available at https://na.theiia.org/Pages/IIAHome.aspx

Institute of Chartered Accountants in England & Wales. (2016). *Auditor independence approach.* Available at https://www.icaew.com/en/technical/ethics/auditor-independence/auditor-independence-approach

PricewaterhouseCoopers (PwC). (2012). *Point of view: Governance and transparency of the audit.* Available at https://www.pwc.com/gx/en/audit-services/publications/assets/pwc-pointofview-governanceandtransparency.pdf

PricewaterhouseCoopers (PwC). (2012). *Point of view: Independence.* Available at https://www.pwc.com/gx/en/audit-services/publications/assets/pwc-pointofview-independence.pdf

For further reading about ethics and compliance, see:

Cunningham, J. & Jezierski, C. (2015, June 26). Independence day: The separate and equal compliance department. *Global Compliance News.* Available at https://globalcompliancenews.com/independence-day-the-separate-and-equal-compliance-department/

The Society of Corporate Compliance and Ethics website. Available at http://www.corporatecompliance.org/

Volkov, M. (2013, July 17). Empowering the chief compliance officer: A recipe for effective compliances. *LexisNexis Corporate Law Advisory.* Available at https://www.lexisnexis.com/communities/corporatecounselnewsletter/b/newsletter/archive/2013/07/17/empowering-the-chief-compliance-officer-a-recipe-for-effective-compliances.aspx

13

Security Governance

So far, we have talked about how executive oversight and full support of the security program is critical to ensuring a successful program. Governance and support is key to setting up an appropriate department reporting structure in the organization, which in turn, is what allows your team to effectively maintain those essential elements that we discussed in Chapter 12, transparency, independence, authority, and scope. Without *all* these things, your ability to properly interact with all levels of your enterprise, identify risks and risk owners, and to partner with the lines of business on risk mitigation plans is compromised.

In this chapter, you will get a chance to explore how a formal governance structure – including an executive security council of leaders across the enterprise – is the final link in the chain that ties together all the pieces we have discussed so far.

This chapter will help you to:
1. Apply the principles of overall corporate governance to enterprise security risk management (ESRM).
2. Explore the role of a security council in governing your program.
3. Set up a practicing security council and define your role on it.

13.1 What is Corporate Governance?

Essentially, corporate governance is the set of systems and processes that a well-managed company puts in place to ensure that it acts correctly in its relations with all its stakeholders, including its shareholders if it is a publicly traded company, customers, employees, industry partners, vendors, even the larger community. Typical corporate governance documents and standards will address issues such as:

- The role of the CEO and chairman.
- The role of the board of directors.
- The need for audit and oversight.
- The rights of all stakeholders.
- The need for disclosure and transparency in management.

13.1.1 Defining Corporate Governance

A commonly referenced definition of corporate governance came out of the Cadbury Committee, which was set up in the United Kingdom in 1991 to raise standards in corporate governance:

> Corporate governance is the system by which companies are directed and controlled (The Committee on the Financial Aspects of Corporate Governance and Gee and Co. Ltd., 1992).

However, that is a limited definition, speaking only to high-level mechanisms but not to the reasons for the governance.

A more detailed exploration of corporate governance can be seen in the 2015 document, *G20/OECD Principles of Corporate Governance* from the Organization for Economic Co-operation and Development (OECD), an international policy organization with 34 member countries, which either adopt its guidelines or use them as a basis for their own regulations and laws. The OECD is extremely influential, even beyond its member countries, and its *Principles* are widely accepted. These are the guidelines that we would most recommend you look at if you choose to delve deeper into the area of corporate governance.

The OECD website defines corporate governance as:

> Procedures and processes according to which an organization is directed and controlled. The corporate governance structure specifies the distribution of rights and responsibilities among the different participants in the organization – such as the board, managers, shareholders and other stakeholders – and lays down the rules and procedures for decision-making (Corporate governance, 2005).

To put that in the simplest possible terms, that means governance controls:

- How decisions are made and carried out.
- Who has the authority and responsibility to do make those decisions.

Both of those elements are at the very heart of ESRM and ESRM governance.

13.1.2 Why is Corporate Governance Important?

Why is the concept of governance so important? Why do many enterprises have whole teams devoted to governance? Why is the topic rising in importance and expanding in scope?

A glance at the newspaper headlines shows us that *not* taking corporate governance seriously can be extremely damaging to your company, its reputation, its brand, and its bottom line.

Governance Failures – A Decade of Scandal

Governance scandals make the news every day. Below is a quick snapshot of some of the scandals caused in part by poor corporate governance. How many of these stories are familiar to you?

- 2015 – The Volkswagen emissions scandal, in which the auto manufacturer admits installing software on its diesel vehicles to misrepresent their pollution standards. It costs the company roughly $20 million in market value.
- 2014 – The Chinese government fines the pharmaceuticals firm GlaxoSmithKline $489 million for paying doctors to use its drugs.
- 2013 – The collapse of a textile factory in Dhaka, Bangladesh, which manufactured clothing for brands including JC Penney. At least 1,130 workers are killed.
- 2012 – Barclays and other leading banks are implicated in a scheme to manipulate the London Inter-Bank Offered Rate (LIBOR). The chief executive officer (CEO) and chief operating officer (COO) of Barclays, among other leading financial industry figures, are forced to resign.
- 2011 – News Corp, the parent company of Fox News, faces criminal and civil charges from accusations of phone hacking.
- 2010 – An explosion on BP's Deepwater Horizon offshore drilling rig kills 11 workers and causes catastrophic environmental damage in the Gulf of Mexico. By 2015, the company, which pleaded guilty to charges including manslaughter and lying to the US Congress, is estimated to have paid at least $54 billion in fines, penalties, restitution, and cleanup costs.
- 2009 – Bernard Madoff is sentenced to 150 years in prison for a Ponzi scheme that may have cost investors more than $50 billion.
- 2008 – Lehman Brothers, an investment firm founded in 1850, is forced into the largest bankruptcy in US history after it is found to have overstated its assets by some $50 billion dollars.
- 2004-5 – The multinational insurance company AIG is accused of accounting fraud and stock price manipulation. The costs to the company include a $1.6 billion fine and a $126 million regulatory settlement, as well as criminal charges against AIG executives.

In every one of these events, corporate governance policy, process, procedure, and personnel were ignored, gone around, or sometimes even complicit in the wrongdoing. Strong, ethical governance can save organizations from being part of the 24-hour news cycle.

13.1.3 Common Themes in Corporate Governance

Corporate governance has different formal definitions and standards, but there are a few basic governance principles that are generally agreed on:

- Transparency.
- Accountability.
- Fairness.
- Responsibility.

These principles are *essentially* the same ones we talked about in the last chapter, as the basics for a successful ESRM program. They are core principles for any business, and they are concepts that your strategic partners in the enterprise are deeply concerned with. Governance is one of those foundational business topics that, if you are going to work together with business leaders in the enterprise, you must have a firm grasp of.

ESRM is not the only model that relies on governance as the key pillar of a program. Table 13-1 offers a sample of the many standards that identify the need for strong governance to ensure program success.

Table 13-1. Standards and Governance Definitions

Standard	Commentary on Governance	Why Governance Matters in the Standard
National Institute of Standards and Technology (NIST) – Framework for Improving Critical Infrastructure Cybersecurity	"Governance (ID.GV): The policies, procedures, and processes to manage and monitor the organization's regulatory, legal, risk, environmental, and operational requirements are understood and inform the management of cybersecurity risk. • ID.GV-1: Organizational information security policy is established. • ID.GV-2: Information security roles & responsibilities are coordinated and aligned with internal roles and external partners. • ID.GV-3: Legal and regulatory requirements regarding cybersecurity, including privacy and civil liberties obligations, are understood and managed. • ID.GV-4: Governance and risk management processes address cybersecurity risks." (National Institute of Standards and Technology, 2014, pp. 21-22).	The NIST cybersecurity standard is a matrix designed to identify gaps between an existing cybersecurity program and the standards that NIST identifies as best practices for cybersecurity. The need for governance is identified in the very first section of the framework. This shows the importance of having the rest of the policies and processes overseen by a governing body to ensure that the policy is set, roles are assigned and supported, and risks are managed and understood. In fact, the NIST framework is an excellent tool to leverage in your ESRM program when identifying and assessing risks in the areas of cyber and information security.
International Organization for Standardization (ISO) – ISO 31000:2009 – Risk management – Practices and guidelines	"Comprehensive and frequent external and internal reporting on both significant risks and on risk management performance contributes substantially to effective governance within an organization." (International Organization for Standardization, 2009, p. 23).	We have mentioned the ISO risk standard repeatedly throughout this book. It is a comprehensive yet easy-to-understand standard that should be a go-to resource for you in all aspects of running a risk-based security program. Specific to the topic of governance, we will follow up in Chapter 16, which is entirely devoted to the mechanisms of internal and external reporting and metrics. Here, we simply want to note that governance is such an intrinsic part of the ISO

		standard that it is not even specifically called out as a separate need. The need for governance is woven throughout the entire document, as the quote here makes clear.
OCEG GRC Capability Model, 2.0	"In the context of [governance, risk, and compliance], effective corporate governance supported and in layers throughout the organization, with the emphasis in processes that affect and influence Board understanding of critical information that allows good decision-making." (Mitchell & Switzer, 2009, p. 10).	OCEG (formerly the Open Compliance & Ethics Group) is a nonprofit organization dedicated to assisting corporations with governance, risk, and compliance (GRC). The organization's emphasis on governance as a tool for good decision-making aligns perfectly with the ESRM methodology for working with your risk owners to determine the best treatment for security risks. Learning more about GRC through this organization can help you become better-versed in the business language of risk.
ISACA COBIT 5: A Business Framework for the Governance and Management of Enterprise IT	Governance can be applied to the entire enterprise, an entity, a tangible or intangible asset, etc. That is, it is possible to define different views of the enterprise to which governance is applied, and it is essential to define this scope of the governance system well." (ISACA, 2012, p. 23).	ISACA's COBIT 5 is another framework that can be leveraged in information security. It leans heavily on governance as the mechanism for standards enforcement, rather than assigning that task to one specific group. Like ESRM, the COBIT 5 model highlights the need for strong oversight to ensure that risks to the organization are being properly managed.
Federation of European Risk Management Associations (FERMA) – Risk Management Standard	Good corporate governance requires that companies adopt a methodical approach to risk management which: • Protects the interests of their stakeholders. • Ensures that the Board of Directors discharges its duties to direct strategy, build value and monitor performance of the organization. • Ensures that management controls are in place and are performing adequately.	While many of the standards we have discussed are global, some are regional or national. European standards are often stricter than in other regions, because the European Union (EU) is a leading force in the importance of privacy and corporate governance accountability. Both the FERMA standard and the EU Solvency II Directive (below) highlight the need for risk

	(Federation of European Risk Management Associations, 2002, p.12).	management to be controlled by a central governing group. If your company is based in Europe or has a presence there, these two standards should be at the top of your reading list when you are implementing your ESRM governance program.
EU Solvency II Directive (2009/138/EC)	"The system of governance includes the risk-management function, the compliance function, the internal audit function and the actuarial function" (European Parliament and Council of the European Union, 2009, L335/4) "Member States shall require all insurance and reinsurance undertakings to have in place an effective system of governance which provides or sound and prudent management of the business. That system shall at least include an adequate transparent organizational structure with a clear allocation and appropriate segregation of responsibilities and an effective system for ensuring the transmission of information." (The European Parliament, and Council of the European Union, 2009, Section 2 Article 41).	Unlike the voluntary FERMA standards, this directive (known as Solvency II) is a legally binding EU directive. Sometimes governance is simply a good practice to ensure that you are protecting yourself, your stakeholders, and your enterprise. But at other times – as with Solvency II, and with Sarbanes-Oxley in the US – it is the law.

13.2 The Security Council: ESRM Governance

Corporate governance is a high-level concept that covers *all* enterprise activities. To use the term that we discussed in detail in the last chapter, it has an extremely broad *scope*. When you are considering ESRM governance, it may help to think of it as a subset of corporate governance. Because, essentially, governance is governance, and methods for providing governance are generally similar:

- Set policy.
- Guide direction.
- Oversee resources.
- Ensure compliance.

The key difference between governance at the highest levels of the enterprise, and governance of specific programs, is in the *scope* of what is being covered, and of course, who is responsible for it.

- In enterprise governance, the controlling body is the board of directors.
- In ESRM, it is the enterprise's *security council*.

For an ESRM program, the security council is the body that is responsible for creating, maintaining, and approving the enterprise's security policy, and for ensuring that the security program supports the enterprise's goals. It drives the security risk tolerance discussion, and it is the body that has the final word on security and security risk decisions – especially in areas where stakeholders disagree. The security council is the ESRM program's "higher authority," and it is the group that can do the most to help the program evolve and mature.

13.2.1 Who is the ESRM Security Council?

Your security council will be made up of executives and business leaders from across your enterprise. Through your understanding of your enterprise's structure, leadership, and culture, you will have an idea of who to invite to participate. It is key for the council members to understand the need to manage security risk to the enterprise holistically, and to accept the role of the security department as the stewards of that risk management.

13.2.2 The Security Council's Role in ESRM

Having a security council is a clear best practice for the successful design, development, and management of an ESRM program. The council is a driving force for risk management, and is an escalation point for any conflict in the risk management process. It is also a venue to engage leaders in discussions of security topics, and to increase security awareness across the enterprise.

If you take a closer look at just one of the OECD Principles of Corporate Governance that we mentioned earlier in the chapter – The Responsibilities of the Board of Directors – you will see that the standard is intended to address board members at the higher level. However, many of these principles also apply to a properly implemented security council. We have excerpted (and paraphrased slightly) a few of them here:

- Members should act on a fully-informed basis, in good faith, with due diligence and care, and in the best interest of the company and the shareholders.
    - Where decisions may affect some groups differently, the board (security council) should treat all fairly.
- Members should fulfill certain key functions, including:
    - Reviewing and guiding corporate (security) strategy, major plans of action, risk policy, annual budgets, and business plans; setting objectives; monitoring implementation and performance; and overseeing major expenditures, acquisitions, and divestitures.
    - Monitoring the effectiveness of the company's practices, and making changes as needed.
- Consider assigning a sufficient number of non-members who can exercise independent judgment to tasks where there is a potential for conflict of interest. (Organization for Economic Co-operation and Development, 2015, pp. 45-54).

Looking at this list, you can see how the general objectives and standards of corporate governance for Boards of Directors apply to ESRM governance and the security council, as well.

13.2.3 Setting Up a Security Council

Setting up a security council begins with ensuring that the enterprise's senior decision-makers understand and accept the importance of overall governance of the ESRM program. After you have done the basic preparations that you reviewed in the earlier chapters – exploring and understanding the business environment, especially its stakeholders and its assets – you should have enough knowledge to gain the support you need to define and set up the security council – a process with six basic steps.

13.2.3.1 Step 1: Define the Council Structure that Will Best Serve Enterprise Needs

The structure for a security council is driven by the needs and tolerances of the enterprise that it serves. There are a few basic structures that your organization might choose, and each of them serves a different need in overall security risk management. In the white paper, *Security governance - a critical component to managing security risk*, the Global Security Risk Management Alliance outlines three different options to consider.

Model 1 – The Security Risk Council

In this model, a single council of risk stakeholders governs all in-scope security risks. This council could report findings into the executive level, or to a higher-level risk management program in the organization. In this model, the council governs and oversees the tolerance and response to all security risks with one set of council members. Figure 13-1 shows an example of this model council with some possible stakeholder groups (which would, of course, vary depending on your organization).

Figure 13-1. Example of a security risk council approach. (Global Security Risk Management Alliance, 2017, p. 12).

Model 2 – Security Risk Council with Subcommittees

This model, shown in Figure 13-2, also has a single body governing all security risk. The difference is that it adds subcommittees for different disciplines of risk. This would entail the central council dealing with most types of security risk, but putting special groups in charge of certain topics like workplace violence, cyber security, or other areas requiring technical expertise to manage more effectively. The subcommittees report into the main council, which provides the interface to higher level management.

Figure 13-2. Example of a security risk council with subcommittees approach (Global Security Risk Management Alliance, 2017, p. 13).

Model 3 – Security Discipline Councils

Figure 13-3 shows a model that features *no* central body with scope over all security risks. Instead, the enterprise might want specific governance only on individual disciplines, so that it can provide more focused risk management on those risks they wanted governed more closely. The individual councils might report into an executive body, as shown below, or the enterprise might have councils operating without any direct reporting. As with all other aspects of ESRM, the most effective structure is the one that fits the needs and tolerances of the enterprise.

Figure 13-3. Example of multi security discipline council approach (Global Security Risk Management Alliance, 2017, p. 13).

13.2.3.2 Step 2: Define the Security Council Stakeholders

Identify all the groups, roles, and individuals with a stake in protecting the enterprise's assets, and ensure

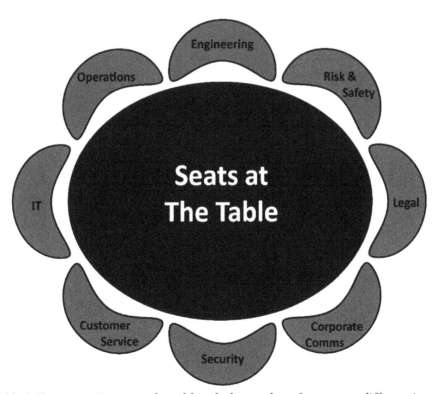

Figure 13-4. Your security council could include members from many different internal organizations and functions that have a stake in security risk governance.

that they all have representation on the security council. See Figure 13-4 for an example of potential council members. (The membership is likely to expand as the council is implemented).

13.2.3.3 Step 3: Define the Mission, Objectives, and Goals of the Security Council and Document Them in a Council Charter

A mission and charter are imperative to ensure that the council members understand the role of the council, their job on the council, the scope of authority of the council, and any specific council requirements that the members might define during the process of setting it up.

13.2.3.4 Step 4: Define Measurements/Project Key Performance Indicators (KPIs) for ESRM

Working with the individuals who are named as members of the security council, develop an appropriate list of measurements and KPIs to track and report to the council, to provide them with the information they will need to direct the ESRM program. We will discuss reporting and metrics in detail in Chapter 22.

13.2.3.5 Step 5: Develop a List of Potential Quick "Wins" for the ESRM Program

Develop a list of open risks that can be addressed relatively quickly if the necessary resources and priorities are assigned to them. This will give the newly developed council targets to focus on from the beginning of the implementation – targets that have a high likelihood of success which will give the ESRM program further credibility.

13.2.3.6 Step 6: Begin the Process of Meeting, Reviewing, and Directing the Program According to the Council Charter.

Once a fully functioning security council is in place, your ESRM program governance is ensured.

> #### Case Study: A New Governance Approach at Stalbridge
> In Chapter 12, we talked about a case of fraud at a financial services provider called Stalbridge. There is more to that story, and delving further into Stanley M.'s decision to implement ESRM at Stalbridge can tell us a lot about ESRM governance.
>
> Stalbridge's general counsel, Stanley M., realized that the company's existing security model did not give the people tasked with securing the company the authority, independence, transparency, or proper scope they needed. He decided that the security function needed to be treated differently. As the person with overall responsibility for Stalbridge's compliance with laws and regulations, he understood risk and how to manage it. But he also understood the company, and he knew that at Stalbridge, change was not easy and was not always welcome.
>
> One reason for that resistance to change was that the company was organized on a regional basis with the regional leaders running things essentially however they wanted. Stanley knew he would need the support of a diverse group of stakeholders with diverse and often competing interests to change the focus of the security team so that it could function effectively across the entire enterprise.
>
> The solution seemed to be a group of stakeholders who could drive the process – a council of peers who would hold responsibility jointly. That was an entirely new approach for Stalbridge, and Stanley was not sure that it could work. While recognizing the critical need for high-level support, he presented the idea, and the compelling reasons for it, to the CEO, and got the go-ahead to try it. These are the steps it took to make it happen:

Step 1: Define the council structure that will best serve enterprise needs.
Stanley understood that the culture at Stalbridge needed a simple, clear solution for security governance. He decided to start under a single overarching security council, knowing that as the council matured, that decision could be revisited, and the model might change into a more diversified council with subcommittees and working groups.

- **Step 2: Define the security council stakeholders.**
  Stanley took the directive from his CEO and then, based his own knowledge of the company, he decided who to initially invite to the council. He met with operational leaders, IT leaders, security managers, other legal personnel, and HR leaders. Some were enthusiastic about the idea of the council, while some thought security should stay right where it was in the organizational structure. But the CEO's mandate made it possible for Stanley to get his stakeholders to a first meeting and at least discuss a security council.

- **Step 3: Define the mission, objectives, and goals of the security council and document them in a council charter.**
  Before that first meeting, Stanley tasked a few of the organization's security personnel to draft a council charter. It gave the council the authority to direct and govern the security program and to fund and require projects to improve security. The draft was intended as the first iteration (recall from Chapters 10 and 11 the concepts of iterative rollout), and he got quite a bit of pushback from the council members. They raised issues like:
  - Where would the project funding come from?
  - Why was the council so powerful?
  - What about the work that already needed to be done? Would it need to just stop and wait for the council to approve?

  Stanley saw that some of their points were valid, and that he might have set too high a bar, at least to start with. The council worked together to craft language that everyone could agree on, and then voted to ratify the charter that they wrote.

- **Step 4: Define measurements/project key performance indicators (KPIs) for ESRM.**
  When they were discussing the roles defined by the charter, the council members were concerned that they might be told that they were responsible for security governance but would not be given any way to carry it out. So, they agreed that part of security's role would be to keep the council informed of its activities, the risks it was identifying, and the mitigations it was implementing. This was not a formal declaration of reporting and metrics, but it was the beginning of what became a quarterly report to the council.

- **Step 5: Develop a list of potential quick "wins" for the ESRM program.**
  Once the charter was in place, the council asked Stanley what he thought the next step should be. He told them that one easy change would be to implement a post-incident reporting process, which would allow security managers to escalate risks to their proper owners. The council agreed, and a formal reporting program was put in place. It was a small victory that the council could build on while they identified other opportunities to push the security program forward.

- **Step 6: Begin the process of meeting, reviewing, and directing the program according to the council charter.**
  Stalbridge built on those first steps, leveraging its easy wins to develop more comprehensive, enterprise-wide programs and processes. Today, the company has a fully functioning security council, and as a result, it has made great strides toward functioning entirely in a security risk management model.

13.2.4 Security's Role on the Security Council: What It Is and What It Is Not

What does all this discussion about roles, responsibilities, charters, and authority mean when it comes time to practice ESRM in your company? What is it, *exactly*, that you are asking of your security council? And what is the dividing line between the *recommendations* made by the security professional, and the *decisions* made by the governing body?

That last question is probably the most important one, because the answer to it lies in one of the foundational principles of ESRM. The basic premise we have stressed repeatedly through this book:

Risk decisions must be made by the risk owner, not by the security department.

In the case of overall ESRM governance, the security council represents the risk owner. Security, working in close collaboration with its strategic partners, will be responsible for setting up the security council and the governance model. And security should *unquestionably* have a seat at the council table. But the security council is *governing* the security program. As such, the leader of the security department cannot ethically "run" the council, nor try to influence it (beyond making recommendations for consideration, the same as any other council member would). That is why the security leader is the one individual who should never be the head of the security council.

It may be tempting to try to "stack the deck," by nominating individuals for the security council whom you think will agree with your recommendations. And it may also be tempting to try to shape the council's agenda by introducing only security risk issues that are important to you. But the result of that would inevitably be a weaker security council, and would make it a weaker ESRM governance process. The council must be as *inclusive* and *independent* as possible, with members who will not just decide on the issues that security raises, but bring their own risk issues and assessments to the table. That way, once the council is in place, and all the members clearly understand their roles, you can be certain that it is looking at what is important to the entire enterprise.

If we once more consider Stanley M.'s experience at Stalbridge with this last point in mind, we can learn from his process. He set up the company's security council, and he was – and still is – a part of it. But as you saw, when there were questions, concerns, or disagreements, he did not try to override them. (In an internally competitive company culture like Stalbridge, that probably would not have worked, and he knew it.) He was not looking for a "rubber stamp" for his own decisions, because his goal all along was to have an engaged and committed group providing oversight for the security function. And that is what he – and Stalbridge – got.

A note on working groups:
One place where security leaders and practitioners can certainly take a lead role is on the technical subcommittees and working groups that might be assigned projects and tasks by the security council. These working groups take direction from the council about what to accomplish but need the subject matter expertise of the security professional to determine how to accomplish it. For example, the leader of the IT security function would clearly make a good chair of a subcommittee on developing a cybersecurity response program, much as an investigations leader might be an excellent choice to lead a working group on threat assessment. Just because it isn't the role of the security leader to be in charge of the overarching security council and the decision-making, does not mean that the valuable expertise that the security leader brings to the table is not critical to the governing process.

Chapter Review

In Chapter 13, you learned:

- The basic principles and standards of corporate governance, how they apply to ESRM, and why they are critical to the success of an ESRM program (See Figure 13-6).
- How a security council can deliver effective security governance enterprise-wide.
- How to set up an effective security council, and what security's role in it should be.

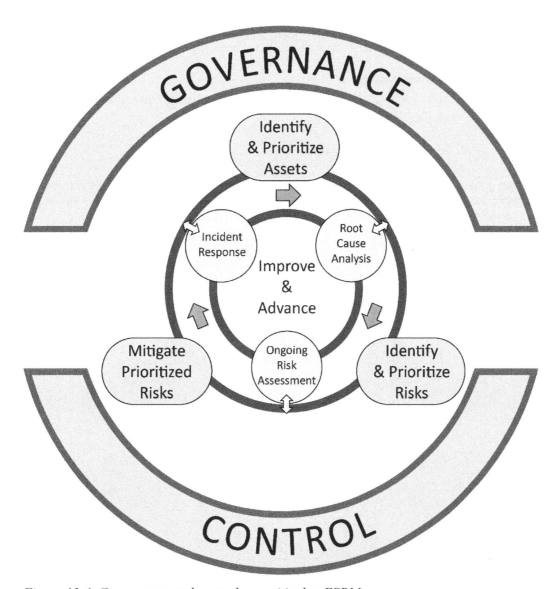

Figure 13-6. Governance and control are critical to ESRM.

Looking Forward

In Chapter 14, we will look at the optimal organization structure, both internally and in the reporting lines of the enterprise, for a well-functioning security organization.

Practitioner steps to consider before moving on to Chapter 14:
- ✓ Determine a list of candidates for inclusion on a security council.
- ✓ Ask executives in your reporting structure about other governance councils that might exist in your organization, and about their experiences with how they work.
- ✓ Draft a sample charter as a starting point for potential members to review and comment on.

Security Program Self-Assessment

In this self-assessment, you should think about the answer to the questions posed, and then see where your program is on the identified ESRM spectrum.

Question	Y/N	Is This ESRM?
Does your enterprise have a security council or a group of leaders who function in that capacity?	☐Yes ☐No	**NO**: If you have no leadership group that functions to champion security issues and to promulgate security policy, this is a suitable place to start your ESRM program. **PARTIAL**: If you have an informal group in place who perform some of the roles of a formal security council, then you are part of the way to an ESRM implementation. **YES**: If you have a formal, named, and functioning security council that is responsible for governance of a risk-based security program, then you are practicing ESRM.

Questions for Discussion

1. How can you leverage your business's understanding of corporate governance to assist with implementing ESRM governance?
2. Why is a security council an important part of the ESRM program?
3. How might implementing ESRM be more difficult without a security council? Give examples of ways the security organization could implement a council-like advisory group if it is not possible to implement a council.

References

Corporate governance. (2005, July). In Organization for Economic Co-operation and Development (OECD), *Glossary of statistical terms*. Retrieved from https://stats.oecd.org/glossary/detail.asp?ID=6778

Federation of European Risk Management Associations (FERMA). (2002). *A risk management standard.* Brussels, Belgium: Author. Retrieved from http://www.ferma.eu/app/uploads/2011/11/a-risk-management-standard-english-version.pdf

Global Security Risk Management Alliance (GSRMA). (2017). *Security governance - a critical component to managing security risk.* White Paper. Retrieved from http://gsrma.net/

International Organization for Standardization. (2009). *ISO/IEC 31000 Risk management – Principles and guidelines*. Geneva, Switzerland: ISO/IEC.

ISACA. (2012). *COBIT 5: A business framework for the governance and management of enterprise IT [preview version]*. Rolling Meadows, IL: Author. Retrieved from https://www.isaca.org/cobit/Documents/COBIT-5-Introduction.pdf

Mitchell, S. L. & Switzer, C. S. (2009, April). *GRC capability model 2.0.* Scottsdale, AZ: OCEG.

National Institute of Standards and Technology (NIST). (2014, February). *Framework for improving critical infrastructure cybersecurity.* Gaithersburg, MD: Author.

Organization for Economic Co-operation and Development (OECD). (2015). *G20/OECD Principles of corporate governance.* Paris, France: Author. Retrieved from http://dx.doi.org/10.1787/9789264236882-en

The Committee on the Financial Aspects of Corporate Governance and Gee and Co. Ltd. (1992). *The report on the financial aspects of corporate governance*. London, England: Gee. Retrieved from http://www.ecgi.org/codes/documents/cadbury.pdf

The European Parliament, and Council of the European Union. (2009). Directive 2009-138-EC on the taking up and pursuit of insurance and reinsurance. *Official Journal of the European Union.* Retrieved from https://www.tsb.org.tr/images/Documents/SolvencyIIDirektifi.pdf

Learn More About It

For more about creating effective teams and teamwork for corporate change, see:

Burtles, J. (2016). Case study: Organic resilience at Rushmore Enterprises. *Principles and practice of business continuity: Tools and techniques*, 2nd Ed. Brookfield, CT: Rothstein Publishing, pp. 357-368.

Graham, J. & Kaye, D. (2006). Culture, strategy, performance, risk and business continuity. *A risk management approach to business continuity: Aligning business continuity with corporate governance*. Brookfield, CT: Rothstein Publishing, pp. 55-70.

Hiles, A. (2014). Group processes to develop consensus for the BCP: Collaborative and creative thinking. *Business continuity management: Global best practices*, 4th Ed. Brookfield, CT: Rothstein Publishing, pp. 401-406.

14

The Security Organization

As you saw in Chapter 13, governance is key to ensuring the necessary transparency, independence, authority, and scope for your security program. Governance alone, however, is not enough to ensure these essential elements. The requirement we will discuss in relation to the program success is the security department structure itself, and the need for proper reporting lines in the enterprise as well as an optimal internal set up for maintaining the Enterprise Security Risk Management (ESRM) methodology.

This chapter will help you to:

- Identify the best lines in your enterprise for the security function to report under.
- Set up a structure for the security department that supports ESRM and risk mitigation technical activities.
- Transition your leadership approach from a tactical to a strategic orientation.

14.1 Where Should Security Report in an Organization Structure?

It can be a challenging exercise to determine where in the enterprise organization the security department should report and how. While the Security Council that we discussed in the last chapter is the *strategic* governing body of the ESRM program, it plays an oversight role, ensuring that the ESRM program has high-level executive input and commitment, as well as authority and independence. The Security Council is not a day-to-day management body. In addition to the strategic guidance of the council, it is important to have an operating structure for the security organization that provides the essential elements for security success. This structure makes it possible for the security team to both manage security risk effectively, and to carry out the tactical risk-mitigation functions of the security program.

When we first adopted the ESRM philosophy and methodology years ago, we discussed reporting lines and functional oversight with many security practitioners, in both large and small organizations. A few of the reporting arrangements we heard about were:

- The security organization sometimes reports to human resources (HR) because the security organization – especially in its physical security activities – protects the enterprise's employees.
- Cyber and information security tend to report through the technology organization either because these are seen as technical functions or because the role is not quite understood outside of the CIO.
- In some enterprises, the security team falls under operations because protecting the enterprise's operational capabilities – its business mission – is its primary purpose.
- We have also seen security reporting to the finance organization because it already has a significant interest in mitigating enterprise risk.
- Security is often placed in the corporate services group because many of the tasks of the security team provide service and support to other departments.
- Facilities is sometimes the organization that controls security because physical security activities like access control and video monitoring happen inside buildings.

These reporting arrangements are all commonplace. However, each of them is also problematic in some way. While it is understandable why some enterprises structure their security organizations this way, in the ESRM paradigm, these fundamentally do not support the goal of enabling successful security risk management.

As we discussed in Chapter 12, reporting to HR, IT, operations, facilities, finance, or any other comparatively narrow-scoped organization almost always delivers less than optimal results. That is because not one of those organizations has enterprise-wide responsibility for corporate governance, risk management, the overarching business mission and goals, or regulatory compliance. Additionally, the security risk manager will often experience problems with authority, scope, and independence when reporting in structures like the ones above.

For most enterprises, we recommend that the security function leader reports where independence, scope, and transparency are optimum and to the highest possible level in the organization – directly to the general counsel, the CEO, or even the board of directors, if possible. These positions have corporate governance and regulatory compliance responsibilities of which security is a key part.

14.1.1 Determining the Optimal Security Organization Reporting Lines

You and your executives should ask a few questions to determine the optimal structure for your enterprise.

14.1.1.1 Question 1 – What Does Security Need to be Successful?

The first question you and your enterprise executives need to ask to determine the best structure for your security organization and your enterprise is:

"What does security need in this enterprise to be successful?"

As we discussed in Chapter 12, the simple, immediate answer is:

- Security needs *independence* to properly identify risks across the enterprise that are within the *scope* of the security role, needs *authority* to make those risks *transparent*, and needs to respond to the risks in partnership with the business leaders.

But applying that simple answer in the real world is not always quite so simple.

One reason for having a Security Council in place as a strategic governing body is that it makes it possible for many different security and risk stakeholders to have a say in very important questions like the one above. All stakeholders and council members have a vested interest in ensuring that the enterprise is handling security risks successfully, and they should all want to set up the security function in the manner most likely to provide those essential elements for success.

14.1.1.2 Question 2 – Which Lines of Reporting Carry Obvious Conflicts?

Operational lines of reporting, as outlined above, carry with them obvious conflicts with the essential elements of security success. A few examples of potential conflicts are:

- If security reports to the finance organization, will it be comfortable investigating the possibility of fraud or other financial misconduct within its own chain of command?
- If it reports to the CIO, will it be comfortable reporting on security risks that reflect poorly on the IT organization?
- If it reports to the COO, will it be comfortable recommending risk mitigation methods that might slow down important business operations?
- If security reports in the facilities group, will it have scope to investigate security risks in other lines of business?

We think the answer to all those questions is clearly "No," and that makes all those structures poor choices for a reporting line.

14.1.1.3 Question 3 – What Reporting Structures are Available in This Enterprise?

Not all enterprises are structured the same, and not all organizations have the same reporting lines *available*. Depending on the enterprise, there might be several options that could provide the optimal levels of independence and authority. A larger organization might have options such as:

- CEO.
- General Council.
- Compliance.
- Enterprise Risk Management.
- Internal Audit.

Smaller organizations might not have all those areas, or the responsibilities might be combined in other groups or positions. In that case, the security leader and the executives in charge of determining structure should find the most appropriate reporting line available.

14.2 The Greatest Success Comes with the Greatest Independence

Based on our own experience and discussions with many other security professionals over the years, we have concluded that the best practice is to have the security department report to functions or departments that, like security, *also* require independence, transparency, authority, and defined scope.

These include the legal/compliance and internal audit organizations, and the board of directors. Obviously, the CEO's office also makes for a high-quality reporting line because of its authority and its legal responsibility to expose risk. Any of these more independent internal organizations would be a good place for the security organization, and the ESRM program, to function in.

As you can see in Figure 14.1, the higher in the enterprise that your security organization reports, the more successful it's likely to be. The key for your program is to have the ultimate reporting line to a leader who has the understanding and authority to ensure the essential elements for security success.

These questions of strategy and direction can be driven by the Security Council if an appropriate reporting structure cannot be developed.

Figure 14.1. The higher the security reporting structure, the more effective it will be.

Questions for the Security Practitioner

- "Do I ever feel that my security organization's reporting structure limits the authority, transparency, or independence of my function?"
- "Does my reporting line in the overall organization allow me the proper scope to manage security risks in all areas of the company?"

14.3 Security Organization Internal Structure

Once it is decided which enterprise reporting structure will house the security function, the next step is to set up an *internal* department structure that will support the ESRM risk-based philosophy and processes, while still providing the technical and tactical expertise needed to perform daily security activities.

The security organization's internal structure can vary widely, according to a broad range of factors, including:

- The size of the enterprise.
- The industry it operates in.
- The degree of regulation it is subject to.

For example, if you look at a very large enterprise in a heavily regulated industry such as a bank, with operations in more than one country, that enterprise will most likely need a sizeable security organization. This hypothetical bank might need:

- A Chief Security Officer.
- Security executives in global regions such as Europe, Asia, and the Americas who understand the regulations and laws that impact those areas.
- Teams of managers and personnel to oversee and perform risk mitigation activities such as:
    - Fraud investigations.
    - Access control and physical security.
    - Video monitoring.
    - Data and information security.
    - Customer protection.

A smaller or less regulated organization, like a small local retail chain, might need a far less complex security structure, with fewer layers of management and possibly shared resources with more general technical duties across the various types of security activity – perhaps a security director and team of generalists.

14.3.1 Defining Strategic Leadership Roles

As we described above, the security department may range from something as small and straightforward as security manager with a few tacticians reporting to her, to a whole suite of vice presidents, directors, and their subordinates, reporting into a chief security officer (CSO).

What matters most here is that strategic security management and direction are provided from the top of the department. At the same time, different areas of technical and tactical responsibility are structured with personnel who have the skillsets to carry out the day-to-day work and tasks, which fall into the security department's scope of responsibility.

Once the reporting structure for the security organization has been defined, and the initial scope of the program has been laid out, the roles lower down the operational ladder will become more clearly defined. These roles could be defined by:

1. Responsibilities:
   (for example, protecting information and systems, conducting investigations, or creating building crisis management plans).
2. Assets that need protection:
   (for example, information, people, or facilities).
3. Geographies:
   (for example, different regions with different regulations or security requirements).

As the roles and responsibilities get deeper into the department structure, they also get more defined and more specific – more tactical – as do the associated functions and skill sets.

In Part 5 of this book, we will delve deeply into the most common tactical disciplines of a security program and discuss how they fit into the ESRM paradigm. For now, we will simply say that the security realm is a complex one with many jobs. Some are similar and can be performed by a security generalist. For example, a physical security installer should easily be able to install either a camera, a door plate, or a badge reader. That same installer, however, might find it difficult to also do a forensic investigation on a compromised computer terminal. Both of those activities are ones that the security department could perform in the mitigation of enterprise security risks. But it's unlikely that a single person would hold both of those responsibilities.

14.3.1.1 Aligning Tactical Skillsets with Strategic Management

Although we can clearly see that it's extremely difficult for a single person to have all the technical security expertise needed to mitigate every type of enterprise security risk, in ESRM, that does not mean that they need to have entirely separate reporting structures in the department.

When looking at security from a strategic, risk-based view, functions at the tactical level that are very different can roll up quite easily under the same strategic role. Why? Because the process of managing risk, and understanding risk management are similar, no matter what the tactical mitigation plan might be at the end of the process.

As an example, look at the skills needed to protect a warehouse full of valuable inventory versus a server full of valuable data. An effective set of tools to protect the warehouse might include access control, alarm, and closed-circuit television (CCTV) systems. The *physical* security specialist would need a specific set of tactical skills, including:

- A technical understanding of the systems.
- The ability to develop and manage an implementation plan (for example, covering camera locations and communication topographies).
- An understanding of how the system would work.

Similarly, an IT security professional tasked with protecting a server may use a firewall to protect the server and encryption for the data on the system. Those tasks require a very different set of skills:

- A technical understanding of the IT security systems.
- The ability to develop and manage an implementation plan (network topographies/encryption key structures).
- An understanding of how the system would work.

These skills are very different. They are also specific and tactical.

However, neither of these very specific skill sets, or any that may be required at a tactical level, are needed to *lead* the security organization, or to manage any area of it at the strategic level. The ability to administer a CCTV system or implement data encryption does not matter at the strategic management level. What *does* matter is an understanding of risks and risk mitigation. An understanding that both cameras and data encryption exist as risk mitigation options to prevent loss of a valued asset is more critical at the strategy level than having the specific technical skill yourself.

The tactical details of the internal structure will depend heavily on your enterprise environment. Our goal is to show that in a risk-based management structure, your options are far more flexible than in the more traditional task-oriented model.

Executive Job Titles: CSO, CISO, or Both?
One area of security organization where things can get very complicated – and very sensitive – is with job titles and the associated responsibilities.

An especially significant point of contention among security professionals today is about the role of the Chief Security Officer (CSO) versus that of the Chief Information Security Officer (CISO).

In most cases, an enterprise with a well-designed ESRM program will not need both, because both individuals have the same basic set of responsibilities. Their role is to provide strategy and execution in protecting the enterprise's assets and making well-informed decisions about security risks and risk tolerances. The only significant exception we have seen to this best practice would be an enterprise that is so complex that it needs a "C-level" information security strategist – a CISO who reports to the CSO.

14.3.1.2 Transitioning Yourself from a Tactical Practitioner to a Strategic Leader
Understanding the ESRM philosophy and applying it to the management of any security risk is critical, and it will become more critical as you climb the ranks, becoming less of a tactical security practitioner and more of a strategic security professional.

At the most senior, most strategic levels, what matters most is aligning the enterprise's security philosophy, strategy, and execution with its business mission. If you are managing security risks using ESRM principles, one philosophy will guide the business through discussions of risk and mitigation, whatever type of risk is being considered and whatever type of asset is being protected.

At that senior level, what you need is not a set of technical or operational skills. It's a comprehensive understanding of the business, its assets, its mission, and its security risk tolerance levels, all of which will make it possible to govern the ESRM process. Those necessary business skills are the ones we are communicating throughout this book. These are what will serve as a foundation as you advance your career in security through ESRM.

Questions for the Security Practitioner
- "What different technical activities in my security organization could be managed as a group in response to a certain type of security risk?"
- "Do I see aspects of my security department that could be organized more effectively under a risk-based structure?"

Chapter Review

In Chapter 14, you learned how to look at and recommend the optimal reporting lines and internal security department structure, based on the needs of your specific enterprise and the need for the essential elements for successful security.

Looking Forward

In Chapter 15, we will begin Part 5 of the book, "Applying ESRM to Specific Security Disciplines." You will have a chance to look at topics such as cybersecurity, information security, investigations, physical security, workplace violence, threat management, BCM, and crisis management, and to review and discuss how these function as part of the ESRM model.

Practitioner steps to consider before moving on to Chapter 15:

✓ Consider how the current security structure might be optimized in an ESRM model.

Security Program Self-Assessment

In this self-assessment, you should think about the answer to the questions posed, and then see where your program is on the identified ESRM spectrum.

Question	Y/N	Is This ESRM?
In the overall enterprise, does your security program report to a department that provides the essential elements for security success?	☐Yes ☐No	**NO**: If you feel that there are limits on the security function that occur due to incorrect reporting lines, then this is a suitable place to start your ESRM program. **PARTIAL**: If you have less than optimal reporting lines in your security structure, but use personal relationships in other areas to work around issues of authority, then you are part of the way to an ESRM implementation. **YES**: If you have a formal reporting structure that enables independence, authority, scope, and transparency inherently, one that is not due to personal influence, then you are practicing ESRM.

Questions for Discussion

1. What are some ways a security department might be structured to take advantage of strategic management of various technical disciplines, rather than just organizing according to discipline?
2. How can understanding risk and risk management help you in developing an optimal structure for your security department?

Learn More About It

For more about creating effective teams and teamwork for corporate change, see:

Burtles, J. (2016). Case study: Organic resilience at Rushmore Enterprises. *Principles and practice of business continuity: Tools and techniques*, 2nd Ed. Brookfield, CT: Rothstein Publishing, pp. 357-368.

Graham, J. & Kaye, D. (2006). Culture, strategy, performance, risk and business continuity. *A risk management approach to business continuity: Aligning business continuity with corporate governance*. Brookfield, CT: Rothstein Publishing, pp. 55-70.

Hiles, A. (2014). Group processes to develop consensus for the BCP: Collaborative and creative thinking. *Business continuity management: Global best practices*, 4th Ed. Brookfield, CT: Rothstein Publishing, pp. 401-406.

Part 5

An ESRM Approach to Tactical Security Disciplines

So far, you have explored ESRM at the general level. You have examined the essential components of an ESRM program and learned how to implement an overarching ESRM program and philosophy in your enterprise. In Part 5 of the book, it is time to go deeper take and take an in-depth look at some of the specific, tactical, disciplines of a security program.

In This Part:
- **ESRM and Investigations**
- **ESRM and Physical Security**
- **ESRM and Cybersecurity and Information Security**
- **ESRM and Workplace Violence and Threat Management**
- **ESRM and Business Continuity and Crisis Management**

15

ESRM and Investigations

Nothing is more basic to security than the investigation – the art and science of figuring out who did what, when, and where. Whether you are investigating a physical incident, a cyber incident, a threat, or anything else, investigations as a discipline is a central component of an enterprise security risk management (ESRM) program. But ESRM takes a different – and somewhat more expansive – view of this discipline from the one that most security professionals are used to. ESRM defines the investigation process, not just as a follow up to a security incident, but as an *integral part* of the risk-management cycle itself. It seeks an in-depth understanding of any security incident and the underlying reasons for it as the main driver of the investigative process, above simply finding out who did it. In ESRM, the investigation process is crucial to addressing and mitigating all present and future risks that stem from a security incident.

This chapter will help you to:
- Understand how security investigations align with and fit into the ESRM life cycle.
- Articulate the differences between traditional views of security investigations and the ESRM methodology.

15.1 How does the Investigations Discipline Fit in the ESRM Life Cycle?

As you conduct your investigation, every process and step fits into the ESRM cycle and should be expressed to your strategic partners as part of the overall paradigm when you discuss those investigations.

Investigations tie closely into the ESRM cycle in three phases.
1. As part of an *incident response*.
2. As a major component of *root cause analysis*.
3. As the foundation of ongoing *risk assessment*.

In a risk-based security management program, investigations are a key piece of the ongoing security life cycle (as shown in Figure 15-1), not merely standalone tasks. They are the way that you and your team find new or previously unknown risks; they are how you work with your strategic partners to uncover issues that exist in their functional areas; and they are how you provide recommendations back to the business about additional mitigation plans that could be put into place.

Figure 15-1. Investigations are part of improving and advancing the ESRM program.

In today's complex enterprise, it is not enough to see an investigation as the process of uncovering the facts which lead to a wrongdoer being caught and punished. Often, just catching and punishing one bad actor most likely will not solve, or even identify, the *underlying* problems that led to the wrongdoing.

Employees and others commit bad acts in a broad range of ways, and for an even broader range of reasons. A security incident may occur because flaws in a process make it possible for an employee to cover up bad acts, or it might happen because of a lack of defined protocols for stopping it, or it could even occur because part of the enterprise environment allows (or does not sufficiently discourage) questionable behavior.

An investigation that does not truly dig deeper to identify the underlying risks and conditions – the root cause – that made an incident possible, will not further the purpose of mitigating it and preventing future incidents. The true role of an investigation in a risk-based security program is identifying the risk that caused an incident, and further, finding residual risk that is impacting the enterprise outside of set risk tolerances.

Questions for the Security Practitioner
- "When performing an investigation, do I continue to check the driving forces behind the violation happening, after I have identified the person responsible?"
- "If so, do I do it every time?"

The investigation process, its resources, and tools, should be part of security risk mitigation planning from the beginning, because risks that are within tolerance and do not have mitigation plans in place, or residual, new, or unknown risks, will always leave some exposure. The ESRM investigation is the method that we use to find out how those residual exposures became incidents, and to assist the business in reevaluating the tolerances and potential new risk mitigation options.

15.2 An Investigation is an Incident Response
As shown in Figure 15-2, in the ESRM paradigm, a security investigation is simply another type of incident response. It is a response to a security risk that has materialized into an incident, and that has had an impact on the asset it is associated with. Having an investigations program in place can provide risk mitigation for a wide number of risks to essentially all enterprise assets and serve all risk stakeholders. It is a shared resource that can protect the enterprise by responding to specific incidents of risk impact, determining the cause, and recommending ways to stop recurring impacts.

Many practitioners who do investigations on a regular basis may not *automatically* think of the investigation as part of an incident response. That is because over time, we have come to think of "incident response" as related to a single point in

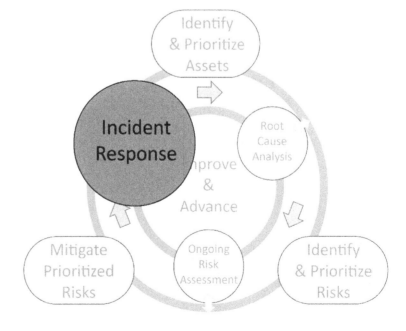

Figure 15-2. Investigations are part of overall incident response.

225

time, as a process that occurs at the same time as the incident itself. But in ESRM, the idea of incident response is holistic, and encompasses everything the security team does in response to a security incident to mitigate both the immediate impact, and future risk exposure to the enterprise.

In ESRM, whatever the incident – a theft, a data breach, a workplace violence incident, or an earthquake – the tactical risk mitigation tasks typically assigned for the security team to carry out are:

1. To stop or lessen the damage being done (immediate response examples would be a physical security action, such as locking down a facility during a civil disturbance or a logical response of blocking network traffic during a Distributed Denial of Service (DDoS) attack).

2. In follow up, once the immediate impact has ceased, a strategic investigation is another response to a security incident which has harmed the enterprise. This includes determining the facts of what happened, and discovering the underlying cause of the incident – tying the investigation to the overall ESRM cycle.

15.3 An Investigation is the Source of Root Cause Analysis

Investigations also tie into the ESRM cycle as the phase of root cause analysis, as seen in Figure 15-3.

The investigation process in ESRM should always include a formal postmortem report. The purpose of the postmortem is to document the root causes as identified in the investigation, with the goal of mitigating potential further risk. That is why the security investigations discipline ties into the cycle at the root-cause analysis phase.

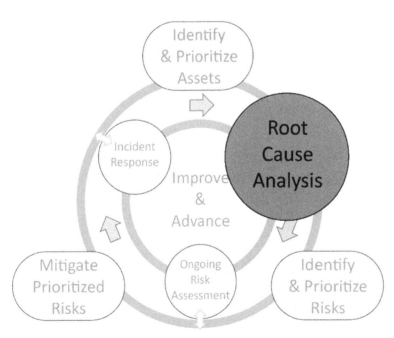

Figure 15-3. Investigations are a part of root cause analysis.

In the rare event that a formal postmortem analysis is not necessary (for example, a security case is so simple that the facts of "who did what" are really all that is necessary), it is still crucial for *process consistency* that the reasoning for conducting or not conducting a formal root cause analysis is documented briefly in the incident report, even though there will be no full post-mortem.

If root cause analysis is not at least considered, *even if it is deemed not needed for a specific case*, the investigation process is incomplete and will lack consistency, which can lead back to the investigation function being perceived merely as a task, and not part of the overall ESRM role of managing security risk to the organization.

15.3.1 Identifying Root Causes Through Security Investigations

In Chapter 9, we discussed some of the elements of *root cause investigation*, seeking the underlying causes of an incident or condition. Whether an investigator is working in a risk-based environment or in a task-based environment, the skills and techniques of investigating are the same. However, there are crucial differences in an ESRM investigation that you will want to consider.

15.3.1.1 Preparing for a Risk-Based Investigation

There is a slightly different focus in the ESRM investigation preparation phase than what you may be used to. From the outset, the investigation is not only focused on determining *who* was involved in the incident, but also what assets, business processes, existing security risk mitigation plans and tactics, and previously identified risks were involved. In an ESRM investigation, there are a few fundamental questions that are always at the forefront of the investigator's mind (in addition to the questions about who was involved or at fault). An investigation in a risk-based environment looks at the incident to determine if it is related to a previously identified and mitigated risk; looks to see if the risk has changed since it was identified; and asks whether the asset owners and stakeholders are still the same. Questions that can help with this pre-investigative step are:

- What asset and stakeholders were impacted?
- Was the risk to the assets known?
- Has the risk changed?
- Is there residual risk?
- Did mitigation tactics exist and fail? Or not exist?
- Are new treatments needed to mitigate any potential impact of new or residual risks?

In the ESRM investigation, a substantial proportion of time is spent on discovering the background of the environment and business ecosystem in which the incident occurred. This allows the investigator to go into the rest of the investigation fully prepared to find not only the accountable party (if there is one), but also – and with equal (or greater) importance – the underlying systems or issues that created the environment in which the incident could take place. This leads into the next ESRM cycle phase of ongoing risk assessment (which we will cover in Section 15-5).

> **ESRM Investigation Case Study: A Theft Investigation**
> As an example of the process of a risk-based investigation, we will look at a simple incident of unauthorized entry.
>
> The scenario: In an engineering lab, a critical piece of research has disappeared and has presumably been stolen.
>
> **Step 1. Preparation – Discover the Existing Risk Environment**
> Professional investigators, in preparing for the investigation, will *already* be asking questions like:
> - What are the assets that were stolen?
> - How was the item taken stored?
> - Who had access to the room?
> - Who physically entered the room during the time frame?
> - How is the room secured?
> - Is there camera coverage?
> - And more…

Adding the ESRM dynamic to the process would bring in risk paradigm components such as:
- Who are the ESRM asset owner and other risk stakeholders?
- What is the impact of the theft on the asset owner and other risk stakeholders?
- Are there any previously implemented security risk mitigation activities for that asset?
- What are the business protocols and procedures around the asset, such as accessing and storage?

These risk and business process discovery questions are just as critical to the preparation of the investigation in the ESRM paradigm as the questions surrounding the logistics and mechanics of this theft.

Step 2. Preparation – Plan Interviews
An investigation would probably plan many interviews in a case surrounding the theft of sensitive information. The investigator would likely:
- Interview witnesses to determine the surrounding case facts.
- Interview potential suspects to determine their culpability.
- Interview related persons who might have relevant input.

The ESRM investigation will *also* incorporate additional interviews, again focused mainly on risks, and impacts to stakeholders. At minimum in this case, the investigator would:
- Interview business process owners to fully understand the procedures involved.
- Interview asset owners and stakeholders to understand impact.

15.3.1.2 During an ESRM Investigation

As the ESRM investigation is proceeding and the investigator is interviewing witnesses, suspects, persons with relevant information, and other people, there are additional, distinct types of questions that they will ask. Beyond ascertaining the case facts, these questions ensure that the investigation meets the goals of the risk-focused program. Some examples might be:

- Has anything concerning the asset changed since the last time the asset in question was identified, valued, and prioritized for risk tolerance, assessment, and possible treatment?
  - Has the asset become more critical or less critical to the enterprise?
  - Has the risk tolerance on the asset changed due to the incident?
  - Is the asset owner the same? Have risk owners changed?
- Was the enterprise or the security organization already aware of the risk that this incident could occur?
  - Were all the correct asset owners and stakeholders aware of the risk and the associated mitigation tactics?
  - Did strategic partners understand their role (if any) in the mitigation plan?
  - Could an awareness and education effort help mitigate any future impact from the same risk?
  - Could data analytics shed more light on additional or changed risk impacts?
  - Was the known risk accepted (not mitigated)?
    - If Accepted, has the risk changed since the original assessment?
      - Does this incident change the priority of the risk?
    - If Mitigated, did the plan function as intended?
      - Has residual risk been discovered through investigation?
      - Could existing mitigation tactics be changed or new ones established to mitigate the risk?

- Is this a new risk brought about by environmental changes?
  - Does this change require a new risk assessment?
  - Has the risk acceptance posture or tolerance level changed?
- Have enterprise priorities changed that could change the criticality of this risk?

These questions are designed to push deep into the causes of the incident and find how known or unknown risk played a part. This difference in focus requires a different attitude on the part of the investigator. It also requires a much-heightened level of awareness about the enterprise, its risk tolerances, and the business drivers that might allow it to accept some level of risk.

The result will allow the security team to guide the business owners through a recommendation process on how they might be better able to mitigate impact from this or a similar risk in the future. Part of transitioning to an ESRM program is ensuring that your strategic partners understand the role of the investigation itself as part of the ESRM cycle of risk response and ongoing mitigation. This allows them to understand that not only will the investigator be providing the facts of who might have perpetrated an incident, but will also be provide recommendations for further risk mitigation that they can consider at the end of the process.

ESRM Investigation Case Study: A Theft Investigation
Continuing our look at a simple incident of unauthorized entry, we have already walked through preparing for the investigation with these steps:
- **Step 1. Preparation – Discover the Existing Risk Environment**
- **Step 2. Preparation – Plan Interviews**
In this phase, we will discuss:
- **Step 3. Execution – The Investigation and Details**
We know that any professional investigator would automatically check who had access to the room, who went in and out and when, look at video surveillance recordings, interview potential suspects, and so on. The investigation report might read, "John S. accessed the room at 8:45 pm. and is the only person to have done so on the day the item went missing." Clearly, this implies that John S. is the prime suspect in the missing research.

That information and identification of the likely suspect is also critical to an ESRM investigation. But in ESRM, it is just as important for the investigator to ask other types of questions to identify risks, root causes, and make mitigation recommendations in the postmortem report. The perpetrator of the incident is part of the risk picture, but not the only part. Other risk factors most likely exist as well.

For the case under discussion here, the investigator might find risks that could have recommended mitigations. For example:
- Question from investigator:
  - "If many people have access to the room, what is the business purpose for that?"
- Answer from business function:
  - "The department finds the process of requesting access control updates burdensome; so they just request access for all new hires."
- Possible recommendations in postmortem report:
  - Does security need to educate the department on the importance of access control?
  - Does security need to make access change requests easier?
  - Does the department merely need to understand the process better so it is not as difficult?

229

    ○   Who is accepting this risk and was that decision made by the right asset owners and stakeholders?

Investigators who have not worked in an ESRM environment before may sometimes feel like these questions are intrusive to their strategic partner. But, if the role of security in the ESRM model is accepted by the business and communicated clearly and consistently throughout all security interactions, then the purpose and intent of those questions will be clear and accepted as part of the investigator's role.

When a security professional asks risk-based questions like these, the incident postmortem report will consider issues beyond whether John S. was the guilty party. It might consider whether he – and others – had any business being in the lab at all. It might consider what mitigation measures, from heightened access controls to improved background checks to better security for specific assets, could be appropriate to recommend to the risk owners.

15.3.2 Reporting Root Causes After a Security Investigation

The last step in the ESRM investigation process is to develop the postmortem report. This is more than just a fact-based incident report. This report identifies all the discovered underlying root causes, and then makes recommendations for the business to mitigate the impact from the same or similar risks in the future. This report is the driving force behind the third place in the ESRM cycle when investigations have the most impact – ongoing risk assessment.

15.4 Investigations Drive Ongoing Risk Assessment

In the ESRM cycle, the ongoing risk assessment phase (see Figure 15-5) of the investigative process is to examine risk and determine what, if any, mitigation plans should be applied against it.

The follow-up questions in proceeding through the ESRM process are:

- Is there residual risk?"
- What is the root cause?
- Could this happen again?"

The root cause analysis exists to find residual risk. This risk must then be assessed in partnership with the asset and risk owners to determine any potential mitigation plans that the business might choose to enact. In many cases in task-based security programs, investigators do push further into these questions, but as we discussed previously, it is the *consistency* of having these follow-up questions *always* be part of the investigation process that truly embeds the investigation in the ESRM cycle and paradigm.

Figure 15-5. Investigations are a part of ongoing risk assessment.

230

Without consistent application of the ESRM principles, without consistently providing your strategic partner with risk follow-up and recommendations, the role of the investigation in the risk-based paradigm could become clouded, as strategic partners would not know what to consistently expect from an investigation.

> **ESRM Investigation Case Study: A Theft Investigation**
> Continuing our look at a simple incident of unauthorized entry, we have already discussed:
> - **Step 1. Preparation – Discover the Existing Risk Environment**
> - **Step 2. Preparation – Plan Interviews**
> - **Step 3. Execution – The Investigation and Details**
> In this phase, we will discuss:
> - **Step 4. Closure – The Postmortem Report**
> In the investigation phase of this example, the investigator determined that, "John S. accessed the room at 8:45 pm and is the only person to have done so on the day the item went missing."
>
> In an investigative interview, John S. admitted to taking the research.
>
> This critical piece of information was detailed in the investigation report and given to Human Resources (HR), who followed their own processes and determined that the company response would be to terminate John's employment.
>
> Additionally, in working with the asset and business owners, the investigator also determined that John S. had no true purpose to be in the room, and he determined that the business processes for granting access to this area with very sensitive information did not explicitly require a sign-off from the asset owner. The investigator noted this in a postmortem report and recommended creating a stricter policy on who could and could not gain access to that specific room. The report was distributed to the asset owner and other impacted stakeholders, who signed-off on the report and acknowledged the possible need for a new process. They determined that they would consider whether they would implement a new process at the beginning of the next quarter.

15.4.1 Postmortem Reporting and Responsibilities

When first transitioning to an ESRM model, the postmortem reporting process can be confusing in one way. The *identification* of root causes and residual security risk is the job of the investigations team. *Enforcing* a risk mitigation on the business is not.

15.4.1.1 Security Role and Responsibilities

In ESRM, for every investigation, the investigator keeps working with the strategic partners in the business to identify controls that potentially could be put in place to lessen the likelihood of the incident happening again. These might include an audit of who actually needs access to the research lab, or putting video cameras inside the room (rather than just monitoring the door) to provide both a deterrent and an investigative tool. If the investigation discovered that the employee had a conviction for a similar offense in a previous job, security could work with HR to identify and close any gaps in the background check process.

If the postmortem identifies a gap in security procedure as a root cause, it is appropriate for the security team to acknowledge the gap; to make recommendations on how to close it; to work with the business to decide whether the recommendations are appropriate; to appoint an owner of the action plan; and to set a time to check back in to see whether that accepted business plan is now in place and whether the risk is being managed within enterprise tolerance.

Questions for the Security Practitioner
- "What are some reasons employees might try to steal from, or otherwise harm, the enterprise I am tasked with protecting?"
- "What could I do to develop a deeper understanding of the employees in the enterprise who are not security stakeholders – not just to understand who might commit bad acts, but also to understand why?"

Analyzing the gap is an effective way to show management and leadership in how to handle these recommended mitigation plans. If the proper and authorized stakeholder makes the decision to *not* address the known vulnerability, proper documentation should be incorporated into the report. As we mentioned above, these reports are part of the regular reporting up to the security council. If the council, as the risk guidance body, sees a risk decision in one of the reports made by the authorized stakeholder that they disagree with, it is the role of the council to discuss with the stakeholder why they feel that the mitigation actions in place are not meeting the security risk management needs of the enterprise.

15.4.1.2 Strategic Partner Role and Responsibilities

Clearly, it is not feasible for an enterprise to identify and prepare for *every* risk, and to plan to eliminate them all. While the goal is ongoing risk assessment, that does not mean all assessed risks end up with associated mitigating activities. That is why your strategic partners must always be involved in ESRM decisions. Sometimes a risk cannot be mitigated, and gaps in protection must be accepted.

A hypothetical example of that case would be attempting to prevent abuse of high-level network access credentials by simply not allowing anyone to have them. There is no way for the business to function in that scenario. That mitigation tactic is unrealistic and unworkable because people would not be able to do their jobs. It is an extreme example, but it makes the critical point that sometimes risks simply must exist to allow the business to achieve its goals – and sometimes those access credentials will end up exposing the company to risk that it must ultimately access to get the mission accomplished.

It is at these times, even when the root cause of a problem has been identified, that gaps exist that could be exploited. However, after ongoing assessments are accepted by the business, the mitigation tactic of an incident response plan and team is required. (For this reason, "Improve and Advance" is a circle within a circle.)

15.5 A Deeper Look at the Role of Investigations in ESRM

A risk-based approach to investigations does not change the basic steps of investigating nor the tools, techniques, and technologies that are used. The main difference that we see in ESRM, is that the investigator's role is broader than in the traditional notion of investigations. In ESRM, that role is tied into the ESRM life cycle to continually improve and advance the enterprise program. The investigator is called upon to be much more aware of the overall impact of any investigation findings to the department(s) involved, and to the enterprise.

15.5.1 Comparing Traditional and ESRM Investigations

We will compare a traditional and ESRM investigation by examining a real-world case study to illustrate the differences between the approaches. The case centers around a problem that is familiar to most security professionals: employee theft.

A Traditional Security Investigation: The Case of the Missing Computer Parts

Steve R., a security manager with a nationwide retail chain in the UK, was tasked with investigating a recurring series of thefts that were reported by the IT desktop support group. For six months, obsolete computer hardware slated for recycling or disposal – monitors, keyboards, desktop computers – had been disappearing.

Steve was assigned to conduct investigations into these thefts – four investigations over the six months. Each time, the investigation led to a warehouse worker who was stealing the computer parts. Each time, the thief was either selling the parts, or was giving them away to friends or family. In each case, Steve referred the investigation results to HR. All four guilty employees were quietly fired.

From Steve's point of view – and from a traditional security point of view – the investigations were a success, and he had fulfilled his responsibilities as an investigator. He did everything he was instructed to do, he did it in a thorough, fair, and impartial manner, and he achieved the goal he set out to achieve, to find the perpetrators of the theft.

But not everybody in the enterprise is pleased with the results.

The warehouse manager, Jennifer G., had a new set of problems on her hands, and from her point of view, these were more serious than the loss of some soon-to-be-scrapped motherboards.

There was high employee turnover in the warehouse. Some experienced employees were being fired, their replacements needed to be trained, and newly trained employees were being lost as well. This was slowing down the operations. Because the cause of the firings was not announced to the general group, employee morale was poor, and it was getting worse. The company's retail outlets started complaining to corporate headquarters about the time it took to get orders filled. And Steve was not the one taking the blame for it all. Jennifer was.

It is important to recognize in this case that Steve really *did* do everything right, at least within the limits of the traditional view of security investigations. He conducted a proper investigation in all four cases, reviewing access logs, interviewing witnesses, and checking video evidence. He caught four bad actors, and the company fired them. But in this case, the traditional view is not adequate to the situation, because his investigations have left the warehouse manager and the people left working for her unhappy. It also left the company's operations with a loss of work capacity. From the point of view of the warehouse manager and the company, the result *was not* entirely the right one. The problem in this case is not with Steve or his investigation, but with understanding the role that the investigation played in the overall scenario and how the success of that investigation was defined.

The Warehouse Investigation: The ESRM Way

What if we look at the same story through an ESRM lens? Here is one way in which it could have come out differently.

In this version, Steve began his investigation after the IT desktop support manager brought the first theft to his attention for an investigation. He still did all the "right" things – checking evidence, looking for witnesses, etc., and he still found the guilty party who was selling the used parts and referred him to HR for discipline.

But now there is a difference. As is called for in the ESRM model, he went on to investigate the factors that led to the theft – the root causes of the incident that we talked about earlier – and he uncovered a hidden problem in the desktop support group's processes.

The unwanted computer parts were not properly tracked for disposal. They were taken out of the asset management, taken to the holding area for donation, and then they were left there until there was a sufficient collection to warrant a pickup by the charity that recycled and repurposed the hardware. The IT group was not managing the items as "assets" anymore and simply assumed that the warehouse team would keep them until they were picked up. That made it incredibly easy for the thief to simply walk out the door with any item he saw that he thought he could sell.

With that root cause identified, Steve took one additional investigation step that is a critical part of the ESRM process. At the end of the first case, after the findings are given to HR, and after HR determined that the course of action they want to take was to fire the employee, Steve then worked with his other strategic partners on the investigation – warehouse, IT, and asset management – to write up a postmortem report outlining the root cause of the thefts and pointing out the lack of adequate controls. The postmortem report recommended that the company's IT organization develop a tracking and management system for assets slated for disposal.

15.5.1.1 One Successful Outcome

The above scenario outlines one *possible* outcome from a change in the focus of the investigation. The difference between the traditional model and the ESRM model is especially clear in the example as we rewrote it the ESRM way. In both cases, an investigation was conducted and a guilty party was identified, referred to HR, and fired. But the ESRM investigation did not stop there. The investigator, as a formal outcome of the investigation, was required to determine the root cause of the problem and recommend measures to keep it from happening again.

The asset owners in our ESRM example were left with a choice to implement the new controls to mitigate additional risk of theft, or not, as their tolerance for additional impact dictates. If they chose to not implement the mitigation recommendations, a documented risk acceptance would happen, in line with ESRM program recommendations. At that point, the risks are identified and transparent and the investigation process concludes.

The success of the investigation is not measured by stopping additional thefts, but by the process of managing the risk. Of course, stopping the theft is important, and if the goal for the asset owners is to eliminate the risk of a similar theft occurring in the future, then the risk mitigation recommendations would be accepted during the postmortem decision-making process, and the report would indicate that. The new process would be implemented by the IT group, as the owner of the mitigation activity. Future measurements of success by averting more theft would be based on whether that process was working.

15.5.1.2 All Successful Outcomes May Not Look the Same

If we take this example one step further and dig deeper into the ESRM way of doing things, we can imagine another way this case could have turned out that might have the same fact pattern as the first, and the same less-than-happy ending, but would ALSO be a successful outcome in ESRM:

1. If Steve had done the same investigation and made the same root cause/policy change recommendations that he suggested above at the end of that first investigation, and…
2. The asset management and warehouse leaders received the postmortem report, considered it, and determined that the mitigation was *not in the best interests* of the operations, and decided to not make the changes, then…
3. As a result, Steve had to still do three additional investigations, and still found the same root cause each time, and three more people were still fired, and the warehouse manager was still unhappy about the situation.

Despite people being unhappy with the ultimate outcome, this is *still* a successful ESRM outcome for Steve. Why? Because for each investigation, he is fulfilling his role, which is guiding the business through a security risk management decision-making process:
1. Identifying the root cause.
2. Suggesting mitigations to the risk and asset owners.
3. Educating all stakeholders in the risk they are accepting.
4. Documenting the acceptance of the risk by authorized stakeholders.

Steve is doing his job, and doing it properly and well. Eventually, if the business decides that the impact had gotten too great and decided to act on his risk mitigation suggestions, then that would also be a decision made by the correct people – the business owners.

Questions for the Security Practitioner
- "Have I ever been involved in an investigation that seemed to be causing problems, instead of solving them? Did my security organization or I change anything to prevent that from happening again?"
- "When I investigated security incidents, have I tried to understand why they happened, or have I been satisfied to figure out who was responsible and report that person to management?"

15.5.2 The ESRM Difference

As mentioned above, in the investigations discipline, the main difference between the traditional view and the ESRM view is not in the *act* of investigating. Understanding security's role in the environment and how the investigation process integrates with the end-goal of an investigation in the risk-based paradigm drives the continual improvement of security risk management by identifying new or residual risk.

15.5.2.1 A Difference in Focus: Fact-Finding Versus Risk Identification

The focus of a traditional investigation is to first uncover the facts of the case and then present them to a decision-maker who will determine what should be done with those facts. Typically, in a business organization, this decision centers on what will happen to the person under investigation. Whether the decision-maker is the security practitioner, the HR or legal organization, or the employee's manager, the traditional focus remains the same: Find the facts and report them to the people who need them. Clearly, there are also times when investigations in the more traditional model investigate underlying causes and make security recommendations. However, the difference is in consistency of focus and consistency in postmortem reporting, which involves the asset owners and risk stakeholders who are impacted.

In ESRM, an investigation into an incident, whether it is an employee theft, a case of workplace violence, or a data breach, always has a more far-reaching purpose, responsibility, and focus. An ESRM investigator consistently is tasked to go past finding the bad actor, to then identify a root cause. Then the investigator must work with the business and risk owners further to develop and recommend potential risk mitigation measures to the strategic partner who owns the asset which was impacted by the incident, and thus avoid additional future impact from that same risk.

Questions for the Security Practitioner
- "Does my investigations program consistently investigate root causes of the incident as a matter of standard practice? Why or why not?"
- "Have I ever performed an investigation that had a clear root cause, but had no engagement from the impacted department to address the root cause?"
- "Throughout each investigation, is the role of the investigation and investigator well understood?"
- "What are the goals of the investigation? The investigator? How does it tie to the overall strategy and goals of the security department in an ESRM environment?"

15.5.2.2 A Difference in Goals – Accountability versus Risk Mitigation

Another fundamental difference between more traditional security investigations and the ESRM view is that there is a very different approach to accountability. Accountability – holding someone responsible for an incident – is often central to the traditional view. It is another aspect of the traditional model that can cause frustration for practitioners, as we discuss in the "think about it" section below.

In an ESRM investigation, by contrast, the goal of holding someone accountable for a given single incident is secondary to the process, at least from the point of view the security organization. Far more important, in most cases, is *identifying and mitigating the risks* that allowed the incident to occur in the first place. Although at the end of an investigation a wrongdoer might be punished, the goal of an ESRM investigation is not solely to hold accountable someone who has done something wrong. More importantly, the end goal is to determine whether the incident exploited a risk that needs to be referred to the risk owners and stakeholders for further mitigation.

> ***Think About It: How can the Traditional Investigation Focus and Goal Cause Security Frustration?***
> The focus on fact finding and identifying a wrongdoer in the traditional investigation model can lead to significant frustration on the part of the security practitioner. Why?
>
> Security investigators are highly skilled personnel. They take pride in what they do and when they perform an investigation, find the facts, and catch the person responsible, the next step in the minds of most investigators is: This person needs to face the consequences of their act. This is a natural extension of the traditional process and mindset, so much so that, as we have seen repeatedly in our careers, the security investigator or manager will wrap up the investigation by going to the human resources department or employee manager, not with a statement of fact such as "John G. has been misusing his company issued credit card against policy," but with a declaration of "John G. should be fired for fraud."
>
> This is where things become frustrating in the task-based model. Human resources or the employee manager may not want to fire John. There may be a host of good (or bad) reasons for this. Maybe John has been a model employee but fell on tough times; temptation led him to make one wrong decision, and the company wishes to give him another chance. Perhaps John is the top sales person in the department, and the

manager cannot stand the idea of losing him. We have even (sadly) seen cases where management was aware of multiple employees violating a policy and refused to fire one because that would lead to losing many other people for the same reason.

Whatever the reasons, in our careers we have heard over and over the lamentations of security personnel that they caught someone "red-handed" and the company has refused to fire them. They feel like all the work they put in was wasted because nothing tangible came of the process. This is naturally and very understandably frustrating for the investigator. However, the reasons for the frustration can be relieved by adopting an ESRM philosophy.

First, in ESRM, while the identification of the culprit is important, it is simply not the end of the process. The real goal is to find out how the incident occurred and identify the risk gap, which means the investigator does not stop at the point of identifying the wrongdoer and then wait for something to happen to that person. They move on to finding that root cause and working with the business to mitigate it. (Note: If the root cause lies completely with the culprit, not any *underlying* business risk, any choice to keep the individual employed should be escalated with a proper risk acceptance at a higher level. This is a necessary part of the ESRM process and a significant security responsibility).

Second, once the ESRM philosophy is embraced, and the role of the security practitioner is truly internalized as *manager of risk*, (not decision-maker responsible for the ramifications of an authorized business decision), the security investigator can rest assured that they have done their job and their work was not wasted. They have rightly educated the company on a risk that exposes the enterprise to harm. That is work they can feel good about, whether the business chooses to act on the awareness or not. The success is in carrying out their role appropriately.

Chapter Review

In Chapter 15, you learned the differences between the traditional view of security investigations and the ESRM model; the importance of risk-based security investigations targeted at understanding the impact on the whole enterprise of a security incident and the associated investigation; and how security investigations are part of the ESRM cycle (See Figure 15-5).

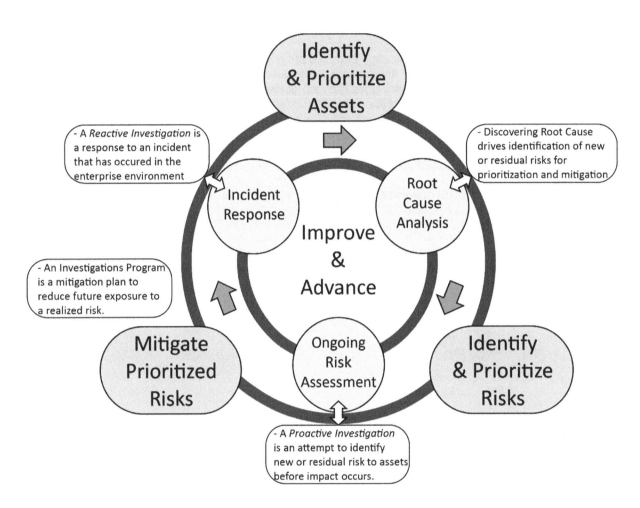

Figure 15-5. Investigations and the ESRM Cycle – A Review.

Looking Forward

In Chapter 16, we will discuss what may be the most "traditional" security discipline of all – physical security.

We will look at ways that the traditional model of physical security is inadequate to address the threats and risks of a changing world, and will consider how a risk-based model can improve physical security.

Practitioner steps to consider before moving on to Chapter 16:
- ✓ What internal and external resources are available that can help me better understand my enterprise's security investigation needs?
- ✓ Are there aspects of my enterprise that make certain approaches to investigations appropriate or inappropriate, for example, the regulatory environment?

Security Program Self-Assessment

In this self-assessment, you should think about the answer to the questions posed, and then see where your program is on the identified ESRM spectrum.

Question	Y/N	Is This ESRM?
Does your security program perform and document root causes of security incidents?	☐Yes ☐No	**NO**: If you do not perform any postmortem or root cause analysis on security incidents, then this is a suitable place to start your ESRM program. **PARTIAL**: If you sometimes perform a root cause analysis, or do so all the time, but without a formal process, or do so and do not share the results with the business, then you are part of the way to an ESRM implementation. **YES**: If you have a formal postmortem incident reporting process to identify root causes of incidents, which you share with impacted stakeholders, and use for ongoing risk mitigation planning, then you are practicing ESRM.

Questions for Discussion

1. Under what circumstances are postmortem reports most appropriate as part of the wrap-up of an investigation? When might a postmortem report be unnecessary? As a security practitioner, how can you show your strategic partner the value of the root cause analysis if they feel that it is unimportant?
2. Why is it especially important that the security investigations processes and procedures be transparent to your strategic partners? How might you benefit from your partners understanding more about the processes of an investigation?
3. How might different members of a security council react to an investigation into wrongdoing in another part of the enterprise? In their own part of the enterprise?

Learn More About It

For further reading about investigations:

American National Standards Institute (ANSI). (2015). *Investigations*. Alexandria, VA: ANSI/ASIS. Available at https://www.asisonline.org/Standards-Guidelines/Standards/published/Documents/INV_ExecSummary.pdf

Association of Workplace Investigators (AWI). (2014, July). *Guiding principles for conducting workplace investigations.* Sacramento, CA: AWI. Available at https://www.aowi.org/assets/GuidingPrinciples/guiding%20principles%2020140707.pdf

Buckley, J. (2015, April 2). *Defining investigation management.* [Web log post]. Available at http://www.resolver.com/blog/defining-investigation-management-2/

Slater, D. (2010, January 25). *Internal investigations: The basics.* [Web log post]. Available at http://www.csoonline.com/article/2124800/investigations-forensics/investigations-forensics-internal-investigations-the-basics.html

For further reading about root cause analysis, see:

ABS Consulting. (2008*). Root cause analysis handbook: A guide to efficient and effective incident investigation* (3rd ed.). Brookfield, CT: Rothstein Publishing.

Forck F. (2016). *Cause analysis manual: Incident investigation method & techniques.* Brookfield, CT: Rothstein Publishing.

Rowe, C. (2017). *Simplifying cause analysis: A structured approach.* Brookfield, CT: Rothstein Publishing.

16

ESRM and Physical Security

Physical security is a foundational building block for all security activities. No matter what other mitigating controls the enterprise uses to manage security risk, if it fails to properly secure the physical environment, then it is missing a vital piece of the overall security framework. All the network security in the world cannot protect against one technician who props the data center door open to make it easier to get in and out, leaving the data exposed to theft or damage from a physical intrusion.

However, while physical security *is* a foundational protection, it is critical to understand it as one aspect of the overall enterprise risk security management (ESRM) program, which is performed as a mitigating response to identified enterprise security risk, not because it is "what security does." The tasks and activities of the physical security discipline fit easily within the ESRM paradigm, and in most programs, they are already aligned with ESRM principles, although possibly not thought of in that way. In this chapter, we will show that alignment and discuss how to ensure that your strategic partners understand it as well.

This chapter will help you to:
- Understand how the physical security discipline aligns with and fits into the ESRM life cycle.
- Communicate the difference between traditional views of physical security and the ESRM methodology.

16.1 How does the Physical Security Discipline Fit in the ESRM Life Cycle?

When many people – even many security professionals – think of security, the first thing that comes to mind is *physical* security. The traditional view of security is so physical-security-centric, in fact, that across the industry, physical security is often actually *called* "traditional security."

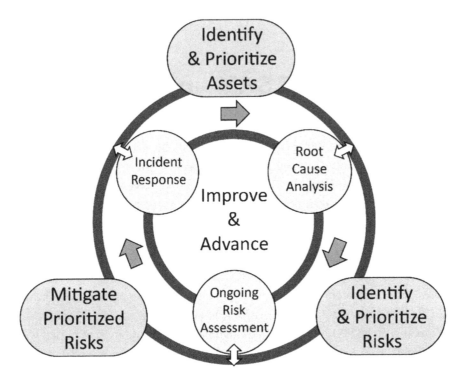

Figure 16-1. Physical security is part of mitigating risks and improving and advancing the program in the ESRM cycle.

However, as seen in Figure 16-1, physical security is a critical component that drives and is tied directly to the entire ESRM life cycle. In an ESRM program, all physical security activities are done to prevent or limit exposure to or impact from a risk. Additionally, while physical security is most often thought of as tied to the risk mitigation portion of ESRM, the skills and processes associated with *securing* tangible assets are, in fact, highly useful in *identifying* assets and risks as well, and are also a key piece of incident response.

16.2 Physical Security Activities Help Identify and Prioritize Assets

In earlier chapters, we discussed topics such as:

- Knowing your organization.
- Understanding where things are and who owns them.
- Recognizing tangible assets.

These activities are the beginning of building out the entire ESRM program, but are especially vital when looking at the physical security aspects of that risk-based program. Asset protection is at the very core of physical security, and assets cannot be protected, nor physical security risks mitigated, without understanding them completely.

Conveniently, identifying the assets that need to be protected with physical security risk mitigation actions can be quite straightforward, due to the expertise already in place in your security department. For example, physical security risk assessments are a baseline skill of most, if not all, physical security practitioners. An excellent way to use the existing expertise of tactical personnel in the ESRM model is to have those individuals from your team who perform facility assessments on a regular basis involved in this first ESRM life cycle step of identifying assets (shown in Figure 16-2).

Figure 16-2. Physical security processes can help identify enterprise assets.

A comprehensive physical security risk assessment program typically establishes a process for asset identification and potential impact to business. If already in place, the same assessment program can be leveraged to provide much of the asset and risk information about the enterprise that your program needs in the beginning. A few extra questions added to the beginning of the physical security assessment process can significantly enhance your initial understanding of all the assets in those facilities. To ensure that a risk assessment contributes additional information for the beginning of the ESRM cycle, add a few assessment categories/questions such as:

- Departments housed in a facility.
- Functions carried out in a campus or other multi-site area.
- Materials stored in a facility, and for what groups.
- Enterprise leaders located in a facility.
- Structures or external storage associated with a function.

These additional questions are aimed at identifying additional asset owners and stakeholders that may not be so apparent from the outset. They are, though, core elements of ESRM, aligned with specific parts of the paradigm.

Another aspect of the ESRM asset discovery step that can leverage existing physical security expertise and personnel is in understanding asset owners. Understanding all your asset risk stakeholders can require more effort than the task of simply identifying the assets. Here again, the physical security team has an advantage for your overall program, in that these are the people who most often interact with personnel and physical assets across the enterprise, and they are the ones in your group who can likely point you in the right direction of the person who is most responsible for risks to that asset. The step of identifying assets is the critical first piece of ESRM, and the cycle cannot move forward without it. Engaging your physical security team in the process provides a critical boost to that step.

16.3 Physical Security Activities Help to Identify and Prioritize Risks

The physical security discipline also plays a leading role in identifying and prioritizing risks to critical enterprise assets. While these are two steps, when it comes to the process of identifying the assets and risks, the processes already happening in the physical security discipline can make them more of a concurrent effort.

Figure 16-3. Physical security personnel have tactical skills to help identify risks to assets.

As we saw with the asset identification step, physical security risk assessments are also a core avenue though which security programs can begin to approach step two of the ESRM cycle (Figure 16-3), identifying and prioritizing risks. Physical security risk assessments tend to be formal questionnaire-type documents that allow each item being assessed to be scored on a matrix. Often the problem with this approach to assessments is that they are done in a "check the box" or "yes/no" template that can deny the physical security professional the ability to apply a more thoughtful approach to the asset being assessed.

But leveraging this process in the ESRM model can have a tremendous impact on this step of program development. With a slight tweak of the questionnaire about a risk-based approach which engages the physical security assessor fully in the ESRM process, the approach might be go from:

A. Using a template/questionnaire assessment that asks, "Does this facility have a security officer assigned?" Answering, "Yes" adds points in the template for a total *Security Score*.

to:

B. A deeper consideration that allows the security team to work with the business owner past that yes/no answer. This becomes a conversation. The building may have a security officer on site, but do the assets in that building require that level of security? Does the business owner of the assets agree? Was the officer put in place due to an impactful risk exposure?

The risk assessment process that engages the physical security professional early in the ESRM process helps to identify assets and risks, and helps to communicate the risk-based philosophy to your strategic partners through these types of conversations.

16.4 Physical Security Activities Serve to Mitigate Prioritized Risks

The activities typically associated with a physical security program are *most* closely tied to the ESRM cycle at the step of mitigating prioritized risks. In the ESRM paradigm, (as seen in Figure 16-4), a physical security control is primarily a mitigation plan or response to an identified risk exposure.

It could be a biometric reader placed on the door to a critical data center, to control physical access to sensitive data housed on company servers and thereby mitigate the risk of a data breach by a someone gaining unauthorized physical access. Or it could be a drop-safe installed in a grocery store, which ensures that significant amounts of cash are taken out of the registers and secured on a regular basis, thereby reducing exposure to the risk of theft. In both cases, it is all about understanding existing risks, recommending appropriate risk mitigation strategies, and finally implementing whatever accepted mitigation plan the business chooses so that it can protect the asset in question.

Every physical security task that any security department does (in an ESRM model or not) is, in some way, a mitigation plan that is in place to protect an asset from harm. Prior to moving into a risk-based program, it is possible that the security

Figure 16-4. Physical security is a risk mitigation activity.

department and personnel may not think of the activities they do as security risk mitigation. But in a risk-based program, it is critical to consistently think of all security activities as mitigating controls that are put in place to treat or respond to the exposure of an asset to security risk. If any activity performed by the security team cannot be tied to the protection of an asset as a mitigation plan that is *accepted by a risk stakeholder*, then it is not an activity that the security group should be doing. That does not mean we are advocating ceasing the activity, but it is necessary to find the assets and asset owners for whom the risk is being mitigated, and ensure that the business accepts that activity as an adequate risk response, to ensure a consistent risk-based approach to the program.

In Table 16-1, we outline some examples of security risk, and the physical security tasks or activities that are mitigating controls for those risks. Again, if the tasks are being done, with ESRM they must be done for a risk-based reason. As you can see in the table, a single physical security activity might mitigate several risks.

Table 16-1. Physical Security Activities are All Risk Mitigation Plans

Example Risk	Example Physical Security Mitigation Activity
Risk of Intrusion	• Access Control • Video Monitoring • Door Locks • Alarm and Monitoring • Security Officer Services
Risk of Theft	• Video Monitoring • Door Locks • Cash Handling Procedures • Loss Prevention Program • Environmental Design • Armored Vehicle Service
Risk of Violence	• X-Ray Inspections • Metal Detectors • Threat Management Programs • Video Monitoring • Security Officer Services
Risk of Business Disruption	• Security Officer Services • Perimeter Control • Mail Room Controls

16.4.1 Turning a Task into a Security Risk Mitigation Activity

A more complete example of how physical security activities are part of risk mitigation planning is with perimeter control. This can be accomplished with guards, fences, cameras, gates, or more likely a combination of all those. These represent a specific risk mitigation plan. That plan is in place to protect multiple assets from the threat of intrusion by unauthorized people. The security organization planned it, and is managing it, so it may seem like it *belongs* to the security organization. But the reality is that the risk belongs to almost every internal team, group, and organization inside that protected perimeter. In most enterprises, there is literally no one who is not impacted by perimeter control. As we mentioned above, when everyone is a stakeholder, it may seem almost as if nobody is. But when a task is stopped, (removing a security guard from that perimeter due to budget cuts, for example), when an impact occurs (a perimeter breach, or break-in), suddenly those stakeholders are very keenly interested in the risk impact that happened to their assets. That makes them risk stakeholders.

Because eventually, a time will come when the stakeholders *will* become interested in that risk impact, whether due to a change in the value of their asset, an impact that came about due to security activities being cut, or a rise in awareness due to some outside news story. Those stakeholders must understand from the beginning of the program that they have a role in physical security decision-making.

Questions for the Security Practitioner
- "Is my team already performing facility risk assessments? How could I leverage those into the overall ESRM cycle?"
- "What assets are already being protected with physical security activities? Do I have a registry of these that I could leverage to begin the asset identification process?"

16.5 Physical Security Provides First Line Incident Response

Moving into the center of the model, incident response is another step in the cycle where physical security fits into the ESRM model (Figure 16-5). Physical security is often thought of as the *primary* avenue of incident response. Alarms, security officers, security operations centers, monitoring cameras, these easily come to mind as security tasks related to a security incident response. The ESRM way of looking at things does not change that. However, as we mentioned in the previous section, the ability to do any of the typical security incident response activities is there because a risk mitigation control was enacted to put that response capacity in place.

One example where the ESRM step of incident response is tied directly to physical security is when the business has implemented a risk mitigation plan to treat intrusion risk by putting security officers in a facility.

Security officers are often the first line of incident response, whether they are helpful front desk attendants, tasked with reporting any incident or suspicious activity to a response group (as you might want in an office environment with a lower identified risk profile), or they could be an armed force, meant to intimidate and deter any potential bad actors (as you might expect to see in a facility with high value or dangerous research, such as a nuclear power plant).

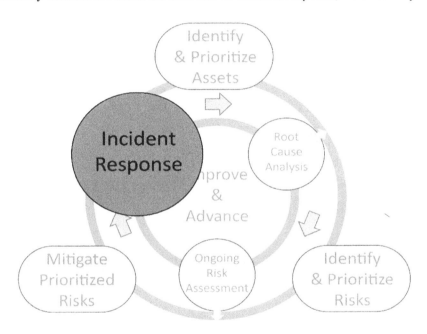

Figure 16-5. Physical security activities are tied closely to incident response.

Another example of a physical security incident response tactic is the use of alarms. Alarms can go off when a door is opened without authorization. Auto-locking mechanisms can be set up to be triggered by a panic button. Motion sensor triggers can issue an alert on movement in an area. Because alarms occur due to risk exposure being realized and turning into a risk incident, these are all forms of physical security that fall into the area of incident response.

16.6 Physical Security Provides Input to Ongoing Risk Assessment

The last place that ties physical security measures very tightly to the ESRM cycle is the step of ongoing risk assessment, as seen in Figure 16-6. Returning to our discussion of physical security risk assessment from earlier in the chapter, we can see how that activity can also help support an ongoing enterprise risk assessment. Risk assessments are a single snapshot in time, and as such must be repeated and updated on a regular (often annual, sometimes bi-annual, basis). The ongoing physical security risk assessment program is one obvious way that physical security activities help enable ongoing awareness and continual security program improvement.

Physical security risk assessments are not the only physical security actions that feed an ongoing risk assessment, though. Many physical security activities and tasks are designed to monitor and report on the physical environment of the enterprise.

- Cameras.
- Access control systems.
- Security Officers.
- Check in processes.
- Status alarms.
- Facility monitoring systems.

These and other physical security programs can be leveraged to monitor enterprise assets to continually identify new risks.

Figure 16-6. Physical security programs can be leveraged for ongoing risk assessment.

For example, if you have a camera system monitoring a parking lot, you can review video from that system on a regular basis to check for changes in traffic patterns, or to see if people are loitering in or near the lot. This can help identify new risks if you see that a significant increase in the number of people walking through the parking lot is correlated with an increase in car break-ins. You can then suggest further mitigating controls to the asset owner and business stakeholders for that parking lot. Monitoring and ongoing assessment is a natural extension of many of the physical security risk mitigation measures that your security department will put in place.

Questions for the Security Practitioner
- "Which ways could I leverage existing physical security functions to become more aware of risks that might be new or moving out of tolerance levels?"
- "What kinds of immediate incident response functions already exist in my enterprise?"

250

16.7 A Deeper Look at the Role of Physical Security in ESRM

The key to approaching physical security using ESRM principles is to ensure that all the various physical security tasks are done, not as independent tasks, but specifically because each activity:

- Is associated with an asset or group of assets that must be protected.
- Is in place to mitigate exposure to or limit impact from risks to those assets.
- Incorporates an incident response into the overall risk management conversation.

It is a subtle difference from the task-based approach, because:

- The tasks are being done in both a task-based and risk-based environment.
- The activities fall into the specialty of the security team, they are being done by the security group in both the task-based and risk-based program.
- A single physical security implementation such as a CCTV system often protects assets belonging to multiple groups, the lack of one *single* owner can make it seem as though the risk owner is the security team.

The risks that are being addressed are basic and familiar, and sometimes can be so self-evident to a security professional that it seems like they do not need to be discussed with other function strategic partners. Risks like:

- Preventing things from getting stolen.
- Keeping people from going where they do not belong.
- Trying to catch people who break the rules.

All these things are practically built into a security practitioner's DNA. As such, we may sometimes not recognize them as risks that need to be explained and related to impacted stakeholders. But just because we, as security professionals, recognize the inherent need for doors to remain closed and locked, that does not mean that the leaders of a warehouse function recognize the inherent risk in propping open a door to make a delivery to save an employee two minutes of time. It is part of the ESRM philosophy to show them that.

16.7.1 Comparing Traditional and ESRM Physical Security Methods

In defining how physical security in the ESRM program functions by comparing it to how physical security functions in a traditional task-based environment, we will look at a real-world case study and see what can happen when physical security tasks are not understood as mitigating specific security risks.

A Physical Security Case Study: The Traditional Approach and Where It Can Go Wrong

Tim W., a midlevel security manager for Kientz Technology (KT), an up-and-coming technology provider, was assigned to create and implement a physical security plan for a new building, still under construction in a suburban office park. The budget for the $100k security project was allocated by the facilities manager, James H., who had overall responsibility for the building project.

Tim developed a security design based on best practices, and on his expertise as a security professional with years of experience in physical security. He was generally satisfied with the design, but he had one specific concern. The new building was still half empty, with a lot of open and isolated areas, especially in the parking lot. Tim thought that more lighting was needed to keep employees and visitors safe at night; so he approached James for the budget to install it.

Tim not only did not get the additional funds, but James – whose overall project was behind schedule and over budget – cut some of Tim's existing security resources. Not only could Tim not install more lights, but he also had to cut down on some of his other protections. He was not happy, but he accepted James's decision, keeping in place everything that was absolutely required by regulations and reducing others, including some perimeter guard controls.

Six months later, an employee was assaulted while walking to her car. The area of the parking lot where the attack took place was poorly lit, there was no video or guard coverage there, and no-one in the security organization was even aware that the assault had taken place until the employee called the police after the attack. In the meantime, her attacker escaped.

The impact of the incident was immediate and profound. Of course, the employee who had been assaulted was deeply shaken and might never again be willing or able to return to work. The company underwent a wave of bad publicity in the local press and on social media. Additionally, many other employees were understandably nervous about working later shifts, and development projects fell behind as a result.

A great many senior decision-makers at KT were furious about what had happened. In addition to the entire organization being shocked by the attack and by the impact to a member of the team. The vice-president for human resources (HR) had to deal with a wave of employee concerns, and at least one very promising employment candidate turned down a job offer because she felt that KT did not care about its employees' safety. The legal organization worked to meet its obligations related to the ongoing police investigation and prepared for the possibility of a long, demanding, and extremely expensive lawsuit. The corporate communications department scrambled to deal with a public relations nightmare.

With all of that going on in the company, the fallout began by trying to identify someone to blame. The person everyone looked at was not the facilities manager who had cut the security budget six months before. It was the security manager, who had made recommendations that were turned down, had done the best he felt that he could with the budget he was given, and who made a seemingly simple decision to trim a physical security implementation that turned out to be extremely damaging to the company in ways that extended far beyond physical security. Tim had simply followed the direction he was given and the strictures that were placed on him. Unfortunately, all those people now dealing with the fallout of the security cut had been originally left out of the decision process. Sadly for Tim, the blame in this case led to him being fired.

The impact of treating physical security in a traditional task-management model can be profound. While this example was admittedly at the extreme end of the scale, the story of Tim taking the blame for an incident that happened because a person who was not the true owner of a risk made a poor risk decision is not unfamiliar in the security industry. But how could the process under an ESRM security program have been different?

A Physical Security Case Study: The Parking Lot Lighting Question the ESRM Way
Returning to Kientz Technology, look at how the story would go if ESRM principles were applied.

Tim W., the security manager, recognized that there was a problem with visibility in the parking areas, and he asked James H. for budget approval to install more lighting. The facilities manager refused, citing cost overruns. Tim, knowing the role of security in guiding the business through a thoughtful risk management decision-making process, followed through with the ESRM model and process. He believed that there were serious risks involved, and that James, being the facilities manager, was not the responsible asset owner or stakeholder to be making decisions on the assets at risk.

Tim worked through the process of asset owner and stakeholder identification, arranged a meeting with the heads of HR to address possible the employee concerns and with the legal organization to discuss legal liability concerns. He laid out his identified risks. He pointed out some of the possible risk impacts of inadequate lighting in the parking areas, the possibility of danger to employees' and visitors' safety, an adverse impact on morale, and company exposure to legal liability. They agreed that more precautions needed to be taken. They presented Tim's plan to the chief operating officer (COO), who then had the choice of whether to approve the necessary budget for adequate lighting in the parking areas.

In this case, the COO made the choice to approve the expense. When the office building opened, the parking areas were well-lighted, presenting a less attractive environment for bad actors. This does not mean that it is impossible for a crime to occur in the parking lot, but the exposure was brought within a tolerance that the business owners agreed on.

But in this same story, even if the COO had not approved the expense, the process still had an inherent risk-decision element. The business could have made the decision to accept a risk as within tolerance. Even if the budget was declined and a crime was committed in the parking lot, the result in ESRM is technically different. The difference is that the risk was made transparent to the proper risk owners and the acceptance decision was made at the appropriate levels of business. The security role and ESRM process were satisfied, and they would be more transparent to the asset owners and stakeholders even if there were a future event that could be tied to the root cause of inadequate lighting.

16.7.1.1 One Successful Outcome

The ESRM version of the story is far less dramatic – and that is a good thing. It is a story of discovering risk owners, educating them on exposure and impact, and allowing them to make an informed decision on a potential cut to a security risk mitigation activity.

In our example, the role of security was well-defined and properly executed. Security practitioners are often faced with answering the questions of, "What happened here?" or, "How could this have happened?" Although those questions are fair, they often are focused on "inadequate security," and as a result imply that the security practitioner had failed to properly protect the environment. If the ESRM process is followed, there is a clear distinction between the role of security in guiding the risk owners through the risk decision-making process, and the failure of the mitigation plan that was transparently chosen, in this case the lighting. The question from the risk owners will not happen in this environment, because they were part of the process of making the decision, and therefore are already aware of both the risk and the decision.

16.7.1.2 All Successful Outcomes May Not Look the Same

There is a paradoxical problem with the no-drama outcome: At best, it is difficult to provide a report of security incidents that *did not* happen, based on mitigation controls. That is why communication skills are so critical to the security professional. It is up to you, in this discipline and all the others, to make sure that physical security stays top-of-mind for all your risk owners and other stakeholders to ensure that they understand the risks clearly, to make sure that you are communicating the risks factually without resorting to fear tactics, and to present appropriate mitigation options for them to consider. If you do that and all risk owners are aware of the risks that their assets face, and how to lessen the impact to within tolerable levels, then you are performing your role successfully, no matter what the ultimate decision on the mitigation of the risk might be. Success is defined in consistency of carrying out the program, as well as protecting the enterprise within the limits of business risk tolerance.

Questions for the Security Practitioner
- "Have I ever faced a situation in which physical security implementations were cut due to budget decisions, without the sign-off of other impacted parties?"
- "In my organization, do asset and risk stakeholders understand that they must also own the risks associated with physical asset protection?"

16.7.2 The ESRM Difference

As we mentioned above, in the physical security discipline, the main difference between the task-based view of security and the ESRM paradigm is in the idea that security tasks performed are just daily security activities versus the understanding that they are implementations in response to identified risks with potential impacts.

16.7.2.1 A Difference in Perception

We have already mentioned the importance of perception: How physical security is seen and understood, inside the security organization and in the entire enterprise. Part of the problem, of course, is that there are a lot of tasks – installing locks, issuing badges, scheduling patrols – that must be done. It is all very hands-on, it is all completely necessary, and it makes it easy to lose sight of the fact that the work of physical security does not end, or even begin there.

Something else that fuels the misperception that the security function is defined simply by the tasks it performs, is that physical security is probably the most visible component of the security department. For example, the average employee may not *see* cybersecurity measures in action or may not recognize them as such. But every time she swipes her access card through a reader, or has her handbag inspected at the gate, she is aware of physical security. That familiarity leads to the idea that physical security is just "something that security does." And it can lead to people taking it for granted. That is not just a problem with the typical employee who is passing through an access point. It can also have a very negative impact on the perceptions of senior decision-makers, including the very risk owners whose interests we as security professionals are working so hard to protect. As the security risk manager, it is up to you to communicate and educate so that the risk owners fully understand both their roles and yours.

16.7.2.2 A Difference in Approach: Risk Management as a Positive Practice

Communicating effectively about physical security without resorting to overly dramatic fear tactics can be challenging, but it also presents security professionals with significant opportunities to raise security's profile within the enterprise, and to see its value recognized. It is important not to limit yourself to a restrictive view of what security can and should do. Because, while you are communicating about the risks that need to be mitigated, you can also talk about the benefits that the mitigation plan might bring about.

Here are just a couple of examples of how far-reaching the impact of good, risk-based physical security practices can be – without even moving past the front desk.

- Front desk security guards:
  - The security guards you assign to the front entrance are essentially "brand ambassadors" for the enterprise. They are usually the first points of contact for visitors to the enterprise's facilities, and if they are professional and courteous, they give visitors a lasting, and positive, first impression.
- Automated visitor check-in:
  - As a different approach to front desk control – automating access control processes can not only make facilities more secure, it can also improve the visitor experience by reducing the time they will spend waiting to be admitted.

For these two quick examples, take a moment to think about who the stakeholders are for front desk/entrance security: There are the obvious business assets owners who need protection from unauthorized intrusion, but there are a lot more.

- The HR department, for example, wants to make a good impression on job candidates.
- Sales and marketing want current and prospective customers to have a pleasant experience, every time they visit your facilities.
- People in the facility with visitors coming would like the ease of using an automated check-in system to register their guests.

When you take an ESRM approach to physical security and move beyond task management to take a comprehensive risk-based approach, security practices and processes can become value-added services offered to other internal organizations.

Questions for the Security Practitioner
- "What are the three most important physical security risks in the environment that I'm responsible for? Can I identify the owners of those risks?"
- "What are the most important messages about physical security that I need to communicate to risk owners? How can I get those messages across more effectively?"
- "Does physical security offer me any opportunities to change the image of the security organization from one that slows things down, to one that makes things work better?"

Chapter Review

In Chapter 16, you learned:

- The difference between traditional views of physical security and the ESRM methodology and why changing that perception difference is critical to shifting to an ESRM model for physical security.
- How the physical security discipline fits into the ESRM life cycle and how existing physical security activities can be leveraged and modified to drive the ESRM program.

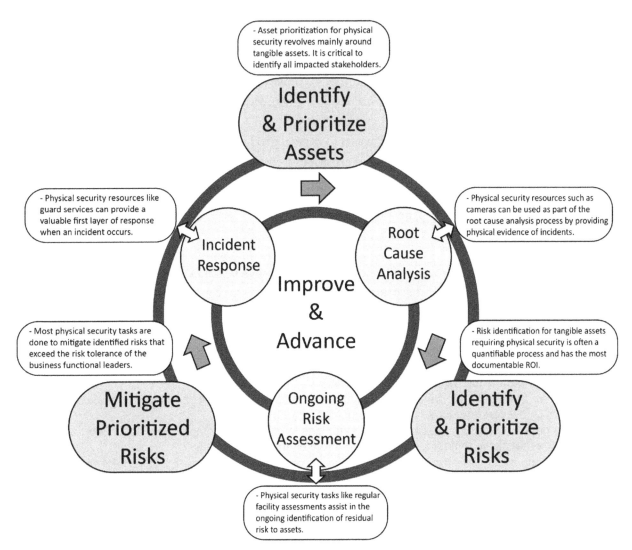

Figure 16-7. Physical security and the ESRM cycle – A review.

Looking Forward

In Chapter 17, we will discuss how cyber security and information security fit into the ESRM paradigm.

> **Practitioner steps to consider before moving on to Chapter 17:**
> ✓ Identify any existing monitoring activities that could be leveraged to help identify new risk.
> ✓ Consider what aspects of your program might be able to help the business with non-security related information or services.

Security Program Self-Assessment

In this self-assessment, you should think about the answer to the questions posed, and then see where your program is on the identified ESRM spectrum.

Question	Y/N	Is This ESRM?
Does your security program incorporate physical security site assessments?	☐Yes ☐No	**NO**: If you do not perform physical security site assessments that include a full investigation of all assets, functions, personnel, and security risks, then this is a suitable place to start your ESRM program. **PARTIAL**: If you perform physical security site assessments, but focus only on "gates, guns, and guards," and do not do a full assessment of all assets, functions, personnel, facility uses, and the risks to them in the location, then you are part of the way to an ESRM implementation. **YES**: If you have a program in place that consistently performs physical security site assessments, which include a full investigation of all assets, functions, personnel, and security risks, then you are practicing ESRM.

Questions for Discussion

1. Does having business partners who perceive physical security as the sum all of security responsibilities truly hurt the department? What if it is the majority of what the department does anyway? What is your opinion of the damage this could do?

2. What topics might be included in an assessment to add to the overall understanding of enterprise assets? Can you think of critical asset areas that are easily overlooked? How can you drive more understanding of the enterprise through an assessment?

3. The process of managing a security risk decision-making process is fundamentally different from managing a risk mitigation activity. What are some effective ways to explain this to the non-security professional?

Learn More About It

For further reading about physical security:

Fennelly, L. (2012, November). *Effective physical security* (4th ed). Waltham, MA: Butterworth-Heinemann.

Knoke, M. & Peterson, K. (2015). *Physical security principles*. Alexandria, VA: ASIS International.

Slotnik, J., Stevens, H., et al. (2012). *Physical security practitioner 2022: An industry look at the future of the physical security industry*. Alexandria, VA: ASIS International. Available at https://my.asisonline.org/Lists/AsisDownloads/PhyS_Physical_Security_Practioner_2022_2012.pdf [Access requires registration and password.]

17

ESRM and Cybersecurity and Information Security

Cybersecurity and information security are two closely related security disciplines. While there are differences between the two, both present significant risks in today's world, and both require a significant amount of attention and security risk mitigation. The *Horizon Scan Report 2016*, from the Business Continuity Institute showed that the top two risks of concern for continuity and risk professionals are cyberattacks and data breaches (Business Continuity Institute, 2016, p. 5).

Similarly, cyberattack ranked five in the top business threats identified in a 2016 PricewaterhouseCoopers survey of top US chief executive officers (CEOs). Clearly, both topics are receiving close attention in the business world, will receive increasing scrutiny as more incidents occur, and they represent a significant part of any well-managed security risk program. However, in your enterprise security risk management (ESRM) program, you can manage these risks just as you would any other type of security risk, through consistent application of risk identification, prioritization, and mitigation, in line with tolerances set by the business. Cybersecurity and information security are technology-intensive, but they are still, at the root, security risks (PricewaterhouseCoopers, 2016).

This chapter will help you to:
- Understand the nature of evolving and emerging cybersecurity and information security threats, vulnerabilities, and risks.
- Understand how cybersecurity and information security fit into the ESRM life cycle.

17.1 How does Cyber and Information Security Fit in the ESRM Life Cycle?

Many people find cyber and information security a challenge if they do not possess a background in information technology (IT). Unfortunately, that can lead to the misconception that cybersecurity and information security are essentially technology issues. However, technical knowledge and understanding do not define the role of a security risk manager. The role is defined by *understanding the security risks* that the technology is exposed to and knowing how to assist the business in mitigating them. ESRM approaches cybersecurity and information security in the same way it does every other aspect of security: comprehensively, holistically, and with an iterative approach that considers every phase of the ESRM life cycle (Figure 17-1). Why? Because, as *security risk areas*, cybersecurity and information security are no different from physical security or any other security discipline.

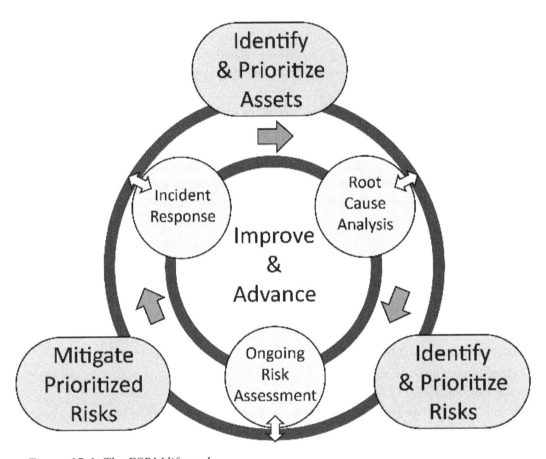

Figure 17-1. The ESRM life cycle.

While the risk mitigation activities for these risks may require highly specialized skills from the technical and technology personnel tasked with carrying them out, the underlying principles of ESRM still apply.

17.1.1 The ESRM Cycle and the NIST Cybersecurity Framework

Before we move forward with examining how the individual steps of the ESRM cycle fit with cyber and information security, we want to discuss a tool that we highly recommend using when examining your existing cyber and information security program or when setting up a new program. The National Institute of Standards and Technology (NIST) offers a best practice framework for cybersecurity – the NIST Cybersecurity Framework.

As we showed you in Chapter 5, the five core phases of the NIST Cybersecurity Framework align well with ESRM and other risk-management models, working under a structure of fundamental risk management principles. Independent standards organizations like NIST offer especially valuable guidance because:

- They typically draw from a broad range of industries, enterprises, and individuals with an equally broad range of experience.
- They update their guidance on a regular basis.

The framework is built as a tool for all types of organizations, which means that you can apply it in your enterprise and your security organization, no matter the industry, as part of aligning information and cybersecurity to a risk-based approach.

The framework (available online at http://www.nist.gov/cyberframework/) is designed to help enterprises:

- Understand, manage, and reduce cybersecurity and information security risk.
- Prioritize their cybersecurity investments.
- Improve risk and cybersecurity management communications among all stakeholders.

The NIST framework has five basic components (shown in Figure 17-2) that can be roughly aligned with the ESRM life cycle. These, with enterprise and industry-specific variations, will prove effective in transitioning your cybersecurity efforts to an ESRM methodology.

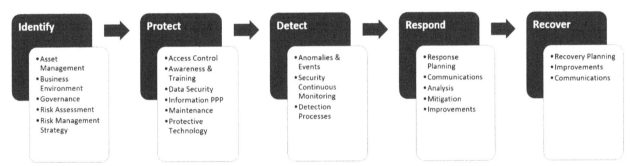

Figure 17-2. The NIST cybersecurity framework has five phases. (National Institute of Standards and Technology, 2014).

Here we will cover only the very basic information, but we encourage you to work through the entire framework with your IT group and other critical technology stakeholders, to determine the state of current cybersecurity, information, and technology security in your enterprise, and to examine how that compares to tolerances.

17.1.1.1 Identify

This framework component involves identifying current and emerging threats, assets, asset/risk owners, and other impacted stakeholders. The primary areas covered are:

- Asset management – identifying and understanding the business assets that need to be protected against cybersecurity threats.
- Business environment – understanding the enterprise, the industry in which it operates, and factors including the legal and regulatory requirements to which it must adhere.
- Governance – determining the cybersecurity-related decision-making structure, and identifying the roles and organizations with accountability for cybersecurity decisions.
- Risk assessment – assessing the potential impact and exposure of threats to the enterprise (National Institute of Standards and Technology, 2014)

The *Identify* step of the NIST framework correlates to the two steps of the ESRM cycle of identifying first assets, and then risks.

17.1.1.2 Protect
Once risks and other critical factors have been identified, the NIST framework calls for protective measures to be put into place:
- Access control – ranging from policies concerning who has access to what systems and under what circumstances to technological systems that enforce those policies.
- Awareness and training – ongoing programs designed to increase employee awareness of cybersecurity threats, ways to recognize them, and ways to prevent them.
- Data security – protections for business-critical intellectual property, sensitive customer and employee information, and other valuable data.
- Information protection processes and procedures.
- Maintenance – ensuring that both policies and mechanisms are up-to-date and adequate to address identified cybersecurity risks.
- Protective technology – systems and applications designed to detect and protect against a broad range of cybersecurity threats and risk, both external and internal (National Institute of Standards and Technology, 2014).

The *protect* step of the NIST framework correlates to the step of the ESRM cycle of mitigating prioritized risks.

17.1.1.3 Detect
This phase, which will inevitably require extensive involvement by the security investigations function, is designed to identify cybersecurity issues in areas that include:
- Anomalies and events – occurrences that may indicate cybersecurity issues, ranging from inappropriate access, to unusual traffic volumes, which might indicate a distributed denial-of-service (DDoS) attack.
- Security continuous monitoring – ongoing monitoring of cybersecurity processes, mechanisms, and technologies.
- Detection processes – practices and technologies for identifying cybersecurity threats and vulnerabilities (National Institute of Standards and Technology, 2014).

The *detect* step of the NIST framework is analogous to the ongoing risk assessment area of the ESRM model.

17.1.1.4 Respond

The security organization must have processes in place to address cybersecurity issues that will inevitably arise, including:

- Response planning – proactive processes for dealing with both anticipated and unanticipated security incidents.
- Communications – ongoing communications with all risk owners and other impacted stakeholders.
- Analysis – the ability to understand the nature and impact of a cybersecurity incident, before, during, and after a security incident.
- Mitigation – the measures to be taken to address a security incident, and to limit its risk impact.
- Improvements – continuous process improvements designed to enable the security organization to learn from previous incidents, to developing cybersecurity trends, and to develop more effective countermeasures (National Institute of Standards and Technology, 2014).

The *respond* step of the NIST framework is comparable to the incident response step of the ESRM model.

17.1.1.5 Recover

Cybersecurity incidents inevitably have consequences, ranging from the minor to the catastrophic. This phase focuses on addressing those consequences, through:

- Recovery planning – ensuring preparedness for incidents and their impact.
- Improvements – ongoing assessment of the effectiveness of cybersecurity processes and practices, with a view to continuous improvement.
- Communications – ensuring that all strategic partners and other stakeholders are informed of cybersecurity incidents and mitigation measures, and that they have continuous input into associated risk decisions (National Institute of Standards and Technology, 2014).

The recover step of the NIST framework encompasses aspects of root cause analysis and additional risk mitigation in the ESRM model.

We highly recommend using the framework to perform a gap analysis on the current state of cybersecurity vs. the desired state, before moving on to any other implementation steps for the information security and cybersecurity area of your ESRM program.

17.2 Identifying and Prioritizing Assets in the Cyber Environment

Identifying business assets to be protected, and determining which ones need protecting most urgently, the first step in the ESRM cycle (shown in figure 17-3), can be more difficult in the information security and cybersecurity areas, than in many others.

1. Many of the assets are intangible.
2. Information and networks are often widely distributed.
3. Information and date requires both physical and logical protections.
4. Many assets are connected to networks without the business owners even knowing it.

An information asset may simultaneously exist in multiple locations, which means it can come under threat from many different access points. Furthermore, the asset and its location may change constantly as network segments and backup processing centers come online and go offline, in the normal course of business.

In the cyber environment, there is complicated multi-level, cross-departmental reliance and interdependence with distributed networks, databases, applications, and systems. This environment also includes significant third-party provided services and supply chain interface requirements.

However, while complex, this step in the ESRM process can, in fact, help you build valuable bridges between the information technology group, the information security (IS) group (if it is a separate group in your enterprise), and the ESRM security risk manager and team. When identifying and valuing assets associated with information and cybersecurity, it is imperative that the IT

Figure 17-3. Identifying and prioritizing assets may be more difficult in information security, but is critical.

department and any IS security specialists are brought into the process. They will have the most information about what assets exist, where they are, and what they are used for. With information and cyber related assets, any undocumented or unknown assets are a significant danger to the enterprise. Partnering with any groups in the enterprise who can assist in uncovering potential hidden assets will only make the entire environment more secure.

17.3 Identifying and Prioritizing Risks in the Cyber Environment

Identifying and prioritizing risks, the second ESRM step (Figure 17-4), may be the most challenging phase of the ESRM life cycle where cybersecurity and information security are concerned.

The threat landscape (the types of threats, their sources, even their motivations) changes so rapidly that even the most specialized security professionals struggle to keep ahead of them. It is quite literally impossible to identify all current and emerging risks. Oftentimes, the risks in the world of cyber and information security are completely unknown until an attack happens. This makes effective prioritization crucial. This effort will require very close collaboration with your technology partners, because, as always, they are the ones who know what really matters to the

Figure 17-4. Identifying and prioritizing risks may be more difficult in information security, but is also critical.

business. They are also the ones who have the most detailed understanding of the specific technological risks. The partnership between security and IT must be a very close one, to ensure that the enterprise is being protected in the best possible way, by both organizations.

17.3.1 Risk in Cyber and Information Security

We have mentioned that a cybersecurity or information security risk is not really any different from a physical risk, but it may be helpful to have a real-world example. Here is one that will be familiar to practitioners in literally any area of security: risk of intrusion.

Intrusion can fundamentally be described as someone getting into the enterprise who should not be there. The intruder could be using a crowbar to break open a padlock on a warehouse door or a virus to get through an unpatched hole in a network. It does not really matter because, in ESRM, both the risk and the process are essentially the same. In both cases, the ESRM security risk manager needs to work in partnership with any impacted risk stakeholders to assess the risk and to put mitigating plans in place to prevent the intrusion from happening. In both cases, you would start with a set of initial questions, such as the ones outlined in Table 17-1.

Table 17-1: Cyber and Physical Security Risk Similarities

Intrusion Risk in a Warehouse	Intrusion Risk on a Network
• What asset is inside the warehouse?	• What data is on the server?
• Whose asset is it that is being protected?	• Who uses that data?
• How important is that asset to the mission of the business?	• How important is the information asset to the mission of the business?
• What are the security risks to the warehouse?	• What are the security risks to that information?
• Who are the stakeholders?	• Who are the stakeholders?
• What would be the impact to the business if the assets in the warehouse were intruded upon, and potentially stolen or vandalized?	• What would be the impact to the business if the information assets in the network were intruded upon and potentially stolen or manipulated?
• How would you recover?	• How would you recover?

Once you have identified the assets and the associated risks and identified your stakeholders, you will need to develop a mitigation plan.

The technical skills involved are different, whether you are implementing a video monitoring and access control system for the warehouse or running intrusion detection and password management systems for the network. Also, the personnel to whom you assign the actions that mitigate those risks will certainly be different. However, the underlying principle is essentially the same. You are working to ensure that the right people are allowed in, and the wrong ones are kept out.

17.4 Mitigate Prioritized Risks

Risk mitigation – protecting against identified threats, and dealing with ones that have emerged – is the third step in the ESRM cycle (Figure 17-5). Designing the mitigation plan requires a certain level of technical skill and knowledge, and it will certainly require input from technical specialists, either inside or outside the enterprise.

No security leader can be an expert in every mitigating action that can possibly be put into place, but under ESRM principles, that is perfectly fine. As the leader of the security function, you must understand security risk and the need to mitigate them, but you are not personally responsible for implementing every mitigating action.

Just as with physical security, investigations, or threat management, personnel with the specialized technical skillset for mitigating information and cybersecurity risks must be part of the overall security mitigation activities. If your security team is tasked *directly* with providing the technology risk mitigation actions like network firewalls, system architecture, patch management, etc., you

Figure 17-5. Mitigating prioritized risks can require specialized technical knowledge.

will need a greater level of expertise in those areas than if you are *partnering* with a technology team who provides those technical services as part of the overall risk management program. What matters most is that the technical personnel are available to protect the enterprise by mitigating risk and that you, as the security risk manager, are ensuring that all necessary risks are being managed.

17.4.1. Risk Mitigation Planning: The Cybersecurity Framework

For risk mitigation planning, a gap analysis of your enterprise response capacities against the desired capacity recommended by the NIST framework can be immensely valuable. It helps in determining business tolerance to risk and in identifying what assets and risks should have mitigation plans put in place.

The process of performing this gap analysis is relatively simple. It *must* be done in partnership with business leaders, preferably the security council that we discussed in Chapter 13. Many risk tolerance decisions will need to be made, and the security council – or a project working group dedicated to this analysis – is the group with the authority to make those decisions,

17.4.1.1. Performing a Gap Analysis for Risk Mitigation Planning

Each area of the NIST cybersecurity framework allows your organization to identify the level to which the enterprise currently meets the requirement of the area, and the level that the enterprise would like to meet.

There are four tiers that an enterprise can align to. Not all enterprises may choose to meet the highest tier on all areas or even to meet any of them. The key to the gap analysis is to understand the gap between where the enterprise is and where it *wants to be*. To achieve this understanding, the governing body should direct a technical and security working group to:

Phase 1 – Determine Current State

1. Read and fully understand the framework and supporting documents available online at the NIST web site.
   - There are many documents on the NIST website (http://www.nist.gov/cyberframework/) that can assist you and the team with this process.
2. Identify to the security council which technology systems will be considered in scope for measurement against the framework.
   - At this point in your program, you will already have a register of assets, risks, and associated impacts. Only those technology assets and systems with a high enough impact to need security risk mitigation planning should be considered in scope for your analysis.
3. For each item in the framework, identify the current state of enterprise capacity to align with that item.

Phase 2 – Determine Desired State

4. Present the initial findings to the security council or security risk governing body. Include:
   - Assets and processes in scope.
   - Explanation of the tiers and what they mean specific to your industry and enterprise.
   - What the working group has collectively agreed the current state/tier is.
5. Ask the business leaders responsible for cyber and information security governance to determine what tier level meets risk tolerances for the enterprise.
   - This step may require several sessions to ensure that the business decision-makers understand the meanings of the tiers in each area.

Phase 3 – Analyze Current vs. Desired State

6. For any items where the current rating tier is different than the desired tier, determine:
   - The difference in tiers.
   - Steps required to bring that item into the desired security tier.
   - Costs and time associated with completing those steps.

Phase 4 – Governance Review/Changes/Approvals

7. Present the Phase 3 findings to the business leaders who are responsible for cyber and information security governance (the security council).
8. Ask the security council to review the mitigation requirements, and to approve projects to close the gaps, or to determine if costs outweigh benefits. Then ask them to determine new tolerance levels for the enterprise, and set new desired tiers.

Phase 5 – Repeat

9. The assessment process should be repeated every 12 to 18 months, to ensure the continual improvement of the information and cybersecurity posture in the enterprise.

17.5 Improve and Advance

As seen in Figure 17-7, the last step in the ESRM cycle is itself a continuous process of improving and advancing the program. Because both the threats and the associated risks are constantly changing, the cyber environment requires protections to be constantly monitored, reevaluated, and enhanced.

These changes mean that a very minor problem can quickly spin out of control, and a set of protections that was effective yesterday no longer works today. As we saw in our discussion of security investigations in Chapter 15, responding to and investigating a cybersecurity incident requires not only finding out what happened and who did what, but also how and why it happened. Then the investigation must determine the root cause and recommend security risk mitigation plans to ensure that any impact that falls outside of business tolerances for risk does not happen again. As in any other kind of investigation, these are the steps that are necessary to continuous improvement, which makes it possible to keep up with the enterprise's fast-changing cyber-risk profile.

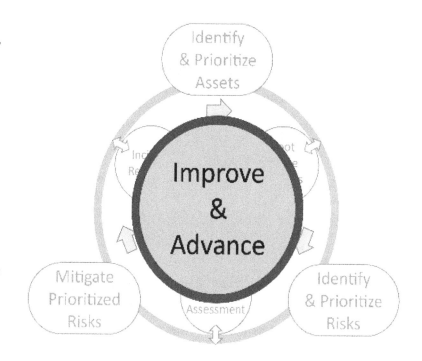

Figure 17-6. Improving and advancing in the cyber realm requires constant vigilance.

17.5.1 Using the NIST Framework to Improve and Advance

To continually improve and advance the risk management program in the cybersecurity area, the business leaders in charge of determining risk tolerance and making decisions on what security risk mitigation activities to implement must have a continual awareness and understanding of the state of cyber and information security risk.

The NIST framework is an excellent risk reporting tool for the security council, or for other governing bodies to understand the current state of technology-related security risk. One of the best methods for reporting this information to the security council on a regular basis is in the form of spider graphs, which show the current vs. desired state in the program, as identified in the original gap analysis. An example of this analysis – from the *protect* section of the framework – is shown in Figure 17-7.

Cyber Security Framework Tier – *Protect*

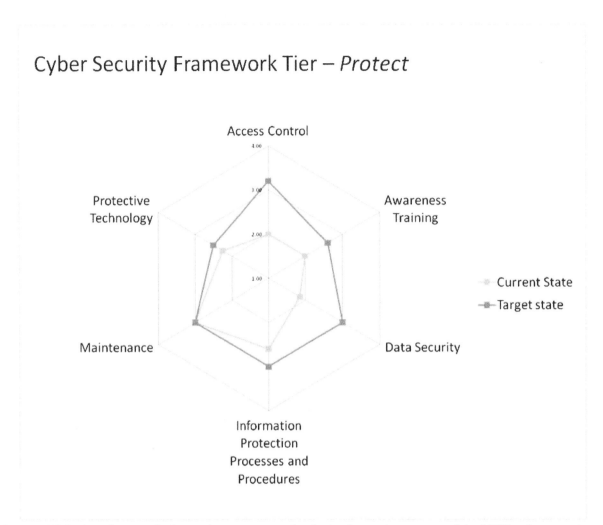

Figure 17-7. A spider graph shows the current vs. the desired state in aspects of the NIST cybersecurity framework.

17.6 A Deeper Look at the Role of Cyber and Information Security in ESRM

As with every other discipline of security that we cover in this book, a truly risk-based approach to cybersecurity and information security requires a comprehensive understanding of both areas of risk. There are some who would argue that cyber and information security are fundamentally just technology problems that belong to the IT department and that department should be left to deal with them.

However, in an ESRM model, the role of the security practitioner and organization is to identify risks that could impact the organization and to work with asset owners to mitigate them. Because these are not just technical problems, bugs, or glitches, this need for cooperation means that securing the cyberenvironment simply cannot be left to the IT organization. They are serious and potentially enterprise-destroying risks. Security must work with the IT organization to identify risks and institute mitigation plans in the same way that security must determine physical risks to locations and partner with the facilities group to mitigate them or seek personnel risks in all areas and work with HR or management to mitigate those.

For a host of reasons, securing technical environments cannot be left solely to the IT department:

1. The IT group can experience significant conflicts of interest when security risk mitigations have the potential to cause project deliverables to run late or budgets to run over. As you saw in Chapter 12, concerning independence, when security personnel are reporting up through the IT structure, the group will likely not have the needed independence to properly manage security risks to the enterprise.

2. If the IT department is regarded as the only owner of the risk to technology systems, they are left to make risk-decisions based on their own perceptions of how the assets in their care impact the rest of the enterprise. If they are missing input from the business owners who use those systems, a security incident might have far greater impact than can be tolerated.

3. As the world gets increasingly more connected and complicated, the cyberenvironment is beginning to encompass far more than just information technology, now encompassing a new area: *operational technology*.

4. Possibly most important, when defining the security role through ESRM as a discipline within the enterprise, the security department *must* be thought of as a standalone department like legal and internal audit, not as an add-on to an existing department. That existing department, like IT in this case, would still own the risk and risk decisions, possibly even the mitigation activities, but the role of guiding the department through the security risk decision-making process would belong to the security department as defined by ESRM.

17.6.1. Operational Technology – More than Just Data

In Chapter 3, we talked about the changing risk conversation. One significant driver of that change is the *internet of things* (IoT), which is the connected network of everything from cars, to refrigerators, to air conditioners. That changing technology environment is increasing the role in all enterprises of *operational* technology. These connected operational systems – factory lines, supervisory control and data acquisition (SCADA) systems, automated delivery systems, and more – are every bit as critical as IT for most enterprises, and for many, it is even more important. In recent years, the world has seen a substantial number of cybersecurity incidents, some of them devastating in their impact, in which data was not the main target, or was not targeted at all. Here are a few recent examples of attacks that struck at operations, rather than data:

- **Stuxnet:** The Stuxnet worm, which many industry observers consider the most complex and sophisticated cyberattack seen to date, targeted Iran's nuclear installations, including both civilian power plants and military facilities. The worm, widely believed to have been jointly developed by US and Israeli intelligence agencies, was embedded in software from the German manufacturer Siemens, sometime before 2010. It was designed not to access data but to damage Iran's nuclear operations by causing a series of "accidents," such as centrifuges spinning out of control. At one point, it was estimated that Stuxnet had destroyed one-fifth of Iran's centrifuges. And here's a sobering thought: The attack didn't stop with its intended target. Stuxnet appears to have "gone rogue," infecting other facilities, including a Russian nuclear plant that it was probably never intended to target.

- **German steel mill attack:** In 2014, cyberattackers used spearphishing and other social engineering techniques to gain access to the office networks of an as-yet-unnamed German steel mill and, from there, accessed the mill's physical systems. Details are incomplete, but clearly, the attack caused physical damage to at least one of the mill's blast furnaces, perhaps unintentionally.

- **Sony:** The 2014 cyberattack at Sony Pictures Entertainment, which the US government has blamed on North Korea, certainly exposed sensitive data. But a fact less covered in the news was that it also installed malware that crippled Sony's networks for months, making internal and external communications extremely difficult, causing lengthy and extremely expensive delays in film and television production. And it was not even the first time that Sony had been hit. In 2011, its PlayStation Network was brought to a standstill when an attack exposed 77 million accounts and prevented users from logging in, forcing Sony to shut down the entire worldwide network for 23 days. Sony estimated the cost of the attack at $170 million.

Movie studios, steel mills, gaming consoles – it is an incredibly wide range of targets. But they all have one thing in common: They are all interconnected. That is what makes operational technology so vulnerable in the global landscape now. Every enterprise has critical systems and applications that are connected to the Internet, and that means that they are literally exposed to the entire world. No matter how sophisticated and elaborate the defenses that we put in place are, there are always people and organizations looking for, and finding, ways to get around them. When we talk about operational technologies, we are talking about:

- Manufacturers' assembly lines, supply chains, and distribution networks.
- The SCADA systems, which manage critical infrastructure like electrical power plants and hydroelectric dams.
- The IoT: The millions and millions of Internet-connected objects, devices, and sensors that constantly transmit and receive information about our businesses, our vehicles, our homes, and even our bodies, through wearable devices like smart watches and fitness monitors.

Everything is a target now. Someone who hacks your environmental systems, for example, is not exposing your data, but the hack can make your facilities uninhabitable, bringing your operations to a complete halt. If you are in manufacturing, your networked robots can be taken offline, stopping your assembly lines. If you are managing a transportation network, communications with your fleets can be cut off so that you do not know if your planes are running on time or if one of your trucks has been hijacked. None of these problems target data, but they are all security risks that are specific to the cyberenvironment. In the connected world within the cyber environment, where networked connections can impact physical assets, the risk owners and stakeholders are significantly changing as well.

Many potentially impacted assets are far outside the scope of the IT department being able to "own" the risk. They must be managed more holistically with all asset-owners and stakeholders involved in the risk decision-making process. It is a significant risk to the enterprise to allow business leaders and executives to continue thinking of cybersecurity as just "data breaches," and to leave the security risk mitigation entirely in the hands of the IT department. The ESRM program must manage all enterprise security risks, no matter if the attack vector is physical or logical, whether the danger approaches over wires or in a vehicle.

Chapter Review

In Chapter 17, you learned how information and cybersecurity risks can impact all aspects of the enterprise, how the traditional approach that leaves technology security in the hands of non-dedicated security groups can lead to unforeseen risks, and how an ESRM implementation can assist the enterprise in securing itself against a fast-changing global technical risk environment. See Figure 17-9 for an overview of some of these points.

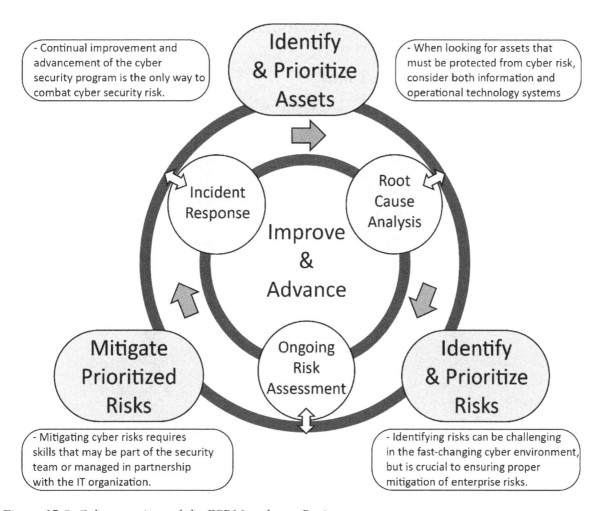

Figure 17-8. Cybersecurity and the ESRM cycle – a Review.

Looking Forward

In Chapter 18, we will learn about measures to address one of the most sensitive and highly publicized risks to enterprises today – workplace violence. We will:

- See how fear of discussing workplace violence has handicapped the process of preventing it.
- Look at how ESRM can engage the right risk stakeholders in the process of managing threats in the workplace.

Practitioner steps to consider before moving on to Chapter 18:
- ✓ Consider the level of cybersecurity awareness across your enterprise. Is it at the level it needs to be? If not, think about what you could do to raise it.
- ✓ Think about the specific skills, technical or otherwise, that your security organization might need to add, to better protect the enterprise against cybersecurity threats.

Security Program Self-Assessment

In this self-assessment, you should think about the answer to the questions posed, and then see where your program is on the identified ESRM spectrum.

Question	Y/N	Is This ESRM?
Does your organization have a defined level of risk tolerance for all technology-based threats?	□Yes □No	**NO:** If you do not consider any threats outside of data breaches in your technical security, then expanding the consideration to operational technology and other aspects of your cyberenvironment is a suitable place to start your ESRM program. **PARTIAL:** If you have some non-data aspects of your enterprise included in your technology security risk management processes, then you are part of the way to an ESRM implementation. **YES:** If you have a formal, documented framework of assets with technology security risk exposure, defined tolerances, and security targets, with oversight of the programs from a governing body, then you are practicing ESRM.

Questions for Discussion

1. If an IT department objects to having a security risk-management program and governing council oversee technology-based security risks to the enterprise, what reasons might they give? Can you think of convincing arguments to counter the objections?
2. In an environment with two separate teams – one for technology-based security and the other for remaining areas of security, such as physical security and investigations – how can the leaders of these two teams partner in an ESRM paradigm? How can they work together to ensure that all enterprise security risks are managed appropriately?

References

Business Continuity Institute (BCI). (2016). *Horizon scan report 2016.* Retrieved from
https://www.bsigroup.com/Documents/BSI-BCI-Horizon-Scan-Report-2016-UK-EN.pdf

National Institute of Standards and Technology (NIST). (2014, February 12). *Framework for improving critical infrastructure cybersecurity.* (pp. 19–35). Retrieved from
https://www.nist.gov/sites/default/files/documents/cyberframework/cybersecurity-framework-021214.pdf

PricewaterhouseCoopers. (2016) *19th annual global CEO survey.* (p. 7) Retrieved from
http://www.pwc.com/gx/en/ceo-survey/2016/landing-page/pwc-19th-annual-global-ceo-survey.pdf

Zetter, K. (2016, January 1). *The biggest security threats we'll face in 2016.* [Web log post]. Retrieved from https://www.wired.com/2016/01/the-biggest-security-threats-well-face-in-2016/

Learn More About It

For further reading about the NIST Cybersecurity Framework:

National Institute of Standards and Technology (NIST). (2017, January 10). *Cybersecurity framework.* Available at http://www.nist.gov/cyberframework/

PricewaterhouseCoopers. (2014, May). *Why you should adopt the NIST cybersecurity framework.* Available at https://www.pwc.com/us/en/increasing-it-effectiveness/publications/assets/adopt-the-nist.pdf

For further reading about cyber-physical security:

Cyber Physical Systems Public Working Group. (2016, May). *Framework for cyber-physical systems release 1.0.* Available at https://s3.amazonaws.com/nist-sgcps/cpspwg/files/pwgglobal/CPS_PWG_Framework_for_Cyber_Physical_Systems_Release_1_0Final.pdf

18

ESRM and Workplace Violence and Threat Management

During the past decade, rates of workplace violence have been rising worldwide. Although there are many types of workplace violence, public perception tends to focus on the more sensational stories:

- The "active shooter," who inflicts mass casualties.
- The "disgruntled employee," who targets and kills his supervisor.
- The "random act of violence."

Although given less media coverage, incidents of robbery and domestic violence are the more commonplace types of violent incidents that occur in workplace settings. Whatever form workplace violence takes, it represents a significant risk to the enterprise and its employees and must be considered in any security program. Unfortunately, implementing a comprehensive workplace violence program in many enterprises can be a challenge. The mindset that workplace violence is a thing that can happen only to other people or in other places can hinder the acceptance of workplace violence as a true risk.

A robust enterprise security risk management (ESRM) program helps lessen that challenge by identifying and engaging all appropriate asset owners and stakeholders. Once risk owners truly understand the full spectrum of workplace violence risk, they can decide on the best approaches to risk mitigation activities in that area. In this chapter, we will look at risk-based workplace violence prevention and threat management to show how the ESRM model works to support the enterprise in mitigating that risk.

This chapter will help you to:

- Explore how a workplace violence prevention and threat management program fits into the ESRM model.
- Understand how risk-based threat management can help your enterprise lessen the likelihood of workplace violence.

18.1 How does Workplace Violence Prevention and Threat Management Fit in the ESRM Life Cycle?

Workplace violence prevention and threat management both have ties to every single step in the ESRM cycle. There is literally no aspect of the ESRM life cycle, seen in Figure 18-1, which does not apply to the design, implementation, and ongoing management of a workplace violence prevention and threat management program. Threat assessment and management, the foundation of workplace violence prevention, is a *fundamentally* risk-based process.

Figure 18-1. Workplace violence is a risk to be mitigated, while threat management is a mitigation plan. Both are tied to the entire ESRM cycle.

18.2 Identifying and Prioritizing Assets in Workplace Violence Prevention and Threat Management Programs

The first step of the ESRM life cycle, seen in Figure 18-2, is identifying the assets to be protected and the owners of those assets. It might seem obvious that, in this discipline, the primary assets to be protected are the enterprise's employees. That is true, but the issue still requires a closer look, because not all employees have the same level of risk, nor require the same types of protective activities. There are certain classes of employees who are at much greater risk of becoming victims of violence in the workplace. It is worth taking the extra time to determine whether your enterprise includes some of these people, who might need extra consideration in your workplace violence program. Here are a few examples of some roles to be considered:

- Medical.
  - Nurse.
  - Physician.
- Mental Health.
  - Professional.
  - Custodial Care.
- Teaching.
  - Pre-school to High school.
  - College/University.
  - Special education.
- Law Enforcement.
  - Police.
  - Correctional officer.
  - Security guard.
- Retail Sales.
  - Convenience or liquor store clerk.
  - Gas station attendant.
  - Bartender.
  - Retail sales.
- Transportation.
  - Bus driver.
  - Taxi driver.
  - (US Department of Justice, 2011).

Figure 18-2. Workplace violence prevention and threat management requires determining the assets most vulnerable to workplace violence.

All the job roles on the list above have an increased risk of being victims of violence at work. If these personnel categories are part of your enterprise, you will want to explore further how risks might be increased in their areas.

18.2.1 Asset Owners and Stakeholders: Everyone Owns Workplace Violence Prevention, Not Just Security

A key component of the ESRM approach to workplace violence prevention is the underlying principle that every stakeholder involved with the asset (in this case, mostly personnel assets) must be involved in designing and developing the workplace violence prevention program, and must ensure that it has enterprise-wide commitment.

In many instances we have seen, a security leader tries to convince senior executives that a workplace violence response program is needed. The security leader is told that it is an employee issue and that human resources (HR) should handle it, or that it is a safety issue for which employee health and safety (EHS) is responsible. In fact, the executives are correct in both cases. That is why you need to engage those, as well as other stakeholders, in discussing and prioritizing the real risks of all aspects of workplace violence, and collaborate to develop recommendations for a comprehensive program. When you present senior management with a program that has the backing of all stakeholders, that program is more likely to be successful than one created by security alone.

Workplace violence is everyone's problem, and everyone – every impacted individual or group – must be part of the solution. (This is an excellent area to apply to the design thinking principles we discussed in Chapter 12.) In Table 18-2, we have listed some groups and their possible stake in the issue.

Table 18-2. Workplace Violence Department Stakeholders

Department or Function	Stake/Concern
Human Resources	HR's stake is the most obvious, as the group with the primary responsibility for employee well-being in most organizations.
Employee Health and Safety	EHS also has a significant role in workplace violence concerns. In many places, they also have a mandate from the national, state, or regional health and safety regulatory bodies. In 2011, for example, in the US, the Occupational Health and Safety Administration (OSHA) issued a specific directive on workplace violence, making handling these cases mandatory, much like the other aspects of work safety they mandate. On the other side of the globe, similar rules are in effect in Australia, based on the Victoria Occupational Health and Safety Act 2004 (the OHS Act). Many other jurisdictions have similar mandates.
Trade Unions and Worker's Councils	In locations where employees are represented by trade unions or worker's councils, these groups have a significant stake in any discussion involving the safety of employees, as well as the rights of any employee who is the victim of violence or is accused of concerning behavior.
Legal and Regulatory Compliance	Any time regulations are involved, the legal and/or compliance department has a significant stake in the discussion. In addition, the legal team needs to be involved in any decisions that impact employment law. All employees have certain rights, and it is important to ensure that processes consider the rights of both employees reported for concerning behavior and employees reporting that behavior. Every investigation and assessment must account for the two (or more) sides of every story. Legal is there to protect the rights of all the employees involved – and of course, the enterprise, as well.
Corporate Communications/Public Relations (PR)	Any act of violence in the workplace is something that will have a significant impact on the corporate communications or PR department. They certainly need a voice in designing the process and program. Additionally, many PR teams have responsibilities for internal communications. In the event of an act of violence in the workplace, this team needs to understand what is going on in order to present the story – internally and externally – and do so truthfully but with sensitivity to all involved.
Facilities	Workplace violence does not just affect people. Violence may be an escalating process, often beginning with vandalism or destruction of property. Not only does the facilities department have an interest in protecting the physical assets of the organization, they may see indications of concern in the form of physical damage to property, prior to any employees' noticing any escalated concerning actions.
Operations	Operations also has a stake in ensuring that a functioning and comprehensive workplace violence prevention policy is in place. They are dependent on a functioning workforce. Incidents of violence, whether

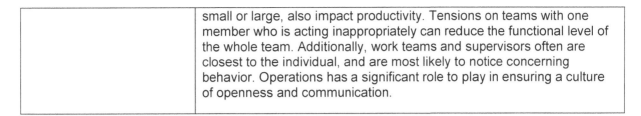

| | small or large, also impact productivity. Tensions on teams with one member who is acting inappropriately can reduce the functional level of the whole team. Additionally, work teams and supervisors often are closest to the individual, and are most likely to notice concerning behavior. Operations has a significant role to play in ensuring a culture of openness and communication. |

In an ESRM program, the role of security in *managing* security risks is separate from the more tactical risk *mitigation* role of responding to incidents when they occur. The role of managing the workplace violence risk requires engaging the appropriate asset owners and stakeholders in the security risk management decision-making process on what risk mitigation plans to put in place.

In many programs, the security risk mitigation activities of incident response and investigations related to threats of violence are then assigned to the security team. In that case, security also becomes a stakeholder, and should weigh in on the security risk decision-making process in that capacity. This does introduce some complexity which must be carefully managed when you and your team fill *all* the roles, risk mitigation task management, risk stakeholder/decision making, *and* ESRM risk-based program management. We have discussed how your role as the security risk manager is not to enforce your opinion of how the security risks should be mitigated. However, *in this case*, as a risk *stakeholder* who will have responsibility for incident response, if you find some aspect of the response plan inadequate, you have a responsibility to yourself and your team to make sure the risk mitigation activities are appropriate for protecting both the enterprise and your personnel.

18.3 Identifying and Prioritizing Risks in Workplace Violence Prevention and Threat Management Programs

Once the assets impacted and the correct stakeholders are identified, the second step in the ESRM model, shown in Figure 18-3, requires that your workplace violence program identify and prioritize the specific types of risks that could be present in your environment. This must be done in conjunction with the stakeholders whom you have identified, so that you can get all perspectives in the potential risks.

According to the National Institute for Occupational Safety and Health (NIOSH), the highest risk factors for workplace violence are:

- Contact with the public.
- Exchange of money.
- Delivery of passengers, goods, or services.
- Having a mobile workplace, such as a taxicab or police cruiser.
- Working with unstable or volatile persons in healthcare, social service, or criminal justice settings.
- Working alone or in small numbers.
- Working late at night or during early-morning hours.
- Working in high-crime areas.
- Guarding valuable property or possessions.
- Working in community-based settings (National Institute for Occupational Safety and Health, 1996).

Figure 18-3. Workplace violence prevention and threat management require risk identification first.

Of course, in the process of risk identification, you may conclude that there are none of these extended risks that are specific to your enterprise. If this is the case, you will still cover the generalized work environment and all the varieties of "everyday" risks.

Workplace Violence Warning Signs
You and your employees must be able to recognize and report concerning behavior to prevent it from escalating to violence. The US Department of Labor provides an excellent high-level guide that could be referenced in any employee or manager training on this topic, and will be especially useful as basic workplace violence training for threat management team members.

Warning signs to look for:
- Early warning behavior.
  o Intimidating/bullying.
  o Discourteous/disrespectful.
  o Uncooperative and/or verbally abusive.
- Escalated behavior.
  o Argumentative.
  o Refusal to obey policies.
  o Sabotage or theft of property.
  o Communicates threats to hurt co-workers or managers.
  o Feels victimized by the company.
- Emergency behavior.
  o Suicide threats.
  o Physical fights.
  o Destruction of property.
  o Display of extreme anger or rage.
  o Using weapons to harm others.

Although the US Department of Labor provides this information, it is highly useful in any area of the globe. Here we have included some of the warning signs to look for, but the full document is available online at https://www.dol.gov/oasam/hrc/policies/dol-workplace-violence-program.htm

18.4 Mitigate Prioritized Risks Through Workplace Violence Prevention and Threat Management Program Design

The third step of the life cycle, in Figure 18-4, is mitigating the defined risks. This process designs, builds, and rolls out your workplace violence prevention and threat management programs. Referring to Chapter 12 and the design thinking process, workplace violence prevention and threat management programs – because they rely on multiple stakeholders – will need to be designed and rolled out in a highly collaborative manner, gathering all feedback, and making changes as the programs evolve. In an area that is as sensitive and fraught with complex feelings as workplace violence, you will need to take extra care as you go through the process to ensure that all input is weighed and given appropriate consideration. Some general principles for mitigating security risks of workplace violence are having the program include:

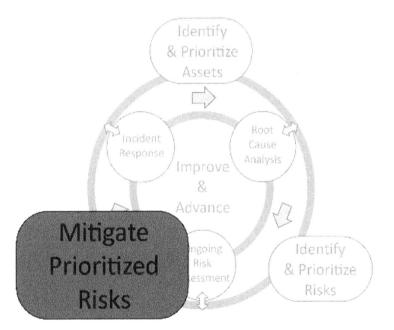

Figure 18-4. Workplace violence prevention and threat management programs are both risk mitigation activities.

285

- Employee awareness.
- Mandatory reporting of concerning behavior and events.
- A threat assessment and management team and process.
- Ongoing testing.
- Reporting to a governing body on the ongoing results of the program.

Multiple standards exist that can assist you in building a program that best suits your enterprise and its needs. As with all security programs, the best program for *your* enterprise is the one that works to mitigate those specific risks to which the organization is exposed.

Questions for the Security Practitioner
- "What can I do to identify the individuals and roles most likely to be threatened by workplace violence?"
- Who in the enterprise – whether inside or outside the security organization – can help me make that assessment? Who can help me develop my skills in this area?"

18.5 Incident Response in Workplace Violence Prevention and Threat Management Programs

In terms of workplace violence, the ideal incident response is to investigate a *report* of concerning behavior that has *not yet* escalated into a violent incident. That aspect of response consists of:

1. Having the capacity to receive a report or complaint or take a witness account.
2. Responding appropriately, using threat assessment and management techniques (like the ones we outline in Table 18-3) to manage a threat and move an individual away from the risk of violence. That response to a concern is typically referred to as a *threat management program.*

We also must recognize and consider the unfortunate possibility of having to respond to an incident where a violent act has already occurred or is in the process of happening. This second aspect of workplace violence response involves teaching employees the skills to react to an act of violence as it is taking place. But in the ESRM model, shown in Figure 18-5, that incident is only one part of the overall holistic program, not the entire – or even the primary – focus of the program.

Figure 18-5. – Incident response to workplace violence includes responding to reports of concerning behavior or actual violent incidents.

Threat Management Case Study, Part 1: Receiving a Report of a Workplace Violence Threat

Bob R., a longtime assembly line worker at a manufacturing plant, had begun displaying disturbing behaviors. His work had always been excellent, but recently it had suffered in terms of both productivity and quality to the point that mistakes he made stopped the assembly line completely. Of even more concern, he began to angrily yell at co-workers and throw tools on the factory floor. Several of his co-workers, worried about his safety and theirs, reported that they suspected him of drinking on the job.

When the foreman called him in to speak with him about these issues, the encounter went very badly. The foreman noted that Bob's eyes were bloodshot, his hands were trembling, and his breath reeked of alcohol. He was extremely angry at having his work criticized, and he stormed out of the foreman's office, kicking over a chair as he left. Shaken by the encounter, the foreman went to the plant manager, and demanded that Bob be fired – immediately. (In Part 2 of the case study, we will see how the plant manager handled this situation.)

18.6 Root Cause Analysis in Workplace Violence Prevention and Threat Management Programs

When dealing with workplace violence – both reports of concerning behavior and actual incidents – the root cause analysis step of the ESRM cycle, as we see in figure 18-6, is essential. It is the key to determining how to prevent concerning behavior from escalating into violence or determining whether environmental factors can be modified to reduce probable future incidents.

Consider an example in a storefront customer service center of a rural power provider, where people came in to pay their bills in person. This location saw a considerable number of angry customers – often people whose power had been shut off for some reason. These angry people yelled at or sometimes threatened the counter staff, with security called out at least twice a month for several months to escort a customer from the premises.

The company's security manager discussed the issue with the director of customer service centers, and they decided to perform a deeper root cause investigation. This showed that in 80% of the cases, the customer had been attempting to correct a collections issue. But the counter staff had no authority to try to resolve problems in collections

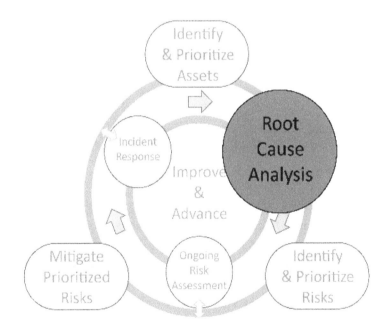

Figure 18-6. Root cause analysis is critical to removing residual risk of violence from the workplace.

cases. All they could do was to tell the customer to call the company's customer service line. This simply escalated the situation, making angry customers even angrier. The customer service director, discussing the options with the security manager for mitigating the risk, decided that at least one manager at the center could be trained in dispute resolution, and would have the authority to work with customers on the collections issues. The result: The number of incidents of threatening customers declined sharply.

In workplace violence and threat management, the root causes of actions are often cloudy, with many contributing factors. Consistently looking for patterns in location or similar incidents over time can help the program identify emerging and changing risks, or ones that are beginning to creep out of security risk tolerance levels, and help to avert future risk impact if mitigation plans are updated.

> ### Threat Management Case Study, Part 2: Analyzing a Potential Workplace Violence Threat
> The plant manager, aware that Bob had been an employee in good standing for many years, decided not to fire him – at least not immediately. Over the foreman's vehement objections, and according to the program policy he was trained on, the manager called in the security organization's threat assessment team. An investigator assigned by the team interviewed Bob's co-workers and learned that they were genuinely concerned about him. He was going through a bitter divorce and custody battle and had been working overtime to pay for child support. His co-workers believed the last straw was that his ex-wife was making plans to take their children and move to another state.
>
> Toward the end of the investigation, Bob himself was interviewed. He acknowledged that he had been drinking heavily, including at work, and that he was depressed and extremely angry. He was worried about losing his children and his house and now his job. And he told the investigator, "Maybe it'd be better if I was dead," and muttered something about "taking everybody with me." The investigator interpreted that final remark as a clear threat, not only to Bob himself but also to others. (In Part 3 of the case study, we will see how the threat management team resolved this situation).

18.7 Ongoing Risk Assessment in Workplace Violence Prevention and Threat Management Programs

Finally, the last piece of the ESRM cycle, shown in Figure 18-7, involves the continual assessment of existing risk to see if incidents or impacts are within set business tolerance levels, and scanning for new risk or emerging risk patterns, which feeds workplace violence prevention and threat management program improvement. Conducted in conjunction with oversight of the security council, the assessment of new, previously unknown risks, or risks identified in post-mortem reviews on incidents, is a key piece of ensuring the ongoing safety and security of the workplace, and keeping it free of acts of violence.

Employees involved in threat situations, or who display concerning behavior, are

Figure 18-7. Ongoing risk assessment is critical in workplace violence cases to ensure mitigation plans are carried out and effective.

oftentimes not fired for the offense if they can correct the behavior, and if it was not egregious enough for immediate termination (for example, an angry outburst is potentially correctable, a death threat is another level altogether).

However, the original behavior did require an investigation. Thus, ongoing risk assessment within the structure of a threat management and workplace violence prevention allows the threat management team to monitor the situation moving forward to ensure no residual risk behavior occurs, which would require additional action.

> ### *Threat Management Case Study Part 3: Mitigation Planning for a Workplace Violence Threat*
>
> The investigator, like the foreman, clearly recognized that Bob's words and actions represented a threat. But working together with representatives from the threat assessment team, he reached the decision that Bob should not be fired for his remarks, at least not at that time. The point of this process is to reduce the potential for violence and other disruptive behavior, and firing Bob, further adding to his very real troubles, might actually make violence more likely.
>
> The assessment team moved to escort Bob from the workplace. They referred him to the company's employee assistance program (EAP), which offered him counseling and alcohol treatment, both of which were mandatory if Bob were to keep his job. He went on short-term disability, with ongoing monitoring by the EAP and HR – which is mandated by OSHA rules in the US. At the end of three months, Bob was alcohol-free, and his counselor determined that he could manage his personal problems well enough to return to work.
>
> The assessment team accepted the counselor's recommendation and allowed him to return to the workplace under certain strict conditions. He had to continue alcohol treatment and submit to regular drug testing. He was instructed to apologize to his co-workers – something he did willingly because he was genuinely remorseful for his behavior. He also was not permitted return to the same assembly line but was to be moved to a different part of the plant where his skills were needed.
>
> Bob's story does not have a perfectly happy ending. He remained employed, but his custody battle ended badly with his kids moving out of state, and his financial troubles resulted in his losing his house. ESRM does not guarantee that every ending will work out better than an ad hoc approach. However, it does provide a much more consistent and defined role and responsibility for everyone engaged in the process. As anyone who has dealt with a workplace violence threat has come to realize, everyone is a security expert after the incident. With workplace violence assessments, there are no right answers, but there are many options. Some options can work out better than others, and it is the asset owners and stakeholders who collectively should work through them and decide which option is the best avenue for each individual case. Security's role in guiding the risk owners through that process, as well as being a subject matter expert to help with the conversation, will more uniformly and comprehensively address these security risks, and help in developing a well thought out workplace violence prevention program.

Questions for the Security Practitioner
- "Do I understand human behavior well enough to tell the difference between an immediate threat and something that can be dealt with over the longer term?"
- "Who can I call on to help me make sound assessments of workplace violence threats?"
- "Is a team in place to make these assessments? If not, who should be part of that team?"

18.8 A Deeper Look at the Role of Workplace Violence Prevention and Threat Management in ESRM

The ESRM workplace violence prevention model is different from most other approaches – in focus, in ownership, and in culture. In a risk-based security management environment, the discussion of workplace violence is much broader, involves more stakeholders, focuses on more areas of impact, and is generally a more holistic approach than we often see in those proposed workplace violence prevention programs that so often struggle for traction.

18.8.1 A Difference in Focus: Holistic Workplace Violence Prevention and Threat Management Programs vs. Workplace Violence Response Training

The holistic approach to workplace violence prevention is not a new one, and we are not suggesting that there are not already high-quality programs in place in enterprises worldwide. In fact, there are many excellent standards and workplace violence prevention programs available to use as the foundation for an ESRM workplace violence prevention program (see Table 18-3) if your enterprise chooses to implement one.

Table 18-3. Standards for Implementing Holistic Workplace Violence Prevention and Threat Management

Workplace Violence Prevention Standard	Key Features
Workplace violence prevention and intervention: American national standard. ASIS International, and Society for Human Resources Management (SHRM).	According to ASIS International and SHRM in a 2011 press release: "The Standard reflects a consensus from professionals in the fields of security, human resources, mental health, law enforcement, and legal. It serves as an important tool to help organizations evaluate current practices; develop or enhance workplace violence prevention and intervention programs; and effectively manage post-incident issues... [and] defines the recommended scope of an organization's efforts to prevent and manage workplace violence; describes the key stakeholders within an organization who will be responsible for this issue; delineates the components of a workplace violence prevention and intervention program; outlines intervention techniques; and addresses post-incident issues" (Society for Human Resource Management, 2011).
Risk Assessment Guideline Elements for Violence: Considerations for Assessing the Risk of Future Violent Behavior (RAGE-V). Association of Threat Assessment Professionals.	This guide is intended specifically for the threat assessment portion of a workplace violence prevention program and includes practice advisories for information gathering, legal considerations, and psychological considerations. An assessment flowchart is included to allow threat assessor to walk through an assessment in a more structured manner. From the guideline itself: "The RAGE-V is an exploration and explanation of *interrelated* processes and activities that will assist in evaluating the potential risk of future physical violence from a known individual, including those inspired or

	motivated by group philosophy or beliefs." (Association of Threat Assessment Professionals, 2006, p 5).
Guidelines for Preventing Workplace Violence for Healthcare and Social Service Workers US Department of Labor, Occupational Safety and Health Administration – OSHA 3148-06R 2016.	While this guide is specific to preventing violence in a health care setting (healthcare workers being one of the most impacted occupations, along with taxi drivers, when it comes to workplace violence), this guide offers solid guidance for almost any practitioner wanting to set up a workplace violence prevention program, and it covers multiple aspects of setting up a program, including: 1. Management commitment and employee participation. 2. Worksite analysis. 3. Hazard prevention and control. 4. Safety and health training. 5. Recordkeeping and program evaluation. (Occupational Safety and Health Administration, 2016).
The Prevention and Management of Violence in the Workplace National Occupational Standards	This British standard from the National Occupational Standards organization aims to provide employers and workers in the UK with the tools and information to prevent violent acts in the workplace. While this standard is more training-focused, it has a significant scope of helpful information. (Skills CFA, 2013).

These models are excellent background reading for setting up a workplace violence prevention and threat management program in your enterprise.

Of course, the specifics of the program that works best for your enterprise will depend on many factors in your organization. But there are some best practices that we believe apply to any comprehensive, effective workplace violence prevention program. They include:

- Ensuring that all impacted stakeholders are involved in developing the program.
- Encouraging or mandating the reporting of concerning behavior.
- Having a formal structured threat assessment and management team in place with processes mapped out.
- Educating and communicating to management, employees, and assessment team members about the vital importance of awareness and prevention.
- Training people on what to do if workplace violence occurs – the run/hide/fight decision. But there should also be stress on the fact that preventing violence in the first place is always preferable to reacting to it.

We will discuss some detailed specifics and recommendations in the remainder of this chapter.

Case Study: Holistic Workplace Violence Prevention Programs Work
Susan J. was a teller in a branch bank in Texas in the US. She recently left her husband, Frank, after being married for 12 years. Her boss, the branch manager, Danielle M. was aware of the divorce, but Susan never told her about the history of domestic violence in the relationship, something that Susan did not like to discuss and did not want known at work.

Rhonda C., another teller at a different branch of the bank, was a friend of Susan's. She kept Susan's confidences about all the circumstances of the marriage and divorce because she felt that it was Susan's personal business and not something that anyone at work needed to know about.

However, one week, Rhonda had been disturbed by some posts that Frank, whom Rhonda also knew outside of work, had been making on his social media accounts. Frank made comments online about how angry his was with Susan for leaving him and made some vague statements about getting even with her. He also posted a picture on his site with a new shotgun that he said bought for hunting. These things combined to make Rhonda feel as though Frank might be a threat to Susan. She told Susan about it, but Susan said she was done with Frank and had a restraining order to keep him away. She said everything would be fine.

Rhonda had gone through workplace violence prevention training that was delivered by her bank's security team. She was taught that workplace violence is more than just the possibility of an active shooter, or even (although more likely in a bank) an armed robbery. She learned that, actually, the most significant source of workplace violence in most organizations was domestic violence that spilled over into the work environment. The training stressed that it was every employee's responsibility to report concerning behavior of any kind – anything that felt like it could threaten the safety of the workplace. Although Rhonda felt very bad about bringing Susan's personal business into work, she just did not feel that she could ignore the signs she was taught about in the workplace violence prevention training she received. So, she called the security reporting hotline number and told them about the disturbing posts she had seen.

The company threat management team received the report and investigated the situation. The security manager, Craig D., reached out to his local law enforcement contacts to alert them to the posts. Since Susan did have a restraining order, the police were interested in what Frank had said online. They went to Frank's house to ask him about the posts, but Frank was not home. His roommate said he had been agitated lately and that he had said he was going to go do some target practice. The police were concerned and went back to the bank branch to talk to Susan to make sure she was okay. Luckily, when they got there, one of the officers saw Frank's car at a gas station across the street from the bank. They went over to assess the situation and saw Frank in his car. They observed that he was drunk and had several loaded guns in his car. The police arrested him and took him to the police station.

This was a close call for Susan and for the company. The training that Rhonda received from her company's workplace violence prevention program was responsible for averting what very likely would have been a tragedy. The clearly predefined roles of each group also allowed for expediency in response and reporting.

18.8.2 A Difference in Culture – Workplace Violence Awareness

Effective workplace violence prevention is not something that can be achieved overnight. It certainly will not be achieved by a single training session telling people what to do if someone appears in the workplace with a weapon. It is more focused on prevention, on receiving reports, on assessing and managing threats, and moving behavior *away* from potential violence in any given situation.

A cultural shift involves all employees embracing their role in workplace violence prevention by reporting concerning behavior, by wearing their identification to show that they belong in the workplace, by inquiring politely if they can help people who appear *not* to belong, and by reporting to security if they feel something is not right. Moreover, it is a shift away from people "just minding their own business," to people feeling comfortable about saying something when a co-worker is exhibiting concerning behaviors.

Workplace violence *prevention* is a long, complex, demanding process, based on risk assessment, management, and education. Ultimately, it will help to prevent violence from happening, not just teach employees how to react to violence when it does occur.

Workplace violence is an area where the partnerships developed as part of the ESRM program can assist the security team in communicating the message that workplace violence prevention is everyone's responsibility. In ESRM, the consistent message in all security risks is that it is the role of the business to determine which security risk mitigation plans are used to bring the risk in line with the tolerance set by the business. In that environment, the idea that the business is responsible for the same things in a workplace violence prevention and threat management program will not be new or surprising to your strategic partners. It is not that much further to bring them into the more active role of participating in the mitigating activities, such as making security reports and (if appropriate to their role) participating on the threat management team.

Questions for the Security Practitioner
- "What kinds of workplace violence should I be concerned about, in my enterprise, in my industry, and in my location? What are the factors that contribute to my views about this?"
- "Would I know how to identify concerning employee behavior if it was brought to my attention? What individuals and organizations within the enterprise could help me to enhance my skills and understanding in this area?"
- "Who are the key stakeholders in workplace violence prevention and management in the security area I am responsible for?"

Chapter Review

In Chapter 18, you learned about workplace violence, what it is, how to implement programs to prevent it, and how to manage threats of violence in the enterprise workplace.

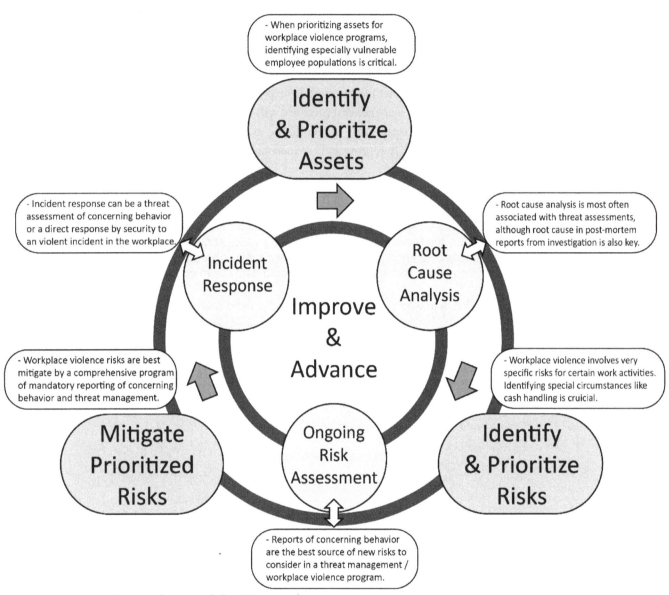

Figure 18-8. Workplace violence and the ESRM cycle – A review.

Looking Forward

In Chapter 19, we will move on to look at one more aspect of an ESRM security program – Business Continuity Management.

Practitioner steps to consider before moving on to Chapter 19:

✓ Consider the level of workplace violence awareness across your enterprise – is it at the level it needs to be? Do you have training programs? Is the current program effective?

✓ Think about the specific skills – technical or otherwise – that your security organization might need to add to protect the enterprise against workplace violence threats.

Security Program Self-Assessment

In this self-assessment, you should think about the answer to the questions posed, and then see where your program is on the identified ESRM spectrum.

Question	Y/N	Is This ESRM?
Does your organization have a holistic workplace violence prevention and threat management program?	□Yes □No	**NO:** If you do not have a workplace violence prevention program, then instituting a program, and building a threat management team is a suitable place to start your ESRM program. **PARTIAL:** If you have some training available on workplace violence response or aspects of workplace violence, but have no formal threat management program, then you are part of the way to an ESRM implementation. **YES:** If you have a formal, holistic program to train employees on workplace violence prevention, and to manage threats of violence in the workplace, then you are practicing ESRM.

Questions for Discussion

1. Business leaders may argue that that discussing workplace violence is too scary and disturbing to employees. What are some ways you could counter these objections?

2. How can increased visibility of a specific type of security incident, like workplace violence in this case, help or hinder a security program? Can you think of instances in which news events have led to a disproportionate concern about one specific type of event?

3. How could awareness of domestic violence in the workplace help convince employees that they should be more vigilant in helping to enforce a security culture in your organization?

References

ASIS International and Society for Human Resources Management (SHRM). (2011, September 2). *Workplace violence prevention and intervention: American national standard*. Arlington, VA: ASIS International.

Association of Threat Assessment Professionals (ATAP). (2006, September 4). *Risk assessment guideline elements for violence*: *Considerations for assessing the risk of future violent behavior*. Sacramento, CA: Author. Retrieved from https://c.ymcdn.com/sites/www.atapworldwide.org/resource/resmgr/imported/documents/RAGE-V.pdf

National Institutes of Health and Safety (NIOSH). (1996, July). *Violence in the workplace.* (DHHS (NIOSH) Publication, Number 96-100). Retrieved from https://www.cdc.gov/niosh/docs/96-100/risk.html

Occupational Safety and Health Administration (OSHA). (2011, September 8). *OSHA issues compliance directive to address workplace violence.* Retrieved from https://www.osha.gov/news/newsreleases/trade/09082011

Skills CFA. (2013, January). *The prevention and management of violence in the workplace: National occupational standards.* Retrieved from https://www.skillscfa.org/images/pdfs/National%20Occupational%20Standards/Industrial%20Relations/2007/The%20Prevention%20and%20Management%20of%20work-related%20violence.pdf

Society for Human Resource Management (SHRM). (2011, October). *ASIS International and SHRM release joint workplace violence prevention and intervention ANSI standard.* Retrieved from https://www.shrm.org/about-shrm/press-room/press-releases/pages/workplaceviolencepreventionandinterventionstandard.aspx

US Department of Justice. (2011, March). *Workplace violence,1993-2009: National crime victimization survey and the census of fatal occupational injuries.* Special Report, NCJ 233231. Retrieved from https://www.bjs.gov/content/pub/pdf/wv09.pdf

US Department of Labor. (N.D.). *DOL Workplace Violence Program.* Retrieved from https://www.dol.gov/oasam/hrc/policies/dol-workplace-violence-program.htm

19

ESRM and Business Continuity and Crisis Management

This chapter covers a specialty area that at times is included under security's area of responsibility – *business continuity management* (BCM) and *crisis management*. Unfortunately, many enterprises consider BCM and crisis management to fall outside the realm of security. They may decide it belongs in information technology (IT), in a company operational group, or even in the facilities area. Nevertheless, the idea that BCM and crisis management make up a mitigation activity designed to protect enterprise assets the way that security risk management does not necessarily fit with the view of BCM or security held by many business leaders. In this chapter, we will show why this view should be challenged. We will show how BCM truly aligns with other security disciplines overall, as well as protecting the enterprise from risk by preparing ahead of time for all types of incident response.

Because BCM and crisis management are already risk-based disciplines, they may possibly constitute the one area that is most easily brought into an enterprise security risk management (ESRM) approach. BCM requires the same risk assessment and mitigation planning steps as ESRM. While crisis management and emergency response – the other pillars of the continuity management discipline – are another kind of incident response, they are also based on risk mitigation planning.

This chapter will help you to:
- Understand why BCM and crisis management should be part of your ESRM program.
- Learn how to implement a BCM program in the ESRM model.

19.1 How does Business Continuity and Crisis Management Fit in the ESRM Life Cycle?

The crisis management and business continuity process is already risk-based, and in fact, follows a very similar path to the ESRM cycle.

In Table 19-1, we compare the ESRM life cycle to the Plan/Do/Check/Act model espoused by both the International Organization for Standards (ISO) and the American National Standards Institute (ANSI) in their respective BCM standards documents. In the table below, you will see how the BCM standard model relates to the steps in the ESRM life cycle with which you are already familiar.

Table 19-1. Comparing BCM and ESRM Life Cycles

ESRM Life Cycle	ISO and ANSI Plan/Do/Check/Act
1 Figure 19-1. BCM requires a life cycle very similar to ESRM, which makes it a natural fit for an ESRM program.	*2 Figure 19-2. Both ISO 22301 and ANSI BCM 01.2010 use a Plan/Do/Check/Act cycle for BCM. (International Organization for Standardization, 2012, & American National Standards Institute, 2010).*
1. Identify and Prioritize Assets ESRM and BCM programs both require practitioners to fully understand the assets of the enterprise. **2. Identify and Prioritize Risks** ESRM and BCM both call for the practitioner to identify the risks faced by the organization.	**Establish (Plan)** This step in the ISO and ANSI model looks for, "…objectives, targets, controls, processes and procedures relevant to improving business continuity in order to deliver results that align with the organization's overall policies and objectives." (International Organization for Standardization, 2012, & American National Standards Institute, 2010) In other words, what are the assets that are important to the business, and what controls need to be put in place to deal with the risks that the business wants to mitigate.
3. Mitigate Prioritized Risks In both ESRM and BCM programs, risk mitigation is a key aspect of dealing with the potential impact to assets by harmful things.	**Implement (Do)** This step is for writing and enacting the, "…business continuity policy, controls, processes and procedures." (International Organization for Standardization, 2012, & American National Standards Institute, 2010).

4. Improve and Advance	Monitor and Review (Check)
• **Incident Response** • **Root Cause Analysis** • **Ongoing Risk Assessment** ESRM and BCM programs both require continual review and improvement to ensure the best enterprise protection.	This step calls for the BCM program to, "Monitor and review performance against business continuity policy and objectives, report the results to management for review, and determine and authorize actions for remediation and improvement." (International Organization for Standardization, 2012, & American National Standards Institute, 2010). This statement essentially covers the ongoing risk assessment and general improvement aspects of the program. **Maintain and Approve (Act)** The last step, according to ISO and ANSI is to, "maintain and improve the BCMS by taking corrective action…" (International Organization for Standardization, 2012, & American National Standards Institute, 2010). This aligns with responding to incidents, and seeking root causes of issues to make changes to the program as needed.

As you can see, the cycles are very similar, and working BCM into the overall ESRM program is not too difficult a task if the BCM practitioners on your team understand and align with the ESRM philosophy.

19.2 Identifying and Prioritizing Assets and Risks in a Business Continuity and Crisis Management Program

The first two steps in BCM and crisis management planning are to:

1. Determine the impact of functions and assets to the enterprise.
2. Determine how they are at risk, what the likelihood of those risks occurring are, and whether those risks will be included in the risk mitigation, continuity, and crisis planning programs, as they move forward.

These are the same as the opening steps of the ESRM cycle, seen in Figures 19-3, and 19-4. It is so similar because, like the ESRM philosophy, BCM and crisis management already function in an *inherently risk-based model.*

There are some benefits your ESRM program rollout can gain by incorporating BCM into the ESRM program, or, if it is not possible to do that, in partnering closely with the team responsible for enterprise BCM and crisis management during the ESRM rollout. When implementing an ESRM security program, much of the work already done by your BCM team can come into play. Two areas specifically can benefit tremendously from the outset.

Figure 19-3. The BCM process also begins with identifying and prioritizing assets.

1. Security can leverage any business impact analysis (BIA) and risk assessment already completed by the BCM team: to identify many existing assets, departments, and functions; to understand the impact they have on the overall enterprise; and to find a registry of the risk they are exposed to.

2. The BIA and risk assessment process from BCM has likely already allowed the BCM team to develop a deep understanding of the business, assets, and stakeholders. This knowledge can be shared with everyone involved in setting up the ESRM program, and could be used as step one of the ESRM process, or at least as a solid base to expand on.

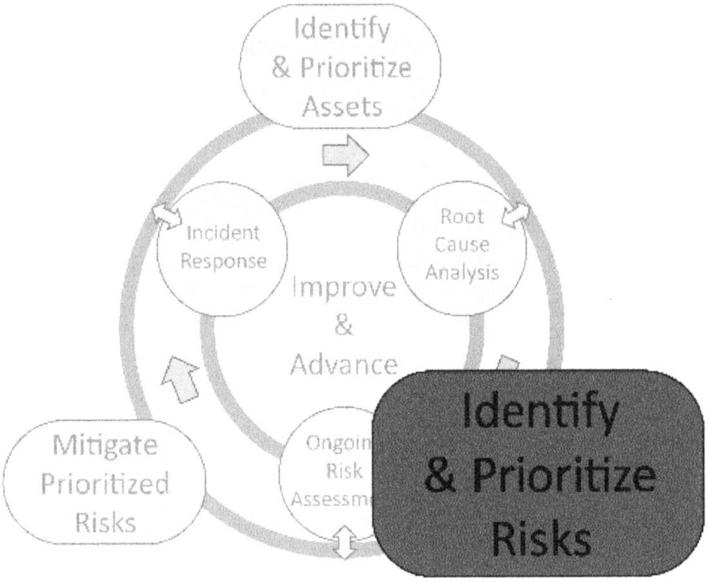

If there is no pre-existing crisis and/or BCM program in your enterprise, the discipline of continuity and crisis management is a great way to begin your ESRM implementation.

The concepts of continuity and crisis management are familiar in the business world, and many of your strategic partners will already understand business impact analysis in that setting. This familiarity makes the crisis preparedness discussion an excellent way to engage new strategic partners, and to begin a further ESRM discussion based on determining how to handle crisis and continuity.

Figure 19-4. BCM and ESRM must both identify and prioritize risks.

302

19.3 Mitigating Prioritized Risks in a Business Continuity and Crisis Management Program

In BCM and crisis management, once the impact of assets and critical functions on the business – and risks to those assets and functions – have been analyzed, the next step is to determine the strategy for crisis response and recovery, and then to write plans to help mitigate the impact of an interruption of business operations. This follows right along with the ESRM step of mitigating the risks as determined by the business, seen below in Figure 19-5.

From a BCM perspective, the mitigation process requires asking what the business wants out of the crisis program. The answers to the questions will drive the level and detail of planning, and determine whether backup sites or workaround processes are put in place.

Typical BCM planning questions that must be answered are:

- Does the business want to plan for quick recovery?
- Does the business want to have alternate methods of function already in place, prior to a crisis?
- Is the business more comfortable with having only plans for recovery in place, without active backups already existing?
- Which details will the business need to recover operations?
- Is there a deep field of redundant knowledge that can be called upon in a crisis?
- Are tasks so specialized that detailed instructions are needed?

Figure 19-5. BCM planning and crisis response are additional ways to mitigate prioritized risks.

These are just a few representative questions to ask to help the BCM planner, and the functional subject matter expert (the asset owner or risk stakeholder in ESRM terms) to put together a continuity and crisis management plan. But in BCM, just as with all ESRM risk decisions, the options must be decided upon by the business owner, based on their ability to tolerate risk, and would not be dictated to them by the BCM professional assisting them in their planning efforts.

Another aspect of the BCM function that directly parallels the ESRM step of mitigating risks is the task of putting the crisis risk mitigation activities into place. Besides writing plans, this could include getting backup equipment in place; setting up contingency plans to have alternate work locations in a crisis; building crisis teams, and training them on crisis activities, and more. In this aspect of mitigation, some enterprises assign the tasks to the BCM team, making them not only the managers of the risk of crisis events, but also risk stakeholders who carry out actual mitigation activities. In other organizations, the BCM team only provides expertise and guidance to the business owner, and that business owner is responsible for ensuring that they provide their own mitigation activities. This is essentially the same as the other disciplines we have discussed in previous chapters, where the security department might own the security risk mitigation activity that is protecting the assets, or a business owner might be responsible for the mitigation plan.

19.4 Incident Response in a Business Continuity and Crisis Management Program

Business continuity management and crisis management are activities that, at the core, are targeted directly at incident response. Crisis management is a direct response to an incident – an incident that may have a much larger scope, impact, and required reaction than some other security incidents, but an incident response, nonetheless. Like other security incident responses, crisis management requires:

- An immediate response to crisis level incidents.
- A coordinated and organized approach following an existing mitigation plan.

Eventually, the immediate crisis ends, and then the secondary incident response of getting the organization back to normal levels of functionality comes into play, by invoking the continuity plans that have been put in place to get the business back up and running. These will:

- Provide a roadmap to get each function back to work.
- Allow employees to understand the state of their function, and when it will resume normal operations.
- Allow the enterprise to have a timeline and an organized process for bringing functions back online in order of priority.

Figure 19-6. Continuity and crisis planning all focus on responding to a crisis incident then recovering from it.

The incident response phase of BCM and crisis management, as with the ESRM cycle as seen in Figure 19-6, consists of activities that the team carries out in support of the risk mitigation decisions, made by the strategic leaders in the enterprise.

Questions for the Security Practitioner
- "Does my BCM team perform and publish postmortem reporting on all crisis events and exercises?"
- "Have I ever participated in a BIA or risk assessment with the BCM team in my organization?"
- "Have I participated in BCM or crisis plan writing in my organization?"

19.5 Root Cause Analysis in a Business Continuity and Crisis Management Program

BCM best practices require every crisis response or BCM plan activation to go through a postmortem reporting process, to determine several things including lessons learned, and the root cause of an incident, which is the same as root cause analysis in the ESRM model (Figure 19-7).

The formal BCM root cause analysis might look a little different from the one we discussed in Chapter 15 on investigations, but it is necessary for continual program improvement in BCM in the same manner that it is for all the other security disciplines. The information from the postmortem report is used to update crisis and continuity plans, just as it is used in other security risk areas to suggest additional mitigation activities.

A sample of items that would be included in a postmortem for a crisis event are listed below:

- Description of the incident.
- Timeline of events.
- Impact of the crisis on the enterprise and on individual functions.
  o Human impact.
  o Asset impact.
  o Financial impact.
  o Regulatory impact.
  o Brand impact.
- Declaration of crisis.
  o Incident commander.
  o Crisis team participants.
  o Plans invoked and followed.
- Close of the crisis phase.
  o Transition to continuity.
- Lessons learned.
  o What worked according to plan.
  o What gaps were found.
  o How plans and responses can improve.
- Risk Identification.
  o Known risk vs. unknown or residual risk.

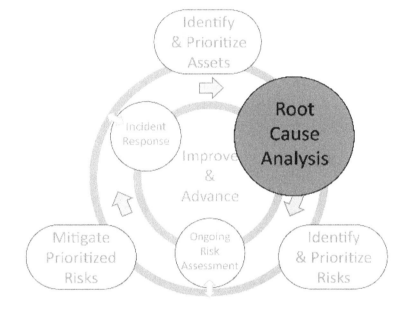

Figure 19-7. Post mortem reporting and root cause analysis is a key aspect of the BCM program.

Root cause analysis is a critical component of ongoing business continuity planning, and of ensuring the enterprise organization is protected from crisis events to the tolerance levels set by the business.

19.6 Ongoing Risk Assessment in a Business Continuity and Crisis Management Program

Just as we have discussed in the ESRM paradigm (Figure 19-8), ongoing risk assessment is as critical to BCM as all other aspects of security. Ongoing risk assessment in BCM consists of updating plans in response to the root cause analysis, and continually testing and training plan participants.

The postmortem reports that we discussed in the previous section, are used to drive continual preparedness improvement, and to better the plans and program overall.

Identified good practices and gaps are communicated to asset owners and to risk stakeholders, allowing them to update their continuity and crisis plans in order to:

- Adopt good practices from other groups
- Change practices in their plans that did not work during their response and recovery
- Change practices in their plans in response to impacts other groups had during the crisis.

These practices allow the enterprise BCM program to benefit from both positive and negative lessons learned on an ongoing basis. These lessons learned and plan updates are not only made in response to a crisis, however.

For the ongoing risk assessment to occur and program improvement to happen, it is not enough to wait around for a crisis incident to come about. Training crisis response team members, putting them and their plans through regular exercises, and doing the same root cause analysis on those exercises that you would do in a real crisis are also imperative for ongoing improvement of the BCM function.

Figure 19-8. Ongoing risk assessment is critical in BCM to make sure the enterprise is always prepared for crisis.

19.7 A Deeper Look at the Role of Business Continuity and Crisis Management in ESRM

Business continuity and crisis management fit very well into an ESRM program. There are significant advantages to both the BCM team and the security team when they are part of a common group.

The advantage for BCM is:

- ESRM can provide much of the support and traction that a BCM organization needs – the strategic partnerships, inherent authority, scope, and independence that allow the BCM program to operate efficiently – without requiring the BCM team to struggle to find traction with a high-level sponsor or reporting structure of its own.

The advantage for the security team is:

- BCM professionals already operate in a risk management mindset. They understand much of what will be needed for the security program to shift to the new ESRM model, and they can be a significant help.
- The BCM group typically already has an intimate knowledge of the entire organization, and they can be a source of critical information in the ESRM implementation.

The main advantages that can come about if BCM and crisis management are part of the risk-based security program are tied to the essential aspects of successful security, as we will now explore.

19.7.1 A Difference in Authority – Getting Traction

When operating in an ESRM model, a BCM program that operates under the security umbrella can take advantage of the fact that the *acknowledged authority* of the security team is already in place to manage security risks, in partnership with other functional leaders. Once that mission is established, the business continuity team is simply another aspect of the overall mitigation of risk in the enterprise. A prevalent view in BCM professional circles is that BCM must report into a C-level executive or some similar high place in the enterprise so that the rest of the organization understands that it must comply with the BCM program. This is not needed once BCM is operating under the authority of the ESRM program, which (by the time it is rolled out) has a well understood role to manage all security risks in the enterprise.

Chief executive officers (CEO), chief operating officers (COO), and other senior executives have limited bandwidth for multiple programs all reporting to them separately. By rolling business continuity and crisis management into the overall ESRM program, it will have the proper traction to go out into the business and help people manage their continuity risks as part of the mission of the security department, while removing the need to have a direct line of reporting to a top executive for the crisis program.

19.7.2 A Difference in Transparency – Driving Acceptance Through Simplification

In many BCM programs that we have seen over the years, the planning process is complicated, lengthy, and documentation-heavy. Anyone reading this book who has ever participated in a BCM planning session is likely familiar with this tendency. Those things can combine to make the BCM discipline seem like something that is too difficult for the business functions to deal with and can lead to the people being placed in charge of contributing to plans, but putting limited effort into completing an onerous planning process, only doing enough to get it marked as "complete," and then returning to running their business in the same way as before.

Note: We are certainly not claiming that this tendency to complicate things is done deliberately to obfuscate the process. It is often a result of:
1. Traditional training in the BCM discipline, focusing on extensive documentation and detail.
2. A general mindset of people who like to be prepared (BCM planners certainly fit in that category) also usually liking to be over-prepared, which leads to requests for increasingly complex documentation.

No matter the reason, the complexity of BCM programs gets in the way of their success. The remedy for this is transparency – making the process understandable for everyone, not just the crisis and continuity planners.
- Simplify the process.
- Make the plans less weighty and nimbler.
- Focus only on planning for what the business identifies as the critical aspects to cover.

These steps are the path to having a transparent program, which your strategic partners will accept. When added to the portfolio of services provided by the security program, a transparent and simplified BCM program can become a valuable addition to the services you provide to your strategic partners, rather than a burdensome process they are required to slog through every year or two. A simple and transparent crisis/continuity program will drive adoption in the lines of business by making it easy for them to participate and still be fully prepared.

19.7.3 A Difference in Independence – Ensuring Participation Through an Overarching Program

The essential component of independence is just as key for a BCM program as it is for other security disciplines. Business continuity and crisis management impact the entire enterprise. None of the functions avoid exposure to potential crisis events; whether it is a critical function of the firm, such as just-in-time delivery and shipping to customers; or 24/7 call-center operations that must be recovered immediately; or a function such as audit or marketing, which might have the potential to stop operations for a few days without a significantly harmful impact to the enterprise. These all would still have impact from a crisis level event occurring in the enterprise.

Independence is a necessary attribute for BCM if it is to reach and cover these functions. As we mentioned in Chapter 14, reporting lines matter.

- If the continuity team reports to IT, what is its ability to reach out and have a group like accounts payable work with the process?
- If the crisis team is part of operations, will they even remember that perhaps someone from marketing might be impacted as well as what they view as their core business function?
- If the continuity group is a function of facilities, will they be able to ensure that the IT disaster recovery plans are in place?

Reporting lines in companies often determine what is prioritized for each team. Right or wrong, work coming in from an outside team "next to" the department (as it could be seen) is typically given less importance than work coming down from the top.

A BCM and crisis function operating under the umbrella of an ESRM program has the necessary independence to work with all areas of the organization. Like other independent groups – compliance, legal, audit, etc. – the BCM and crisis function can gain traction with the leaders of that organization if those leaders understand that the continuity and crisis team is there to educate them about the risks they face, and to implement mitigation tactics that they feel meet their acceptable risk levels.

19.7.4 A Difference in Scope – Leveraging Resources for Success

In an ESRM security program, scope is necessary for understanding what does and does not fall into the realm of managing security risk in the enterprise. The BCM program, if part of the defined scope of managing enterprise security risk, can do more and better work in all aspects of planning and preparedness. This comes from leveraging the authority, independence, and transparency of the ESRM program, but also from leveraging the resources of the security team itself.

In typical, more traditional organizations, crisis management and BCM are usually either one person or a very small group of people. These BCM professionals often find that they lack the capability to truly implement a quality program, due to a lack of time and available manpower for performing all the needed activities like planning, testing, training, and more.

However, security teams are usually at least a little larger, and there is much that the BCM program leader can leverage in a security department to tie into security processes, and gain input for the BCM program. This sharing goes both ways, with investigators or other security personnel able to leverage the holistic knowledge of the BCM team about the enterprise's departments, structure, and critical functions.

An ESRM program can integrate BCM into security by creating a matrix of local security personnel to cover typical BCM/crisis activities things like:
- Interfacing with local emergency management, police, fire, etc.
- Building relationships with local businesses.
- Assisting with coordinating meetings to identify connections for BCM planners with local management.
- Leading BCM exercises locally.
- Incorporating BCM training into basic security training.
- Acting as incident commanders if needed during a crisis.
- Incorporating continuity and crisis risk questions into a facility security risk assessment.
- Using physical security assets such as facility camera feeds during a crisis to assess impacts remotely.

At the same time, there are aspects of crisis and continuity processes that the security manager can leverage as part of the ESRM cycle:
- Using the BCM asset identification and risk identification process for overall ESRM asset/risk identification.
- Leveraging lessons learned from exercises and tests to identify new security risks to improve the holistic ESRM program.
- Incorporating security mitigation plans into other crisis readiness mitigation tactics for increased efficiency.

These differences between a traditional BCM program, and a BCM and crisis function as implemented in an ESRM modeled security group, can make the ultimate difference in the acceptance, adoption, and participation of all enterprise functions in the BCM processes.

Questions for the Security Practitioner
- "Does the BCM function in my organization already operate in a similar fashion to the ESRM model as described?"

Chapter Review

In Chapter 19, you learned about business continuity and crisis management in the ESRM model, and how an ESRM approach to business continuity and crisis management can increase adoption of the program.

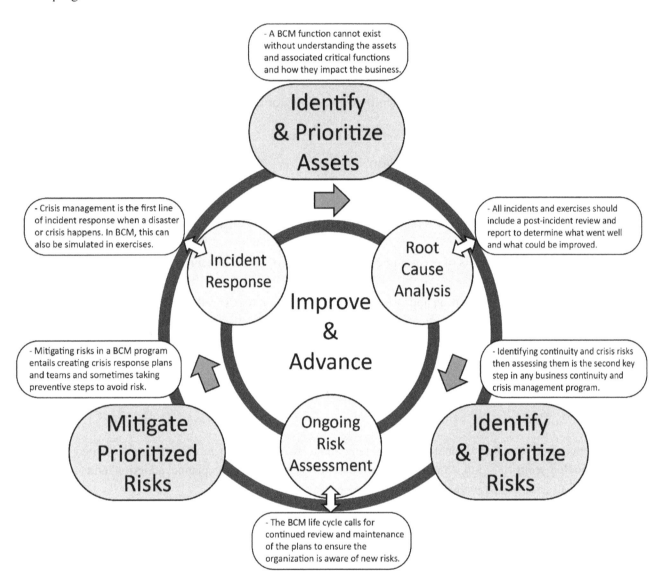

Figure 19-9. BCM and crisis management and the ESRM cycle – A review.

Looking Forward

Part 6 of this book begins with Chapter 20. In Part 6, we will explore concepts of program performance, beginning with what executives need to know about ESRM, what they should expect from the ESRM program, and how to educate them on ESRM topics to drive acceptance and support of the program.

Practitioner steps to consider before moving on to Chapter 20:
- ✓ Consider the steps you can take immediately to align your organization's BCM program more closely with your ESRM security philosophy.
- ✓ Think about whether your strategic partners consider the organization's BCM and crisis management program to be user-friendly and accessible. What could make it easier for them to participate in it?

Security Program Self-Assessment

In this self-assessment, you should think about the answer to the questions posed, and then see where your program is on the identified ESRM spectrum.

Question	Y/N	Is This ESRM?
Does your organization have a comprehensive business continuity and crisis management program reporting to the security function?	☐Yes ☐No	**NO:** If you do not have a BCM and crisis management program, then instituting a program and building crisis and continuity teams and plans is a suitable place to start your ESRM program. **PARTIAL:** if your organization has a BCM and crisis management program that covers all or part of the enterprise, but does not report to the security function, then you are part of the way to an ESRM implementation. **YES:** If you have a formal, documented, BCM and crisis management program that reports into the security function, and is designed in a simple, strategic, and service-oriented way, then you are practicing ESRM.

Questions for Discussion

1. Why might some continuity and crisis professionals insist on complex plans, teams, and programs, even in industries and organizations where regulations would not require them? What arguments might sway these types of planners to a simpler program?

2. How can a well-functioning continuity and crisis program assist with all areas of an ESRM security program? How can the partnerships formed on the crisis team assist with implementing other aspects of the security program?

References

American National Standards Institute (ANSI). (2010). ANSI/ASIS Standard BCM.01-2010. *Business continuity management systems: Requirements with guidance for use.* Alexandria, VA: American National Standards Institute (ANSI) & ASIS International.

International Organization for Standardization (ISO). (2012). ISO 22301:2012 *Societal security – Business continuity management systems – Requirements.* Geneva, Switzerland: ISO/IEC.

Learn More About It

For further reading about BCM programs:

Burtles, J. (2016). *Principles and practice of business continuity: Tools and techniques* (2nd ed.) Brookfield, CT: Rothstein Publishing.

Business Continuity Institute (BCI). (2013). *The good practices guidelines.* Reading, UK: Author. Available at https://shop.thebci.org/shop/shop.php?sid=144 [Free to members, available for purchase for non-members.]

Hiles, A. (2015). *Business continuity management: Global best practices* (4th ed.). Brookfield, CT: Rothstein Publishing.

Lindstedt, D. & Armour, M. (2017). *Adaptive business continuity: A new approach.* Brookfield, CT: Rothstein Publishing.

Loyear, R. (2017). *The manager's guide to simple, strategic, service-oriented business continuity.* Brookfield, CT: Rothstein Publishing.

For further reading about BCM tests and exercises:

Burtles, J. (2016). *The manager's guide to business continuity exercises: Testing your plan.* Brookfield, CT: Rothstein Publishing.

Rothstein, P.J., editor. (2007). *Disaster recovery testing: Exercising your contingency plan.* Brookfield, CT: Rothstein Publishing.

Part 6

ESRM Program Performance and Evaluation

In the first five parts of this book, you discovered what ESRM is and how it can help you and your security program more successfully manage security risk in your organization. You learned how to set up an ESRM program and how to relate ESRM to specific security disciplines. Now, in Part 5, it is time to look at ESRM program performance – how to evaluate your program's performance, how to communicate it to executives, and how embracing an ESRM approach might potentially lead to a converged security function as the program matures and grows.

In This Part:
- **ESRM for Business Executives and Boards of Directors**
- **Risk-Based Security Budgeting Process**
- **Reporting and Metrics That Matter in ESRM**
- **ESRM and the Path to Security Convergence**

20

ESRM for Business Executives and Boards of Directors

Communicating the benefits of enterprise security risk management (ESRM) to your enterprise executives can potentially be a lengthy and daunting process. Presenting the benefits and advantages of risk-based security to executives with limited time and hundreds of other concerns is a complex task, requiring clear, concise communication of the main points necessary for understanding ESRM. This chapter offers guidelines to help you with your presentation and to provide a basis for executive conversations about adopting an ESRM approach in the enterprise. Some of the information presented may appear similar to information we have covered earlier in this book, but here we tailor it to the critical aspects you need to communicate to your executives.

This chapter will help you to:
- Understand the key points of ESRM that are critical for an executive to know.
- Define and communicate the role of the executive in supporting an ESRM security program.
- Explain to executives and the board of directors what they need to know about risk-based security management and what they can to expect from the program.

20.1 What do the executives need to know about ESRM?

To properly support risk-based security, your executives must first come to agreement with you on:

- The need for and value of ESRM.
- The premise behind the philosophy of the role of security in the enterprise.
- An understanding of the executive's role in relation to managing a security program.

When discussing ESRM with senior executives, there are a few main points that are critical to communicate about the philosophy and program. We recommend focusing on just these main points, especially at first, since the opportunity to speak at length or in depth may not always be available.

20.1.1 Point 1 for Executives – Understand What ESRM is and the Value of Implementing ESRM Within the Organization

In communicating ESRM to enterprise executives on what ESRM is and what the value of the program is, the first thing you need to do is to clearly define:

"What is ESRM"?

Discuss this in simple and defined terms to set the baseline understanding of what *enterprise security risk management* is, as quickly and easily as possible.

First, go back to the definition of ESRM to ensure that you can concisely explain each part.

Enterprise security risk management (ESRM) is the application of fundamental **risk principles** to manage all **security risks** – whether information, cyber, physical security, asset management, or business continuity – in a comprehensive, holistic, all-encompassing approach.

The fundamental role is to guide the business through a security risk management decision-making process.
- **Enterprise:** An organization, business, or company.
- **Risk Principles:** Risk management should:
    - Be part of an ongoing decision-making process.
    - Be transparent and inclusive.
    - Be dynamic, iterative, and responsive to change.
    - Be capable of continual improvement and enhancement
- **Security Risk:** Anything that threatens harm to the enterprise, its mission, its employees, customers, or partners, its operations, or its reputation. (International Organization for Standardization, 2009).

These points are the underlying start of the conversation, simply to ensure that everyone in the conversation is clear regarding what we mean when we say ESRM.

20.1.2 Point 2 for Executives – Understand the Underlying Philosophy of ESRM and the Role of Security

To truly understand ESRM and how it will benefit the enterprise, your executives will also need to recognize the role of security and the role of business function leaders in the risk-based security program. These roles are outlined in Table 20-1.

Table 20-1. The Partnership Between Security and Other Enterprise Business Functions

The Role of Security	The Role of Business Function Leaders
Manage security risks to enterprise assets.	Understand the role of the security department in helping the business carry out its operational mission, and align the security department in the organization to allow it to manage the security risks in a transparent and independent manner.
Monitor risks to ensure impacts stay within defined tolerance levels.	Define an acceptable level of security risk tolerance to assets in their area of responsibility.
Provide subject matter expertise on risk mitigation options.	Make quality, educated decisions on security risks to assets in their area of responsibility.
Carry out risk mitigation tasks that require technical security skills in support of the security/business partnership.	Carry out risk mitigation tasks that require business function involvement in support of the security/business partnership.

To narrow everything in that table down to an even more concise message, you might say:

A. The role of security is to manage security risk.
B. This means the security team provides security guidance and subject matter expertise to business function leaders to help them make quality security risk decisions in their areas of responsibility.

20.1.3 Point 3 for Executives – Essential Requirements for Security Success

To communicate the basics of the ESRM philosophy, you will need to make sure your executives have a good understanding of the essential foundational elements of a successful ESRM program, which are:

- **Transparency** in identifying all risks and communicating those risks and their root causes to all appropriate parties, as well as communicating the processes and procedures that the security department follows.
- **Independence** in making risks transparent, and when necessary, escalating improper risk acceptance decisions.
- **Authority** of the security department's role.
- **Scope** of responsibility.

When discussing these points with your executives, you will want to be sure that you have a clear understanding yourself, so that you can communicate what each of these things mean.

20.1.3.1 Transparency

In ESRM, executives need to know that security *transparency* means being open and honest and clear with all our strategic partners in the enterprise about what security is doing, why we are doing it, and what we need from those partners. In ESRM terms, transparency has two key dimensions: risk transparency and process transparency.

- **Risk transparency:** Clearly and completely reporting all security risks that impact company assets to all the impacted asset owners and risk stakeholders.
- **Process transparency:** Communicating clearly the entire security risk decision-making process – how you arrived at your recommendations to the risk owners, and why, and the possible outcomes if those recommendations are, or are not accepted.

20.1.3.2 Independence

When you are discussing security independence with executives, make sure they understand that it means that the security organization:

- Must have the freedom to point out *any* security risks across the enterprise, without the fear of obstruction or retaliation from the leaders of the organization or function where that risk exists.
- Must have appropriate "reach" into the entire enterprise to enable it to consider security vulnerabilities *wherever* they exist,
- Must have information about all aspects of the business and the business' assets so that when responding to an incident, they can clearly identify its root causes.

The executive must understand that without these aspects of independence, the function of security will be severely hampered.

20.1.3.3 Authority

Executives should be made aware that in the risk-based security program, "authority" is not referring to the security function having the power to coerce or force functional leaders to take specific actions, nor is it somehow allowing the security function to impose its own ideas on the functionality of the enterprise. Instead, in ESRM, authority refers to the idea that the security function has the role of:

- Identifying security risks.
- Finding all the stakeholders.
- Ensuring that stakeholders are given the opportunity to have input into risk-response decisions for that asset.

Additionally, the security function has the authority to escalate the risk decision to a higher level of the organization if a person who is not an appropriate risk owner tries to take control of that risk decision-making process.

20.1.3.4 Scope

Finally, the executives need to understand that a defined scope of operations must be determined for the security group. Such scope is needed for the independence and authority inherent in the security risk management program to operate within specific boundaries of what the enterprise defines as appropriate for the function.

20.1.4 Point 4 for Executives – Understand ESRM Parallels with Other Risk-Based Functions

Change can be difficult, especially in large enterprises, where making fundamental shifts in philosophy requires time and can impact significant populations. In all instances, communicating the need for change must be clear and factual. In Part 3 of this book, we discussed how an effective persuasion tool can be to draw parallels with other areas that have the same protective function and goal as security.

The last point that we recommend communicating to your executives in the process of gaining their buy-in for the ESRM program is that security, when practiced following ESRM principles, shares many traits with audit, compliance, legal, and other risk management functions. As we mentioned in Chapter 12 about security essentials for success, no executive would expect an internal auditing team to do an effective job if the organization being audited were not required to be open, honest, and forthright. Nor would they recognize an audit as valid if the function being audited was in some position of authority over the audit team. An executive over a large organization will clearly understand that the ethics and compliance organization would be unable to enforce the standards of business conduct they are charged with ensuring, if they did not have enterprise authority and scope to do it. By drawing comparisons to what audit teams and compliance and other legal teams do, and what *their* success factors are, you can better convince executives of the need for transparency, independence, authority, and scope in your ESRM program.

20.1.5 Tailoring the Conversation

When presenting to your executives, you can tailor your message to include as much or as little information on risk-based security management as needed. To have an effective conversation, you will need to conform to what you learned about your enterprise and leadership throughout the course of understanding your organization.

You are in the best position to understand how to communicate with the executives in your organization. If you are not already used to having these conversations, we recommend that you speak to some of your strategic partners in the enterprise to find out how they recommend presenting to the executive level of your organization.

Whatever way you decide to do it, it is critical that you get executive buy-in and support for the ESRM program. Without that executive support, you will have trouble getting the needed independence, transparency, authority, and scope, as well as the other types of support that you need for your program.

One of the core benefits of ESRM for the executives is that the intent of the program is to ensure a process where the risk owners and executives are more educated when making their security risk decisions. Their decisions may not necessarily change, but all decision-makers will be better informed for the decision-making process. This a great premise to start from when building your presentation strategy and material for executives, since you will likely be hard-pressed to find an executive business leader who wants the people in the enterprise making decisions on behalf of the business to be *less* informed about the decisions they are making.

> ### Think About It: Presenting to Executives
> Presenting to a C-Level or other Senior Executive audience can be challenging. The executive decision makers are typically extremely busy, have tight schedules, and are required to make many critical decisions each day on a wide-ranging number of topics. You may only be allotted a brief amount of time, and so it's important to plan and make the most of the opportunity to communicate your message successfully. Here we have put together a list of tips to consider when preparing to present to a senior executive audience.
>
> ### Tip #1 – Know Your Executive Audience
> - Ask others in the organization who have done presentations to the group that will be in attendance for input on audience members

- Ask questions like:
  - How do the people in the audience like to receive information?
  - Do they prefer hard statistics, numbers, and metrics? Or do they want to hear the "story" of what you need and why?
  - Will they want to see graphs and charts? Or will words on the screen engage them more?
  - Will they want a mostly verbal or written presentation of the main points?
  - What are the typical words and phrases that the audience uses?
  - What are the current executive buzzwords that will most grab their attention?
  - Are there any preferences/pet peeves to be aware of when presenting?
  - Will anyone in the room be threatened by the recommendations?
- Keep in mind that you are presenting to them, seeking their agreement and approval. However, understand that while they are executive decision makers, they are also just people.
  - Be respectful of their titles and roles, but not intimidated.
  - Keep the focus on "What's in it for them." That means, how will your request drive the business mission and success?
  - Present on what they asked for or what you have agreed to discuss before attempting any other topics.
  - Be aware of their time pressures and respect the allotted time.
- Link your content to corporate objectives.
  - Remember the big picture/enterprise mission and goals. How does your presentation support that?
  - Know the hot-button topics: Is it Strategy? Profitability? Revenue? ROI?

Tip # 2 – Prepare, Prepare, Prepare
- Do a Content Review.
  - Have someone with experience presenting to the audience look at your material and give feedback.
- Prepare supporting data.
  - Understand all the consequences and implications of what you are seeking and be ready to discuss all the pros and cons.
  - Anticipate the questions you might receive, and prepare answers ahead of time.
  - Think about what might not be clear.
  - What might the audience disagree with?
  - Play devil's advocate with the content as you prepare it.
- Verify all your data.
  - Do not use material that you are unsure of, which could be outdated or incorrect.
- Prepare back-up material/appendices.
  - Do not include all the detailed information in the presentation.
  - Make sure all the detailed information is available for questions – either as takeaways or just data for presenter to use as reference.
  - Do not rely on improvisation.
- Have multiple copies of the presentation ready in several formats to hand out or email afterward.

Tip #3 – Plan Your Time Wisely
- Prepare material that will take a third to half of the time slot given to account for questions, interruptions, late entries, etc.
  - Make sure you cover all content in the allotted time.
  - Leave time at the end for questions and discussion.
  - No one minds a meeting ending early if you do not fill all the time.
- Get directly to the point.
  - State the topic up front, to remind them of why you are meeting.
  - Plan to make all the major points in the first five minutes.
- Establish a clear direction and desired conclusion from the beginning.

- Start by defining your desired conclusions or end state.
- Clarify the expectations for the presentation.
- Outline the benefits of the topic.
- Stay on topic, and make sure that all information supports the stated conclusion.
- Focus on the bottom line.
  - Executives do not have time to be experts on your topic. Make sure you keep the discussion high-level, and keep the focus on how they can help you to help them and the business.

Tip #4 – Tailor Your Presentation or Handouts

- Structure the presentation around high-level concepts and make sure it is strategic, not operational, or tactical. Keep slides to a minimum if you use them at all. If you have a slide deck:
  - Keep it clean and simple.
  - Favor charts and graphics over words.
  - Avoid using animations of slides or PowerPoint "tricks."
  - Leave out anything that has a chance of not working at a crucial moment.
  - Avoid using non-standard fonts.
  - Leave out YouTube or other streaming video links.
  - Leave out any online content.
  - Avoid using animated gifs.
  - Keep the audience focused on you, not the screen.
  - End with a blank screen to bring focus back to speaker.

Tip #5 – Flexibility is Key

- Expect interruptions during your talk. In fact, welcome them – it means your information has sparked ideas or questions.
- Determine whether the audience is expecting a discussion or a speech, and deliver accordingly.
- There might be questions.
  - Anticipate every question you can and plan a response.
  - Redirect if you have no response – you might ask someone else to comment on what was asked.
  - Rephrase and confirm what was asked to ensure that you understood the question and can answer it appropriately.
  - "I Don't Know" is a valid answer – it is better to admit that you don't know and promise a follow-up response than to provide an incorrect answer.
  - Bring questions/discussions back around to your main point.

Tip #6 – Finish Strong

- Remember to add a call to action at the end, what is "The Ask?" Why were you presenting? Be specific about what you have done and what you need them to do.
  - Do you want approval to move forward?
  - Do you need them to send a message to the team/company?

Tip # 7 – Why Presentations Fail

As we have mentioned before, there isn't just one piece of set-up advice that will work in every enterprise. These are just a few tips that we have found to be useful over the years when presenting information to company executives. The tips above are about succeeding in your presentation, but below we also include some items we have seen derail a meeting. Presenters can go wrong when they:

- Provide too much detail up front.
- Do not link to corporate objectives.
- Cannot answer challenging questions.
- Have too many topics in one presentation.
- Have too many distractions from the focus.

20.2 What is the Role of Executives in an ESRM Program?

The first step in talking with your executives is to explain the basics of ESRM, help them to understand the overall concept and philosophy, and get them to agree to the role of security and other business function leaders in a risk-based security program. That discussion and agreement is essential before you can move to the second step, which is that they not only understand the role of the security team and the other business leaders, they also understand the role of executives and even the board of directors, in promoting security success across the enterprise.

At its most basic, the executive level of any enterprise is responsible for ensuring that the business meets the mission and objectives that are laid out for it by the board of directors (or other owners in a non-board-directed organization). The top leaders are there to lead strategically, and it is their role to ensure that all the other personnel and groups in the organization have what they need to perform their roles in meeting those strategic objectives.

20.2.1 The Executive Role of Ensuring a Definition of Security Success

As we have discussed in several previous chapters, your security program cannot be a success if the enterprise you operate in does not agree on a definition of a successful security program. That success measurement must be defined by the business – by what the business wants to protect and how they are willing to protect it. It cannot be defined by security, at least not in a vacuum. Some questions that must be answered for a common definition of success for the ESRM program are:

- What is the overall security risk tolerance for the enterprise?
- Are there areas with a higher or lower tolerance for security risk?
- What is the measurement of tolerance discrepancy?
- By what methodology will the security team be judged as fulfilling the mission of managing security risk?
- How will the performance of security tasks that mitigate risk for the business be included in the definition of security success?
- What are the thresholds of tolerance where security risks need to be escalated?

Answers to these questions will give security leadership the ability to fulfill their role of managing security risk, and of performing risk mitigation activities as deemed appropriate by the business.

It is the executive role to ensure that the security leader has the proper access to all business leaders to discuss these questions and get a consensus answer. Additionally, the executive will need to review and agree to whatever definition the security and business leaders that report to him or her have decided is appropriate or make any changes as desired. This definition of what the enterprise expects of security – to consider it successful – will drive the entire ESRM program set-up, rollout, and ongoing operations. Once the security program is functioning within these set guidelines for success, the security leader and team and their strategic partners will all have a clear understanding of what is expected of them.

20.2.2 The Executive Role of Ensuring the Correct Security Skillsets

Once the business has defined the criteria of success for the security program and executives have accepted this definition, they need to ensure that the security team has the correct skillsets for carrying out both the risk management strategic function and the risk mitigation tactical function.

Setting the security team up for success means first ensuring that the security leader has the right skills to manage the ESRM program. Some questions for your executives to ask about potential security leaders are:

- Does the security leader understand business concepts?
  - o Business communications.
  - o Personnel leadership.
  - o Finance and budgeting.
  - o Reporting.
- Is the security leader able to interface with business professionals, functional leaders, business executives, and board members?
- Does the security leader appropriately understand technical security topics that fall into the scope of risk mitigation tactics?
- Does the security leader have the experience needed to lead a risk-based, not task-based, security function?
- Do the members of the security team understand risk management topics?
- Do the members of the security team have the needed security technical expertise to mitigate security risks to the business?
- Do the members of the security team embrace the ESRM philosophy?

If the security team is lacking in critical skills for protecting the enterprise from security risk in a manner consistent with the security role, it is imperative that the executive either provide training and education to close the skills gaps quickly, or find alternate or additional resources for the security team.

When you are communicating this concept of ensuring needed skills to your executive, it is imperative that you, as the security leader, identify exactly how you fit into the needed skillsets for the role. We have suggested in many places in this book that you examine your own skills and abilities to effectively embrace and implement an ESRM program. Key questions are:

- Do you have the requisite communications skills?
- Do you understand the relevant business concepts?
- Are you able to collaborate with your strategic partners?

These are skills that every security leader needs. If you feel like any aspect of these skills is an area where you could improve your personal performance, then do so. These business skills can be obtained in continuing education programs, workshops, online classes, or even formal degree programs. Just as the security program must continually improve and advance to adapt to a constantly changing security risk environment, so must you, as a security professional, also continually improve and update your skills to effectively lead the program.

Think About It: Law Enforcement is an Experience, not a Skillset

We have heard repeatedly from business leaders who have been given responsibility for security functions in their enterprise that they need to recruit a former law enforcement agent, or a military retiree to lead the program. The argument on the part of the business leader is invariably based on the idea that if the candidate can perform those types of activities in the public sector, then they will be able to do similar tasks in the private sector. This is sometimes a correct assumption, depending on the organization. However, very often we have seen both the business organization and transitioning public sector person served badly by the assumption that the law enforcement "skillset," based *solely* on the law enforcement or military background of the person hired, will carry over to the enterprise organization and provide a successful security program.

Law enforcement and military service is an excellent experience, to be sure. However, it is just that – an experience – not a *skillset*. Not all law enforcement and military personnel have the same jobs or roles, nor use the same skills. The job of a detective in a municipal police force is different from that of a solider, which is different from a government security analyst. But these differences are often overlooked by business leaders in a quest to simply have a candidate with a law enforcement background.

We realize that law enforcement and military candidates possess many critical security skills that have been honed through their career experience, which do apply to a business security setting. The critical thing in choosing the correct candidate to lead or be part of an ESRM program is for that person to have the skills needed to identify and manage security risks in partnership with the other business leaders in the enterprise. These skills will be highly specific to the enterprise you are operating in, and should be listed out, and then matched to the best candidates, whether they are transitioning from the public sector, or not. In our time in security, we have seen excellent security leaders come from many different backgrounds:

- Internal Audit.
- Risk Management.
- Human Resources.
- Facilities.
- Legal.
- Technology.

Of course, we know excellent security leaders who have come from a military or law enforcement background as well. The point for executives to keep in mind when looking for a security leader is to find one with the skills that will allow them to succeed in the culture of the enterprise they are joining. Some skills that are necessary for a security leader in an ESRM program are:

- Communication.
- Executive interactions.
- Collaboration and partnership.
- Risk management.
- Basics of finance and planning.
- Project management.
- Understanding various security disciplines.

This is clearly not an exhaustive list, but as you can see, these are skills that people from many differing backgrounds might have. We highly recommend that no matter the background, the security leader for any enterprise also have a deep understanding of (or even a degree in) business management concepts and topics.

We certainly encourage all enterprises to look at transitioning military and law enforcement personnel when seeking candidates for enterprise security positions.

However, we feel that merely hiring based on the previous job title of law enforcement or military may not bring these critical leadership skills. It could be setting up both the security program and the person hired to lead it for difficulties and potential failure if that new hire does not have the skills needed in the specific enterprise.

20.2.3 The Executive Role of Ensuring the Essentials for Success are in Place

Once your executives understand that transparency, independence, authority, and scope are essential elements, then their most critical role is to align the security department in the overall organization where those elements will allow it to succeed and make sure those essential elements exist in the organization. Your enterprise executives in an ESRM program must commit to providing support to the security leaders and the team in cases where other business function leaders question or push back on the independence, authority, transparency, or scope of the security group.

These essential needs for the security team can be controversial when first rolled out. It is possible that the security team might be thought of as overstepping their boundaries if the enterprise is accustomed to seeing the role of security as managing tasks such as badges, cameras, and passwords. ESRM is a different philosophy and mindset. Executive support is critical in ensuring that the entire enterprise understands the role of security, and how they will be partnering with the business leaders to help them protect the assets in their area of responsibility.

Additionally, your executives must ensure that as the security leader, you have access to the other business leaders and are meeting with them on a regular basis to ensure proper management of enterprise security risk. Some organizations have tricky political relationships; some are highly competitive, and business leaders will see any change in the scope of another program as a threat to theirs; sometimes groups in enterprise organizations have fierce competitions for resources and support. (We will mention here that certainly not all organizations have these aspects, but these are the types that might have the most trouble accepting the change). The support from the executives in your role – and the mandate that the security team is responsible for managing all security risks – will go a long way in making sure you can have an effective partnership with all your new strategic partners in security risk management.

20.2.4 The Executive Role of Ensuring the Correct Reporting Structure

The organizational reporting structure of the security department is one of the most influential aspects of the security program, which will drive the essential elements listed above. As we have outlined already, independence of reporting lines is unquestionably crucial to the success of the security organization. The role of the executive in ESRM is to ensure that independence, by placing the security organization in the part of the company that will provide the clearest lines of independence and authority for the program.

Depending on the enterprise, there might be several options that could provide this. A larger organization might have options such as:

* Legal.
* Compliance.
* Enterprise risk management.
* Internal audit.

Smaller organizations might not have all those areas, in which case, the executive's job is to find the most appropriate reporting line.

We recommend, of course, that the security department should report to senior management directly. And, depending on the nature and impact of risk to the enterprise, even have C-level leadership of the security department as a chief security officer (CSO), reporting directly to the chief executive officer (CEO). If that is not possible, a CSO reporting to the general counsel is also a good option.

20.2.5 The Executive Role of Ensuring that the Board or Enterprise Ownership is Aware of the Role of Security and of Security Risks as a Business-Critical Topic

Just as it is critical that the executive level make sure other functions inside the enterprise are aware of the role of security, it is also incumbent upon the executive leadership to make the board of directors aware of how of security helps the business protect itself from harm from security risks. Some topics that the board should be aware of are:

- Significant security risks to the enterprise critical functions.
- Changes in major risk categories, due to environmental changes in business products, program, mission, or goals.
- Material and significant security incidents that violated tolerance levels as set by the board or executives.

These are aspects of security risk management that truly rise to the level of material consideration of the board of directors. Many boards are now beginning to take an active role and interest in information security. In an ESRM paradigm, the topic of enterprise security risk is expanded to include much more than data. The executive level of the organization is the path for ensuring that the board or other ownership understands that many types of security risk can impact the organization, and that their interest should encompass all of those.

Providing transparent reporting to the Board can also help with protecting senior management from controversy in risk decision making. If the risks are all transparently reported and documented, then the Board, in receiving those reports and overseeing the program, is also playing a role in the decision-making process. This can protect the executives from appearing to have made a risk decision in a bubble, or even appearing that they were making some attempt to conceal a risk.

Questions for the Security Practitioner
- "Do I understand what skills will be needed to lead an ESRM program in my enterprise?"
- "Am I willing to identify skills gaps I might have for leading an ESRM program and work on closing them?"

20.3 What Should Executives and Boards of Directors Expect From ESRM?

We have covered many things in this chapter about what the executives need to know about ESRM, and what they can provide to the security team to ensure a successful security program. But there are also many things that executives and boards of directors should expect from a security group that operates in an ESRM methodology.

20.3.1 Reporting and Metrics

The ESRM program allows the security team to assist the enterprise in protecting itself and its mission. Enterprise leadership will need a constant awareness of how the security organization is doing that, and what the current level of security risk to the enterprise is. Reports and metrics that the executive should expect to receive from the security leader are:

- Regular reporting on current and future security risks that are material to business success.
- Regular reporting on the efficient use of enterprise resources in mitigating security risk.
- Regular reporting on the security risk landscape inside and outside of the organization.
- Regular reviews of the business functions that security has met with and partnered with in managing enterprise risk.

Many of these items should be delivered to executives on a regular basis as part of regular reporting and metrics. In Chapter 22, we will cover how security can build quality reports that assist the business in understanding the current risk picture, and that give a view of potential future risks that are on the strategic horizon.

20.3.2 Transparency of Risk

We spoke earlier in the chapter about how the ESRM program must operate with transparency, honesty, and openness, to be successful. In this area, the executives should expect that the security program will be thorough in finding and planning responses to risk, in partnership with the business. Executives must expect the security team to identify risk exposure in all areas of the business, and to make sure that the asset owners and stakeholders are responding to them in line with identified risk tolerances. Because of this expectation, the executives should also expect to occasionally be brought into further discussions about:

- Escalation of security issues that exceed the tolerance levels set by executives or the board.
- Escalation of security response conflicts with stakeholders that cannot be resolved at any lower level of the organization.
- New risks that might come about from strategic business decisions that take the enterprise into innovative areas of business, or product lines that might have unclear risk stakeholders, due to newness.

20.3.3 Communications, Notifications, and Awareness

Above all, in a risk-based security program, the executives and business leaders in the enterprise must expect and be able to rely upon the security leader for timely awareness of any security issues, risks, or potential incidents that rise to the level of needing executive attention.

This may mean different things in different organizations, but the key is that the security leader must be trusted to understand what executives consider as integral to the areas of interest for them, and to communicate standard notifications on all events, incidents, or intelligence that fall into those areas of executive interest. This process of determining the correct level of interest may take time, but it is the security leader's responsibility to both escalate information that the executives need to know about, and to ensure there is not over-communication, which can lead to the escalations and notifications being thought of as simply communicating business as usual.

Chapter Review

In Chapter 20, you learned the elements that executives need to understand about ESRM and their role in ensuring a successful ESRM program including:

- The necessary basics of ESRM.
- The role of the executive in ESRM.
- The expectations for security that pertain to executives.

Looking Forward

In Chapter 21, we will look at ways to involve your strategic partners and asset owners in the security budgeting process, to build a stronger case for security risk mitigation programs.

Security Program Self-Assessment

In this self-assessment, you should think about the answer to the questions posed, and then see where your program is on the identified ESRM spectrum.

Question	Y/N	Is This ESRM?
Does your organization have an executive level sponsor or other support for the security program?	□Yes □No	**NO**: If you do not have any executive level exposure for the security functions, then beginning this awareness campaign is a suitable place to start your ESRM program. **PARTIAL**: If your organization has some executive support, but no ongoing access, then you are part of the way to an ESRM implementation, and might consider trying to get at least an annual meeting at the executive level, if not quarterly. **YES**: If you have a high-level security leader with regular access to, and meetings with the C-Level of the organization, then you are practicing ESRM.

Questions for Discussion

1. In what circumstances – and why – might executives fail to recognize security risk as something that needs to be managed at the enterprise level? What are some ways that you could show the importance of security risk to enterprise operations?

2. What arguments or objections might you expect to receive from the executive level on the importance of managing security risk in a department that has transparency, independence, authority, and properly defined scope? How would you counter these?

References

International Organization for Standardization (ISO). (2009). *ISO/IEC 31000:2009 Risk management – Principles and guidelines*. Geneva, Switzerland: ISO/IEC.

Learn More About It

For further reading about making presentations to the C-Suite:

Gilbert, R. (2012, October 12). *Four presentation strategies for a C-level audience*. [Web log post]. Available at https://www.td.org/Publications/Magazines/TD/TD-Archive/2012/10/4-Presentation-Strategies-for-a-C-Level-Audience

Gilbert, R. (2011, August 10) *Nine rules for pitching ideas to C-level executives*. [Web log post]. Available at http://www.industryweek.com/companies-amp-executives/nine-rules-pitching-ideas-c-level-executives

Iannarino, A. (2011, August 14). *How to be interesting (and useful) to C-level executives*. [Web log post]. Available at https://thesalesblog.com/2011/08/14/how-to-be-interesting-and-useful-to-c-level-executives/

Reiffenstein, K. (2010, May). Speaking up: 10 tips for making a C-level presentation. *T+D Magazine.* (American Society for Training and Development [ASTD]). Available at http://andnowpresenting.typepad.com/files/speaking-up-10-tips-for-making-a-c-level-presentation.pdf

21

Security Budgeting Process

Now that you have seen the essentials of a successful security program – *independence, authority, transparency, scope* – and discussed the need for partnership with and support from enterprise business leaders, it's time to consider another critical aspect of any program – *budget*. There is no escaping the fact that even in a security risk management approach, with all security activities planned in alignment with business tolerance, the risk mitigation activities taken on by the security department will cost money – and it will need to come from someone's budget. In this chapter, we will review the traditional way of looking at security budgeting and contrast it with the enterprise security risk management (ESRM) approach. We will also introduce you to a financial concept – value chain theory – that will help you to better communicate the value of security risk mitigation activities to your strategic partners. Finally, we will discuss the process of converting from a traditional, often dispersed, security budgeting model to a unified ESRM budget model that allows business leaders to more effectively recognize, track, and control security costs.

This chapter will help you to:

- Recognize the pitfalls of the traditional security budgeting process.
- Communicate the value of security risk mitigation activities as part of the business value chain.
- Develop and defend an annual security budget in partnership with risk owners and stakeholders by using ESRM principles.

21.1 How has Security Budgeting been Approached Before?

Traditionally, security is seen a *cost center* in enterprise operations – much like facilities, maintenance, utilities, information technology (IT), payroll, and benefits. Generally, in business, a *cost center* is an essential department that costs the organization money to operate but does not add directly to overall profit. While the contribution of a cost center to a company's profitability is only indirect, a *profit center* contributes to the enterprise's profitability *directly* as part of its operation. Most often, in the minds of the executives and business leaders, security falls into the realm cost centers that do not contribute directly to the profit of the company.

In the financial mindset of categorizing expenses as either cost centers or profit centers, the unfortunate reality is that when cuts to expenses need to be made, costs are reviewed long before looking at the profit side. This thought pattern leads to a few typical reactions by security professionals, as they try to continue to protect company assets with shrinking budgets. Those reactions include:

- Using fear to sell security activities in the organization.
- Making security decisions based on the amount of money available to spend rather than according to the true needs of the organization.
- Cutting protective activities, and when security incidents occur, shifting blamed for the failure to budget cuts.

These thought patterns put the security leader in an unenviable position that often feels like a no-win situation. Unfortunately, streamlining budgets without a deeper exploration of the enterprise impacts that those budget cuts may have can lead to increased risk exposure that, if the business leaders were made fully aware of them, might clearly fall outside of business risk tolerances. Using ESRM principles helps guide the security leader through these budgeting landmines by ensuring that the conversation stays focused on the assets and security risks throughout the budget lifecycle, effectively moving the conversation away from defending individual tasks and activities to a broader conversation on security risks, and the role of security in managing those risks for the enterprise.

21.1.1 Fear, Uncertainty, Doubt – The FUD Factor

The *FUD factor* is a notion often heard about in the security industry. It plays on the fear, uncertainty, and doubt that leaders can feel about making major decisions, and it capitalizes on those feelings by exaggerating possible outcomes, or by playing up bad things that have happened to other people. In practice, this can take the form of:

- Using news stories where incidents have happened to other companies to request funding for security activities that would mitigate the risk of that happening in the practitioner's company – regardless of whether the company in the news shares any risk factors with the practitioner's enterprise.
- Exaggerating the potential impacts to enterprise assets to gain approval for security expenditures that may not correlate to the true impact.
- Focusing on extreme examples of risks, or high-impact/low probability risks, to get the attention of decision-makers.
- Continually bringing up bad news or events to create a continual feeling of fear in the enterprise.

Using FUD *can* bring short-term success in getting security budgets increased or approved, but it has many drawbacks that ultimately make it a bad base to build from.

1. Fear and emotion eventually wear off, and the security department will lose credibility when the business asks for metrics on the effectiveness of the security implementation.
2. Executives begin to filter out the steady drumbeat of trouble, often beginning to avoid the bearer of continual misfortune (if possible).
3. Using FUD for security expenditures, rather than solid business arguments, creates the perception that the security executive is not part of the business conversation, but is an "emergency responder," who should be called in only when danger is present.

Certainly, dramatic anecdotes and news stories can be useful in bringing attention to a possibility or probability. However, these stories can lose their effectiveness quickly, and they are used too commonly as an attention-grabbing basis for budgeting requests. Using a formal, risk-based approach to security budget management eliminates the need to use scare-tactics to get funding for security activities.

21.1.2 Making the Best of What You are Given, and the "Blame Game"

Another response often seen to budget limitations is to simply take what is given and try to make the best expenditures on security within those limits, often providing only bare minimum protections. This may seem like the only option in a business environment where financial executives control the budget, and then hand it to the security practitioner in a "no arguments" form, but unfortunately this leads to:

- The security professional, not the asset owner, making all the decisions on what security to keep and what to limit.
- Inadequate security protections that can lead to eventual failure.

This more passive tactic does not allow the security professional to fulfill the mission of protecting the enterprise assets in the way the business needs to be protected. The outcome of a potential security failure usually ends with the blame for that failure landing, not on the finance or budget decision-maker who did not provide enough funding to protect enterprise assets, but on the unfortunate security practitioner who was merely attempting to do a difficult task with inadequate resources.

In a risk-based environment, we see a subtle difference in the ownership of risks that enables the security leader to avoid these issues. Because in an environment where ESRM is fully implemented, security does not "own" the risks. The security group is simply a steward for the budgeted dollars assigned to protect a specific set of assets. If the business leaders, once fully educated on the risks and available mitigation options, choose at the appropriate level of authority to not implement a risk mitigation tactic, or to cut an existing one, that is 100% their role and authority in the budgeting process. Having all budget adjustment decisions (decreases or increases) supported by the asset and risk owners avoids putting the security leader in a defensive position, trying to justify each task or activity as if they were somehow partitioned from the overall mission of the organization.

Questions for the Security Practitioner
- "When you have been faced with an annual budget cut in the past, what has been your response?"

Think About It: The "Cut Your Budget" Conversation
Before we begin our discussion of the ESRM approach to security budgeting, we would like to discuss a story direct from our own experience. A couple of years into our first ESRM implementation, Brian was in a meeting for the annual budget cycle and the following conversation took place (edited for brevity, of course).

Finance Leader: "We need you to cut the security budget by 50%."

Brian: "Okay, let me get back to you."

The end.

This is a significant departure from what most security professionals would do in a *non-ESRM* environment. Brian did not argue that the cuts were too much, or try to convince the finance leader that terrible things would happen to the enterprise if security was slashed by 50%. Instead, he simply said he would return with a plan for the finance leader at the next meeting on how to cut security expenditures.

After that conversation, Brian went to all the leaders in his security group and asked them to look at their current programs. He asked them to identify:
1. The assets those programs were protecting.
2. The asset owners and stakeholders
3. The potential impacts of a 10%, 20%, 30%, or 50% budget cut.
4. The potential risk exposures that would increase as the programs were cut by the stated percentages.

From there, he went to each asset owner and stakeholder, reviewed the potential cuts and how those could impact the protection of their assets, and got their feedback on the resulting exposures. He found out that the current budget could sustain somewhere between a 10% and 15% cut before the expectations and tolerances of the asset owners and stakeholders could no longer be met.

At the next budget meeting, the conversation on cutting the budget went like this (again, edited for brevity):

Brian: I have looked at the security budget, and we can sustain a 12.5% cut in budget before we begin to have significant impacts to the business. Anything larger than that, and we will need to bring our strategic partners into this meeting to discuss the cuts, because neither of the two of us is the risk owner who can decide on the acceptable risk to the assets.

Finance Leader: 12.5% is fine. We'll leave it there.

Of course, the budget discussion is not always going to go this way. However, what set the stage in this story was that the security role of being a guide for the business though the security risk decision-making process was clearly defined, long before that budget meeting. Rather than making a knee-jerk defense in the initial meeting, or trying to immediately negotiate a lower number, Brian came back with a defensible and documented position of what was and was not his risk to accept in the security risk decision process. At this point, he was able to guide the finance team through their role, which was also not to accept risk on behalf of other asset owners and stakeholders.

This scenario could have ended quite differently, and would still have been acceptable in a risk-based security program. If the chief financial officer (CFO) had brought in the asset owners and stakeholders, and worked through a change in the risk tolerance level with the oversight of the security governance group, then certainly cutting the security budget 50% could have still very well been on the table. And if the security risk management process was followed and the appropriate asset owners and stakeholders accepted the new risks, the 50% would have been fine. Of course, nobody wants to cut their budget by 50%, but security's role is not to build budgets or maintain a certain headcount on a team, it is to follow the risk tolerance level set by the leaders of the business. It may seem like a cold approach, but that is the way of business, and managing risk to a set level of tolerance is security's role in that business paradigm.

In this case, the business appreciated the transparency of the process, and the CFO also understood security's role in the process. The CFO could see that the security team was efficiently stewarding resources to meet strategic partner expectations, and was aligned with the overall business objectives of asset and risk stakeholders.

This exercise was a significant test in ESRM practice. It worked well and further solidified the role of security in the organization through the budgeting process. In fact, process worked so well that from then on, every year it became a part of the strategic cost-savings/waste minimizing activity for the whole group to undertake, ensuring the responsible stewardship of security dollars over time, and always aligned to the assets and asset owners.

Now, with that story in mind – how would you handle that budget conversation today? How could ESRM help you make it differently?

21.1.3 Return on Security Investment

We hear the term *return on security investment* (ROSI) quite a bit when talking with our colleagues in the security profession, usually as part of the question, "How can I prove ROSI to my executives?"

We have a very concise answer to that question: "Don't."

For the security department in a traditional environment, ROSI is a trap. The request to "prove" ROSI is setting the security leader up for failure because it is inherently asking that the security function itself be a source of profit, or at least expense offset.

21.1.3.1 Return on (Non-Security) Investment

In business, *return on investment* (ROI) describes the measurement of the amount of return on an investment compared to its cost as a percentage. By using a percentage, it is simpler to compare the cost/benefit ratio of other investments within the organization.

Your strategic partners in the business think of ROI in this way. They look for the percentage of return on the money spent on security in order to compare it to the percentage of return on the money spent on other investments. This mindset is problematic because the calculations for ROSI are different, even though the phrasing of the terms implies that it is similar.

Look at a typical example of a ROSI argument:

- To determine ROSI, begin with the annual loss expectancy (ALE) – which is what the enterprise expects to lose in a year – of a specific risk, and then subtract it from the annual cost of the security mitigation task.

Such an approach is problematic because you are using a mathematical term that in *other* functional areas uses very well-defined and defended numbers. In the ROSI definition, the "expected loss" is an estimate, which is typically extremely hard to prove. Financial experts, when looking at budgets for areas of savings will immediately zero in on this concept of "expected" loss vs. "proven" loss. The argument that "we stopped terrible things from happening" is rather easily offset by "prove it."

Additionally, this formula is not truly measuring the "return" on an investment; rather, it is highlighting the efficiency and effectiveness of a control on a risk impact. Looking at security budgeting in this manner starts partitioning security activities as if security should be judged by its task effectiveness. This goes back to treating and defining security by the tasks it is assigned, which is what we are trying to get away from by using a risk-based model.

This measurement issue is why we refer to ROSI as a trap. Security's budgets, even as assigned to a single mitigation plan, should always be tied to a security risk-management-decision conversation with the business, not a conversation about the efficiency of the task management.

21.1.3.2 Whose "Return" is It?
In addition to the issue of having fewer hard numbers than regular ROI calculations, the traditional concept of ROSI is also problematic because it directs the focus of the calculation directly back to security, rather than to the asset owner whose asset is being protected.

The return to the enterprise of protecting assets is in being able to continue the mission and function of those assets. The business and the asset owner benefit from the security risk mitigation activities, not the security department. Security provides a service that enhances the asset's ability to provide its own ROI, but does not provide funds to the business itself (in most cases). Any security leader attempting to defend expenses based on ROSI is being set up for failure. The true return on a security investment is that the business' products did not get stolen, or were protected from impact from a security risk that was outside of the set tolerance level. ROSI muddies the role of security by asking it to justify an expense, rather than to manage the risk on behalf of an asset owner.

21.2 The ESRM Approach to Security Budgeting
ESRM is centered on the premise that all risk decisions, including whether a security risk is mitigated or not, are made by the business. Therefore, risk mitigation activities are *funded* based on decisions by the business. It is the job of the security leader to ensure that the asset owners and risk stakeholders understand the risk, the potential impact, the mitigation actions, and the costs to gain the support of the strategic partners in funding those activities. Your challenge is to better communicate to your strategic partners how security can support their overall business value and show that your team is a mindful and careful steward of the dollars given towards mitigating security risk in the organization. One budgeting theory that could help you is the *value chain theory*.

We first heard about the idea of using the value chain theory in relation to security budgeting from noted security expert Dave Tyson, in his book *Security Convergence: Managing Enterprise Security Risk*. Although our approach is somewhat different from his, the ideas he originally proposed formed the beginnings of how we now view value chain and security budgeting. We list his book in the "learn more about it" section at the end of this chapter, as recommended further reading on this topic.

21.2.1 Value Chain Theory

Value chain theory is a strategic management model described by Michael Porter of Harvard Business School, in his book *Competitive Advantage: Creating and Sustaining Superior Performance*. Essentially, Porter's theory is that the value chain is the set of activities that an organization performs to bring something of value (a product of service) to the marketplace. It goes on to differentiate those activities in two categories, primary activities and support activities (Porter, 1998, p. 38).

Primary activities are the ones that directly contribute to the increased value of the product. They are listed in the model as:

- Inbound Logistics – The steps involved in bringing in the raw materials (or ideas, etc.) used in the production process, like receiving and inventory management.
- Operations – Refers to all the steps and actions used to turn raw materials into a final good or service. This will vary widely from product to product, and could be anything from assembly line work on vehicles, to computer programming on a latest technology gadget, and even to dance training if your product happens to be a musical theater production.
- Outbound Logistics – The methods and processes by which the good or service gets to the consumer, including things like distribution, warehouse operations, or digital distribution platforms.
- Marketing and Sales – Includes actions like advertising, selecting distribution channels, pricing, etc., which ensure that the product reaches the right market at the right price (value) point.
- Service – Refers to activities that are required post-production, such as maintenance and training, and other post-production services. (Porter, 1998, p. 39).

Support activities are what businesses commonly refer to as "overhead," those things that the enterprise does that allows them to accomplish the primary activities. In the model, they are shown as:

- Enterprise Infrastructure – The enterprise's administrative, accounting, finance, strategic planning, quality control, and other functions that support the capacity of the enterprise to function.
- Human Resource Management – Hiring and retaining an appropriate pool of personnel for all organization activities.
- Technology Development – Refers to all activates such as research and development, process automation, or other technical activities that are used in the organization.
- Procurement – The methods by which raw materials are obtained (Porter, 1998, pp. 40-43).

Traditionally, security activities in most businesses are thought to fall into the enterprise infrastructure category. Later, our ESRM view of the value chain will show that it does not (wholly) belong there.

339

Figure 21-1 is a diagram of Porter's standard overall value chain.

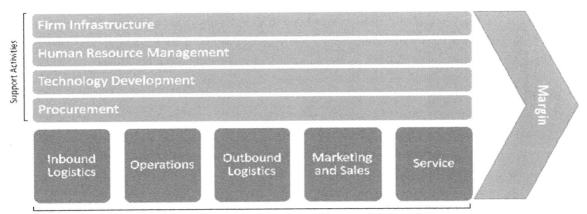

Figure 21-1. Porter's value chain analysis diagram. (Porter, 1998, p. 37).

The essence of the value chain theory is that at each step along the chain, some activity happens within the organization that adds value to the good or service that is offered at the end of the chain. The amount of value added over the course of the production or creation process drives the amount that the firm can ask from a consumer of the good or service, and in turn, drives the profit margin at the end of the chain (Porter, 1998, p. 38).

As an economic model, it makes sense, and many firms and business leaders who have never heard of Michael Porter or value chain theory, still operate under this model, because it is easy to see in action: You take raw materials or ideas, you perform actions on them, and you have a product at the end. So, from a business perspective, it makes sense that a savvy business leader wants to put as much as possible in resources into the activities that *add* value to the product, and as little as possible on the things like rent or electricity, which are important to getting the product made, but do not *directly* make the result more valuable to the consumer. Unfortunately, when budgets get tight, this type of thinking often results in those leaders making cuts to what they see as support activities, like security, which appears to produce less value. But using this same economic theory, you can show your strategic partners how the security risk mitigation activities that your team performs to protect the business are truly adding to the end margins of the product value.

Questions for the Security Practitioner
- "What are the primary drivers of value for my organization's product or service?"
- "How is the value of support activities viewed in my enterprise?"

21.2.1.1 Increasing Value to your Primary Function Strategic Partners

There are two avenues through which this business approach can help you educate your strategic partners on why certain security risk mitigation activities are beneficial to them.

- Educate the owners involved in the primary activities about how security risk mitigation can assist them to ensure the ability to consistently fulfill their mission by avoiding downtime, damage, or loss due to a security incident.
- Show enterprise executives the ways in which security could be considered a primary activity itself, contributing value directly to the profit margin, along with the production process.

To demonstrate value to your strategic partners, you may find Porter's concepts helpful. We will discuss each of the five *primary* activities as identified in Porter's value chain (depicted in Figure 21.1). For each of Porter's activities, we apply the activity to ESRM, and explore how security risk mitigation activities can protect that activity from losing value and/or increase its value.

1. Inbound Logistics

Inbound logistics includes supply chain management, warehousing, or facility access for receiving goods. Inbound logistical activities often function in a "just-in-time" manner, meaning that any disruption in the supply chain or problem in the warehouse can impact the entire production process. Security risk mitigation activities can provide increase efficiency and availability for these logistical functions. The value of security risk mitigation activities to the leaders of inbound logistical functions could include:

- Vendor risk assessments.
  - Whether the vendor is a provider of raw materials from the other side of the globe, or a hosted software service that tracks assets and inventory, assessing the security risk of the vendors used by the inbound logistics function helps them to ensure a source of materials from a vendor that does not expose the supply chain to too much risk of disruption, or a software system that does not expose the enterprise to cybersecurity risk of hacking or other interference.
- Global security awareness.
  - The inbound logistics team can rely on the security group to maintain a level of awareness about the global security situation, and notify the supply chain manager of any events that might require switching to a secondary vendor, or arrange to provide extra security protections to specific inbound shipments of goods.
- Continuity planning for disruption.
  - Crisis management and continuity planning can help ensure the supply chain is operational at acceptable levels, regardless of what events or incidents might be happening in the community or world.
- Physical security (closed circuit television [CCTV], access control, guard force management).
  - Warehouse operations deal with critical assets and physical security activities can protect those assets from theft and loss through multiple control activities.

2. Operations

Operational activities vary widely, but regardless of the activities that take place to convert the raw materials to the finished product, security risk mitigation activities can help those operations run more smoothly and avoid costly business interruptions. Security risk mitigation activities to discuss with operational leaders could include:

- Network security.
  - Today's networked environment is vulnerable to attacks, which can significantly disrupt operations activities. Automated manufacturing lines, processing services provided by software-as-a-service vendors, heating, ventilation, and air conditioning (HVAC), and other facility systems all require protections to reduce exposure to the risk of external interference. The cybersecurity risks your enterprise is exposed to may not even be on the radar of your operational leaders. Educating them on the potential risks is critical to the overall risk posture of the enterprise.

- Physical security (CCTV, access control, guard force management).
  - Just as the virtual environment must be protected from impact, so must the physical environment in which operations activities occur. Identifying the risks specific to your enterprise will help you discuss with the operational leaders how their environment could benefit from any risk mitigation activities that they choose to implement.

3. Outbound Logistics

Outbound logistics are similar to inbound logistics, only with goods and services flowing out of the organization instead of in. The same benefits apply here as in inbound logistics, but in outbound logistics, you add an aspect of organization employees who are potentially interacting far more with the public and distributing goods in many several types of environments. Employee security issues might be something you focus on with this functional area:

- Personnel security training.
  - Personnel who are involved in distribution to areas with higher security risk profiles might benefit from training in how they can function more securely while performing their jobs. This lowers the risk profile of employees and keeps them safer, reducing turnover from personnel who feel unprepared to function in riskier situations.

4. Marketing and Sales

Marketing and sales is a group that might not initially be aware of the security risk it is exposed to, or how to mitigate that exposure. But marketing deals with confidential intellectual property that must be protected to maintain a competitive advantage. For marketing and sales, discussions could focus on:

- Information security and control.
  - Advertising campaigns and pricing decisions are just two areas that could benefit from information security protections to reduce the risk of premature release.
- Internal Investigations.
  - Unfortunately, with sales often being a commission-based function, it is exposed to a significant risk of fraud. Internal investigations can, with the business owner, develop markers to indicate unacceptable sales practices, and assist with identifying possible exposure to fraud risk.
  - Service
    Like outbound logistics, service is exposed to security risks that revolve around personnel being in contact with the public. For service, which includes things like on site installations and maintenance, discussions could focus on:
- Personnel background checks.
  - When dealing with high value goods and when interacting with customers, the service function can benefit from ensuring high-integrity employees. Background checks help bring in personnel who meet set standards.

21.2.1.2 Is Security a Support or Primary Activity?

In some models, security risk mitigation can also stand alone as a primary value-contributing activity. Just as marketing adds value by convincing the consumer that they want a product or service adds value by ensuring the customer has a pleasant experience after purchase, the security function can add value to a good or service by giving the consumer a better opinion and feeling about it.

For example, if the product is installed in a customer's home, a risk mitigation tactic that provides the customer with the installer's name and picture ahead of time can give a level of comfort about the installation and could increase customer goodwill and brand reputation. Another example might be a firm that hosts software services in a shared data center environment. The security risk mitigation actions protecting the data center, the servers, and the network are truly part of the value chain – an insecure hosting service will not find many customers. Globalization and networked enterprises are making security considerations and risk mitigations more critical to the value chain of many organizations. This business-based message can help you educate your strategic partners on security risk in their areas.

21.3 Changing from a Traditional Security Budget to an ESRM Budget

The process of changing your enterprise security budget from a traditional security budget to an ESRM model is not an overnight switch. Finding all security tasks being performed across the enterprise, who is performing them, what resources are being applied to them, and then determining how they can be transitioned into your ESRM program is a long-term project. However, it will ultimately provide a much more focused security risk management program, which is aligned with the business mission and priorities. Additionally, you are likely to find financial and resource efficiencies when unifying security tasks under a single group of personnel with the correct technical expertise and skillsets.

It is essential, though, that the security risk management and partnership role, scope, and authority are well-defined and understood first. That understanding and acceptance lays a foundation for this exploration.

21.3.1 Discover Existing Security Tasks and Activities

The first step in the process of moving from a task-based security program to a risk-based security program, is to understand what security activities are *currently* happening in the enterprise. Whether these activities end up being performed by the security team in the new risk management paradigm, or remain with the group that is doing them, it is critical that the security leadership knows that these security activities are going on (and that they are using resources they might not realize are currently being applied to "security").

In this discovery process, you can look at several areas (depending on your enterprise operations and functions) that might be performing security activities. Some examples might be:
- Customer facing security activities.
- Internal or external investigations.
- Information security systems (firewalls, network security, etc.).
- Fraud (ID theft/internal).
- Physical or cyber forensic activities.
- Physical security systems (access control, CCTV, etc.).
- Business continuity/crisis management.
- Subpoena or other regulatory compliance.

With your understanding of your organization and security, you will be able to put together a specific list of the places to look for groups in your enterprise that might be doing these tasks.

Here are some questions to consider when looking for security risk mitigation activities that might be happening in your organization, but are not being performed by the security team:

- Do any departments or groups in your enterprise hold special events for either internal or external audiences? If so, how do they provide security for these events? Do they work with the security group or go outside?
  - Example: Marketing events, community events, employee parties, board meetings, stockholder meetings.
- Do individual facility managers work through security to provide any guard services needed? Can they or do they reach out locally and hire services?
- Does your enterprise have areas that handle cash? Is security involved in cash-handling decisions? In moving cash? Or do the departments that handle cash set their own policies, handle their own cash pickups, and transfers?
- With each of these programs and security practices, are they tied to specific assets? Are the assets prioritized to the overall business mission? Has there been an overall balancing of asset prioritization, risk identification, and associated resources applied to security risk mitigation?

21.3.2 Personnel Discovery

After determining what security activities are happening in the enterprise, and what departments are either doing them or managing contracted services to do them, the next step is to determine the assigned personnel who are doing those activities, and the percentage of their time devoted to them.

For each of the activities that you identify, determine:
- Inventory of personnel with responsibility for a security risk mitigation activity.
  - Identify personnel with 100% of dedicated time to security activities.
  - Identify personnel with some lower percentage of dedicate time to security activities.

In many cases where we have performed these inventories, we find dozens of people across a large enterprise performing similar or identical security tasks as part of a non-security job. This can include things like having administrative personnel creating and handing out access control or ID badges. We have also seen facilities personnel tasked with maintaining cameras or alarm systems, or human resources (HR) groups responsible for contracting guard services to provide security in higher risk buildings. These situations involved non-security personnel performing security activities that they are not subject matter experts in, and are not focused on as part of their *core* job functions.

In an ESRM program, significant time-management and efficiency gains can be made by consolidating these types of activities under the security department to have them carried out in a uniform manner across the enterprise, by personnel who have the proper training and expertise to perform them.

21.3.3 Financial Discovery

After looking at the human resources that are performing security tasks across the enterprise, the last step of the discovery process is determining the financial resources that are being spent on security risk mitigation activities. This discovery process uses accounting systems and coding to do data discovery on invoices have been paid for security activities.

Look for invoices that have been coded to:

- Operational expense:
  - Guard contractors.
  - Computer forensics.
  - Special events.
  - Investigation costs.
  - Alarm management.
  - Access management.
  - Video management.
  - Cyber response consulting.
  - Investigative consulting.
- Capital expense:
  - Physical security infrastructure.
  - Facilities security.
  - IT security infrastructure.
- Physical security system maintenance and upgrades.

Also check for missing or unaccounted-for expenses buried in operational expenses under various line-items:

- Repairs and maintenance – Hardware.
- Repairs and maintenance – Labor.
- Marketing events.
- Consultants (Private Investigators).
- Legal (investigations).
- Contract labor.
- Outside services.
- Small tools and equipment.

If necessary, in systems where there are no accounting codes dedicated to security categories, another way to use data mining in the accounting system is to search for invoices using key word searches:

- Alarm.
- Security.
- Investigations.
- Guards.
- Protection.
- Large agencies.
- Monitoring.

Once discovered, the personnel and financial resources that are being spent in non-security departments across the enterprise can be targeted for identifying efficiencies and reducing expenses overall.

21.3.4 Building the Unified Budget

Unifying a budget takes time. No leader in a business organization likes to give up budgeted resources. In the business world, budget equals control and responsibility – a significant indication of status, and often tied to the leader's sense of place, person, accomplishment, and self-worth. This is a large hurdle to overcome. It is also difficult for a business leader to give up control of a security activity or task if they feel as though they may ultimately be held accountable for the outcome of any failure in the risk mitigation activities protecting their assets. Ultimately though, if all risk decisions are made in alignment with the set tolerance levels of the business, the proper risk-decision-making process protects all participants through process transparency. To facilitate the transition, costs may continue to be managed through different business functions or departments, until there is a comfort level that the security budgeting process and experience are the same, no matter the scope of responsibilities. When ESRM is executed appropriately it will eventually become apparent to the business that the security budgeting process is based on core risk principles that are the same, no matter who controls them.

This is part of the iterative approach to rolling out a security program that we discussed in Chapters 10 and 11. It can also ease the transition process to offer oversight and control of the transition to the security governing body as the budgets for all security risk mitigation tasks and activities are consolidated into a single unit.

21.4 Ongoing/Annual Budgeting

The initial process of building an ESRM program budget is a starting point for the first year of ESRM operations. After the first cycle, however, you will most likely have to go through an annual budgeting process. The annual budget review is an activity to ensure that the decisions originally made to mitigate security risk are still valid and meet the levels of risk tolerance set by the business. It is also an exercise to ensure that the security department is spending the dedicated security dollars in the most efficient way possible to provide the desired level of protection.

21.4.1 Budget Updates

Our recommendation for annual budget review is to take the same steps we outlined in our first story at the beginning of this chapter.
1. Look at all existing security expenses.
2. Determine the impact to security risk mitigation services if spending on that activity is cut 10%, 15%, or 20%.
3. Understand the gaps between the expected/agreed upon service levels and the levels that could be delivered at each level of expense cuts.
4. Determine the level of funding needed to meet the minimum service level agreement to strategic partners (whether this means a cut or increase in budget dollars).

Questions for the Security Practitioner
- "What is the main driver of budget conversations in my organization?"
- "Do I involve any departments besides security in my budget discussions?"

21.4.2 Budget Decision Making and Risk Tolerance

Once you understand the budget's needed to deliver security risk mitigation services for the asset owners and risk stakeholders in your enterprise, you will have documented information to bring to the annual budgeting process from your discussions with those leaders. You can show the financial decision makers how budgeted dollars are tied to mitigating risk for your strategic partners. If the finance group disagrees with the requested annual budget, you will be able to explain to them that the risk tolerance discussion of reducing budget below the requested amount must involve your strategic partners, since neither the security, nor finance groups are the appropriate decision-makers on risks to those assets.

Involving the security council in the budget process is also a good plan. The governance body can provide an overall picture of the security risk tolerance level, set by the executives or board, and can provide the necessary support to the security department to carry out their role during the budgeting process. The security governance can clarify the role of security past the task based model, assisting security in moving the scope of the budgeting process from defending the budgeting for individual tasks, to defending the security risk mitigation efforts based on a pre-defined tolerance level.

21.5 Procurement Partnerships and the Role of Procurement in the Budget Process

Another business function that security consistently interacts with that can sometimes complicate the budgeting and expense process – whether it is the annual budget or budgeting for a single project or implementation – is procurement (also called purchasing). At a management level, it is procurement's role in the organization to purchase goods and services on behalf of the company, and to negotiate favorable terms to get the best price-point possible – conserving company resources. The group is a critical part of efficient business management, but it can sometimes be at odds with groups that are attempting to purchase goods and services that are complex in nature – as security may often be.

When practicing ESRM, the interactions with procurement change as well. While the procurement function *is* to ensure that company resources are spent wisely and not wasted, it is *not* to define or accept a security risk in the process of seeking the most favorable purchasing option they feel is available. However, the procurement process *can* have that unintentional impact when a product or service is substituted that is not truly comparable, and it is security's role to identify and escalate when those situations occur.

For just one example of how this can work, imagine that the security group is implementing a software solution to minimize an identified risk that has been deemed by the asset owners and stakeholders to need mitigation. A software is chosen, but there are multiple providers of similar types of software. If the procurement manager, as part of the purchasing process, identifies a lower cost solution which isn't as comprehensive or truly comparable, and determines that the company will not accept the chosen tool, in the ESRM paradigm, that decision falls outside of the risk acceptance capacity of that procurement manager. If the lower-cost option would not satisfy the risk tolerance needs, then it would be a mistake for the security department or procurement to move forward on that transaction, before a new risk assessment could completed and signed off by the risk stakeholders.

This same type of scenario applies to any security purchasing project. Guard services, CCTV equipment, network monitoring tools, and more. If a guard services company were chosen by simply identifying the cheapest provider based on hours and cost, the entire conversation about the role the security officers are playing to protect asset(s) from risks is shoved aside. That does not mean procurement negotiating these contracts is a mistake. If the cheaper company mitigates the same risk to the same level as the more expensive company, and the security risk assessment was completed, then finding efficiency in cost is a good thing, and the security risk decision did not truly change. However, if the cheaper guard company hires cheaper guards, who are not as well-trained, professional, or alert, or who lack needed skills, there very well may be a change in the risk profile.

The success of the procurement group is often driven by how much money they save the company, so it is easy to see how at times there could be competing interests with the needs of the groups on whose behalf they are purchasing. Nevertheless, there is no need for the relationship with the purchasing function to be adversarial in any way. They provide a critical service to the enterprise that is recognized by business executives. It makes sense to establish the security and procurement relationship before there is any conflict. When done this way, a good partnership with procurement can also be another set of eyes for the security group when identifying security risks. Oftentimes, as other departments work through their own projects with procurement, certain aspects of those projects get cut to squeeze a project within a certain budget. If part of the project that gets cut could have an impact on a security risk, procurement can be a great ally to bring those risks to security's attention and get them in the loop. This is more likely in a well-understood and cordial relationship.

Questions for the Security Practitioner
- "What is the main driver of budget conversations in my organization?"
- "Do I involve any departments besides security in my budget discussions?"

Chapter Review

In Chapter 21, you:

- Considered the differences between a traditional budgeting process and the ESRM approach.
- Looked at the *value chain theory* to place values on the contributions of various primary and support activities in an organization, and discussed how security can be positioned as part of the primary chain of activities.
- Discussed how partnering with other groups in the enterprise can assist in the budgeting process, and how a partnership with the procurement group specifically can help the security function be more efficient with expenditures when each group understands their role.

Looking Forward

Chapter 22 will cover the metrics and reporting needs of executives who interact with an ESRM security program.

Practitioner steps to consider before moving on to Chapter 22:

✓ Consider your existing budgetary process and how it may or may not align with the ESRM way of budgeting.

✓ Think about how you can use the concept of value chain theory to explain the benefits of mitigating security risks to primary activities.

Security Program Self-Assessment

In this self-assessment, you should think about the answer to the questions posed, and then see where your program is on the identified ESRM spectrum.

Question	Y/N	Is This ESRM?
Does your security budgeting process align all security expenses across the enterprise to a single budget and a protected asset, and does it ensure asset-owner support of the expense?	☐Yes ☐No	**NO**: If you do not have a singular budget process aligned with protected assets and stakeholders, then this is a suitable place to start your ESRM program. **PARTIAL**: If your organization has some expenses aligned to specific assets or aligns them all, but in distributed budgets, then you are part of the way to an ESRM implementation. **YES**: If you have all your security expenses contained in a single budget that is aligned with specific asset owners and stakeholders, then you are practicing ESRM.

Questions for Discussion

1. What are some potential obstacles that could happen in the process of building a unified budget?
2. What are some of the aspects of the security budgeting process that require strong partnerships with other departments in the enterprise? What are the advantages of developing strong partnerships prior to beginning a unified budget discussion?

References

Porter, M. E. (1998). *Competitive advantage: Creating and sustaining superior performance*. New York, NY: The Free Press. [Text copyright 1985. Introduction copyright 1998.]

Learn More About It

For further reading about value chain theory:

Arline, K. (2015, January 26). What is a value chain analysis? *Business News Daily*. [Web log post] Available at http://www.businessnewsdaily.com/5678-value-chain-analysis.html

Tyson, D. (2007). *Security convergence: Managing enterprise security risk*. Burlington, MA: Butterworth-Heinemann.

22

Reporting and Metrics That Matter

Just as it is crucial for you to gain executive and strategic partner support for implementing your enterprise security risk management (ESRM) program, you also need to engage them through regular communications, metrics, and reports on program progress. In this chapter, you will see how reporting metrics in an ESRM implemented program is different from how metrics traditionally are looked at in many security programs. Then you will dig into some specifics of how to present risk-based data and information to your direct management, strategic partners, and executives to allow them to monitor and measure the success of the ESRM program.

This chapter will help you to:

- Understand the different reports and metrics to use to communicate with different audiences.
- Build effective metrics and reports for measuring your ESRM program.
- Tailor your message so that it neither over-communicates nor under-communicates to your intended audience.
- Build strategic reports that your partners and leaders can use to understand their risk condition.

22.1 Why are Security Metrics Important?

Security metrics are important because a risk-based security program is centered on the need for business leaders to set risk tolerance, making risk decisions to ensure that the business is operating within that tolerance. Thus, a key piece of your ongoing ESRM program is to continually communicate the status of all enterprise security risk as it relates to the set tolerance. Besides that, in almost every business organization, the bedrock upon which most strategic and tactical decisions are made is made up of the daily, weekly, monthly, quarterly, and annual reports that go from the lowest levels of the organization up to the highest. Your message needs to be clearly and appropriately crafted to show your audiences exactly what they need to know about the status of security risk as it pertains to them and the decisions they need to make.

Of course, not all your audiences need the same information. Some of the people you need to communicate to are making more tactical choices and will need more task-oriented details. These audiences might include:

- The functional leaders to whom security reports, who control the budget, payroll, and expenses for the security group.
- Asset owners, who provide direct financial support for some of the risk mitigation activities that the security team carries out.
- Security department personnel, who need to understand what others in the security department are doing.
- Procurement teams, who work on hardware, software, and personnel contracts for the security team.

Those groups need a different level of data and information than audiences who operate with a more strategic outlook for the enterprise:

- The board of directors or other leadership/owner group, tasked with ensuring oversight of all enterprise risk.
- Company senior executives, who need to understand the overall security risk picture.
- The security council, who will want to understand how the program is managing various security risks, and how the risk tolerances are being maintained.
- Your functional area strategic partners in the enterprise, who will need to know the status of the security risks impacting their area.

Questions for the Security Practitioner
- "What security metrics and reports do I currently build? Do I think that the audience reading them can use any of it to make business decisions?"
- "What are the security aspects that I would like to make my stakeholders aware of? Am I conveying what I want them to know in my reports?

Regardless of the audience, in an ESRM environment, you will report on risks or groups of risks that are:

- Associated with an asset or departmental group of assets.
- Tied to the risk interests, concerns, and the appropriateness of the risk owner or stakeholder.
- Applied to a business-defined risk tolerance.

Such reporting will drive the metrics that you deliver in a contextual way, focused on audience needs.

22.2 What is the Traditional View of Security Metrics Reporting?

In many conversations with security professionals across the years, we have heard that it is extremely difficult to develop metrics that allow professionals to gain traction for their security program. Some of the reasons we have heard about the difficulty of creating useful reports are:

- "You cannot build a report on incidents that do not happen or are avoided, and you cannot count how many were averted."
- "If we report on the number of incidents that occur, we will be showing that we do not stop them all."
- "My leaders do not want to see a graph of guard-post hours or cameras monitored."
- "Our incident reports are interesting, but too long to report them all."
- "Management does not want to know about (insert your organization's controversial incident type here) because they are afraid of the information getting out."

To echo our premise at the start of this book, we would argue that these concerns with reporting are a direct result of operating a security program in a task-oriented manner rather than in a risk-based manner. Some of the types of reports that we see in a more traditional security environment are based on reporting incidents, efficiencies, or quantities of tasks being performed, which could include:

- Security guard hours and performance.
- Security incident numbers by type or location.
- Number of cyber threats averted.
- Numbers of IDs passwords or access badges processed.
- Loss/shrinkage numbers for assets.
- Cameras maintained or replaced, or door locks installed.
- Number of investigations completed.
- Number of calls taken and responded to.

These reports might have their place for some audiences, but they are certainly not the kind of reports that could be used for strategic business decision-making. Task-based reports tend to focus on budget efficiency and justification, or incident trends, either realized or averted. If the tasks that security does defines the role of the department, then these metrics make sense, because they show how much work the department is doing, and show the trends of the kinds of work being done. They will also come in handy when having to justify a budget or move personnel around. The team can point to a trend of more incidents of type A and say, "Look, we do a lot of that. Let's add a person to do more," or, "We are seeing less of type C, so we can cut funding there, if you insist." The issue here is that assigning resources based on trending does not deal with whether those trends and resources are tied to a risk that the business has determined a tolerance level on. If the trends show that incidents of theft are rising, does that mean the business needs more "security?" In absence of a strategic look at the risks associated with those thefts, it is hard to say. It might be that a policy change is needed, or staggered employee shift changes, or any other change that could be found in a risk-analysis-focused investigation, not just a trending chart.

The focus on ESRM metrics and reporting is on the risk and risk owner. Each metric must be relevant and specific to that the needs and interests of the report reader and the impact that the reported security risks may have on that reader's goals and objectives. Thus, the metrics being reported need to be developed in *partnership* with the business leader to establish relevancy. A threat to an asset that causes concern from a security practitioner's perspective may not be impactful at all to the business stakeholder's objectives. Developing a risk-based metric specific to a business leader's asset and mission will help establish the relevancy of reports, and in turn, it can lead to an understanding of security's efforts on behalf of that business leader.

22.3 What is the ESRM View of Security Metrics Reporting?

Reporting metrics in ESRM is very different from reporting metrics in a more traditional security environment. In ESRM, the types of reports that you will most often provide might be:
- Incident levels that indicate security risk tolerance exceptions.
- New or residual risks identified since the last report period.
- Metrics of mitigation activities as related to risk categories, and the effectiveness of those mitigation activities.
- Specific reports on/for individual assets, risks, risk owners, or business objectives.

When we look at reporting and metrics in an ESRM environment, the reports can be broken out into a few categories, including:
- **The Focused Risk Status Report**: This report is focused on a specific risk, an asset, a business function, a project, or a leader, for example. It delivers a specific message on the risk, tolerances, variances, and concerns around a specific topic.
- **The General Risk Status Report**: The report measures more generally how the security risks identified by the business as their critical concerns are being managed, and how they are faring in relation to the set tolerance level, all in context with the interests of the audience of specific report.
- **The Metrics and Efficiency Report**: This report details risk mitigation activity/task management, and efficiency of resource use in the department, more like the traditional types of reporting. However, even these task-focused reports should always include a tie to the asset, risk, and asset owner of the risks that the tasks are being performed to mitigate. Especially at the beginning of your ESRM journey, you do not want these efficiency-focused reports to blur the role of security as performing these tasks for the sake of "doing tasks," not in service of mitigating a risk for an asset owner.

All these reports are important in their way, but the audiences are different and the uses of the reports in the ESRM environment are also different.

22.3.1 Metrics of Risk Tolerance

In a traditional security department, the kinds of reports that are sent to management tend to focus on how busy the department is, how much work it is doing, how many types of responses it has done, and how many hours were spent on security tasks. In contrast, ESRM places a much larger focus on reports that directly communicate to the business function leaders how the mitigation plans are working to ensure that risks to the enterprise assets are remaining within the boundaries of tolerance. This is not a method of reporting that many security professionals are used to doing, and it will be a shift in how you think about and develop reports.

The best way to communicate to your audience about the metrics of risk tolerance is to ask some basic initial questions and think about them from the point of view of your strategic partners who will be receiving the reports. Table 22-1 offers some questions to ask and points to think about for each question as you develop reports based on your ESRM program.

Table 22-1. Questions to Consider for Reporting Risk Metrics

Question	Thoughts to Consider
Who is the audience for this report?	• You will most likely need to create separate reports for each line of business, due to disparate risks and areas of interest. • The security council and executives will have different interests and want higher level reports than the functional leaders in the organization • Internally, your department might want to see metrics on how their efforts to control specific risks are working.
What are the risks that the audience is most concerned with?	• One general report on all risks will likely include too much information, much of it not relevant to all functions. • When creating the reporting material, you might consider building a large master report and then breaking it out into smaller reports with different areas of interest for different audiences.
What metrics will indicate to the audience whether the risk mitigation tasks are keeping the risk within tolerance levels?	• Development of metrics should be in partnership with the risk owners to enable a relevant report, tied to a measurable tolerance level. • Tolerance level thresholds should be established to indicate when a risk is exceeding (or falling below) tolerance, and should trigger an established review or response from the business or security leaders. • Metrics to consider would include, reporting trends, changes in the threat environment, or even a security department assessment tied to the risk(s) in the report.
What metrics will indicate that a previously acceptable risk might be rising to exceed set tolerances?	• Are security responses or investigations rising in a previously unmitigated risk area? • Are risks that have previously had little identifiable impact occurring with greater impact?

22.3.1.1 Metrics of Risk Tolerance for Security Disciplines

Some metrics of risk tolerance you might consider are below.

For all disciplines, you will want to report on:
- Risks in the enterprise that are currently exceeding tolerance.
- Risks that need to be escalated due to prioritization conflicts.
- Conflicts in mitigation plan decision making that need to be escalated to executives or the council.
- New risks identified through reporting processes.
- New risk mitigations in place.

Additionally, for specific disciplines, you will want to focus your reporting on such topics as:
- **Investigations**
  - Residual risks found in the postmortem process.
  - New environmental risks found through internal and external risk scanning.
  - Trends in investigations that might indicate risk tolerance levels are near non-compliance.
- **Physical Security**
  - Residual risks that were discovered through incident response.
  - Availability of new mitigation techniques and technology.
  - New environmental risks found through internal and external risk scanning.
- **Information and Cyber Security**
  - Residual risks that impacted the enterprise beyond tolerance levels.
  - Availability of new mitigation techniques and technology.
  - New environmental risks that are found through internal and external risk scanning.
  - Trends in network or other awareness measurements that might indicate risk tolerance levels are near non-compliance.
- **Workplace Violence and Threat Management**
  - Trends in reports of workplace violence of a specific type, or associated to a location or function.
  - Trends outside the enterprise that might change the perspective on risk tolerance inside the organization.
  - Trends in any of the key risk indicators (KRI) that might indicate risk tolerance levels are near non-compliance.
- **Business Continuity and Crisis Management**
  - Residual risks that impacted the enterprise beyond tolerance levels during a crisis event or that were identified in an exercise as probable excess impacts.
  - New environmental risks found through risk scanning and awareness.

22.3.2 Metrics of Security Efficiency

Although reporting in the ESRM model is mainly focused on metrics of risk tolerance and variance, there are still instances where metrics of efficiency are important. It is important to be able to show that we are being responsible stewards of those funds assigned to risk mitigation activities. Metrics of efficiency are excellent reports for audiences, such as:

- The direct security management structure.
- Finance or other budgetary control groups.
- Functional leaders who directly fund security activities in support of their assets and areas of responsibility.

For those audiences with an interest in the metrics of efficiency, these types of reports are ideal for communicating security metrics, such as:
- Incident response.
- Investigations.
- Business Support.

In reports to security leadership, some metrics of efficiency that you might consider including are:
- **Investigations**
  - Number of investigations completed.
  - Number of investigations by type or location.
  - Number of postmortem reports completed.
  - Number of business partner meetings.
  - **Physical Security**
  - Numbers of hours worked by guards.
  - Facilities protected by security guards.
  - Security alarms responded to.
  - Access control credentials processed.
  - Security reports received.
  - Background checks performed.
- **Information and Cyber Security**
  - Number of attempted attacks.
  - Number of incidents responded to.
  - Patterns of incidents types or attacks.
  - Number of incidents by type or location.
- **Workplace Violence and Threat Management**
  - Number of workplace violence training sessions completed.
  - Number of reports of concerning behavior received.
  - Number of threat assessments performed.
- **Business Continuity and Crisis Management**
  - Number of crisis team activations.
  - Number of exercises performed.
  - Number of new or updated plans/teams.
  - Number of training exercises.
  - Number of relationships with local emergency responders or law enforcement agencies maintained through contact or exercise participation.

22.3.3 Comparing ESRM and Traditional Security Reporting

As we have seen, the process of reporting metrics is significantly different for an ESRM program than a traditional program. In Table 22-2, we will take another look at the issues we heard from our security colleagues in the past regarding difficulty in producing viable metrics – and show how these issues are dealt with in a risk-based security program.

Table 22-2. Traditional Security Reporting Concerns and the ESRM Response

Traditional Security Reporting Concern	ESRM Response
"You cannot build a report on incidents that do not happen or are avoided, and cannot count how many were averted." And "If we report on the number of incidents that occur, we will be showing that we do not stop them all."	In ESRM, the business owner sets the tolerance for each type of risk and chooses what they consider to be an acceptable response to mitigate the risk. Therefore, the need to claim that any specific number of incidents was avoided becomes unnecessary. An ESRM report on any risk impact occurring at a level that is within set tolerance is an excellent metric to measure the status of a risk mitigation. Additionally, a trend that shows the type of incident moving out of tolerance can show the risk owner that a different plan might be needed.
"My leaders do not want to see a graph of guard-post hours or cameras monitored."	In an ESRM program, reports and metrics are tailored specifically to the needs of the audience, and metrics of efficiency are not needed for all audiences. They may even be completely irrelevant to some people, including executives. However, they could be highly valuable to others, like security managers.
"Our incident reports are interesting, but too long to report them all."	Sometimes incident summaries point directly to security risk trends, and can be included in an executive level report for illustrative purposes on a risk tolerance level. However, you would not automatically include a report of all incidents in a report unless they communicated a specific message on a security risk that needed to be looked at by risk owners or other audiences.

| "Management does not want to know about (insert your organization's controversial incident type here) because they are afraid of the information getting out." | This issue points out a core difference in the ESRM philosophy. The idea that there is a risk that is deliberately ignored because "management" does not want to see it is not possible in an ESRM program. The ESRM process requires all risks to all assets are identified, prioritized, and responded to by an appropriate level of the business.

While it is possible that enterprise leaders may have determined that they have an extremely high tolerance for some types of risk, and do not want reports on them, that is a decision that they are allowed to make as the risk owners. But even in that case, it is still incumbent upon the security team to make sure the threat, exposure, and potential impact are monitored on a regular basis, and if any change occurs to the risk, to ensure that the tolerance of the enterprise for that risk has not changed. |

Think About It: The Controversial Security Risk

We have, unfortunately, seen instances where security personnel have been specifically forbidden to mention certain types of incidents. Whether this is because a department does not want the information to reach the attention of enterprise leaders, or because they think it might have a bad public relations impact (or any other reason), the underlying idea is that if a risk is not reported on, it does not actually exist. As a security professional, you know this is not true, but if ESRM accepts that the role of the business is to determine the tolerance level for risk, what should you do?

The answer is simple. The role of the security manager is to ensure that all risk stakeholders are aware of security risks. This means that if *one* group would like to either accept or ignore that risk, you have the chartered responsibility to make sure that *every* risk stakeholder for that risk is aware of and agrees with the idea of accepting or ignoring that risk. If they do, then it is further the role of the security manager to continually monitor that risk, and to bring it forward in the form of a report any time the risk or potential impact of that risk changes.

An example of this kind of controversial risk has been seen on some college campuses with administrators, who are mainly concerned with ensuring that the enrollment numbers remain high for their school, not wanting to report on or track cases of rape or sexual assault on the campus. We have spoken with security professionals who have begun tracking these types of assaults, and they have been told that, "There were no assaults before, and now you are showing that there are. We cannot send that message to students' parents," or even, "Those numbers will scare students, we need to stop collecting them."

While the administrators are certainly one risk owner of this risk, there are others that can and should be brought into the conversation:
- Student advocates.
- The legal group.
- Public affairs.
- Campus safety.
- Parent advocates.
- Marketing.

These groups all could have an impact from the risk of campus assaults, whether due to being a victim of a risk they were not aware existed, or having a lawsuit brought for not protecting students, or having bad publicity for the perception of incidents being hidden somehow.

These are all aspects of the risk that must be considered. While it is possible that if all these groups were consulted, the business might still decide to accept or ignore a controversial risk, it is far less likely with more people involved. If they do, however, you can know that ESRM processes were followed.

22.4 Building Metrics Reports

Once you have determined your report audience, you also want to consider the best presentation of the data to communicate the information clearly, concisely, and with the least opportunity for confusing the message of the report.

22.4.1 Communicating to an Executive Audience

We wrote in Chapter 20 about some of the tips for communicating in person to an executive audience. Some of those also carry over into written reporting. When designing a report for senior executives, remember some of these aspects of crafting communications for the executive level.

- Make sure your data tells a story (it has a reason for being in the report). What is being communicated to the reader? Is it clear, concise, and relevant?
- Use graphics to present numeric information as much as possible, rather than tables and writing.
- Keep reports short and to the point.
- Present the data on a regular schedule (quarterly is recommended for executives).
- Use only up to date information in reports, avoid estimates as much as possible.
- Have appendices and backup details ready for executives who request further information based on your basic report.

22.4.1.1 Planning a Security Report for Executives

The executives are responsible for running the company at a long-term strategic level. The reports you prepare for them should not include daily tactical information unless it is indicative of a trend that requires a strategic response or correction. Tactical metrics, of course, should always be available as supporting material if needed. In ESRM, the most important purpose for reports and metrics is to ensure ongoing awareness of the status of security risks and tolerances. Reporting the number of incidents or averted incidents, although may show off some excellent work by the security department, may not be relevant to the executives if it is not associated with a specific risk, and in context with the executive's goals and missions.

When planning a report for your executives, some questions to ask are:
- What are the new risks the company is facing in the next quarter or year?
- What risks have executive attention, and which need to have a tolerance status reported?
- Are any high-impact risks beginning to move out of tolerance?
- Are any types of risk making news headlines, and likely to be something the executives have on their minds? Is there information to present on that?
- Where has the focus of the security team been during the time this report is covering?
- Are there existing or new security risks that could have a potential impact on business goals and objectives?

22.4.1.2 Building a Security Report for Executives

We recommend a structure that includes a past/present/future focus that are each tied to a defined risk tolerance such as:

Past: Trends from the reporting period just ended (quarter or month).

- Current trends being seen around the trackable risks that the executives are concerned with.
- Metrics/Charts/Graphs in support of those trends.

Present: Environmental trends that might impact risk in the next reporting period.

- Projected increases or cuts that could impact mitigation activities.
- Business changes that could impact risk.

Future: Long term trends or activities to watch.

- Emerging risk trends.
- Future mitigation activities and projects planned.

22.4.2 Communicating to the Security Council Audience

The security council is interested in whether the security risk management program is functioning appropriately and if it is meeting the tolerances they set for it in the initial phases of program implementation. They are likely to be interested in the report you prepare for the executives; however, the security council will also need to have some more detailed reports to show them how the security program is meeting the objectives for risk mitigation assigned to it. They will wish to see:

- The status of any risk mitigation projects that are assigned to be monitored at the council level, and a red/yellow/green rating to indicate the degree to which they are on target for time and budget.
- The status of long-term gap analysis remediation, with spider charts showing current vs. desired state.
- Audit reports of how the program is functioning and adhering to the policies and guidelines set for it and agreed to by the council.
- A continuous assessment of procedures.
- Status updates on the establishment and regular review of security risk tolerance thresholds.

22.4.2.1 Planning a Security Report for the Security Council

The security council has a very specific area of interest in their view of the security program. Just as with the executives, they are not going to be interested in the day-to-day metrics of efficiency. Their attention will be drawn to metrics that reflect how a specific risk mitigation project is performing or metrics that indicate a place where resources might be shifted to be better used in another risk area, an action requiring a council decision. The reports for the security council should focus on the key performance indicators (KPIs) that you and the council have agreed upon in your council charter.

When planning a report for your security council, some questions to ask are:

- What risk mitigation projects has the security council assigned to carry out and what is the status of those projects?
- What specific risks have the council named as risks to monitor for compliance to tolerance levels?
- How does the risk profile of the enterprise measure against the targets set by the council?

22.4.2.2 Building a Security Report for the Security Council

Once you determine what the security council wants to see reports on, you can determine the best format for those reports.

Spider Graphs/Radar Chart of Risk Tolerance: Spider graphs are so named due to their superficial resemblance to a spider web with radial lines and the graph plotting points of current data vs. target data. They are an excellent way to present information on multiple aspects of your security risk management program, and they show visually how they relate to the target. Some examples of data that can be shown on a spider graph are:

- Number of incidents of a certain type compared to the target number that would indicate exceeding tolerance.
- Program maturity of the current tier/rating of aspects of a program compared to the future desired tier.
- Residual risk exposure compared to pre-mitigation risk exposure.
- Risk assessment results of physical security protections versus the baseline target for protection.

Mitigation Project Status Reports: A second type of report that you can use with the security council is a project status report that shows how various projects of interest to the council are performing. The council report on project status should not be the same type of *detailed* report that a project manager would use to communicate a weekly status to a project team, but it needs to be at a higher level showing all relevant projects. Information included in the report would be:

- Project name.
- Brief description.
- Target asset and risk mitigation.
- Target end date.
- Status in simple terms such as:
  - Green/Yellow/Red.
  - On Schedule/Delayed.
  - Planning/Executing/Complete.
  - Any significant issues associated with the project.

22.4.3 Communicating to a Strategic Partner Audience

Communicating to your strategic partners is a hybrid approach to what we have already discussed – with the same types of information, but with a smaller scope, related to the assets and risks that impact a specific area.

22.4.3.1 Planning a Security Report for Strategic Partners

To plan your report for your strategic business partner, you will want to ask questions like:

- Who is the functional leader/asset owner/risk stakeholder for this report?
- What are the risks that the audience is most concerned with?
- What assets do I need to report on?
- What metrics will indicate to the audience whether the risk mitigation tasks are keeping the risk within tolerance levels?
- What metrics will indicate that a previously acceptable risk might be rising to exceed set tolerances?

22.4.3.2 Building a Security Report for Strategic Partners

When building the report for your strategic partners, you can use the formats we discussed already, but tailor the risks and projects to the area of interest to your audience. Those report formats can be repurposed to cover a variety of different risk topics and areas. You may also find that your partners have reporting preferences that they would like to see, and they can provide you with ideas about how they might like the information delivered.

22.4.4 Communicating to Security Functional Leadership

The audiences we have looked at so far will be more interested in metrics of risk tolerance than in metrics of efficiency. There is, however, certainly an audience of people interested in ensuring the security team is operating efficiently and using security budget dollars wisely and within the bounds that were set. The functional leadership with oversight over the security team will be interested in these reports, as other groups such as finance, or accounting might be. Metrics of efficiency are more straightforward, but you should still plan your report to make it an effective method for telling the story of how you are operating, not merely presenting lists of numbers with no context. Some of these metrics reports might also be interesting to your strategic partners, especially if the assets for which you are providing risk mitigation activities require their financial or budget support.

22.4.4.1 Planning a Security Report for Security Management

When developing a report for your internal security leadership and team, it's important to not overwhelm the reader with data. Reports and metrics of efficiency can certainly be longer, more detailed, and more frequent than the documents that we have discussed so far, but they should keep in mind the interests and attention of the intended audience.

Some questions to ask yourself when planning a report detailing metrics of department activity and efficiency of resource use are:

- Budget-focused questions.
  - What activities require the most budget support?
  - Who is interested in ensuring those budget dollars are well spent?
  - What information would provide a picture of how efficiently we are using these resources?
- Trend-focused questions.
  - What activities do we perform that can be categorized and broken down by type?
  - Who would be interested in the trends shown by the categories identified?
  - What data would show the volume of work performed?
  - What data would show the main "user" of that volume?
- Asset-focused questions.
  - What assets have significant mitigation activities performed to protect them from risks of harm?
  - Are there metrics of work volume that can be show broken down by that asset?

Questions for the Security Practitioner
- "How can I better understand my audience's needs in report writing and metrics?"
- "Am I clearly communicating the important aspects of my security program in my reporting?"

22.4.4.2 Building a Security Report for Security Management

The options for building efficiency metrics reports are widely variable, so below we are going to go through just one exercise exploring a single report focused on the security investigations function.

First, we will begin by asking and answering several questions:
- Q: Who is the audience for this report?
  - A: The functional leader over the security department.
- Q: What activities is this report covering?
  - A: The monthly roll-up of efficiency and trend metrics for investigations.
- Q: What data will show the volume of work performed and the focus of that work?
  - A: A graph or chart showing:
    - The number of investigation performed.
    - The top 5 or 10 categories of investigations.
    - The functional areas that request the most investigations or are the target of investigations.
- Q: What data will show trends in activities that might be cause for adjusting activity levels?
  - A: A chart comparing previous and current time periods.

Again, working with your report audience to clearly define the metrics they are interested in will assist you in narrowing down the information you provide.

Chapter Review

In Chapter 22, you looked at several ways to present information about the ESRM program to various audiences to enhance their understanding of risk and to enable them to make more informed risk decisions.

Looking Forward

Chapter 23 will cover the topic of enterprise security organization convergence.

Practitioner Steps to consider before moving on to Chapter 23:
✓ Consider how you might change your metrics and reporting to better serve your current audiences.
✓ Think about what new audiences might benefit from tailored security reporting and metrics.

Security Program Self-Assessment

In this self-assessment, you should think about the answer to the questions posed, and then see where your program is on the identified ESRM spectrum.

Question	Y/N	Is This ESRM?
Do the metrics you build for your security program focus on risk trends and information?	☐Yes ☐No	**NO**: If you do not include risk trending information in your reporting and metrics, then is a suitable place to start your ESRM program. **PARTIAL**: If you occasionally include risk trending information in your reporting, but focus mainly on efficiency reporting, then you are part of the way to an ESRM implementation. **YES**: If you have reports tailored to specific audiences that present risk trending, and efficiency metrics based on audience interests, then you are practicing ESRM.

Questions for Discussion

1. What are some reasons that people who receive metrics and reports about a traditional security program might not find them relevant? Discuss ways to determine how to enhance relevance in security reporting.
2. Discuss reasons that a "less is more" philosophy towards metrics and reporting might ultimately benefit the overall message of a metrics report.

Learn More About It

For further reading about building metrics reports and communicating with executives:

ASIS International. (2017). *Presenting metrics to senior management.* [Web log post]. Available at https://foundation.asisonline.org/FoundationResearch/Security-Metrics/Presenting-Metrics-to-Senior-Management/Pages/default.aspx

Hanson, M. (2014, October 12). *Creating a web analytics report for the "big picture" executive.* [Web log post]. Available at https://megalytic.com/blog/creating-a-web-analytics-report-for-the-big-picture-executive

Lavinsky, D. (2013, September 6). Executive dashboards: What they are and why every business needs one. *Forbes.* Available at https://www.forbes.com/sites/davelavinsky/2013/09/06/executive-dashboards-what-they-are-why-every-business-needs-one/#20a4ff1b37d1

Smith, N. (2015, October 12). *Designing and building great dashboards – 6 golden rules to successful dashboard design.* [Web log post]. Available at https://www.geckoboard.com/blog/building-great-dashboards-6-golden-rules-to-successful-dashboard-design/#.WVnIcWeWypo

23

ESRM and the Path to Security Convergence

If you have been around the security industry at all in the last 10 to 15 years, the word *convergence* is likely to be familiar to you. Convergence is the idea that all personnel performing security tasks of any kind (physical or logical) should be organized under a single reporting structure, with one executive in charge. While convergence is sometimes cited as a best practice for security management, on the other hand, it is sometimes seen as the worst possible solution to a confusing tangle of skillsets and security management requirements. In our view, convergence has the potential for either strength or weakness. Thus, any discussion of a converged management structure must be predicated on the benefits (or risks) it might bring to an enterprise. While organizational convergence is not a specific goal of enterprise security risk management (ESRM), there certainly could be benefits to the merged structure, as well as situations in which convergence might be a risk mitigation solution that works to reduce enterprise security risk. In this chapter, we will show you where ESRM can help manage risk in an enterprise environment – converged or not.

This chapter will help you to:
- Understand common views of the security convergence concept.
- See how ESRM can work to manage risk in a converged or non-converged structure.
- Explore the benefits and challenges of a converged security environment.
- Analyze how an ESRM paradigm can help you implement a converged structure if your organization chooses to do so.

23.1 The Common View of Security Convergence

The phrase "security convergence" began appearing with some frequency in the industry beginning around 2004 and 2005. During those early years, the definitions of security convergence were really set. If we want to discuss security convergence and ESRM, it is critical that we first understand what the term means in the industry.

On CSO Online, security convergence is defined as:

> Integrating historically stove-piped functions of operational risk management to achieve better security, oversight of enterprise-wide risk and cost efficiencies (Slater, 2005).

A somewhat more formal definition comes from Dave Tyson, in his book *Security Convergence: Managing Enterprise Security Risk:*

> Security convergence is the integration, in a formal, collaborative, and strategic manner, of the cumulative security resources of an organization in order to deliver enterprise-wide benefits through enhanced risk mitigation, increased operational effectiveness and efficiency, and cost savings (Tyson, 2007, p. 4).

Notice that both definitions refer to risk management and security risk – these were also the foundational beginnings of the ESRM concepts we have been discussing in this book.

The concept of convergence essentially means managing all your security risks within one central organizational structure and in the same way – as risks – and ensuring that no matter if the mitigation tactics put in place are physical or logical, they are doing what they are supposed to do, protecting enterprise assets from harm.

The convergence conversation has moved on since the early 2000s, in part because the conversation around this topic has matured through continued dialogue, but also because technology has moved on as well, and has created a whole new world of logical risk associated with physical objects that are now connected to networks. These changes have led to the melding of logical and physical security risks *and* mitigation solutions, regardless of whether they are being treated by two separate security departments or under one functional security organization that has responsibility for all security risks.

The nature of logical – or cyber – risks is changing at such a furious pace, and carries such potential for significant operational disruption, that it is forcing businesses to re-examine how cyber and technology risks are being managed throughout the enterprise. The discussion of logical risk is transforming from a focus on "information security" to the risk of cyber-attacks that can have significant impact to any aspect of the business. Thus, the conversation has changed from a technical dialog focused on data, to a business resiliency dialogue focused around proper security risk management.

Questions for the Security Practitioner
- "How do the physical and logical security groups interact in my organization?"
- "Do different teams doing security in my organization work *'across borders'*?"

23.1.1 Technological Convergence

Convergence of technology is a fact. Within the last decade, the access control systems, door locks, alarms, cameras, facial recognition systems, and many other kinds of physical security implementations have moved to operate on the very same networks as the rest of the company – likely along with operational systems that the company relies on. Whether the security industry is ready for it or not, technology risks and solutions have converged, meaning that the security risks that used to be able to be treated as either "physical" or "informational" have also merged.

But one thing that often fails to get mentioned in the conversation about technology convergence is that the risk *environment* that the security team is responsible for managing is also converging. There is a business *and personal* reliance on networked "things" for everything from running manufacturing lines to banking and finance to keeping in touch with grandma over social media. Just a few examples of how our online world makes risk a cross-technology-border concern are:

- An employee claims she is being harassed and threatened at work by another employee. While 20 years ago, this might have been a "traditional" security response with an investigator investigating the claim, today this investigation could not happen without also involving multiple digital channels and potentially a forensic examination of the employees' computers.
- Also, 20 years ago, you only had to worry about physically securing your customers' walk from the car into your retail environment when you wanted to sell them something or allow them to come and pay their bill for services. Now, you are responsible for keeping customers and their accounts safe as they access your business from anywhere on the planet via a website or dedicated app.
- In the past, if employees were let go from the company, you had to ensure that you collected their key to the office. If they posed a risk to the company, you had to ensure that you notified security personnel to be on the lookout for them coming back and to stop them from entering the facility. Now, you must ensure that all their network rights, digital access, and passwords are revoked. But that is the easy part. If they pose a risk of retaliation for their firing, you must be on the lookout for anything they might have left behind on the network or watch for them sneaking in through a digital "back door" they might have installed themselves.

This list could go on, and we are sure you can think of several risks and threats yourself that cross the line between the physical and virtual world. This technology convergence is not just in security; it is universal, which makes securing that converged universe even more critical.

Programs and procedures used by both traditional and logical security programs perform essentially the same risk mitigation role – protecting assets from harm. Although the skillsets to manage these risks are different, advances in technology mean that the tools and resources are starting to converge even those differing skillsets, because there are efficiencies and tactical benefits when performed together, even by the same person. Investigators, physical security implementers, continuity planners, threat managers, *and* technology security personnel are all beginning to use these technically advanced tools in a cross-functional way.

The convergence of technology is a fact. Even the staunchest opponents of the idea of our next type of security convergence – organizational convergence – cannot argue that.

23.1.2 Organization Convergence

Somewhat more controversial in the security world is the idea of organizational convergence. This is the idea of taking all the personnel who perform security tasks of any kind (physical or logical, or increasingly, both at the same time, as technology merges), and aligning them under one single reporting structure, typically recommending a chief security officer (CSO).

Although ESRM does not require convergence, later in this chapter we will discuss how and why ESRM programs often end up organizationally converging, as well as why many people in the security field still believe that the concept is too challenging to implement (and therefore still find it controversial). For now, we will look at what kind of convergence the ESRM approach *does* require – a convergence of operating philosophy.

23.2 The ESRM View of Security Convergence

Organizational security convergence may or may not be a risk mitigation choice for the business. But even in an environment that has multiple teams of personnel in different structures, who are responsible for the tactical activities of security risk mitigation, ESRM allows for a different kind of convergence – convergence of philosophy.

23.2.1 Convergence of Philosophy

What does it mean to operate under a *converged philosophy*? It means that all leaders and personnel in the organization who perform security risk management activities or risk mitigation tasks, operate under the ESRM understanding that security risk decisions must be *made* by the business, but must be *managed* by the security team and leader. And it goes further. Operating under a converged ESRM philosophy means:

- All security teams adhere to a clearly defined security risk management role, based on common risk principles.
- The security team follows a formal and consistent process to document the risk identification and decision-making process.
- No matter which team is responsible for responding to a security incident, that team follows the same approach of postmortem investigations and root cause analysis to continually improve the security risk situation of the enterprise.
- All security teams are provided the same level of transparency, independence, authority, and scope to do their work in the right way, and ensure that the risk decision-making processes align with the ESRM program as implemented in the organization.
- All security teams report on the risks that are in their scope of responsibility in the same way.
- All security risks, no matter which team performs activities associated with mitigation, are overseen by the ESRM governance body.
- Security teams work in partnership with one another, ensuring open communications and collaboration across department lines.

Essentially, we mean that the ESRM program, philosophy, approach, and implementations, are fully embraced by all teams that perform any activities done in response to security risks. There is no room for "turf battles" over scope of responsibility. Those battles often lead to a lack of information-sharing about security risks across departments, which limits transparency and can lead to unintentional risk acceptance by the different security groups as they attempt to control what is "theirs," and protect it from the "other" group. If all security teams operate under an ESRM philosophy, no matter who they report to, they understand that security risk management is everyone's role, and that sharing that role does not lessen the status of any of the teams involved in security risk mitigation activities.

In organizations with multiple silos that perform physical, logical, policy, regulatory, or other security activities, leaders of each security function, to ensure that they are operating under a converged philosophy, should ask themselves:

- Do we all have clear goals that align with the business?
- Are we all operating under a defined role?
- Are all of us communicating that our role is to manage security risks, not tasks?
- Are we all ensuring that we work with our business partners in the risk decision-making process?
- Are the members of our individual teams able to work together in situations that cross boundaries of scope?

Many aspects must be coordinated and harmonized across all departments to which security activities have been assigned. More than just the occasional meeting, it takes real commitment from the leaders of those siloed operating groups, as well as from each team member in the various organizations, to achieve true collaboration to ensure that this convergence of philosophy happens. But, in an organization that is committed to ESRM ideals, such collaboration is what it takes to ensure that the enterprise is truly operating from an ESRM playbook.

23.3 Why ESRM Often Leads to Converged Organizations

As security's role becomes clearly defined in the enterprise through ESRM, and as risk principles are allied more consistently, the walls that separate the disparate organizations performing risk mitigation tasks and activities start to fade away. Because of how walls start to come down, ESRM (although we maintain it is not a *requirement* of the philosophy) often ends up *leading* the enterprise leaders and risk stakeholders to the conclusion that a converged security structure is the best practice. That it will allow for the most comprehensive and effective management of the diverse and increasing areas of risk, faced by the enterprise. The rest of this chapter will focus on the concepts of converged organizational structures as that best practice, which we believe the leaders in your organization will eventually embrace as the most efficient and productive structure for a few reasons.

23.3.1 Changed Understanding of Roles Leads to Changed Structures

First, when security is defined by its tasks, (i.e., physical security, information security, investigations, etc.), it inherently relegates the security function into specific institutions within the organization, at times aligned with specific assets or with the activities being performed. For example:

- Information security ends up aligned within the technology group.
- Physical security is lumped in with facilities and administration.
- Workplace violence and threat management becomes associated with human resources activity.

These alignments make sense for executives who might not have a true understanding of what security's real role is. They align the security department where the security tasks and activities are most commonly associated, leading to divergent security groups under various enterprise business silos.

Nevertheless, under an ESRM paradigm, when security's role is defined by risk-based security practices, an understanding of security's role and the needed elements for success helps to provide clarity on a fitting security alignment and structure. To avoid potential conflicts of transparency and independence, leaders often come to see that security should *not* be aligned under an operational owner. If everyone performing security risk mitigation tasks and activities is working within the stated set of ESRM principles, it becomes evident that there is only a need for one security leader – the CSO. This singular role becomes the touch-point at the executive level for all things "security," and we have seen in many organizations that over time, this converged role simply makes more sense until it is finally embraced, and the converged structure is put in place. This does not happen "overnight," but we do see in organizations using the ESRM methodology that it tends to go that way.

23.3.2 Changed Understanding of Risks Leads to Changed Structures

A second reason that embracing ESRM usually leads to the organizational convergence of security structures and groups is that the intersection of logical and traditional risks has become blurred. As discussed earlier, the changing focus of cyber risks has gone from simply information security to a much broader concern about operational technology security risk and reputational risk from cyber events. This change has combined to elevate overall business resiliency concerns around all types of security risk, whether they are cyber, information, terror, human, or mother-nature related. The executive's first concerns are that the business mission succeeds. As the many types of security risks converge and multiply, the solution, approach, and expectations around managing security risks also converge, and the idea of a converged organizational structure and single executive leader in the person of the CSO becomes more frequently explored.

Questions for the Security Practitioner
- "Could I see the leaders in my organization accepting the idea of a converged security structure today?"
- "How might this change in my organization, under an ESRM paradigm?"

23.3.3 Changed Understanding of Practices Leads to Changed Structures

The last factor that often leads to the adoption of a converged security structure once the organization has fully embraced ESRM is that the practices of security in each silo are both very common in their purpose. The purpose and mission of the security role is the same, whether you are:
- Investigating a theft of money from a safe, or doing computer forensics to investigate an unauthorized transfer of money out of a business account.
- Printing badges to control physical access, or providing passwords to control logical access.
- Conducting a risk assessment to determine how to better mitigate security risks against it, or to ensure business continuity in the event of an incident.
- Monitoring behavior for workplace violence threats, or monitoring a network for cyber vulnerabilities.
- Fixing a physical security flaw by fixing a window or fixing a technology security flaw by patching a firewall.

Tactics are different, but philosophies and mission are the same. These conjoined philosophies of all personnel performing security risk mitigation activities eventually bring them together for a common purpose "in the trenches," and that cooperation can "trickle up" to the leaders who come to see the benefits of cooperation and working together.

23.3.4 The Convergence Decision

The need to ensure collaboration, common policy, smooth interactions, communications, and cross-functional handoffs of tasks as security incidents are responded to, managed, investigated, evaluated, and remediated often leads the enterprise to eventually determine that there would be significant benefits to be had from changing the organization structure to a solitary group. However, the idea of that great a change also raises issues. Change and upheaval are never easy, and often those who might have their roles changed or their budgets or headcounts moved to a different area are, of course, concerned by the idea of restructuring into a converged group.

Ultimately, the benefits of reducing risk to the enterprise through a converged ESRM program must, in the eyes of the business, be significant enough to outweigh the challenges. Since the specific benefits and challenges will vary by enterprise, only the leaders of that organization are qualified to make the decision. However, without making any specific recommendations, we will outline the major benefits of having a converged security organization, and then discuss some of the challenges.

23.4 The Benefits of a Converged Organization in an ESRM Security Program

There are significant benefits that most organizations can accrue by converging the structure and management of all personnel who perform security risk mitigation activities under a single leader – the CSO. These benefits might or might not be significant enough in impacting your enterprise risk profile that your business leaders will feel that undertaking the change is worth the effort, but it is certainly worth doing an analysis of your own organization to determine if you would want to make the recommendation.

23.4.1 The Converged Security Team Aligns All Security with the Enterprise Business Mission

The role of the CSO in a converged security structure is critical. That person must be the executive level communicator of the ESRM strategy; the one who works side by side with the other executive leaders to ensure that all security activities are performed in alignment with the business mission, and in within the risk tolerances set for the enterprise. Additionally, one of the CSO's most critical roles is working with the executives and board of directors to *establish* enterprise-wide risk tolerance levels, and to execute the security program in a way that enables proper reporting and governance around those thresholds to help the executives to succeed with their goals. That is quite a significant job description and a tall order. However, that role becomes far more difficult and challenging when:

A. Multiple executives are all attempting to perform that same role, such as when a chief information officer (CIO), chief technology officer (CTO), chief information security officer (CISO), and chief security officer (CSO) all attempt to ensure that their security posture aligns with their piece of the overall business strategy.

B. Or even worse, due to the distributed nature of security activities happening in the enterprise, there are *no* executive level representatives to ensure that the security activities happening in the organization are in fact, aligning with the business mission. In a distributed structure, security tasks often happen under operational groups who may not have security risk alignment as their top priority.

Putting all security responsibilities under the purview of a single executive leader – the CSO – ensures that everything that happens in that aligned organization also aligns with the overall business mission and goals.

23.4.2 The Converged Security Team Helps Change the Perception of Security

Operating in a single structure brings the benefits of a uniform security risk management approach to both the physical and logical security personnel. More importantly, it brings the *defined role of security risk management* to both groups.

In this book, we have discussed at length the idea that the perception of security as "tasks-doers" is detrimental to the overall security of the enterprise. If the security team is viewed merely as a group that "does security things," and not perceived as performing risk mitigation activities in service of managing security risks to the business assets and mission, then those tasks are far easier to cut out, undercut, avoid, or flat-out ignore – reducing the overall security posture of the enterprise, and in fact, exposing it to more risk.

Although we have discussed that perception issue mostly in the context of more "traditional" security, information technology (IT) and technology security personnel often suffer from the same perception issues that plague physical security practitioners. They are perceived as the "password police," or task managers and often are even *less* understood than other security professionals, due to the complex nature of their tasks. Bringing both physical and logical IT security under a single umbrella helps change the perception of both groups into business-benefitting managers of security risk, it and ensures that your internal strategic partners understand the critical risk mitigation activities of all the security policies – including those complex passwords that cause so many complaints.

23.4.3 A Converged Security Program Unifies Security Awareness Efforts

When all security activities happen under a single, unified structure, the enterprise benefits from a capacity to engage and educate all enterprise employees on "security" as an overarching topic, rather than having multiple groups providing awareness materials on differing topics, possibly with non-uniform messages along the way. Many governments around the globe require companies to deliver information security training. Many organizations also want to educate employees on other varying topics of security such as workplace violence, fraud prevention, personal security, and more. However, employees have limited time available in their work lives, and most HR groups limit "mandatory" training hours. This means that typically, the group with the government or regulatory mandate is the one that gets that training time.

But in a converged environment, one, single, unified message can be presented to employees which covers not only the mandated training topics, but the other messaging your security organization needs to convey as well, including risk-reducing topics like:

- What security is responsible for.
- What employees need to do to ensure a secure environment.
- Most importantly – how to contact security for any reason.

Concise, pointed awareness materials will greatly reduce the risk exposure from a human-error security risk perspective, enabling a much more secure environment overall.

23.4.4 A Converged Security Program Reduces Employee Confusion

A converged structure brings another employee benefit – reduced confusion about who to call or contact when there is a security issue. In the past, we have seen where instructions for how to report a security incident in a business organization included at least four separate reporting mechanisms – how to report an information security issue, how to report a general security issue, how to report a regulatory compliance issue, and how to report an anonymous issue. That does not even include the multiple groups to contact if an employee has an issue with a badge to get access to a building, or a password to get access to a network, or who to call to set up a new employee or a guest for access to company resources. At some point, all these various methods of contact serve to do one thing – drive the employee away from reporting anything at all, or if they *must* deal with security, to look on the interaction as cumbersome and unpleasant, not the image your security team is going for.

Most employees do not have a daily exposure to the security team that allows them to get a full understanding of the scope of security's responsibilities, so the idea that they need to reach out to different security departments to fulfill various needs complicates things that should be kept simple. The employee wants to contact security – it is as simple as that. So, for the average employee to know they should reach out to information security for spam, or to the fraud group to report a theft, or to corporate security to replace a lost badge, is much more complicated than it needs to be.

Aligning all security activities under a single security structure allows you to provide a "one-stop-shop" for all security needs. While your team will certainly have many areas of activity and expertise, the initial contact to security can happen through a single point of contact; you can offer employees in the enterprise a single phone number/email address/online reporting system that will then send their communication directed internally and seamlessly to the correct area to assist them.

Another benefit of unified contact and reporting is that the easier you make it to report a security issue, the more likely your employee population will do so. Internal employees are a crucial part of the ongoing security risk awareness effort. The eyes and ears on the front lines of everyday enterprise interactions can provide you with advance notice of problems before they become problems, so long as you provide them with a straightforward way to let you know about them. Of course, this kind of converged reporting is possible under a converged philosophy of ESRM, even in a multiple-leader environment. However, as with many of these benefits, the level of cooperation and collaboration needed for this to happen in a non-converged structure is much harder to reach than in a world where a single leader has the capacity to set the structures up in a collaborative way from the outset.

Questions for the Security Practitioner
- "Does my enterprise currently have any gaps that might benefit from a converged structure?"
- "Do employees in my organization know how to contact security quickly?"

23.4.5 A Converged Security Program Promotes Efficiency of Security Operations

Efficiency of reporting and issue support are emphatically not the only efficiency benefits the enterprise will get from an organizational structure that is converged under a holistic ESRM program. The security organization will realize many efficiency benefits from operating as a unified whole.

- Employees with different skillsets can more easily collaborate on incident response processes.
- Information sharing within a single department is easier than making cross-department requests for data during security investigations that require both physical and logical forensics.

- Team members can be highly cross trained to understand what each other's specialties are, allowing all staff to perform the "basics" on their own, no matter their specialty, while also knowing exactly who to go to when a more advanced skillset is needed.
- Career paths and opportunities in the security group become more diverse, and employees have more areas of expertise to choose from as they learn more, and grow their skillsets and areas of expertise.
- A single budget or accounting structure for all security activities makes the security expenditures of the company more transparent, and it allows the enterprise to understand what activities are happening in the organization to mitigate security risk "at a glance," rather than having to dig into multiple budget areas.
- Consolidating security activities and ensuring streamlined processes saves man-hours and money, allowing diverse security risks to be managed by a single process or mitigation action, rather than spreading them out across multiple groups.
- Budgeting dollars for programs like security awareness, on-call employees for 24x7 coverage, security call-centers, or security operations centers can be combined for all security areas to increase budgeting efficiency.
- Putting reports of risks or metrics reports in a single report to one business leader, who would have otherwise received multiple reports from separate groups, adds to the efficient use of business leaders' time, as well as consistency with the reporting process.
- Other business functions that provide internal support to all teams in the enterprise (i.e., financial department support, human resources and career support, and development,) can also find efficiencies in providing those services to a single security group, rather than many.

As we mentioned in Chapter 21 on budgeting, while the security function does not "own" the risk, we are responsible for performing these activities in service of protecting the assets of our strategic partners. We certainly are responsible for being good stewards of the budgets allotted to us, making effective use of our employees' time and skills, and the tools and equipment they use. A converged structure allows for sharing of resources and cross-functional employees – maximizing the use of all of them.

23.4.6 A Converged Security Program Optimizes the Risk Profile

One last benefit to mention before we move on is a concept discussed by Dave Tyson in his book on security convergence is: Optimizing your risk profile.

> The primary idea to take away from this discussion is that convergence is about optimizing the risk profile so that all risks are identified, considered, and either mitigated or accepted…. Senior management should not be accepting any more risk than they are aware of, and if all the risks are well understood in this new and increasingly complex environment, then the first part of the job is done. (Tyson, 2007, p. 41).

This optimization is much easier in a converged structure because a single leader is responsible for ensuring that all aspects of security are considered, no matter who owns them. In a converged structure, risks that exist simultaneously between the physical and the virtual can be identified, especially those risks that might be missed due to a group thinking the problem is outside of their purview.

Although there are likely more benefits that you could find from a converged structure in your enterprise, these are the most significant ones, and are what you should include in your considerations while you determine whether this path is a good fit for your organization or not.

23.5 The Challenges of Converging an Organization in an ESRM Security Program

Of course, no major change is without its challenges. Converging two previously separate functional departments under a CSO will bring definite challenges. But many of them, if dealt with as part of an overarching ESRM approach, are not as challenging as they might first appear.

23.5.1 The "Culture" Challenge

A very significant challenge, one that is always mentioned when people want to discuss why a converged security organization will never work, is the aspect of differing cultures between the "traditional" security professional and the "IT" security professional. Stereotypes are trotted out to prove that these two groups cannot successfully work together. The IT security people are labeled "geeks." They are pointed at as unprofessionally dressed or too casual, not observant enough, and undisciplined. In many areas, because the IT security practitioners may tend to be younger, generational stereotypes are pulled out and they are accused of being unable to work with other people "face-to-face" or of being afraid to talk to people. All these stereotypes are as untrue as the ones that are then said about the "traditional" security personnel. They are perceived as "ex-cops" who still carry around a law enforcement attitude. They are accused of being skeptical, insular, and part of the "old boys" network (the fact that many are young, or female, notwithstanding). Traditional security folks are said to be only concerned with the Three Gs – gates, guns, and guards.

Why are these arguments made? First, these two groups rarely get to interact, and the old question of perception that we have been dealing with since the beginning of this book is coming into play, only this time *inside* the security group, rather than outside. Second, when you get right down to it, the major obstacle between these two groups is mainly distrust caused by a lack of understanding of what security's role is in managing enterprise security risk. This obstacle leads to divisiveness based on skillsets to perform a specific job rather than cohesion based on a shared philosophy and recognition of the similarities of role.

On the surface, the jobs look so very different. Each group – the physical and the logical security teams – have their own areas of focus and language. While one team is talking about BOLO and CCTV, the other is talking about IPS and NSM. But when you break this down, what is interesting is that both teams are really talking about the same thing – security risk. Look at the acronyms we just mentioned. BOLO in the physical security world means *be on the lookout*. It is an attempt to stop a person from entering a place who should not be there – mitigating an intrusion risk. And IPS stands for *intrusion prevention system* – also in place to prevent intrusion, just by another avenue. CCTV means *closed circuit television*, a way to remotely watch and monitor for evidence of security incidents. But NSM means *network security monitoring*, which also involves watching and monitoring for signs of potential security events. Just because the teams use different acronyms, that does not mean the ultimate goals are different. If brought together under an ESRM paradigm in which all personnel involved understand that the goal is to manage *all* security risk, each with their own special set of skills, then these two groups can soon see that they are not so different after all.

Dave Tyson had this to say on the topic of cultural clashes:

What are they both concerned with? The mantra of the physical security practitioner is to protect people, information, and property, whereas the IT security professional is concerned with protecting the confidentiality, integrity, and availability (CIA) of the organization's data and networks. Essentially, these two missions are neither inconsistent with each other nor mutually exclusive (Tyson, 2007, p. 85).

That is not to say that the cultural difference between these two groups will simply fall away with no effort, but that it is a manageable effort in an ESRM environment. As with all things ESRM, we recommend an iterative approach, with collaboration building first upon joint security projects, cross training, and "cross-border" cooperation on activities like investigations. The key to the breakdown of cultural barriers is in all personnel understanding that they have the same mission. And if that mission is understood, if everyone is on the same page about managing security risk, they will ultimately know that each person's tactics are worthwhile and will come to appreciate the contributions of the others to the overall focus of the security team.

Questions for the Security Practitioner
- "What are the cultural differences, if any, in my organization between physical and logical security personnel?"
- "Do I think the leaders of either the physical or logical security tactical groups in my organization could be brought together under a single leader today? What about under an ESRM paradigm?"

23.5.2 The "Control" Challenge

The second big challenge of building a converged security program is the regular, old-fashioned issue of human beings not wanting to give up control over things they see as theirs. In a converged environment, the CSO will be the ultimate leader of the personnel who perform security risk mitigation activities. That means that someone, somewhere will have to cede control of some:

- Budget.
- Headcount.
- Space.
- Scope of responsibilities.
- Information.
- Authority.
- Prestige.

…and probably more things that we have not mentioned here.

There are different sorts of people who will end up being part of a consolidation effort. As we talked about in Chapter 21 on budgeting, there are asset owners and stakeholders somewhere in your enterprise who have been doing tasks that might be better managed in a converged security environment. These could be facilities people or HR people, but in this convergence situation, these are most likely to be management level IT personnel, such as a CIO, CTO, or CISO. These are not leaders who are used to other people making decisions for them, and they may not initially see the benefits that can accrue to them when the security responsibilities and tasks that used to be "theirs" are performed by headcount in some other department.

At any rate, this challenge can also be overcome with an ESRM approach. The message that will help overcome resistance to change is to assure the previous leaders that they will not be losing any level of security for their assets. A key ESRM point is to show them how the converged organization under the ESRM paradigm can, in fact, increase the level of security that their assets have. That's because you and they are working in partnership to manage all the risks. The assets are still theirs. The risk mitigation decisions are still theirs. In fact, with independence and transparency, executives will most likely have a *deeper* view into the risks within their department. The converged security team is simply there to help them, as well as all the other stakeholders in the enterprise, to make those decisions in the most informed and educated way possible and to perform the technical risk mitigation activities in service of all departments as well.

23.5.3 The "Different Tasks" Challenge

A third challenge to converged environments is the idea that the tasks and skills of a physical and logical security team are so wildly different that they cannot possibly exist in a single organization structure.

However, this argument also breaks down in an ESRM environment because the ESRM model treats all security risk the same, while the tactics for mitigating those risks might be highly divergent. As long as the leaders of the converged security organization understand the concepts of risk management and have a grounding in all the varied tactics of risk mitigation which can be employed by the personnel in the security organization, everyone can be in alignment. Then, there is no reason at all that one employee mitigating access control risk through a badging system while another employee mitigates access control risk through a network password system should pose any kind of problem for the ultimate goal of managing access risk.

Noted security expert Steve Hunt made this point quite succinctly in 2010 on CSO Online:
> It is not our job to secure the building.
> It is not our job to secure the network.
> It is our job to secure the business (Hunt, 2010).

In the past, we also thought that it would be difficult to manage the many varied tasks that need to happen in a comprehensive security program. However, when we began to truly understand that *all* security tasks are mitigating activities to reduce *some* type of security risk, we realized that it is quite possible to manage these activities in a synchronized whole.

In Table 23-1, we show a comparison of the kinds of tasks that security groups do, and how they are just responses to the same security risks.

Table 23-1. Physical and Logical Security Similarities

Physical Does This	Logical Does This	Because of This
Gates and Fences	Firewalls	Intrusion Prevention
Door Locks	Passwords	Access Control
Investigations	Forensics	Incident response
Alarm Monitoring	Network Monitoring	Threat Detection
Business Continuity Teams	Cyber Response Teams	Crisis Management

Security Gap Remediation	Patch Management	Break-Fixes
Incident Reporting	Incident Reporting	Incident Response
Security Awareness	Security Awareness	Security Culture
Business Impact Analysis and Risk Assessments	Business Impact Analysis and Risk Assessments	Security Risk Management

23.6 Executive Leadership of a Converged Organization in an ESRM Environment

If your enterprise leaders do find that the benefits of a converged organization are something they would like to take advantage of to reduce overall security risk, while gaining the efficiencies of a centrally managed complete security organization, then the organization will need an executive leader – the CSO. This role is critical to the success of the converged ESRM organization, and it is a substantial job, requiring a highly skilled and intelligent leader. Derek Slater, writing for CSO Online described the job of the CSO in a converged environment as:

Chief Security Officer means what it sounds like: The CSO is the executive responsible for the organization's entire security posture, both physical and digital. CSOs also frequently own or participate closely in related areas such as business continuity planning, loss prevention and fraud prevention, and privacy (Slater, 2005).

The CSO is a leader, a visionary, and a motivator. This job is not for a tactician. It is not necessary for the CSO to personally perform any of the technical tasks that are done by any of the security personnel. Of course, they do need to understand what kinds of tasks can be used to mitigate all the risks that the enterprise faces. More importantly, they *must* be able to understand that risk environment, anticipate new security risks, see how security risks might change in exposure and impact, help the enterprise understand those risks, and make decisions on how to respond to them.

23.6.1 CSO Requirements in a Converged ESRM Organization

The qualities needed to be a good CSO of a converged security environment operating in a ESRM model are many. The CSO:

- Must be a people leader and security risk manager, not a manager of tasks.
- Must be intelligent, articulate, and persuasive.
- Can serve as an effective member of the senior management team.
- Understands the necessity of communicating the ESRM philosophy at all levels of the organization.
- Should have a background that includes leading many different security disciplines.
- Should understand compliance, resilience, auditing, and risk management.
- Can build commitment in the enterprise, and communicate the role of the security organization.
- Can lead change at all levels of the enterprise.
- Must be a great collaborator and business partner.
- Understands that the business has a business to run – everything ties to the bottom line.
- Needs to consider some certifications, such as the CPP from ASIS International, the CISSP from ISC2, the CISM from ISACA, CFE from ACFE, and the MBCP from DRII, or FBCI (or other certification level) from the BCI. (We include links to these certifications in the Learn More About It section at the end of this chapter).

Getting to the level of CSO in the security organization does not require any specific security background. Many high quality CSOs have started in IT security, investigations, law enforcement, security services, business continuity, and a multitude of other diverse starting points. The key to moving into the top spot in the ESRM paradigm is a keen understanding of business, the ability to talk the business talk, and a willingness to get out of the silo he or she started in, explore other territories, and then combine that experience into a holistic view of the converged security operating environment.

Questions for the Security Practitioner
- "Does my organization have a CSO? A CISO? What are the differences?"
- "What other representation does security have at the executive level in my enterprise?"

23.7 If Your Enterprise Chooses to Converge

The process of converging your security organizations is a big one. In this book, we have talked about designing a program, and touched on how to structure and budget for a program as well. But the "how to" of building out a converged organization is too large a topic to include in this book. It is, in fact, a whole other book – one that has been written quite a few times by different people. We have quoted several times in this chapter from Dave Tyson's seminal work on converging organizations, and would recommend that as a starting point. The book was written in 2007, but while much of the specific technology has *certainly* changed since then, the core ideas on how to build a converged physical/logical security team have not. At the end of this chapter, we list that and other references for learning about the convergence process.

The key to the change, like any other ESRM-based change, is education of your enterprise strategic partners: Involve them in the process, ensure everyone is "on the same page," make the changes iteratively, and ensure you continually improve. Above all, focus on the security risks you are mitigating with this change, ensuring that you are in no way making the enterprise *less* secure or less prepared anywhere in the process.

Chapter Review

In Chapter 23, you examined the concept of converging physical and logical security teams into a single organizational structure, the benefits, and challenges, and how such a structure would be possible in an ESRM environment.

Security Program Self-Assessment

In this self-assessment, you should think about the answer to the questions posed, and then see where your program is on the identified ESRM spectrum.

Question	Y/N	Is This ESRM?
Does your security organization manage all personnel who perform any security risk mitigation activities under a single organization structure?	□Yes □No	**NO**: If you do not currently have all personnel with security risk mitigation tactical responsibilities reporting into a single organization, then consider this as a suitable place to start in your ESRM program. **PARTIAL**: If your organization has most personnel with security risk mitigation tactical responsibilities reporting into a single organization, then you are part of the way to an ESRM implementation and might consider either aligning philosophically with the other departments, or beginning a discussion on any possible benefits of convergence. **YES**: If you have all personnel with security risk mitigation tactical responsibilities reporting into a single organization, then you are practicing ESRM in a converged environment.

Questions for Discussion

1. What are some political challenges that you feel are worth and not worth overcoming to gain the benefits of a converged environment? Are there scenarios you can think of where you would or would not broach this as a topic for the business to consider?
2. If you were the executive in charge of a siloed security organization today, what would your opinion of managing a converged security structure be? In a task-based department? In a risk-based department?

References

Hunt, S. (2010, March 1). *Convergence: The semantics trap.* [Web log post]. Retrieved from http://www.csoonline.com/article/2135065/security-leadership/convergence--the-semantics-trap.html

Slater, D. (2005, April 15). *Security convergence, defined.* [Web log post]. Retrieved from http://www.csoonline.com/article/2118703/security-leadership/security-convergence--defined.html

Slater, D. (2005, December 1). *What is a chief security officer?* [Web log post]. Retrieved from http://www.csoonline.com/article/2122505/infosec-careers/it-careers-what-is-a-chief-security-officer.html

Tyson, D. (2007). *Security convergence: Managing enterprise security risk.* Burlington, MA: Butterworth-Heinemann.

Learn More About It

For further reading about security convergence:

LaRoche, G. (2012). Information and physical security: Can they live together? *Information Systems Security.* Available at http://www.infosectoday.com/Articles/convergence.htm

Liscouski, B. (2014, June 1). Using security convergence to enable the enterprise. *Security Magazine Online.* Available at http://www.securitymagazine.com/articles/85551-using-security-convergence-to-enable-the-enterprise

For further reading about security certifications:

CPP (Certified Protection Professional) from ASIS International: https://www.asisonline.org/Certification/Board-Certifications/CPP/Pages/default.aspx

CISSP (Certified Information Systems Security Professional) from ISC2: https://www.isc2.org/cissp/default.aspx

CISM (Certified Information Security Manager) from ISACA: http://www.isaca.org/certification/cism-certified-information-security-manager/pages/default.aspx

CFE (Certified Fraud Examiner) from ACFE: http://www.acfe.com/become-cfe-qualifications.aspx

MBCP (Master Business Continuity Planner) from DRII: https://www.drii.org/certification/mbcp.php

FBCI (Fellow, BCI) (or other certification level) from the BCI: http://www.thebci.org/index.php/membership/membership-categories

Credits

Kristen Noakes-Fry, ABCI, is Executive Editor at Rothstein Associates Inc. since 2011. Previously, she was a Research Director, Information Security and Risk Group, for Gartner, Inc.; Associate Editor at Datapro (McGraw-Hill), where she was responsible for *Datapro Reports on Information Security*; and Associate Professor of English at Atlantic Cape College in New Jersey. She holds an M.A. from New York University and a B.A. from Russell Sage College. She is currently based in St. Petersburg, Florida.

Cover Design and Graphics:	Sheila Kwiatek, Flower Grafix
eBook Design & Processing:	Donna Luther, Metadata Prime
Copy Editing:	Anne Younger
Senior Copy Editor:	Nancy M. Warner

Philip Jan Rothstein, FBCI, is President of Rothstein Associates Inc., a management consultancy he founded in 1984 as a pioneer in the disciplines of Business Continuity and Disaster Recovery. He is also the Executive Publisher of Rothstein Publishing.

Glyn Davies is Chief Marketing Officer of Rothstein Associates Inc. He has held this position since 2013. Glyn has previously held executive level positions in Sales, Marketing and Editorial at several multinational publishing companies and currently resides in San Francisco, CA.

Rothstein Publishing is your premier source of books and learning materials about Business Resilience, including Crisis Management, Business Continuity, Disaster Recovery, Emergency Management, Security, and Risk Management. Our industry-leading authors provide current, actionable knowledge, solutions, and tools you can put in practice immediately. Rothstein Publishing remains true to the decades-long commitment of Rothstein Associates, which is to prepare you and your organization to protect, preserve, and recover what is most important: your people, facilities, assets, and reputation.

About the Authors

Brian J. Allen, Esq. **CISSP, CISM, CPP, CFE** has more than 20 years' experience in virtually every aspect of the security field and is founder of the Security Risk Governance Group (www.esrm.info), an executive advisory firm that provides security management solutions and implements enterprise security risk management (ESRM). Previously, as Chief Security Officer (CSO) of Time Warner Cable  (TWC), he was responsible for protecting TWC's assets worldwide. He coordinated TWC's crisis management and business continuity management (BCM) programs, managed the cybersecurity policy, and led the security risk management program. In addition, he managed TWC's security policy and relations with law enforcement and government authorities, as well as all customer security risk issues, oversaw internal and external investigations, and headed the company's workplace violence program. Before joining TWC in January 2002, he was Director of the Office of Cable Signal Theft at the National Cable and Telecommunications Association, Washington, DC, and the owner of ACI Investigations, a provider of security guard, investigative, and consulting services.

Brian earned his Bachelor of Science degree in criminal justice from Long Island University and received his Juris Doctor degree from Touro Law Center in New York. He is a member of the New York State Bar Association, a Certified Protection Professional (CPP) with ASIS, a Certified Information Systems Security Professional (CISSP) with ISC2, a Certified Fraud Examiner (CFE) with the ACFE and a Certified Information Security Manager (CISM) with ISACA. Brian is also a member of the International Security Management Association and the Association of Threat Assessment Professionals.

Brian is an Adjunct Professor at the University of Connecticut, School of Business MBA Program and is active in industry organizations. He served as a member of the Communications Infrastructure Reliability and Interoperability Council (CSRIC), an FCC appointed position, and co-chaired its working group on Cybersecurity Best Practices and the Cybersecurity Framework. He is one of four elected communications company representatives to serve on the Executive Committee of the US Communications Sector Coordinating Council (CSCC). He works with the Cross Sector Cybersecurity

Working Group, established by the U.S. Department of Homeland Security (DHS) under the Critical Infrastructure Partnership Advisory Council. Brian has served on the board of directors of ASIS International, and the board of trustees of ASIS International's Foundation. He is currently a member of the Board of Directors of the Domestic Violence Crisis Center in Connecticut.

With Rachelle Loyear, he co-authored *The Manager's Guide to Enterprise Security Risk Management: Essentials of Risk-Based Security* (Rothstein Publishing, 2016).

Rachelle Loyear, MBCP, AFBCI, CISM, PMP, has spent over a decade managing various

projects and programs in corporate security organizations, focusing strongly on business continuity and organizational resilience. In her work life, she has directed teams responsible for ensuring resilience in the face of many different types of security risks, both physical and logical. Her responsibilities have included: Security/business continuity management program design and development; crisis management and emergency response planning; functional and location-based recovery and continuity planning; training personnel in crisis management and continuity; operational continuity exercises; logistical programs, such as public/private partnership relationship management; and crisis recovery resource programs.

She began her career in information technology (IT), working in programming and training design at an online training company, before moving into the telecommunications industry. She has worked in various IT roles – including Web design, user experience, business analysis, and project management – before moving into the security/business continuity arena. This diverse background enables her to approach security, risk, business continuity, and disaster recovery with a broad methodology that melds many aspects into a cohesive whole.

Rachelle holds a bachelor's degree in history from the University of North Carolina at Charlotte, and a master's degree in business administration from the University of Phoenix. She is certified as Master Business Continuity Professional (MBCP) through DRI International, as Associate Fellow of Business Continuity International (AFBCI), as Certified Information Security Manager (CISM) through ISACA, and Project Management Professional (PMP) through the Project Management Institute (PMI). Active in multiple business continuity management industry groups, she is vice-chair of the Crisis Management and Business Continuity Council of ASIS International as well as serving on the IT Security Council.

She is the author of *The Manager's Guide to Simple, Strategic, Service-Oriented Business Continuity* (Rothstein Publishing, 2017). In addition, with Brian Allen, Rachelle co-authored *The Manager's Guide to Enterprise Security Risk Management: Essentials of Risk-Based Security* (Rothstein Publishing, 2016).

390

When the Stakes Are This High, Learn from the Best

Rothstein Publishing Presents 11 New and Current Books/Templates on Business Continuity, Disaster Recovery, and Risk, Crisis, Emergency Management

NEW DIGITAL FORMATS! Get it by the Chapter or by the Book

Make your own eBook – choose only chapters you need from each book, or mix/match chapters from any Rothstein books listed here. See www.rothsteinpublishing .com for details!

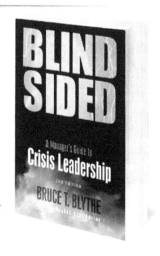
391

State-of-the-Art Exposition of the "Twin Disciplines"

Business Continuity and Risk Management:
Essentials of Organizational Resilience
By *Kurt J. Engemann*, PhD, CBCP and *Douglas M. Henderson*, FSA, CBCP

Business Continuity and Risk Management are now considered twin disciplines and this new text offers a state-of-the-art exposition of the global body of knowledge for their interrelationship.

» 10 chapters cover Business Continuity principles and practices; 3 focus on Information Technology and Emergency Management; and 4 explain Risk Modeling for those wanting statistical underpinnings in Risk Management.

» Extensive Instructor Resources are available for college courses and professional development training, including syllabi, test bank, discussion questions, case studies, and slides.

Authors are a college professor who is also editor-in-chief of the International Journal of Business Continuity and Risk Management, and a Business Continuity consultant with 25+ years of experience.

It's difficult to write a book that serves both academia and practitioners, but this text provides a firm foundation for novices and a valuable reference for experienced professionals.

— Security Management Magazine

©2012, 370 pages, glossary, index ISBN 978-1-931332-54-5, paperback 8 5 x 11
ISBN 978-1-931332-73-6, PDF/eBook   ISBN 978-1-931332-89-7, ePub

---

Demonstrates That Systematically Managing Individual and Collective Workplace Emotions Is Critical to Risk and Crisis Management

The Cost of Emotions in the Workplace:
The Bottom Line Value of Emotional Continuity Management
By *Vali Hawkins Mitchell*, PhD, LMHC

Finally – a people management guide that goes way beyond the typical "problem employee" books to help you understand and manage the entire emotional culture of your organization.

» Introduces the rising field of Emotional Continuity Management (ECM) and provides a tested system to observe, predict, prepare, and write policy to manage the full range of workplace emotions productively – to stop workplace problems before they start.

» Offers tools to quantify bottom-line costs of disruptive emotional incidents, from bad managers, emotional terrorists and office bullies to workplace violence, and includes real-life examples, tips, tools, checklists, forms, and sample plans.

"Dr. Vali" is a Certified Traumatologist, holds a Doctorate in Health Education, and is a highly regarded speaker, consultant, educator, and counselor to victims of major disasters, including 9/11 and Hurricane Katrina.

You'll look with new eyes at the enormous role played by human emotions in today's business. I endorse it as a guide for the 21st century global workforce.

— James J. Cappola, MD, PhD, Medical Director, Medical Affairs, Harvard Clinical Research Institute

©2013, 300 pages, glossary, index ISBN 978-1-931332-58-3, paperback 6x9   ISBN 978-1-931332-68-2 PDF/eBook
ISBN 978-1-931332-84-2 ePub

Easy Workbook Format Shows Managers New to Business Continuity Planning How to Develop a Basic Plan and Keep It Updated

Business Continuity Planning:
A Step-by-Step Guide with Planning Forms, 3rd Edition
By *Ken Fulmer*, CBCP

If you've been tasked with developing a basic business continuity plan and aren't sure where to start, this workbook with sample forms, checklists, and plans will walk you step-by-step through the process.

» Extensive, easy-to-use downloadable resources include reproducible worksheets, forms, templates, questionnaires, and checklists for various natural disasters and special hazards such as power outages, boiler failures, bomb threats, hazardous material spills, and civil unrest, along with a checklist for vital records storage.

» Straightforward explanations emphasize non-technical aspects of Business Continuity Planning/Disaster Recovery.

Kenneth L. Fulmer, a 30+ year veteran of the computer industry, has published, trained and spoken on business continuity throughout his career.

This excellent primer sets out a simple, concise, and, most of all, logical roadmap both for developing the justification for a business continuity/disaster recovery program as well as for developing and maintaining the resultant plan.

— Larry Kalmis, FBCI, Project Executive, Virtual Corporation and Chairman, Business Continuity Institute

©2008, 190 pages, + Downloadable Resources, glossary ISBN 978-1931332-21-7, paperback 8 5 x 11
ISBN: 978-1-931332-80-4, PDF/eBook ISBN: 978-1-931332-90-3, ePub

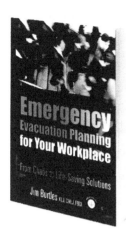

First All-in-One, Practical Resource That Integrates Workplace Emergency Evacuation Planning with Business Continuity

Emergency Evacuation Planning for Your Workplace:
From Chaos to Life-Saving Solutions
By Jim Burtles, KLJ, CMLJ, FBCI

Whether you work in facilities management, HR, or emergency, risk and business continuity management, this groundbreaking new book will become your go-to resource for safely evacuating people of all ages and health conditions from workplaces of all kinds.

» Based on 12 years' research into global best practices, it includes a comprehensive package of 600+ pages of book and downloadable resources with tools, templates, case studies, sample plans, forms, checklists, articles, and practical tips.

» Selected by the International Facilities Management Association (IFMA) and endorsed by The Business Continuity Institute (BCI).

Jim Burtles is an internationally acclaimed Business Continuity consultant with 35 years' experience in 24 countries. A founding Fellow of the Business Continuity Institute, he received BCI's Lifetime Achievement Award in 2001.

Unique, comprehensive, important guide and reference for anyone interested in workplace safety and emergency evacuation planning. Recommended.

— Choice Magazine, Association of College and Research Libraries

©2013, 340 pages + Downloadable Resources, glossary, index ISBN 978-1-931332-56-9, casebound 6x9
ISBN 978-1-931332-67-5, PDF/eBook ISBN: 978-1-931332-85-9, ePub

---

Selected One of "30 Best Business Books of 2013" by Soundview Executive Book Summaries

Lukaszewski on Crisis Communication: What Your CEO Needs to Know About Reputation Risk and Crisis Management
By James E. Lukaszewski, ABC, APR, Fellow PRSA

America's Crisis Guru draws on four decades of consulting experience confronting crises of every kind to advise you exactly what to do, what to say, when to say it, and when to do it while the whole world is watching. He uniquely emphasizes how to manage the victim-driven nature of crisis.

» Tells how to get heard by management and gives step-by-step details for creating a practical crisis communication plan and putting it into action in the real world of victims, media relations, social media, litigation, and activists.

» Packed with case studies/examples, practical tools, charts, checklists, forms, and templates.

James E. Lukaszewski (loo-ka-SHEV-skee), profiled in Living Legends of American Public Relations, was invited by Penn State University to speak at its 2013 Bronstein Lecture in Ethics and Public Relations and was recognized by the Minnesota Chapter of Public Relations Society of America with the Donald G Padilla Distinguished Practitioner Award for his role as a PR educator, ethicist, and ambassador.

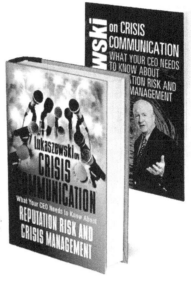

"Jim is one of the most knowledgeable people on earth about crisis management and his counsel has saved the reputation of many corporations and individuals."

— Jay Rayburn, PhD, Fellow PRSA, Division Director, Advertising/Public Relations, School of Communication, Florida State University

©2013, 400 pages, glossary, index ISBN 978-1-931332-66-8, hardcover 6x9
ISBN 978-1-931332-57-6, paperback 6x9 ISBN 978-1-931332-64-4, PDF/eBook
ISBN 978-1-931332-81-1, ePub

Selected by Risk and Insurance Management Society (RIMS) and American Society for Quality (ASQ)

Root Cause Analysis Handbook:
A Guide to Efficient and Effective Incident Investigation, 3rd Edition
By ABS Consulting; Lee N. Vanden Heuvel, Donald K. Lorenzo, Laura O. Jackson, Walter E. Hanson, James J. Rooney, and David A. Walker

Reach for this bestselling handbook anytime you need to identify and eliminate the root cause of incidents with quality, reliability, production processes, and environmental, health, and safety impacts — and their attendant risks.

» THE most complete, all-in-one package available for root cause analysis, including 600+ pages of book and downloadable resources; color-coded, 17" x 22" Root Cause Map™; and licensed access to extensive online resources.

» Based on a globally successful, proprietary methodology developed by an international consulting firm with 50 years' experience in 35 countries.

A global classic called "in a league of its own" and "the best resource on the subject."

©2008, 300 pages + Downloadable Resources, fold-out map, glossary ISBN 978-1-931332-51-4, paperback 8.5x11
ISBN 978-1-931332-72-9, PDF/eBook, ISBN 978-1-931332-82-8, PDF/eBook

New eBooks
From The Rothstein Publishing eBook Collection

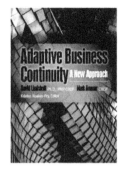

Adaptive Business Continuity: A New Approach
David Lindstedt, Ph.D., PMP, CBCP and and Mark Armour, CBCP
Kristen Noakes-Fry, ABCI, Editor
(A Rothstein Publishing Collection eBook) June 2017
ISBN: 978-1-944480-4-0 (EPUB)
ISBN: 978-1-944480-41-7 (PDF)
172 pages

The preparedness planning industry is at a turning point. Circumstances demand that professionals look at business continuity (BC) and its practice in new ways. Adaptive Business Continuity: A New Approach offers an alternative to make your BC program more effective. Adaptive Business Continuity will improve your organization's recovery capabilities.

The Manager's Guide to Simple, Stategic, Service-Oriented Business Continuity
Rachelle Loyear, MBCP, AFBCI, CISM, PMP Kristen Noakes-Fry, ABCI, Editor
(A Rothstein Publishing Collection eBook) May 2017
ISBN: 978-1-944480-38-7 (EPUB)
ISBN: 978-1-944480-39-4 (PDF)
145 pages

You have the knowledge and skill to create a workable Business Continuity Management (BCM) program –but too often, your projects are stalled while you attempt to get the right information from the right person. Rachelle Loyear takes you through the practical steps to get your program back on track.

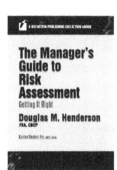

The Manager's Guide to Risk Assessment: Getting It Right
Douglas M. Henderson, FSA, CBCP Kristen Noakes-Fry, ABCI, Editor
(A Rothstein Publishing Collection eBook) March 2017
ISBN: 978-1-944480-38-7 (EPUB)
ISBN: 978-1-944480-39-4 (PDF)
114 pages

Risk assessment is required for just about all business plans or decisions. As a responsible manager, you need to consider threats to your organization's resilience. But to determine probability and impact – and reduce your risk – can be a daunting task. Guided by Henderson's The Manager's Guide to Risk Assessment: Getting It Right, you will confidently follow a clearly explained, step-by-step process to conduct a risk assessment.

ROTHSTEIN PUBLISHING
A Division of Rothstein Associates Inc.
Brookfield, Connecticut USA
www.rothstein.com

f www.facebook.com/RothsteinPublishing

in www.linkedin.com/company/rothsteinpublishing

🐦 www.twitter.com/rothsteinpub   I

New eBooks
From The Rothstein Publishing eBook Collection

The Manager's Guide to Cybersecurity Law: Essentials for Today's Business
Teri Schreider, SSCP, SISM, C | CISO, ITIL Foundation Kristen Noakes-Fry, ABCI, Editor
(A Rothstein Publishing Collection eBook) February 2017
ISBN: 978-1-944480-30-1 (EPUB)
ISBN: 978-1-944480-31-8 (PDF)
168 pages

In today's litigious business world, cyber-related matters could land you in court. As a computer security professional, you are protecting your data, but are you protecting your company? While you know industry standards and regulations, you may not be a legal expert, but fortunately, in a few hours of reading rather than months of classroom study you could be.

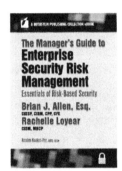

The Manager's Guide to Enterprise Security Risk Management: Essentials of Risk-Based Security
Brian J. Allen, Esq., CISSP, CISM, CPP, CFE
Rachelle Loyear MBCP, AFBCI, CISM, PMP Kristen Noakes-Fry, ABCI, Editor
(A Rothstein Publishing Collection eBook) November 2016
ISBN: 978-1-944480-24-0 (EPUB)
ISBN: 978-1-944480-25-7 (PDF)

Is security management changing so fast that you can't keep up? Perhaps it seems like those traditional "best practices" in security no longer work? One answer might be that you need better best practices!

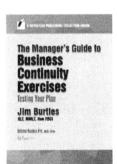

The Manager's Guide to Business Continuity Exercises: Testing Your Plan
Jim Burtles, KLT, MMLT, Hon FBCI Kristen Noakes-Fry, ABCI, Editor
(A Rothstein Publishing Collection eBook) November 2016
ISBN: 978-1-944480-32-5 (EPUB)
ISBN: 978-1-944480-33-2 (PDF)
100 pages

Your challenge is to maintain a good and effective plan in the face of changing circumstances and limited budgets. If your situation is like that in most companies, you really cannot depend on the results of last year's test or exercise of the plan.

A Division of Rothstein Associates Inc.

Brookfield, Connecticut USA
www.rothstein.com

f www.facebook.com/RothsteinPublishing

in www.linkedin.com/company/rothsteinpublishing

www.twitter.com/rothsteinpub

II

New eBooks
From The Rothstein Publishing eBook Collection

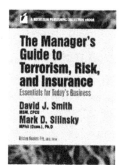

The Manager's Guide to Terrorism, Risk, & Insurance: Essentials for Today's Business
David J. Smith, MSM, CPCU Mark D. Silinsky, MPhol (Oxon.), Ph.D
Kristen Noakes-Fry, ABCI, Editor
(A Rothstein Publishing Collection eBook) October 2016
ISBN: 978-1-944480-26-4 (EPUB)
ISBN: 978-1-944480-27-1 (PDF)
120 pages

As a manager, you're aware of terrorist acts, are considering the risks, but sense that you need more background. How might terrorism occur?

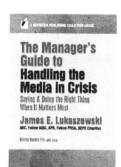

The Manager's Guide to Handling the Media in a Crisis: Saying & Doing the Right Thing When It Matters Most
James E. Lukaszewski, ABC, Fellow IABC, Fellow PRSA, BEPS Emeritus
Kristen Noakes-Fry, ABCI, Editor
(A Rothstein Publishing Collection eBook) September 2016
ISBN: 978-1-944480-28-8 (EPUB)
ISBN: 978-1-944480-29-5 (PDF)
120 pages

Attracting media attention is surprisingly easy – you just want it to be the right kind! If an event causes the phone to ring and TV cameras to appear in your lobby, you need confidence that the people who happen to be at your worksite that day are prepared.

The Manager's Guide to Quick Crisis Response: Effective Action in an Emergency
Bruce T. Blythe Kristen Noakes-Fry, ABCI, Editor
(A Rothstein Publishing Collection eBook) August 2016
ISBN: 978-1-944480-23-3 (EPUB)
ISBN: 978-1-944480-22-6 (PDF)
117 pages

Avoid being "blindsided" by an unexpected emergency or crisis in the workplace – violence, natural disaster, or worse!

ROTHSTEIN PUBLISHING
A Division of Rothstein Associates Inc.
Brookfield, Connecticut USA
www.rothstein.com

f www.facebook.com/RothsteinPublishing

in www.linkedin.com/company/rothsteinpublishing

y www.twitter.com/rothsteinpub

III

New eBooks
From The Rothstein Publishing eBook Collection

Introduction to Emergency Evacuation: Getting Everybody Out When It Counts
Bruce T. Blythe Kristen Noakes-Fry, ABCI, Editor
(A Rothstein Publishing Collection eBook) July 2016 ISBN: 978-1-944480-14-1 (EPUB)
ISBN: 978-1-944480-15-8 (PDF)
120 pages

When it's not just a drill, you need to get it right the first time. If an emergency alert sounds, are you ready to take charge and get everyone out of the office, theater, classroom, or store safely?

The Manager's Guide to Bullies in the Workplace: Coping with Emotional Terrorists
Vali Hawkins Mitchell, Ph.D, LMHC, REAT, CEAP Kristen Noakes-Fry, ABCI, Editor
(A Rothstein Publishing Collection eBook) July 2016
ISBN: 978-1-944480-12-7 (EPUB)
ISBN: 978-1-944480-13-4 (PDF)
120 pages

As a manager, you can usually handle disruptive employees. But sometimes, their emotional states foster workplace tension, even making them a danger to others.

Creating & Maintaining Resilient Supply Chains
Andrew Hiles, Hon FBCI, EIoSCM Kristen Noakes-Fry, ABCI, Editor
(A Rothstein Publishing Collection eBook) July 2016
ISBN: 978-1-944480-07-3 (EPUB)
ISBN: 978-1-944480-08-0 (PDF)
120 pages

Will your supply chain survive the twists and turns of the global economy? Can it deliver mission-critical supplies and services in the face of disaster or other business interruption?

ROTHSTEIN PUBLISHING
A Division of Rothstein Associates Inc.
Brookfield, Connecticut USA
www.rothstein.com

f www.facebook.com/RothsteinPublishing

in www.linkedin.com/company/rothsteinpublishing

🐦 www.twitter.com/rothsteinpub

IV

398

45990861R00236

Made in the USA
Middletown, DE
22 May 2019